NESTED NATIONALISM

Portrait of a woman and girl in national costume, Astara District, late 1950s–1960s. Courtesy of the Archive of Atiga Izmailova.

NESTED NATIONALISM

MAKING AND UNMAKING NATIONS IN THE SOVIET CAUCASUS

Krista A. Goff

CORNELL UNIVERSITY PRESS
Ithaca and London

Publication of this book was made possible, in part, by grants from the First Book Subvention Program of the Association for Slavic, East European, and Eurasian Studies and from the Office of the Dean in the College of Arts and Sciences at the University of Miami.

First published 2020 by Cornell University Press

Library of Congress Cataloging-in-Publication Data

Names: Goff, Krista A., author.
Title: Nested nationalism : making and unmaking nations in the Soviet Caucasus / Krista A. Goff.
Description: Ithaca [New York] : Cornell University Press, 2020. | Includes bibliographical references and index. |
Identifiers: LCCN 2020009681 (print) | LCCN 2020009682 (ebook) | ISBN 9781501753275 (hardcover) | ISBN 9781501753299 (pdf) | ISBN 9781501753282 (epub)
Subjects: LCSH: Minorities Azerbaijan History 20th century. | Minorities Caucasus, South History 20th century. | Nationalism Azerbaijan History 20th century. | Nationalism Caucasus, South History 20th century. | Collective memory Azerbaijan History 20th century. | Collective memory Caucasus, South History 20th century. | Azerbaijan Ethnic relations. | Caucasus, South Ethnic relations.
Classification: LCC DK509 .G64 2020 (print) | LCC DK509 (ebook) | DDC 323.1475—dc23
LC record available at https://lccn.loc.gov/2020009681
LC ebook record available at https://lccn.loc.gov/2020009682

In memory of my father, Thomas Michael Goff, Sr.,
who inspired me to become a historian

Contents

Abbreviations   ix

Explanatory Note   xi

Introduction   1

1. Making Minorities and National
   Hierarchies   19

2. Territory, War, and Nation-Building
   in the South Caucasus   61

   Interlude: After Stalin: Reform
   and Revenge   94

3. Defining the Azerbaijan Soviet
   Socialist Republic   106

4. Scholars, Politicians, and the Production
   of Soviet Assimilation Narratives   144

5. Minority Activism and Citizenship   179

   Conclusion   214

Notes   241

Bibliography   289

Acknowledgments   309

Index   313

Abbreviations

ADR	Azerbaijan Democratic Republic
ASSR	Autonomous Soviet Socialist Republic
CPSU (Russian initials: KPSS)	Communist Party of the Soviet Union
Kavburo	Caucasus Bureau of the Russian Communist Party
Minpros	Ministry of Enlightenment (Education)
Narkomindel	People's Commissariat for Foreign Affairs
Narkompros	People's Commissariat of Enlightenment (Education)
Narkomzem	People's Commissariat of Agriculture
NKAO	Nagorno-Karabakh Autonomous Oblast'
NKVD	People's Commissariat of Internal Affairs
Politburo	Political Bureau of the Central Committee of the Communist Party
RSFSR	Russian Soviet Federated Socialist Republic
Sovmin	Council of Ministers
Sovnarkom	Council of People's Commissars
SSR	Soviet Socialist Republic
TSFSR (Russian initials: ZSFSR)	Transcaucasian Socialist Federated Soviet Republic
Zakkraikom	Transcaucasian Regional Committee

Explanatory Note

During the period covered in this book, many of the peoples and places of concern were renamed—sometimes multiple times. For the most part, I follow the nomenclature prevalent in sources, changing terms in the text as they change over time, making reference to contemporary names, but not projecting them onto the past. As for proper names, people in the Soviet Union often existed in multiple cultural-linguistic worlds. Most political elites used Russianized surnames, at least in their public lives and in the official correspondence preserved in state and party archives. In most cases, I follow this convention (Bagirov rather than Bağirov, Ibragimov in place of İbrahimov, Musabekov instead of Musabeyov, etc.). I have also included, however, many of the contemporary Azerbaijani (or, when relevant, Talysh, Lezgin, etc.) variants for reference. For place names, I have tried to stay with the local national version, with exceptions made for established English-language spellings, including Baku in place of Bakı and Nagorno-Karabakh instead of Dağlıq Qarabağ. To that end, although Nagorny Karabakh is linguistically more correct, I have opted to write Nagorno-Karabakh, the adjectival form derived from Nagorno-Karabakhskaia avtonomnaia oblast' (Nagorno-Karabakh Autonomous Oblast') because this is more commonly used in English.

Borders were also in flux, with territories sometimes changing hands; at other times expanding, contracting, or disappearing—as was the case for the Soviet Kurdistan *uezd*, which was disbanded in 1929. There are two maps available in this text, including a political map of Soviet Azerbaijan in the late 1980s and a map of the broader region today. Some names for regions, towns, and villages in Azerbaijan changed many times in the Soviet and post-Soviet periods. In the text, I replicate place names as they are found in sources, in most cases also referencing their contemporary equivalent. When the name has changed since the late 1980s, I often reference that variant as well for the purposes of rendering the map useful to the reader.

The contemporary regional map, situated at the start of chapter 2, is included here to help readers understand the basic geography of Soviet Azerbaijani,

Armenian, and Georgian pretensions to Iranian and Turkish territories during World War II. In the case of Iran, there have been significant administrative changes since the 1940s. Most notably, the Iranian Azerbaijan province has been separated into the East Azerbaijan, West Azerbaijan, and Ardabil provinces. Khorasan Province has also been subdivided into South Khorasan, North Khorasan, and Razavi Khorasan, and Golestan carved out of Mazandaran. The Turkey portion of the map also reflects contemporary realities. While different national communities might have different names for some of the same sites, I use the standard national variants on this map.

Russian and Azerbaijani are the most common languages transliterated here, but names and terms in Talysh, Lezgin, Georgian, and other languages are also included. For Russian, I have used a simplified version of the Library of Congress system, with some changes, including writing "ц" as "ts" and "ий" as "ii." I made some exceptions for names and terms that have been commonly rendered differently, such as Lavrentiy Beria and Politburo. Some of these languages underwent multiple script and orthographic reforms during the period in question, including Azerbaijani which had four official scripts (Perso-Arabic, Latin, Cyrillic, and, now, a new Latin alphabet) over the course of the twentieth century. I transliterate Azerbaijani sources according to the contemporary Latin script and have opted not to use all of the Azerbaijani diacritics, hoping that the resulting transliteration will make Azerbaijani pronunciation more accessible to a broader audience, while remaining recognizable to those who are familiar with the language. To this end, I have made the following changes, rendering "c" as "j," "ə" as "a," "ğ" as "gh," "ç" as "ch," "ş" as "sh," and "x" as "kh." I also generally include Azerbaijani words with full diacritics in parentheses for reference. For Talysh transliteration, I am mostly working with sources written in the Cyrillic script, which is no longer in common use in Azerbaijan (it is still often the standard for Talyshes in other parts of the former Soviet Union, while Talyshes in Iran use the Perso-Arabic script). Since there is no standardized transliteration system for Talysh in Cyrillic, I elected to translate Talysh and reproduce the Cyrillic Talysh script in those cases where I felt it would be helpful for the reader to see the original phrasing.

NESTED NATIONALISM

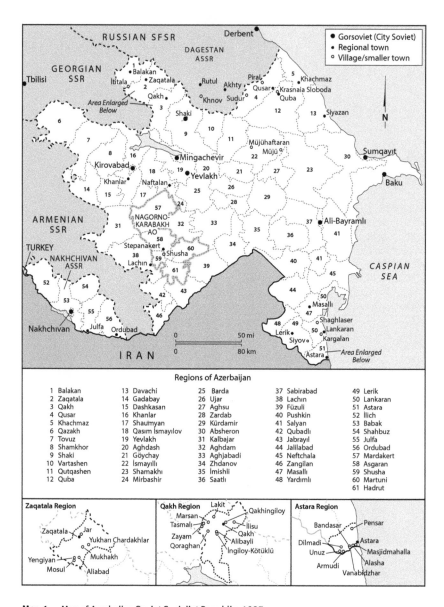

Map 1. Map of Azerbaijan Soviet Socialist Republic, 1987.

Introduction

In 1962, anonymous petitioners from the northwest corner of the Azerbaijan Soviet Socialist Republic (SSR) wrote to First Secretary of the Communist Party of the Soviet Union (CPSU) Nikita Khrushchev. As might be the case with many readers today, they expected that he might not know much about Georgian-Ingilois, who probably accounted for only 15,000 of the more than 208 million people living in the Soviet Union at that time. Coming from this mixed community of Muslims and Orthodox Christians, they acquainted Khrushchev with problems they were experiencing as minorities in Soviet Azerbaijan and begged him to help secure their precarious national future. In writing and sending this petition, they joined long-standing debates about how the state might best manage national imbalances in the Soviet Union's diverse republics, where titular nations that shared the name of those republics enjoyed greater access to power and cultural privileges than the minorities who also lived there. And, as practiced members of the Soviet world, they employed the rhetoric of Soviet multinationalism with aplomb: "We love the languages of all republics of our Soviet Union and their culture," they explained, so "why not love our language and our culture"?[1]

It was a valid question. Soviet residents, including these petitioners, had long been told that the USSR was a place where different nationalities could blossom in tandem thanks to the success of the world's first socialist state. Politicians, writers, artists, and activists had declared loudly and frequently that the

Soviet Union celebrated and protected national self-determination and equality. The preface of the *Atlas of the Peoples of the World*, published by the Soviet Academy of Sciences in 1964, replicated in print what all Soviet citizens far and wide were expected to know:

> In the Soviet Union, the national question has been solved on the basis of Leninist national policies that proclaimed the principle of full equality for all nations and their right to self-determination. In the big family of Soviet republics, representatives of all nations, large and small, live, work, and successfully develop their own culture together. They are united by common interests in life and one goal—communism.
>
> In contrast with the socialist countries, the majority of capitalist countries have no national equality [*natsional'noe ravnopravie*].[2]

Leninist nationality policies thus generated expectations, but also grievances. The Georgian-Ingiloi petitioners who reached out to Khrushchev knew that the multinational goals of the Soviet Union and its realities were not the same. They wrote, hoping that violations of their national rights could be corrected, that the core Soviet values they had imbibed could be made more real, and, ultimately, that their national community could flourish.

Nested Nationalism examines the world that pushed these petitioners to anonymously contact Khrushchev at the center of the Soviet Union to try and negotiate a different national future for the republic in which they lived. At the heart of this study are questions about the lived experience of "titular" and "nontitular" populations in the Soviet Union, how these experiences triggered different responses that still affect the region today, and how the masking tendencies of state-driven paper trails have shaped the histories written about Soviet republics and their afterlives. At its core, the book seeks to explain why history writing about nontitular minorities in the Soviet Union, and in Azerbaijan in particular, has proven so problematic.

This story revolves around Azerbaijan because of the variety of nontitular communities that live there and the many ethnic conflicts that emerged during its transition to independence in the late 1980s and early 1990s. Yet, as *Nested Nationalism* is about not only state structures but also the peoples living within them, its geographical range is broader and intersects with the history of Iran, Turkey, and neighboring republics in the Soviet Caucasus, namely Armenia, Georgia, and Dagestan. It moves across different spatial scales—from Caucasian villages, republican capitals, and halls of governance and academia in Moscow to international arenas of diplomacy and dispute—to describe a regional world that extended beyond Soviet borders and to argue that uncovering nontitular histories helps us better understand both Soviet and post-Soviet ethnic conflicts.

As is widely acknowledged, the national federal structure of the USSR and other foundational Soviet nationality policies worked to simultaneously consolidate Bolshevik power, disarm nationalism, and contend in a revolutionary manner with the Russian Empire's imperialist legacy. One of the central tenets of this politics was that the diverse population of the former Russian Empire needed assistance to evolve past the historic phase of national consciousness and reach the point at which communism could emerge. As Stalin explained in the 1920s, "We are undertaking the maximum development of national culture, so that it will exhaust itself completely and thereby create the base for the organization of international socialist culture."[3]

What did it mean to "undertak[e] the maximum development of national culture"? One manifestation of this effort was the ethnoterritorial structure of the Soviet Union, which divided the country into national territories (including republics, subrepublics, and districts) generally named for a titular, or principal, nationality living in that space. There were also "nativization" (korenizatsiia) policies that aimed to develop national cultures, identifications, elites, workers, and languages in these areas. From the very beginning of the Soviet project, the Bolsheviks touted their commitment to national equality and to the elimination of the national oppression, hate, and inequities they associated with the Russian Empire's colonial regime and the capitalist world. Correspondingly, equal political, economic, state, cultural, and social rights irrespective of an individual's national or racial background were hallmark provisions of Soviet constitutions on both the all-Union and republic level.

These rights were extended to all Soviet citizens, including peoples who did not have republics named after them—the commonly termed "nontitular minorities." As Soviet historian Terry Martin correctly notes, "Soviet policy was original in that it supported the national forms of minorities rather than majorities. It decisively rejected the model of the nation-state and replaced it with a plurality of nation-like republics."[4] So, for instance, the nontitular Georgian-Ingiloi petitioners (with whom this introduction began) by law had the same rights as other nationalities in Azerbaijan, including the titular Azeris. In practice, however, state and party officials did not treat all peoples equally. This raises an important question. The Soviet state supported the development of minorities to counter the colonial legacy of Great Russian chauvinism and secure its power, but were all non-Russians in the Soviet Union minorities? *Nested Nationalism* re-examines, through the example of Azerbaijan and surrounding territories, the concept of the minority by shifting its gaze away from the all-Union scale to the republics, where people characterized as "minorities" in the all-Union context often formed the majority.

Evolving power differentials between titular and nontitular nationalities in Soviet republics became more salient as time went on. The primary beneficiaries of nativization policies and practices were often exactly those who we would expect: the titular nationalities whose names matched the Soviet republics in which they lived, like Azeris in Azerbaijan, Uzbeks in Uzbekistan, Armenians in Armenia, and so on. This was even more the case after the 1930s, when nontitular minorities, such as Georgian-Ingilois, Talyshes, Kurds, and others, experienced limited—or no—access to comparable national "rights," including national cultural support, native language development, and recognition in the "big family of Soviet republics." In between these two broad categories of titular and nontitular—in terms of access to support and recognition—were the principal nationalities that inhabited lower-level ethnoterritorial units embedded in union republics, like Abkhazians in the Abkhaz Autonomous Soviet Socialist Republic (ASSR) in Georgia.

National proliferation was a starting point rather than an end goal of these practices and policies, which aimed to move the Soviet Union closer to a communist future that transcended national-cultural divisions. In this sense, *korenizatsiia* and corresponding measures were part of a broader process that Soviet historian Francine Hirsch has termed "double assimilation," that is "the assimilation of a diverse population into nationality categories and, simultaneously, the assimilation of those nationally categorized groups into the Soviet state and society."[5] The lower-level part of this process affected nontitular peoples who increasingly faced assimilatory pressures to identify as part of other nationality categories, whether a larger, "more developed" nationality or, more often, the titular nationality of the republic in which they lived. The other type of assimilation, meanwhile, described the eventual merging of recognized nationalities into a Soviet nation united through the Russian language. This higher-level assimilation was more developed in theory than in practice. The state never aggressively undermined the ethnonational titular foundations of the Soviet Union, but the notion of creating one nonnational (but in many ways Russian-defined and dominated) Soviet nation nonetheless felt threatening to those who feared it might affect their own national futures.

To date, scholars have taken a critical and limited approach to analyzing the Soviet Union through a colonial lens. Central Asia has been the focus of these studies, but many who put this region in conversation with European overseas colonialism also take care to highlight key limitations to this comparison.[6] Having analyzed the arc of these studies, Moritz Florin concluded that they ultimately "remind us of the futility of any attempt to accept or deny unequivocally the colonial nature of Soviet rule in Central Asia."[7] Yet, layered inequalities in the Soviet world have meant that this question repeatedly has been raised, and not only in relation to Central Asia. Although titular populations like Azeris were comparatively privileged within the boundaries of "their" republics, members of these communities sometimes chafed at both Moscow's control over republican affairs and at the all-Union hegemony of the Russian language and culture. In this way, Russian hegemony sometimes acted as a unifying force among non-Russians in the Soviet Union, like British or Spanish hegemony did throughout much of the rest of the world. Both titular and nontitular people alike could find common ground and identify with one another through their shared experience vis-à-vis Moscow. They were one in as much as they were not the ones in power.

What are some particularities of post-Soviet postcoloniality? As Maria Todorova has observed, "The emancipatory mantle of postcolonialism all too often serves as a cover for the perpetual lament of self-victimization." In the post-Soviet case, this strong declaration could be considered an understatement. Serguei Oushakine has adroitly highlighted why this is the case, showing how postcolonial narratives in the Soviet context have been characterized by an emphasis on "the brutality of the colonizers" rather than by the search for subaltern agency.[8] Embedded in this focus on the external colonizer is a distancing of oneself or one's nation from agency or responsibility for things that might have happened in the past. Indeed, in many post-Soviet states like Azerbaijan the Soviet experience has been inscribed in a framework that highlights how Moscow and Russians, as the proxy nation of Soviet power in the periphery, marginalized and discriminated against non-Russian peoples and republics, rendering all non-Russians equally innocent and equally disenfranchised from the power structures in which they lived. This narrative is blatantly untrue. The Soviet system was committed to national equality in some very real ways, but also fostered structures of inequality.

The center-periphery approach, thus, sometimes masks the complicated power dynamics within Soviet republics. For many nontitular peoples, titular nationalism—not Russian or Soviet colonialism—is to blame for the base level inequalities experienced over generations. At the local level, titular communities were often the ones that were most visibly privileged and empowered. Indeed, the creation of titular nationalities in Soviet republics generated a status-based ranking of ethnicity that paved the way for others to be designated minorities in those spaces. Titular peoples could at once be minorities (on the all-Union scale) and form the majority (in "their" republics). They sometimes experienced violent nation-building processes, as well as discrimination, on account of their nationality, but they were also known to enact some of these same practices to marginalize and violate nontitular communities and identifications.

As national affiliation gradually superseded class as the most significant marker of social identification in the USSR, there were many occasions when ethnonational communities were bureaucratically erased or otherwise pressured to assimilate into titular majorities, making minority erasure and subordination a central element of titular nation-building in the Soviet Union. These discriminatory or exclusionary practices sometimes fostered a backlash, stimulating minority nationalisms that, like titular nationalisms, drew on the elusive promise of national equality. In this way, key components of Leninist nationality policy, including ethnoterritorialism and *korenizatsiia*, contributed to nested nationalism—a recursive, enduring, and symbiotic relationship between majority-minority nationalisms in the Soviet Union. *Nested Nationalism* explores how this dynamic between peoples grew, mutated, and was hidden and re-remembered by all involved. As the Soviet Union strove to render nationalism impotent, a world of searing nationalist actors—aggressors, victims, and everything in between—emerged.

Interest in these dynamics has focused to date on the Stalin era and the breakdown of the USSR—the causes célèbres of Soviet history—overlooking the core years this book identifies as the incubator of what was to come. Little attention has also been paid to the history of nontitular communities, even when they have been at the center of post-Soviet ethnic conflicts. The prime reason for this is not just ideological; it is a question of source base availability, political censorship, and methodology. Many nontitular minority communities were not bureaucratically recognized after the 1930s, making them much harder to trace in Soviet archives. There are also significant gaps in history writing and ethnographies of nontitular minorities because of repressive state practices. During the Great Terror some scholars from these communities, as well as some who studied them, were intentionally targeted, leading not only to an erasure of existing knowledge, but also indicating to all who survived that the study of sub-republic minorities was potentially dangerous.[9] Thus, lacking robust narratives of post–World War II nationality politics and nontitular histories, Soviet historiography mostly leapfrogs over decades of evolving practices, theories, and experiences in this arena, drawing tenuous connections between the 1930s and 1990s and overlooking the formative postwar decades that gave rise to significant national movements.[10]

The constructivist turn in the 1990s that described the Soviet Union as a maker rather than a breaker of nations has also shaped the way histories have been produced.[11] Writing against an older narrative that dismissed Soviet nations as artificial and nationality policies as a disingenuous and manipulative mask for a repressive state, these scholars understood all nations to be constructed and took Bolshevik nation-building efforts seriously.[12] Focusing on the ways that the Soviet system shaped national identifications and nationhoods, and working at a time when Soviet archives were made newly accessible, these scholars often oriented their studies around the Soviet bureaucratic structures that were reproduced in those archives. Thus, when the state closed many of the programs and departments that dealt with nationality issues and assumed a more assimilationist posture toward nontitular minorities in the late 1930s, these changes were often mirrored in the histories being written about these topics. In essence, after the state curtailed outward support for nontitular minorities in the 1930s, historians also stopped looking past that period to study them.

There were two primary exceptions to this trend. National deportations continued to generate a substantial amount of paperwork about targeted minorities deported before, during, and after World War II. This unique history and the subsequent visibility of deported peoples like Crimean Tatars, Meskhetian Turks, and Poles in Soviet archives—as well as in memoirs and other types of sources—generated significant studies that set some of these communities apart. A handful of monographs also blended archival or published source research with ethnographic fieldwork or oral histories. This mixed methods approach allowed authors to extend the timeline of their narratives beyond the 1930s and to ask questions that were unresolvable in archivally constrained projects, including about the diversity of minority subjectivity, identification, and experience throughout the Soviet period and about the construction of categories and the internalization of and engagement with state efforts at cultural construction.[13] This book expands on this approach, nesting its study of peoples rarely found in archives with the oral traces of lives lived outside the state's conceptual limitations.

Kinship networks are at the heart of this story. A range of political actors in Communist Party structures, national movements, and minority communities sought to extend their cultural spheres of influence and make contingent use of kin minorities to advance national claims to neighboring republics and international states.[14] Through these networks, *Nested Nationalism* connects local narratives to global events such as World War II and the Cold War in pursuit of the politics, cultures, and communities that were layered across internal and international Soviet borders, ultimately exploring a regional world that transcended the political borders dividing the Soviet Caucasus from Iran and Turkey.

By cross-referencing and piecing together oral, visual, and written sources, I foreground the otherwise obscured mechanisms of cultural and identity organizing among peoples who often lacked meaningful state support and rec-ognition. Moving into the postwar and post-Stalin eras, this method helps to show how wartime experiences generated different ways of imagining and po-licing nontitular communities in the USSR. Even though Soviet officials de-clared that they had solved the nationality question in the 1930s, local residents, activists, academics, and politicians continued to contest national rights and nationality practices. Despite ethnographers making propagandistic appeals to the Third World by depicting the disappearance of nontitular minorities in the face of Soviet modernity, and republican officials pursuing assimilatory mandates and practices, nontitular identifications obtained in the Soviet and post-Soviet worlds. In short, the story of nontitular national rights and com-munities in the Soviet Union continues long after the 1930s. The bold dis-courses and strategies that national activists employed in grassroots campaigns for national cultural support and recognition in subsequent decades speak to their ongoing engagement with the rights of Soviet citizenship.

Nested Nationalism explores wide-ranging experiences and identifications and shows that people often had conflicting interpretations of their per-sonal and collective identifications and futures. While some minorities sought to assimilate into titular nationalities or saw them as their "natural" community—thus rejecting state or ethnographic attempts to categorize them other-wise—others defined themselves and their communities in opposition to assimilationist policies that encouraged the national consolidation of republic populations. To this end, it is helpful to keep in mind Rogers Brubaker's cri-tique of "groupism," including the "tendency to treat ethnic groups, nations, and races as substantial entities to which interests and agency can be attrib-uted."[15] To the extent that sources make it possible, this work is attentive to the range of opinions and orientations among peoples categorized as part of one national community or another and rejects the tendency to reify the pri-mordial or essentialized views of nationalized actors and agitators. This also means that differences of opinion about minority rights are considered dis-agreements between people with contrasting viewpoints rather than conflicts between bounded ethnic groups.

"The Less You Say, the Longer You Live": Working in the Margins

In the late 1930s, as the Soviet leadership consolidated population categories around key nationalities and drastically reduced its infrastructure for nontitu-lar national support (soviets, schools, presses, etc.), correlated bureaucratic processes that once generated knowledge about these populations also declined, further pushing minority identifications to the margins. Since archives function as a type of state politics, reflecting the epistemologies of the time in which they are created, the archival visibility of nontitular minorities in the Soviet Union decreased as the state started to view them as sites of assimilation rather than preservation.[16] This creates both practical and conceptual hurdles to archival research. In Azerbaijan, for example, various archive directors and employees informed me that I was wasting my time and theirs because it was anachronistic to study national minorities after the 1930s.

The arc of Soviet nationality historiography parallels that of the archive, focusing on titular populations in the early decades, when relevant archival records proliferated across myriad bureaucratic structures. Yet, the archives that historians work in are not merely repositories of facts or sources but places that exclude more than they preserve—sites that must be examined even as we work within them.[17] Although nontitular minorities are catalogued less frequently in Soviet archives as time goes on, this does not mean that these communities ceased to exist or that people stopped demanding recognition of and support for the nationality categories that government agents insisted had been left in the past. Minority histories can also be found in sites of their erasure, in places where one would expect them to be but cannot find them.

Gyanendra Pandey, drawing on Antonio Gramsci's point that subaltern histories are "necessarily fragmented and episodic" because of their relationship to the state, has observed that the "narratives that are preserved by the state in archives and other public institutions and that appear in the wider public discourse originate for the most part with the ruling classes, and owe their existence largely to a ruling class's need for security and control."[18] Indeed, archival absences function as a type of power and enter into the historical record at various points—when sources are (or are not) created, when they are (or are not) preserved or made accessible, and when historians or other narrators do or do not make use of them.[19] Thinking critically about the underrepresentation of nontitular communities in available state documents can thus offer a path to understanding those who were producing and reproducing the systems of power that generated those erasures in the first place.

The political situation in post-Soviet states that have recent histories of ethnic conflict can also complicate studies of minority communities in those places. In Azerbaijan, my archival access was severely constrained by the ongoing Nagorno-Karabakh conflict with Armenia and by Azerbaijan's recent history of autonomist and separatist movements. I benefited greatly from the support of archivists and colleagues who have asked to remain anonymous, but generously extended their time and expertise. Yet, there were also clear institutional constraints. In a number of instances, archivists told me that files I had ordered from the finding aid were now closed or had been destroyed. In one regional archive, the director told me that the records I was looking for had been burned in a bonfire. I struggled in particular with access to the former Communist Party archive in Baku. I briefly worked there in 2008, but was subsequently unable to access documents. During an attempt a few years later, I was admitted to the archive, but not allowed to view any files because, as one archivist quietly told me, my project was "not allowed" (*ne razresheno*). After a few days, the archive director denounced me as a separatist in front of archival staff and seized the pass that allowed me to enter the building. Personal experiences aside, these limitations of source access and institutional support do not just circumscribe the histories that are available to us; they also help explain why nontitular minorities are underrepresented in the historical record as well as why so many want to keep it that way today.

These sorts of obstacles are not just products of past violence; current political tensions make it unlikely that these histories will be easy to find anytime soon. The large Armenian population in Soviet Azerbaijan and the unique challenge Armenian separatism in Nagorno-Karabakh posed to the republic mean that this case is always looming in the background. For these same reasons, however, Armenians do not occupy a central role in this book. Facing frequent accusations in Azerbaijan that I was an Armenian spy or intended to commit treason or sow separatism because I studied minority communities, it was not possible for me to order files about Armenians while conducting research in Azerbaijani archives. Armenians also had a unique minority experience in Azerbaijan. They were vulnerable to discriminatory practices (like many nationalities living outside "their" republic in the Soviet Union) and there were limits to their national-cultural development and political power, but, due to their size, the special status of the Nagorno-Karabakh Autonomous Oblast', and the existence of the adjacent Armenian SSR, Armenians were always a recognized nationality in Soviet Azerbaijan. Many of Azerbaijan's Armenians experienced relatively stable access to native-language educational materials, schools, newspapers, radio broadcasts, and other forms of cultural support. The same cannot be said for other minorities living in the republic.

In cases like these, oral histories are one means of accessing histories that states have tried (and are still trying) to hide. Knowing that I would experience a variety of conceptual and political archival constraints, I started the oral history portion of my project in 2007 during my first research trip to Azerbaijan. My hope was that these interviews would help me explore both minority subjectivity and the lived experiences of formal and informal state policies and practices. I also anticipated that they would give me a better sense of where to look in archives and enrich what was available in those research sites. Indeed, many people provided me with copies of photos, letters, articles, and books that they had saved to document their lives and their interactions with state officials. Living in minority communities also helped me better understand what I was reading in written sources and hearing in interviews. To this end, I conducted more than 120 interviews throughout Azerbaijan as well as in Moscow, Makhachkala (Dagestan), Tbilisi and eastern Georgia, and the Netherlands (with people from Azerbaijan who, for the most part, have since obtained asylum status there). I conducted the interviews myself in Russian, Azerbaijani, or a mix of those languages. Others sometimes joined in the conversation to help facilitate, translate, or offer their own insights. When I spoke with people who only knew Georgian, for example, they would often ask a trusted relative or neighbor to help translate between Russian and Georgian. I interviewed some people multiple times across years and others only once. I tried to ask some of the same questions in all of the interviews, but otherwise conducted them more as open-ended conversations rather than as structured interviews. Concerned about the political environment and research ethics particularly in Azerbaijan, I kept oral history interviews anonymous during the collection process and only provide loose identifying information in this book when it is needed to illustrate points being made in interviews.

Oral histories have unique methodological challenges but no more than archival sources. Archived documents are produced, filed, and preserved by individuals whose perspectives and motives are shaped by the historical moment in which they are acting. Oral sources are similarly created in the environment of the interview and molded by a host of social and political influences, including the subject position of the interviewer and who or what she represents to the interviewee. As historians we have to evaluate the context and subjectivity of this oral narration just as we would a written source made available in an archive.

Among historians, ethnographers, and others who work with oral histories in this region, there are evolving conversations about the specificities of these sources and how the Soviet legacy might mediate interviews. Irina Sherbakova, for example, argues that it is challenging to conduct oral histories in the shadow of the USSR because Soviet officials conceived of memory as a threat and treated it accordingly.[20] Daria Khubova, Andrei Ivankiev, and Tonia Sharova, meanwhile, identify two crises of memory in the former USSR. They find that former Soviet citizens were unmoored by the breakdown of hegemonic narratives and sudden changes before, during, and after the transition from Soviet to post-Soviet life and thus "find it very difficult to make sense of their own memories without an accepted overall public historical story to relate them to."[21] Khubova and her coauthors also identify fear as a complicating factor in oral histories. They cite in particular a "cumulative effect of fear of public remembering" and historical experiences of repression.[22]

Both points require further exploration. I sometimes found myself confronting what has been described as the "drone" or "other side" of silence in interviews, the times when people were preoccupied with the sensitivity of my research and could not or did not want to speak.[23] There were different ways in which people signified their discomfort, including shielded answers, purposeful misremembering, selective amnesia, pointed silences, refusals to speak, and requests to talk in remote outdoor locations (to shield them from neighbors who might report them to security agencies). These examples reminded me to keep sight of the difference between memory and remembering, and to confront both what it means for informants to be asked to remember and the historical significance of contemporary remembrances.[24]

Although it is generally recognized that these sorts of responses signify the agency and subjectivity of individuals in oral histories, deep debates about the crisis of memory, its meaning and subjectivity, and the purpose of oral history research have only hinted at the importance of the here and now in interviews. When informants raised examples of repression as explanatory factors for being guarded in an interview, they showed that both past and contemporary experiences continue to shape collective memory and the interview environment in the post-Soviet space. Some people, for example, argued that few Talyshes had agitated for cultural rights in the Soviet period or wanted to talk about them now because Talyshes had been collectively silenced by the harsh repression of their cultural leaders in the 1930s.[25] Others explained their reluctance to discuss Talysh history by pointing to more recent lessons they learned about the disciplining power of the state, citing specifically the suppression of people who participated in the short-lived Talysh-Mughan Autonomous Republic of 1993 and the 2007 politically motivated arrest of Novruzali Mammadov (Novruzəli Məmmədov). Editor of the Talysh newspaper *Tolishi Sado* and a respected linguist at the Academy of Sciences in Baku, Mammadov was charged with treason and inciting national, racial, or religious hostility.[26] When informants brought him up, they sometimes lowered their voices to a whisper, instinctively reinforcing the discomfort they were verbally articulating. A curtain seemed to fall around him after his premature death in prison in 2009.

People from other minority communities explained their silences or the sensitivity of our conversations in similar ways. In the north of Azerbaijan, a widespread hesitancy to speak about the Soviet-era Lezgin rights movement Rik'in Gaf (РикӀин Гаф) was connected to both historical and contemporary experiences. One major concern was Sadval, a Lezgin movement that was established in Dagestan in 1990, but involved Lezgins from Azerbaijan as well. Sadvalists agitated for the unification of Lezgins in Azerbaijan and Dagestan, arguing that this was the only way they could realize their cultural, political, and socioeconomic potential. In 1994, however, the Azerbaijani government blamed Sadval for a bomb that killed fourteen people on the Baku metro. Sadvalists were arrested, labeled terrorists, accused of collaborating with Armenian secret services, and sentenced to lengthy prison terms or death. The politically motivated imprisonment of other accused Sadvalists soon followed. One person whom I interviewed explained Lezgin collective fear in the following way:

> KG: Do you think that the majority of the population in Qusar knew about Serdechnoe Slovo [the Russian name for Rik'in Gaf]?
>
> INFORMANT: They knew. Everyone knew, but they [local officials] slandered them, in the sense of "they agitate against the state, against the party, against Azerbaijan, against the Soviet Union." They promoted such an understanding . . .
>
> KG: In the Soviet period?
>
> INFORMANT: Yes, even then. And everyone, when they saw them, they were afraid to be connected to them . . . afterward several of them were arrested and harassed—people like Bagishev [member of Rik'in Gaf]—and the nation, in general, was frightened. Well, who wants to be taken to jail for nothing? No one wants that . . .
>
> KG: But why are people still afraid to talk about Serdechnoe Slovo?
>
> INFORMANT: They think that Sadvalist members are all like K'vat'al [КIватIал is the informal Lezgin name for Rik'in Gaf] members. Because K'vat'al members in the 1960s were dispersed, well, I would say, were liquidated . . . They are afraid of this. Sadval developed in 1990 in Dagestan, not here, but [Azerbaijani officials] began to make it seem as if the two movements were one and the same. That's why people are still afraid to speak about Serdechnoe Slovo.[27]

Another Lezgin individual, who sought me out after hearing that I was in Qusar, was nonetheless extremely cautious when we were talking. I asked why and this was the response:

> INFORMANT: It's hard here, it's hard. We're not even allowed to speak openly. Someone will sit with you, have a nice conversation, and afterward he gets up and someone sells him out: he said this and that. Therefore, it's dangerous here. It's so dangerous with them, I saw and I know these types of situations, I've seen a lot. A friend could come

to me, I could welcome him with an open heart, sit with him, and afterward he could pass on to them . . . he's doing this, he's writing these sorts of things.

FRIEND OF INFORMANT: If right now the KGB or local government knew that I hosted this type of person and I spoke with him, oooh, this would be a big deal.

INFORMANT: "Oooh, why did you sit there? She's an American, she lives there, why did you go over there? Why did you sit there? What's your connection?"[28]

FRIEND OF INFORMANT: "Why" they ask and peck at you: "Why, why, why?"

INFORMANT: "Why, what did he want? What do you want? Do you also want . . . to be in jail?"

KG: How would they find out?

FRIEND OF INFORMANT: Well, it happens that walls also have ears.

INFORMANT: Yes, yes, the walls . . . Yes, there is that type of saying. Look, for example, one person had to have said something. But I say that I didn't say anything, and he says that he didn't say anything. That means that the walls also have ears, it's not really clear who . . .

In conclusion, the informant mused, "The less you say, the longer you live."[29] This person experienced low-level repression when agitating for national rights in the Khrushchev era, but it became clear in the interview that post-Soviet experiences have also been sobering. In a similar interview with a Georgian-Ingiloi individual, I mentioned an Azerbaijan Communist Party document that described how Georgian-Ingilois in one village requested that their Georgian-language school be replaced with an Azerbaijani one. This informant instinctively and loudly denounced this claim and then muttered, "Man, if they hear me, they will arrest me."[30]

Khubova and her coauthors may go too far in describing a Soviet state that had near totalizing control over the memories of its inhabitants, but the restrictive political culture of the Soviet Union and many of its successor states increases the likelihood that individuals will be familiar with both canonized histories and the politics of remembering experiences that oppose those politicized narratives.[31] This is no less the case for this project. In Azerbaijan, national historical narratives and memories have been politicized to produce a charged, affective, and nationalized "us versus them" culture wherein minority public figures such as Novruzali Mammadov and his successor Hilal Mammadov (Hilal Məmmədov) are called separatists and traitors or conflated with an Armenian other who is the enemy of the "Azerbaijani nation." Hilal

Mammadov, who revived *Tolishi Sado* after Novruzali's arrest and untimely death, was himself arrested in 2012, accused of politically motivated crimes that echoed Novruzali's, and subsequently spent nearly four years in prison.

In early 2011, Azerbaijani president İlham Aliyev (İlham Əliyev) neatly summarized the official Azerbaijani position at the Baku-hosted World Forum on Intercultural Dialogue—Azerbaijan is and always has been a model of tolerance: "Everyone lives like one family in Azerbaijan. No national or religious confrontations or misunderstandings have existed here."[32] To be sure, as Rogers Brubaker, Margit Feischmidt, Jon Fox, and Liana Grancea found in their study of nationalist politics and ethnicity in Cluj, Romania, ethnicity is more of an "*intermittent* phenomenon," which "*happens* at particular moments, and in particular contexts" than a "continuous" or "everyday preoccupation."[33] Nonetheless, it does "happen" that people interpret everyday experiences, and channel identifications and self-understandings, through the lens of ethnicity (or nationality, as is more often used in the Soviet/post-Soviet context). It is also the case that there have been plenty of national and religious contestations in Azerbaijan, and that it is risky to remember or recount stories or experiences that run counter to the state's master narrative of eternal brotherly love and peace.[34]

Some scholars argue that what they call external and subjective factors such as these can compromise the integrity, validity, or usefulness of an interview. Khubova and her colleagues, for example, portray fear as a complicating factor that negatively affects oral history collection. Others favor relying on the authenticity of memory rather than focusing on the myriad factors that mediate oral history accounts.[35] I argue that the subjectivity of oral sources—like written sources in archives—should not be downplayed or overlooked, and that it is impossible to control for external influences or anxieties that provoke silences, amnesias, or purposeful misremembering in interviews. Further, it would be misleading to dismiss interviews marked by silences as invalid or unproductive because they fail to provide necessary or expected "historical information." These interviews also have analytical and methodological significance.

In this regard, I draw on an approach to subjectivity that finds value in these source particularities. As Alessandro Portelli puts it,

> The importance of oral testimony may lie not in its adherence to fact, but rather in its departure from it, as imagination, symbolism, and desire emerge. Therefore, there are no "false" oral sources. Once we have checked their factual credibility with all the established criteria of philological criticism and factual verification which are required by all types

of sources anyway, the diversity of oral history consists in the fact that "wrong" statements are still psychologically "true" and that this truth may be equally as important as factually reliable accounts.[36]

Portelli reminds us that remembering is an active process, that there is a historical context to the interview itself, and that changes may be wrought not only by faulty or misguided popular memories but consciously or subconsciously because of the meditation of other variables.

Liisa Malkki poses a similar challenge to researchers in her study of Hutu mythico-history among refugees from Burundi. She takes care to differentiate this from oral history, but the point that she makes about reading or using these types of sources is nonetheless helpful for thinking through oral history subjectivity: "the more challenging approach to such narratives . . . is not to sort out 'true facts' from 'distortions' but to examine what is taken to be the truth by different social groups, and why. Different regimes of truth exist for different historical actors, and particular historical events support any number of different narrative elaborations."[37] Instead of focusing on whether what we hear in an oral history interview is "true" or "authentic," we can ask whether the narrator thinks it is, and what that does or does not signify. Further, the subjectivity of the narrator exposes ways in which the past becomes a part of the present, how the past is used to interpret the present, and how people understand, assess, contextualize, and represent their own life experiences.

Interviews where informants expressed amnesias, misrememberings, or silences produced useful research insights. They show how past and present experiences are negotiated in oral histories conducted in contemporary Azerbaijan's minority communities and draw attention to events and individuals of particular sensitivity or significance. These interviews should be kept in mind as a backdrop to all the interviews cited in this book, including those where informants did not share—or better concealed—their collective and individual concerns.

As mentioned above, *Nested Nationalism* is a study of the politics and practices of managing nontitular minority communities and identifications in the Soviet Union and the consequences of these efforts. Its chronology runs from the early years of Soviet power to contemporary minority experiences, with a particular focus on the midcentury decades of the Soviet Union. Chapter 1 traces the evolution of Soviet nationality policies in the 1920s and 1930s and highlights early attempts to layer *korenizatsiia* across titular and nontitular communities in Azerbaijan. It pushes us to think more critically about what it meant to be a minority in the Soviet Union and about the process of minoritization there. By describing an informal hierarchy that began forming among nationalities in those early decades and kept shifting in subsequent years, the chapter shows that the nontitular category itself cannot be taken for granted or read as monolithic.

Chapter 2 asks how World War II and its aftermath were experienced in the Soviet Union and, in particular, how geopolitical conflicts intersected with national consciousnesses, relations, and politics in the South Caucasus. Toward the end of the war and in the immediate postwar period, the Soviet leadership tested the boundaries of its power by fostering national liberation movements among Kurds and Azeris in Iran and advancing territorial claims against Turkey. Against a backdrop of local assimilatory policies, national actors in Soviet republics repurposed these discourses of national extraterritoriality for their own nation-building ends, reigniting dormant national disputes in the Caucasus and consolidating transborder alliances and insecurities.

Chapter 3 begins a multichapter exploration of the afterlife of early Soviet nationality policies and wartime territorial disputes. In these chapters, I engage with historiographical debates about Soviet citizenship, the depth and social meaning of Khrushchev's Thaw, and post-Stalin Soviet society and governance, as well as conceptual questions about identification, minority subjectivity, and nationality theories. After Stalin's death in 1953 and the subsequent repression of then First Deputy Chairman of the Council of Ministers and Minister of Internal Affairs of the Soviet Union Lavrentiy Beria and Azerbaijan Communist Party First Secretary Mir Jafar Bagirov (Mir Cəfər Bağırov), a new leadership cohort led by Mirza Ibragimov (Mirzə İbrahimov), imam Mustafayev (İmam Mustafayev), and Sadıq Ragimov (Sadıq Rəhimov) took charge of Azerbaijan. They pursued a nationalizing course that contributed to their respective dismissals at the close of the decade. Despite the way in which they left office, during their brief time in power they oversaw a series of nativization efforts that helped Azerbaijan to become "Azerbaijani" after decades of uneven titular nation-building. This chapter incorporates nontitular minorities into the history of Azeri nation-building in the 1950s. Nontitular populations are key to this story because republican elites strengthened the republic's titular identity in part by weakening competing identifications and claims to the republic.

In the next two chapters, I turn my attention more directly to the nontitular experience, the different ways in which people from nontitular communities responded to their circumstances and the mechanisms of cultural and identity reproduction in national communities that generally lacked state support. In chapter 4, I focus on the trajectory of Talysh national identifications and classifications. When some nontitular minority activists were agitating for—and realizing—the expansion of their national rights in the 1950s, the Talysh nationality category was being erased from the public sphere in the Soviet Union. This chapter explores why Talyshes were vulnerable to this assimilatory politics and the architecture of Soviet myths of nontitular assimilation. It argues that theories of Soviet modernity, as well as Talysh ethnonational ties to Iran, are key variables that shaped Talysh experiences in the Soviet Union.

In chapter 5, I show how minority activists took advantage of political de-Stalinization and the Thaw to advance national claims and interests. In the 1950s, new grassroots movements emerged, challenging nationalizing policies and practices in the republics. Illustrating the evolving political atmosphere in the USSR after Stalin's death, these minority activists engaged in rights negotiations with the state, and some of them regained access to national rights lost in the 1930s. Their successes—and failures—expose the possibilities of this period but also ongoing debates about the meaning and limits of Soviet constitutional guarantees of national equality and Leninist nationality politics.

Taken altogether, *Nested Nationalism* recovers a historical experience of how Soviet nationality policies and practices promoted and erased the memory of a dynamic, interwoven experience of community building, rebuilding, trauma, erasure, and activism among millions of people in the hopes of creating a communist world for the good of all. Many people suffered during these projects; this book recovers their traces. Many on the local level actively participated in bringing these events about. This book assesses the hows and whys. Today's post-Soviet world is a direct consequence of these experiences and how they were processed. As an answer to the 1962 petition that asked Khrushchev why the greater community could not also love the Georgian-Ingiloi language and culture, this book shows that it was not a problem of love, it was a question of belonging: who belonged in the Soviet republics; who belonged in the Soviet future; and who had the power to determine that belonging?

CHAPTER 1

Making Minorities and National Hierarchies

"I RECEIVED THE TELEGRAM. ANSWER SPECIFICALLY WHY THE FAMILY DOES NOT ANSWER. IS THE FAMILY WELL? KISSES = ZUL'FUGAR." Strips of yellowed paper affixed to a telegram preserve the anxious message that Zulfugar Ahmedzade (Zülfüqar Əhmədzadə / Зульфугар Ахмедзаде) sent from Suslovo, part of the Gulag complex in Western Siberia, to his son, Ayyub (Əjjub), in the Azerbaijan Soviet Socialist Republic (SSR).[1] Desperate communications like Ahmedzade's reflect the tragic circumstances of repressed people throughout the Soviet Union who, in the midst of their own tragedies, worried about the families they had been forced to leave behind and with whom they remained tenuously, if at all, connected. Extrajudicially sentenced to imprisonment by the Special Council of the People's Commissariat of Internal Affairs (NKVD) on August 23, 1938, Ahmedzade never saw his family again.[2] He died in 1942 in Mariinsk, the administrative center of Siblag, the sprawling central prison-camp of the Western Siberian Gulag (*Glavnoe upravlenie lagerei*; or main camp administration).

Who was Ahmedzade? Born in 1898 in Pensar village in what is now the Astara region of Azerbaijan—an area populated mostly by indigenous Talyshes whose Iranic language bears the same name—Ahmedzade joined the Bolshevik Party in 1919. Trained as a teacher, from the early 1920s until his repression in 1938, he worked his way up through Azerbaijan's political and national cultural ranks. He led Communist Party organization and instruction

(Orgotdel) departments, a land department, and executive committees throughout the republic, including in Lankaran (Lənkəran), Kurdistan, Zaqatala, Aghdam (Ağdam), and Astara.[3] He also worked for the Azerbaijan SSR Commissariat of Enlightenment (Narkompros) and from 1934 to 1938 headed the national minority department at the republic's publishing house, Azerneshr (Azərnəşr).[4] By the 1930s, then, Ahmedzade was one of the most prominent Talysh cultural and political figures in Azerbaijan. He produced literary materials in the Talysh and Azerbaijani languages, published poetry and fiction in both languages, created Talysh-language textbooks for new Talysh-language schools, and translated significant texts into Talysh, including *The Communist Manifesto*, *Robinson Crusoe*, and children's stories such as *Qaraca Qız*, by Azerbaijani writer Süleyman Sani Akhundov (Axundov).[5]

As nations are created, determining who does and does not belong, and eliminating, marginalizing, or otherwise silencing those who represent competing identifications and ways of being, are standard and often violent activities. For many years, political and cultural elites in various Soviet republics, including Azerbaijan, debated the contours of their nationhoods among themselves and with Moscow's representatives as part of the USSR's ongoing effort to standardize and define national cultures, traditions, and boundaries.[6] Purges of political and cultural workers in the 1920s and 1930s were part of this process. Although there has been a historiographical tendency to contrast "authentic" national actors (many of whom were eventually repressed) with "inauthentic" others who repress them, some of the victimizers were also enacting their own national agendas.[7] That is, there was no requirement to disavow the nation, however one defined it, when joining the Communist Party or working for the Soviet state. As Adeeb Khalid has pointed out in the context of Uzbekistan in the 1920s, "The new political elite, those whose work lay primarily in the party or the soviet apparatus, was equally invested in the nation, and they had no problem assimilating it to their idea of the revolution . . . The nation had become the common currency in which political elites conducted their business."[8]

The surge of violence and repression in which Ahmedzade was trapped, later known as the Great Terror, began in 1936. In the South Caucasus, it overlapped with the dissolution of the Transcaucasian Socialist Federated Soviet Republic (TSFSR) and the ensuing emergence of full-fledged Armenian, Azerbaijani, and Georgian SSRs.[9] As part of this process, the state started to classify the Tiurks of Soviet Azerbaijan as Azerbaijani in part to establish a titular nationality for the republic. Prior to this, things were blurrier. In the imperial period, the state ordered the population mainly according to religious confession and many people understood themselves in these terms as well. Therefore it was not uncommon for people in the area that became Azerbaijan and elsewhere in the Russian Empire to see themselves in religious rather than national ways. Myriad ethnonyms were also at play, including Tiurk and Türk. The Russian language distinguished between Tiurks (*tiurok*) and Turks (*turok*), but neither term was used in a consistent manner. Further, no comparable differentiation existed in the Azerbaijani and Turkish languages, meaning that until this ethnonymic break, Azerbaijani Tiurks and Turks were both commonly identified as *Türk* in those languages.

With Moscow and Ankara's relationship worsening, these sorts of muddled ethnic boundaries were increasingly undesirable. Thus, although the idea of an Azerbaijani nation can be traced to the local intelligentsia in the late imperial period, theirs was generally an expansionist vision that included pan-Turkish elements and linked Azerbaijanis in the Russian Empire to Azeris in Iran.[10] In contrast, the Bolshevik definition of the Azerbaijani nationality in the late 1930s looked inward, seeking to root Tiurks-cum-Azerbaijanis in the USSR and isolate them from the Turco-Persian world that extended beyond its borders. During the Great Terror, many historians, linguists, and writers associated with pre-Bolshevik or Turco-Persian understandings of Azerbaijani nationhood were repressed as the party standardized its definition of the Soviet Azerbaijani nation.

These geopolitical anxieties also disrupted the nascent national hierarchies and nontitular communities that are my focus here. The term *minority* had always been ambivalent in the Soviet context. Because national minorities (*natsional'nye men'shinstva*, or *natsmen*) were negatively stereotyped as backward, they were targeted, for better or worse, by various forms of national cultural programming that aimed to mature and standardize their national cultures and consciousnesses to advance their ethnohistorical development. The term *natsmen* sometimes was used broadly to describe all non-Russians, but increasingly came to denote nontitular minorities.

It also acquired overwhelmingly negative connotations over time.[11] Janet Klein has defined minoritization as a process through which minorities start "to be regarded as threats to the territorial integrity and sovereignty of 'the nation' and to the imagined privilege and power of the dominant (named) group, now envisioned as the 'majority,' or the *real* citizen."[12] During the Great Terror, political leaders in both Moscow and the republics increasingly conceptualized nontitular minorities as potential threats both to the security of the Soviet state and to the viability of titular nations. As the rights and visibility of nontitular minorities were curtailed and the complicated hierarchy of nationalities simplified to advance titular nation-building and Soviet ethnohistorical progress, prominent members of these national communities like Ahmedzade became marked.

This chapter traces this uneven process of minoritization from the early 1920s through the late 1930s and makes a case for rethinking some conventional understandings of early Soviet nationality policy. Although we write in broad strokes about nontitular and titular nationalities in the Soviet Union, inconsistent national cultural investments meant not only that Moscow treated various titular populations differently but also that there was often little coherence to the nontitular category. The example of Azerbaijan shows us that national cultural resources varied widely across nontitular populations throughout this period. *Korenizatsiia*—the striving to promote native languages and cadres in governmental affairs, education, workspaces, and cultural arenas—continued, and even expanded, in some communities even as others were being erased. Avars and Lezgins, for example, maintained census and passport recognition in Azerbaijan but lost access to other institutional forms of state support at the close of the 1930s. Others, such as Kurds, faced deportation as well as assimilation (at least from the state's perspective) into the Azerbaijani nationality category. Georgians and Armenians in Azerbaijan, meanwhile, entered the 1940s with comparatively stable access to native-language schools, media, and books, as well as representation in censuses and, to a lesser extent, local governance. Although consistently categorized as national minorities alongside other non-Tiurk/Azeri communities in Azerbaijan, Georgians and Armenians were also distinct because they had titular co-ethnics in neighboring republics. Throughout the Soviet period, they received external support from Soviet Georgia and Soviet Armenia, allowing them to be treated more like people who had a kin republic in the Soviet Union than nontitular minorities.

More generally, viewing Soviet history through the nontitular lens offers new ways of thinking about early nationality policies. Multiple scholars have argued, for example, that the drive for centralization during the cultural revolution of the late 1920s and early 1930s impaired *korenizatsiia* in national republics. This argument has intersected with debates about whether these changes precipitated a "Great Retreat" from or prefigured an intensification of extant efforts to amalgamate national groups and achieve ethnohistorical progress over the course of the mid- to late-1930s.[13] The period looks quite different, however, when the nontitular perspective is taken into account because it was only at this time that many nontitular minorities were first brought into *korenizatsiia* and—years after most titular nations—started to experience well-known aspects of Soviet nationhood, including access to state-sponsored national cultural resources and local political representation. In a pattern that repeats itself throughout the Soviet era, the disciplining of titular nations and some titular elites during the cultural revolution created new opportunities for nontitular development. This, in turn, reinforced an emerging dynamic wherein nontitular and titular national interests were often counterposed to one another.

Shifting the perspective from titular to nontitular nationalities similarly decenters debates about Russifying policies in the 1930s. When nontitular minorities were expunged from the census in 1939 they often were folded into the titular nationality of the republic in which they lived. People who might have been categorized as Tats in the 1926 census, for example, would now be Azerbaijani (and not Russian) in 1939. Similarly, it was common to convert nontitular schools to titular-language schools rather than to Russian ones when the Soviet minority school network was stripped down in 1938. In Azerbaijan, for example, curtailing national rights in nontitular communities at the close of the 1930s had an overwhelmingly Azerbaijanifying effect, not a Russifying one. Nested in the republics beneath the "big" titular nationalities, national minority experiences form a counternarrative to many of the defining chronologies and frameworks of Soviet nationality histories.

National Minority Differentiation in the 1920s

For some years, scholars have noted that Soviet history looks different when viewed from the periphery. Assuming the nontitular perspective shifts the standard narratives even further. The term "minority" has commonly been applied to all non-Russians in the Soviet Union, but the case of Azerbaijan shows that there was a much more complicated hierarchy of peoples in the USSR. From the first days of Soviet power, Azerbaijan's Narkompros defined *natsmen* not as all non-Russians but as "all non-Russian-speaking and non-Tiurk-speaking *national'nosti* and *narodnosti*" in the republic, including Armenians, Persians, Jews, Georgians, Lezgins, Greeks, Germans, and Poles.[14] The status of the titular or principal nationality (*osnovnaia natsional'nost'*) was set apart from that of nontitular peoples, meaning that there was an early precedent to handle Tiurks and non-Tiurks differently in the republic.

Terms and concepts were often used imprecisely. Tiurks, Uzbeks, and other titular or principal populations, for example, were sometimes referred to as minorities. This was particularly the case early on when they were stereotyped as backward "eastern nationalities" whose historical development had been stunted by Tsarist-era oppression and inequalities. Blurred boundaries aside, ongoing juxtapositions of titular and nontitular populations made clear both that there was a hierarchy even among these supposedly backward peoples and that they would be treated differently according to their place in the new system being constructed. Tiurks in Azerbaijan were specifically referred to as the principal nationality of the republic or as the "national majority," which was contrasted with "national minorities." Discourses of backwardness were also used against non-Tiurk minorities and minority cultures to favor or advance the Tiurk nation. In 1921, for example, the economist M. G. Veliev contrasted the dominant Tiurk language in Azerbaijan with the "obsolete" languages of the republic's minorities, namely Tats, Talyshes, Lezgins, and Kurds.[15] His use of "obsolete" to describe minority languages is illuminating. According to Veliev, these minority languages were weak not because the minority populations that used them were small or declining, but because the languages were archaic remnants of the past in a way that the Tiurk language was not.

As elsewhere in the Muslim areas of the Soviet Union, Tiurk women were constructed as a symbol of the civilizational backwardness that the Bolsheviks would help Tiurks overcome. In early Azerbaijan Communist Party reports, Tiurk women were criticized for their continued entrapment by the "remnants of everyday practices and religion" (*neosvobodilas' ot bytovykh i religioznykh perezhitkov*) and their "slavish dependence" on men.[16] Yet their purported backwardness was nothing when compared with that of women in Azerbaijan's national minority communities. In a 1927 report on minorities in the Quba region, the authors note, "If we frequently speak in relation to the Tiurk population about the need to fight the old traditions, polygamy, early marriage, the liberation of women and cultural backwardness in general, then with regard to the Mountain Jews we need to raise these questions with even more energy since the latter in this regard are even more backward, even more conservative."[17] Though Tiurks were frequently disadvantaged by imperialistic discourses of backwardness, they could also be uplifted through comparisons with more evolutionarily cursed natsmen living in the same republic, like these Mountain Jews, who descended from an ancient Jewish community in Azerbaijan and spoke a dialect of the Iranic Tat language.[18]

The point here is not to compare who had it worse but to illustrate that once a person was labeled as a part of this or that national grouping, their social, political, cultural, and economic experiences—in short, their public lives—were often mediated by that classification. In general, Russians were privileged over so-called principal or titular nationalities that, in turn, were treated better than national minorities, and so on. Even among nontitular minorities there was a wide range of national cultural support and recognition.

Figure 1. "Azerbaijani women at the school for the elimination of illiteracy." Republic of Azerbaijan State Archive of Film and Photo Documents (Azərbaycan Respublikasının Dövlət Kino-Foto Sənədləri Arxivi), or ARDKFSA, 2-1554.

FIGURE 2. "The shepherds of the Kalinin collective farm in the Ganja region mastering literacy skills" (1934). ARDKFSA 2-6684.

The lived experience of being a minority thus meant different things to different people.

From the start, Tiurk *korenizatsiia* attracted more attention and investment than the development of nontitular communities, which were only inconsistently supported. Primary issues of concern in the republic included increasing the number of Tiurk workers and party cadre members, battling Tiurk illiteracy, and developing a Latin script for the Tiurk language. Problems abounded and state officials faced real challenges indigenizing the republic, but by 1925, the party declared that political-administrative structures in rural Azerbaijan had been successfully Tiurkified. That year, Tiurks accounted for nearly 85 percent of workers in Azerbaijan's executive committees, *uchispolkom*, and village soviets outside of Baku and the Baku region (*uezd*). Russians (just over 3 percent) and Armenians (just over 11 percent) made up the rest of this workforce, typically in communities where they were demographically dominant.

If anything, Tiurks were overrepresented in republican governance outside of Baku. These figures come from a report that the Azerbaijan Communist Party sent to the Transcaucasian Regional Committee, or Zakkraikom. The authors use the 1921 population census of Azerbaijan to measure their successes and failures in indigenizing the republic. Russian and Armenian administrative representation outside Baku roughly matched census figures for both of those populations. When it came to Tiurk census figures, however, the report authors were more vague, grouping Tiurks with all "other eastern *narod-nosti*" to account for the remaining 83.6 percent of the republic's population.[19] In reality, Tiurks only accounted for approximately 59 percent of the population in that census. In conflating Tiurks with the "other eastern *narodnosti*," they obscured the substantial size of the republic's natsmen population and used this inflated category to characterize 85 percent Tiurk representation in rural Azerbaijani administration as a success.

Rural Azerbaijan was one thing, indigenizing the capital Baku and its surrounding region was a more challenging task—herculean, some might say. Over the course of the late nineteenth century, the demographics of the city radically changed in step with the developing oil industry and strengthening Russian influence in the region. In 1843, Muslims accounted for more than 90 percent of the population, but by the turn of the twentieth century they had declined to less than 40 percent. Muslims also owned most of the real estate in Baku and there were prominent Muslim oil magnates, but they also dominated the unskilled workforce in and around the city and tended to be more transient than others who lived in the area, maintaining close ties with their home villages and living a semi-proletarian lifestyle.[20] Russians and Armenians more commonly occupied skilled positions and exerted outsized influence in this economically dynamic city. By the 1920s, significant communities of Tiurks, Armenians, Lezgins, Jews, Iranians, Georgians, Tats, and others lived and worked in Baku, but Russians—at 44 percent—were socially, economically, and politically dominant. This meant that class and political divides fell along national lines in the republic, with Russians far more economically privileged than Tiurks and proportionally more likely to be party members. Party officials at the time focused on building a larger Tiurk proletariat, believing that this would increase Tiurk party membership and representation at higher levels of republic governance, as well as better integrate the Tiurk population into powerful sectors of the republic's economy.[21]

Some indigenization gains were made in the 1920s, but others took much longer. After the 1933 appointment of Mir Jafar Bagirov as first secretary of the Azerbaijan Communist Party, this top party position in Azerbaijan was always occupied by a male from the republic's titular nationality, but only two of the seven men who preceded Bagirov at the top of the party were from Azerbaijan—Mirzadavud Hüseynov (1920) and Levon Mirzoyan (1926–1929).[22] The other five, including Sergei Mironovich Kirov and Grigory Naumovich Kaminsky, were from Ukraine, Russia, and Georgia (displaying once again the belief that the titular nation had a unique claim to "their" republic, Mirzoyan is also often counted as "other" since he was from Azerbaijan but ethnically Armenian). Bagirov, like other republican first secretaries, answered above all to Moscow rather than to the republic, but he was not an empty figurehead put in place to indigenize the republic's leadership on paper. He was a strong and influential leader, who had close personal ties to the leadership in the Kremlin, and especially to Lavrentiy Beria.

Bagirov's appointment aside, efforts to Tiurkify Baku and, more broadly, to make Tiurk (Azerbaijani)-language knowledge more prestigious and commonly used in republican governance extended well into the post-Stalin era. It was only in the 1970s that Azeris (that is, Tiurks) became demographically dominant in the capital city of their eponymous republic. Although some historians and commentators have made much of the point that it took so long for Baku to be "indigenized," implying that certain nationalities are or are not native to Azerbaijan and thus belong in Baku or don't, to others, including Stalin, the multinationality of Baku represented an example of harmony among peoples and the future of national development.[23] This was also not a unique trajectory in the region. Tbilisi, the capital of neighboring Georgia, was a similarly multicultural space in which the titular nationality—in this case, Georgians—were a demographic minority until the 1970s.

Support for evolving national cultures and communities in the USSR— whether titular or nontitular—was continuously disrupted by a multitude of variables, including budget shortfalls, infrastructural shortcomings, postwar conditions, familial or community opposition to nationality categories ascribed by state officials, and a lack of political will.[24] There were also significant conceptual problems. While the Soviet state policy was to divide the population into essentialized nationality categories it recognized, government workers found that many people did not think in national terms (or at least not in those accepted by the state) and that even those who identified (or could be persuaded to identify) as part of one nationality or another did not necessarily speak the language the state associated with that identification. This was problematic not least because state officials generally considered language to be a reliable indicator of ethnicity and native language education was a centerpiece of Soviet nationality policy. They would thus classify some children as part of one nationality and expect them to study in that group's native language despite parents not identifying with that group and/or wanting their children to study in a different language.

At a meeting of Azerbaijan's Narkompros Department of Education of National Minorities in 1920, department workers detailed the basic ways in which these hurdles obstructed their work. They were focused on building a native-language school network in the republic, but how could they do this when there were no trained teachers, native-language educational materials, or other classroom resources? Further, what about the languages that lacked written forms? And where did you educate students whose language competencies matched neither Tiurk-language schools nor native-language schools (in the rare cases when non-Tiurk schools were available)?[25]

Natsmen work in the republic was further hindered by state and party workers who opposed—and attempted to obstruct—national minority development. Within Narkompros and the Communist Party in Azerbaijan, there were different schools of thought about how to deal with the nationality question in the republic. Some officials viewed national minority cultural and community development as a path toward building equality and dampening national conflicts in the region, but others disagreed.[26] Bureaucrats who prioritized Russian language learning at the expense of *korenizatsiia* worked at cross-purposes with those who wanted to cultivate a Tiurk-dominated republican culture that assimilated minorities and redirected resources intended for them to Tiurk communities and Tiurk cultural development. National minority communities became a battleground of sorts in this push and pull over the proper interpretation of Bolshevik nationality theories and policies.

Central Bolshevik policymaking for the South Caucasus, meanwhile, rested on assumptions that the early leadership—notably Stalin, as Commissar of Nationality Affairs and General Secretary, and Grigorii (Sergo) Ordzhonikidze, head of the Zakkraikom—held about the region, one of which was that that it was consumed by intractable, centuries-old religious and ethnic hatreds. As Stalin remarked at the Twelfth Congress of the Russian Communist Party (Bolsheviks) in 1923, "From early times, the Caucasus represented an arena of slaughter and squabbles and then, under Menshevism and nationalists, an arena of war." Citing the case of Zangezur (which corresponds roughly with contemporary Armenia's Syunik province), where he argued that Armenians massacred all the "Tatars" (Tiurks), and Nakhchıvan (Naxçıvan), where he claimed "Tatars" massacred all the Armenians, he declared that massacres were "a known form of solving the national question. But this is not the Soviet form of resolution." The Soviet form, of course, was the Transcaucasian Federation, which Stalin described as an "organ of national peace that could settle friction and conflict."[27]

Bolshevik leaders shaping policy in the South Caucasus were indeed preoccupied by myriad land disputes in the region, including in Nagorno-Karabakh, Zangezur, Nakhchıvan, Akhalkalaki, and Zaqatala, as well as violence that had recently played out in surrounding communities. State reports from this period, even those about banal or unrelated matters, are studded with casual mentions of recent ethnic violence, including references to villages whose inhabitants had been driven off or killed. A summary of educational development among Tats in Quba, for example, nonchalantly noted that cultural work among the Jews of Krasnaia Sloboda (at the time referred to as either Evreiskaia slobodka [Jewish settlement] or simply slobodka) had been paralyzed by a Musavat pogrom that killed up to 200 people during the period of "national hostility between Tiurks and Armenians" in 1918.[28]

In terms of nontitular minorities, then, archival records suggest that the communities that received the most attention in Azerbaijan in the early and mid-1920s were those that reinforced these assumptions of ethnic strife, either because of ongoing land disputes or because of the potential to generate new ones; minorities with foreign connections that could be useful or dangerous, depending on the context; and those characterized in ways that did not correlate to Bolshevik ideology. Sometimes these features overlapped. Greeks received an outsized amount of attention regionally, as did Jews. There were four recognized settlements with "native" (korennoi) Jewish inhabitants: Vartashen (now Oğuz) in Nukha uezd (952 inhabitants), Jewish slobodka in Quba (5,816 inhabitants), Miudzhi Gavtaran (Mücühaftaran) village in Göychay (382 inhabitants), and Miudzhi (Mücü) village in Shamakha uezd (489 inhabitants).[29] These figures accounted for some of Azerbaijan's Mountain Jew population, but Mountain Jews and "European" Jews also lived elsewhere in the republic, particularly in Baku. As of 1928, the state recognized more than 36,000 Jews in Azerbaijan.[30]

From the mid-1920s through the early 1930s, the Azerbaijan Society for the Settlement of Jewish Toilers on Land (the Azerbaijani office of the all-Union OZET [AzOZET]) and the Azerbaijani branch of the all-Union Committee for the Settlement of Jewish Toilers on Land (AzKomzet) targeted these communities for resettlement to newly created Jewish national regions in Crimea and Birobidzhan (also referred to as Bir-Bidzhan). These relocations were part of a broader effort to rejuvenate the USSR's agricultural potential and change the economic culture of Soviet Jews by transforming small-scale traders (purportedly petty bourgeois elements potentially hostile to Sovietization) and unemployed persons into "productive agricultural workers."[31]

High rates of unemployment (and underemployment) were of particular concern. In 1927, people categorized as merchants comprised only 15 percent of the population of Jewish slobodka in Quba; this figure was dwarfed by the nearly 74 percent classified as part of the rural proletariat (batraki), who perhaps had a small plot of land but sold their labor to get by; the poor (bedniaki); and seasonal workers (sezonniki). Increasing pressure pushing merchants to abandon their profession ensured that the number of poor and unemployed persons would only continue to grow. Officials planned to solve this "land question" by reallocating local land for agricultural purposes, but also by resettling people from this community to Crimea and other Jewish-designated agricultural settlements outside of Azerbaijan.[32] Although these were internal Soviet resettlements, a significant foreign dimension was also at play: foreign aid, including from the Joint Distribution Committee (also known as the Joint or the JDC), the Jewish Colonization Association, and others, supported these migration projects, which, ultimately, complemented other efforts to transform the economic, religious, and cultural life of Jews who remained in their home communities.

The "Kurdish problem" was another nationality question that attracted significant attention. The Kurdistan *uezd*, also known as Red Kurdistan or Azerbaijan Kurdistan, was established in Soviet Azerbaijan in 1923, amidst debates about the incorporation of the Autonomous Oblast' of Nagorno-Karabakh and the Nakhchıvan Autonomous Soviet Socialist Republic into Azerbaijan. In 1922, the Central Committee in Baku created a special commission to determine the boundaries and structure of Kurdistan and Nagorno-Karabakh. The two issues were discussed in tandem, but, while there was apparently no question by this point that Nagorno-Karabakh would have some form of autonomy in Azerbaijan, Kurdistan's status was far more contested.

From the close of 1922 to the summer of 1923, the issue was repeatedly discussed and debated at the presidium of the Azerbaijan Central Executive Committee. In early July 1923, it was raised at a meeting of the aforementioned commission. One faction proposed establishing a special administrative Kurdistan *uezd* subordinate to the center, arguing that it had a sufficiently large population, was far from Baku, and was isolated from lower Karabakh. A different group, however, favored a centralizing approach and preferred to create a Kurdistan district (*raion*) with no special status, subordinated to lowland Karabakh. Soon after, on July 7, 1923, the commission went in an entirely different direction, deciding to form an "Autonomous Kurdistan" with borders delimited in coordination with the establishment of an "Autonomous Nagorno-Karabakh." There is still much to be learned about what pushed the commission in this direction, as well as why higher authorities ultimately rejected this proposal, instead creating a Kurdistan *uezd* that was a special administrative unit, but lacked the autonomous status granted to Nagorno-Karabakh.[33] Some supporters of Kurdistan, which was based in Lachın and located between Armenia and Nagorno-Karabakh, were disappointed with its limited status and frustrated that the city of Shusha was granted to Nagorno-Karabakh rather than to Kurdistan. The chairman of Kurdistan's *uispolkom* (*uezd* executive committee) even wrote an article to this effect in *Bakinskii rabochii*, but an Azerbaijan Communist Party resolution in October 1923 confirmed that Shusha would remain in Karabakh.[34]

In 1929, the Kurdistan *uezd* was dissolved in connection with an administrative restructuring of Azerbaijan that abolished this type of administrative unit. Its territory was initially annexed to the Autonomous Oblast' of Nagorno-Karabakh, but a new Kurdistan *okrug* was soon established. Larger than the earlier *uezd*—it reached to the Iranian border—the *okrug* encompassed all of the *uezd*'s territories in Kalbajar, Koturli, Lachın, and Qubadlı, and expanded into the Zangilan region and parts of Jabrayıl previously in the Karabakh Oblast'.[35] It was nonetheless short-lived. There were ten *okrug*s at the start of 1930 in Azerbaijan, including Zaqatala, Baku, Mughan, Nukha, Quba, Lankaran, and Kurdistan, but they were broken up later that year when the republic was once again reorganized, this time into sixty-three regions. When the *okrug* was dissolved, most of the 43,000 recognized Kurds in Azerbaijan lived within its boundaries. Both Lachin and Kalbajar were understood to be "almost exclusively Kurdish regions."[36]

This administrative change was part of a broader reform that abolished most *okrug*s in the USSR, but this does not satisfactorily explain why Kurdistan disappeared from the map of Azerbaijan. There is much we still do not know about the battle for Kurdish autonomy there, but, taking a comparative perspective, it is clear that the benchmarks for achieving national status and territorial autonomy in the USSR were subject to contestation and negotiation, with the adversaries in these disputes often taking the side either of minority autonomy or republican territorial integrity (and titular nationhood). As Arsène Saparov has argued, "a detailed analysis of the creation of national autonomies in Transcaucasia indicates that in each case the decision was made on the basis of the current state of affairs on the ground, as well as taking into account the situational, short-term interests of the Soviet leadership. There was no general conflict resolution plan or strategy according to which national minorities could gain political autonomy."[37] It is indeed easy to find instances where populations with stronger cases for autonomy and cultural privileges than the Kurds also lost out on their autonomy bids. A similar debate unfolded in neighboring Georgia, where the Georgian Party leadership parried demands for Mingrelian autonomy, recognition, and national privileges.[38] In the case of Azerbaijan, the location of Kurdistan no doubt strengthened centralizers' resolve to undermine Kurdish autonomy; Armenians and Tiurks had recently battled—with words and arms—over control of the *okrug*'s surrounding territories—Zangezur in southern Armenia and Nagorno-Karabakh and Nakhchıvan in Azerbaijan.

Kurdish autonomy was contested in Baku, but Bolshevik leaders also had broader concerns about Kurdish foreign connections. As Michael Reynolds has pointed out,

Empires know no necessary or obvious limits to their borders. This boundlessness offers pliability but also breeds insecurity. This held especially true for the Ottoman and Russian empires, whose vast territories were contiguous and whose populations overlapped. Kurds, Armenians, Circassians, Greeks, Tatars, Caucasian Turks, Assyrians, and Cossacks among others inhabited both empires and moved back and forth between them. The imperial states were interpenetrating. They could, and did, project their influence and power beyond formal borders to challenge the authority of the other inside its own territory.[39]

These insecurities and interpenetrations extended to the Persian Empire, which had significant overlapping communities of Armenians, Azeris, Talyshes, Kurds, Shahsevans, Turkmen, and others. Russian imperial agents had fretted about these interconnections amid Russo-Ottoman and Russo-Persian tensions in the nineteenth and early twentieth centuries, and they remained a concern for the Soviet government.[40] There has recently been new research on how Armenian flight to the Caucasus during the Armenian Genocide disrupted ethnic relations in that region and shaped nation-building practices and policies there.[41] Less studied are Kurdish migrations across the late Ottoman/Turkish, Persian/Iranian, and Russian/Soviet borders.

How did the treatment of Kurds in any one of these political spaces ripple through the broader region? Reza Shah's centralizing policies in interwar Iran disrupted Kurdish communities and inspired outmigration to the Caucasus, among other places, but Kurds also moved to the Caucasus from Turkey. From 1916 to 1934, the Young Turks and Kemalist state pursued a "two-track" deportation policy to Turkify Anatolia. Kurds were deported from the eastern provinces to western Turkey in three waves—1916, 1925–1927, and 1934. Young Turk propaganda and policies that accompanied Kurds' physical removal sought to erase the Kurdish nationality and assimilate them into the Turkish nation by renaming them "mountain Turks" (*dağlı Türkleri*), banning the use of Kurdish in public places including schools, blocking the official use of the term Kurdistan, Turkifying Kurdish toponyms, and disrupting social ties. Forced migration also flowed eastward, but those migrations were of "culturally Turkish" settlers displaced from Yugoslavia, Bulgaria, Greece, Syria, and elsewhere who were sent to Anatolia to settle in Kurdish lands and Turkify eastern provinces like Diyarbakır, from which Kurds and, before them, Armenians and Assyrians had been deported and in some cases genocidally killed.[42]

The middle years of displacement in the 1920s overlapped with a large uprising in Turkish Kurdistan driven by a political movement fronted by Shaikh Said. He sought to establish an independent Kurdish state ruled by Islamic principles on the heels of Ankara abolishing the caliphate and pursuing the Turkification of Kurds and Kurdish territories. Shaikh Said's revolt, which started in 1925 and simmered through an amnesty in 1928, was not the first and would not be the last or largest among Kurds in the Turkish Republic, but it triggered extensive repression, even among those who did not participate in the rebellion, and signified the emergence of successful nationalist organizing among Kurds.

The Bolsheviks told Shaikh Said's emissary that they were "not in a position" to assist them, but also pledged to remain neutral should Turkey ask for help suppressing the uprising.[43] The Bolsheviks thus declined to outwardly support Shaikh Said, but their stated sympathy for the Kurdish situation in Turkey and refusal to back Ankara made the Soviet Caucasus a potential destination for Kurds seeking to leave Turkey. Yet Kurds who migrated to the Soviet Caucasus did not always conform to the preferences of their new hosts, who often preferred that they settle in interior sites far from the Turkish and Iranian borderlands. In 1926, 1,422 members of the "Bruk ki" tribe arrived in Soviet Azerbaijan from Turkey. Soon afterward, the Zakkraikom ordered that they be moved to the Nukha (later Shaki) *uezd* in northern Azerbaijan. Dissatisfied with this resettlement, tribal members migrated back to the Turkish border region in Armenia and Nakhchıvan, where they started reaching out to Turkish authorities about the possibility of returning to Turkey.

Soviet authorities disliked having these Kurds in the border zone, but they also worried that Kurdish flight would damage their regional status. This external dimension guided a myriad of internal decisions about Kurds and Kurdish national cultural development in the Caucasus. In 1931, for example, an expert commission met in Tiflis to discuss Kurdish alphabet reform amid a broader movement for Latinization not only in the Soviet Union, but in neighboring Turkey as well. By the time the meeting was convened, an All-Union Committee in the USSR had already approved Latinized alphabets for Azerbaijani (Tiurk), Chinese, Tajik, and thirty one other languages. A Kurdish Latin alphabet had been under development for a couple of years by this point, but disagreements among Armenian, Azerbaijani, and Georgian representatives had delayed the final resolution of this project. Part of the impetus behind shifting Soviet Kurds from an Arabic script to a Latin one was that Latin was considered to be a unifying system that would help Kurds move toward a shared proletarian culture and evolve from "dark masses" into a cultured *narod*. It was also characterized as an "international" script and explicitly contrasted with proposals to adopt a Kurdish Cyrillic script, which, it was argued, would represent a turn away from internationalism. This was particularly important in the Kurdish context because of perceived competition for Kurdish influence in the broader region. "Agents of English imperialism" were purportedly making inroads with Kurds in Iran and Iraq, plus there was awareness that Ataturk's language reforms were altering the linguistic landscape in Turkey. These experts wanted the script they were designing to benefit not only Kurds in the Soviet Union, but Kurds abroad as well. They figured that if they adopted a Kurdish Latin alphabet then Soviet Kurdish publications could spread among the much larger Kurdish populations in Iran, Iraq, and Turkey.[44] The international dimension of the Kurdish question was always at the forefront of Bolshevik planners' minds.

General uncertainty about how to handle the Kurdish question in Baku also stymied planning for Kurds arriving from abroad.[45] This fact was sometimes exploited by those who pushed for Kurdish autonomy, but, despite these concerns, Kurdish cultural resources in the 1920s did not significantly differ from most other national minorities in Azerbaijan—that is, they were equally badly served. In the 1925–1926 academic year, there were 1,440 schools servicing 150,460 students in Azerbaijan. The language of instruction was overwhelmingly Tiurk (1,057 schools), with Russian (132) and Armenian (190) the next most commonly taught languages. Forty schools offered instruction in multiple languages and the remaining twenty-one schools were German (seven), Jewish (two), Volga Tatar (four), Greek (two), and Assyrian (one).[46] As yet, no schools offered instruction in major minority languages in the republic, including Lezgin, Talysh, and Kurdish.

Thus only five years after Sovietization, Bolshevik officials in Azerbaijan could brag about an educational system that taught in eight different languages, but the network still worked best for those who spoke Tiurk, Armenian, or Russian. This included some minorities whose first language was one of these languages rather than the "native" language of their nationality. It worked less well for those who had no choice but to study in languages they didn't know or didn't know well. This remained the case for the next few years, meaning that, despite the Tiurk elite's success at finally realizing Mirza Fath ali Akhundzade's nineteenth-century dream of a Latin script for the Tiurk language, by the end of the 1920s little had been done to create approved alphabets and other native-language resources for most natsmen in Azerbaijan. Indeed, slow progress in this sphere handicapped broader efforts to integrate minorities into the Soviet project.

Talyshes are another example of a natsmen community that raised security concerns but experienced little national development or support in the 1920s. As with the Kurds, discussions about Talyshes in Azerbaijan were influenced by the presence of a large Talysh population in neighboring Iran. At a 1928 party meeting in Baku, for example, officials worried that Talysh alienation from the Soviet project made them vulnerable to foreign propaganda and influences. One proposed solution was opening a cultural front to counter rumors spreading among Soviet Talyshes that better support was available for them in northern Iran.[47]

State officials disagreed about how they could best strengthen Talysh links to the Soviet Union. The Zakkraikom floated the idea of Talysh autonomy, but centralizers in Baku who favored a unified Azerbaijan with a strong Tiurk identity opposed this idea. For instance, a prominent member of the presidium of Azerbaijan's Communist Party, argued that Talysh autonomy should be considered only if Iranian Talyshes were first brought into the Soviet sphere of influence. Barring that unlikely development, he opposed Talysh autonomy, advocating instead for improved Talysh educational initiatives and the creation of a written Talysh language on the basis of Azerbaijan's new Latinized Tiurk alphabet.[48]

Little national cultural or political support was extended to Talysh communities in the 1920s. Between 1920 and 1926, only three new schools were built in the Lankaran *uezd*, home to most of Azerbaijan's Talysh population, as well as to Tiurk, Russian, Jewish, and other settlements. Existing schools were not only in desperate need of repair and resources, they did not teach in the Talysh language.[49] In 1927, Talysh representatives were finally brought into the Azerbaijan Executive Committee's Central Commission on National Minority Affairs (following the suggestion of the Lankaran *uezd* Executive Committee), but significant shortcomings persisted in local Talysh political representation and in the resources allocated to them.[50] Indeed, in the following year, the secretary of the Lankaran regional committee, A. Madatov, informed the presidium of Azerbaijan's Communist Party that the natsmen commission had still not engaged with the Talysh population. With the illiteracy rate among Talyshes hovering at 97 percent, Madatov pushed for greater Talysh representation on central commissions dealing with natsmen affairs and for the creation of a Talysh educational network in Talysh villages.[51] Yet despite significant security concerns, there was little movement on any of these proposals until the close of the decade, and, like Kurds, Talyshes never achieved autonomous status in Soviet Azerbaijan.

The *Korenizatsiia* of National Minorities and Rising National Repression

In the late 1920s, opportunities began to change not only for Talyshes and Kurds but for others as well. The period of the First Five-Year Plan (1928–1932) was when Stalin consolidated his control over the Communist Party and initiated what Sheila Fitzpatrick has termed the Soviet cultural revolution.[52] The revolution increased Moscow's control over the republics by purging national intelligentsias and extending the reach of Moscow-based state institutions like Narkompros. This reinforced Stalin's long-standing desire for greater centralization and his opposition to Lenin's position that, as Terry Martin has put it, "*all* local nationalism could be explained as a response to great-power chauvinism."[53] For Stalin, Russians were not the only potential national oppressors in the Soviet Union. He laid out this position several times, including at the Twelfth Congress in 1923, where he railed against "Georgian chauvinism" and the Georgian leadership's hostility toward the Transcaucasian Federation. As he explained then, the government should ensure that the "needs and requirements" of all nationalities are met in part by guarding against dominant nationalities taking advantage of others.[54]

Historians disagree about how this socialist offensive affected *korenizatsiia*. Yuri Slezkine describes it as a period in which "all of Soviet life was to become as 'national' as possible as quickly as possible," leading to "a feast of ethnic fertility, an exuberant national carnival sponsored by the Party."[55] Martin proposes that its centralizing and statist tendencies "fatally undermined" *korenizatsiia* in Western republics like Ukraine but had different results in the Soviet East, where the presumed backwardness of the local population enabled continued attention to nation-building. Though this was paired with the cultural revolutionary purges of the "*smenovekhovtsy*, the nationalist intellectuals who had accepted the Bolshevik offer to work on behalf of *korenizatsiia*," he finds that the cultural revolution nonetheless favored the East, which "welcomed centralization as it brought with it both greater financial assistance and support in the conflict between Russians and non-Russians, which it received in the form of the campaign against Great Russian chauvinism." Martin concludes that "the zenith of *korenizatsiia* in the east was the period from 1928 to 1932." Audrey Altstadt argues the opposite in her analysis of Azerbaijan at this time, finding that "in Ukraine and other Slavic and 'Christian' republics, *korenizatsiia* continued until 1933," but ended in Turkic or "Muslim" regions when the terror targeted national leaders in the late 1920s.[56]

Adeeb Khalid, meanwhile, redefines the cultural revolution in his study of Uzbekistan, using the phrase to describe "a bout of creativity from below that resulted from the enthusiasms unleashed by the revolution" in the 1920s rather than Stalin's later "revolution from above."[57] To Khalid, the repression of national intelligentsias that Martin and others see as part of the cultural revolution actually signaled its end, "for it transformed the cultural field as it had existed for much of the 1920s and altered the parameters of cultural production."[58] He further finds that *korenizatsiia* played a relatively small role in

Uzbekistan and rejects the idea that this socialist offensive weakened Russian influences in the republic: to the extent that the republic was nationalized at this time, it came at the expense of minorities like Tajiks rather than Russians.[59]

The period of 1928–1933 has been commemorated as a period of national terror in many republics, but Khalid hints at an important question—how did nontitular minorities experience this era?[60] In Azerbaijan, the wide-ranging attack on Tiurk nationalism coincided with a new push to indigenize national minority regions (*natsmenraiony*) and communities. Reports of interethnic anxieties had been building to this point. In a study about national minority work in Azerbaijan's Quba region in 1927, the Commission on the National Minority Question detailed numerous examples of anti-Tiurk tension in the region. Lacking a state-endorsed Lezgin script, Lezgins had to study in the Tiurk language despite not using it in their daily life. This, the commission said, contributed to "abnormal" relations between Tiurks and Lezgins. The situation was reportedly so bad that Tiurk workers could not work among Lezgins. Local Molokans and Tats (Mountain Jews) also apparently harbored anti-Tiurk sentiment. The report blamed this friction on class war and pernicious kulaks who resented losing their privileges, but Tats and Molokans clearly blamed the "Tiurk national government" for their misfortunes, viewing it as a government for Tiurks rather than one serving all the people of Azerbaijan.[61]

In the same 1927 report, dissatisfied national minorities were condemned as national chauvinists, but this was soon to change. Archived records from subsequent years document increasingly critical descriptions of Tiurk governance in national minority areas but also the first steps toward script and educational development for minorities. In 1928, for example, Narkompros developed a Talysh-language alphabet based on the new Tiurk Latin alphabet, enabling the production of the first Talysh textbooks.[62] A second textbook was published for higher grades in the 1930–1931 school year, and plans were made to publish a scientific Talysh dictionary by 1931–1932.[63]

These natsmen resources helped advance native-language education, but national imbalances persisted and local officials were frequently accused of sabotaging this emergent minority cultural and educational work. In 1931, natsmen department officials accused local government representatives of blocking the distribution of Talysh-language texts to delay the development of the Talysh language and protect their own privileges and power.[64] A report produced for Azerbaijan's Narkompros around the same time similarly claimed that first and second grade education had not yet been transferred to the Talysh language because of negligent local authorities.[65] A 1929 report also identified problems with minority education in Zaqatala. For example, the author noted that "Muslim Ingilos" and other national minorities in Zaqatala attended Tiurk-language schools and "Christian Ingilos" attended Georgian schools, but some Muslim students only spoke Georgian and thus had difficulty understanding their teachers. The investigator proposed transferring these schools to the "native language" of these students, but also openly questioned whether the state had enough authority and legitimacy in the area to implement this change.[66] This analysis was based on a review of the myriad ways in which the local population was already undermining the Soviet educational system: mullahs were still operating madrassas and teaching Sharia; nonlocal teachers lacked the authority to influence their constituencies; local teachers were beholden to social pressures and thus unwilling or unable to implement changes; and local government officials were uninterested in the school system and related issues.[67]

Indeed, Zaqatala soon became a major site of rebellion. From 1929–1931, uprisings broke out across the republic, including in Kalbajar, Nakhchıvan, Shamkhor (now Shamkir), the territory of the former Lankaran *uezd* (now Lankaran, Astara, Lerik, Yardımlı, Masallı, and Jalilabad), and in the northern region stretching from Nukha across Qakh and Zaqatala to Balakan. These conflicts were provoked by collectivization (or, in the language of the report, led by kulaks) but also drew inspiration from earlier rebellions and more localized events. The area from Nukha to Zaqatala witnessed one of the most significant anti-Soviet revolts, which security officials partially blamed on nefarious Dagestani, Turkish, and Georgian influences. Here, nearly 900 people were detained, several hundred killed or injured, and a couple hundred arrested.[68]

One of the most cutting criticisms of local nationalism is found in a 1931 memorandum written by Alimadatov, an official reporting to the Zakkraikom in Tbilisi. His wide-ranging study of Azerbaijan's national minority regions was harshly critical of the republic's failure to address natsmen affairs, including cadre development and administrative *korenizatsiia*.[69] He pointed out that non-Tiurks comprised nearly 40 percent of Azerbaijan's population, but Azerbaijan's Central Executive Committee, Party Central Committee, and other government organs did not know which regions were national minority regions in Azerbaijan, the national breakdown of village soviets and collective farms, and the number of party members from Talysh, Kurdish, Lezgin, and other minority communities.[70] Alimadatov was frustrated with the low level of administrative indigenization in Azerbaijan's various regions, and particularly with how this had unfolded in Talysh communities. The Lankaran regional committee, for instance, had forty-six members, but only nine from the sizeable Talysh community. Talyshes were similarly underrepresented on the party side, with only two Talysh members out of fourteen full and candidate presidium members.[71]

He was also concerned that Azerbaijan's Union of Agricultural Collectives had not documented the number of households and rate of collectivization in national minority areas and that village soviets were underdeveloped in these regions.[72] Alimadatov's criticism of Azkolkhoztsentr came at a time when central authorities in Moscow were beginning to attack the Zakkraikom for mistakes made during collectivization. A few months after Alimadatov's report, a Communist Party of the Soviet Union (CPSU) Central Committee resolution harshly evaluated economic work in Transcaucasia and attacked the Zakkraikom for "failing to prepare the peasant masses for collectivization and for [putting] inadequate pressure on the kulaks."[73]

Moscow's criticism of the Zakkraikom soon ramped up, with officials increasingly condemning the local nationalism of Transcaucasia's "principal nationalities"—that is, Tiurks in Azerbaijan, Georgians in Georgia, and Armenians in Armenia.[74] Officials in all three republics were accused of manifesting "great-power" tendencies by ignoring the interests of autonomous and national minority regions in their republics.[75] Finally, in 1932, the presidium of the Transcaucasian Central Executive Committee issued a decree ordering the *korenizatsiia* of national minority regions in the South Caucasus. It called for government affairs and records (legal provisions, protocols, decrees, court proceedings, village soviet records, etc.) to be written in native languages in national minority areas; the improvement and expansion of the school networks; regional executive and technical personnel to know local languages; central authorities to restructure their apparatuses to better serve national minority regions; the end of illiteracy among "culturally backward" *narodnosti* such as Lezgins, Kurds, Assyrians, Tats, Talyshes, and Ingushes; the creation of native teaching cadres; expanded publications in native minority languages; investigations into which language to use where minorities had "lost" their native language (i.e., some Greeks and Armenians in Georgia and Kurds and Tats in Azerbaijan); an increase in the number of national minority workers in Narkompros; and the *korenizatsiia* of village soviets and regional executive committees in national minority regions by January 1, 1933.[76]

According to a report generated later that year, eight of Azerbaijan's forty-four regions were classified as non-Tiurk regions—the Agdzhakend and Narimanov areas north of Nagorno-Karabakh were identified as Armenian; Astara, Zuvand, and Lankaran were defined as Talysh; Qakh was labeled Tsakhur; Gul'ev) was characterized as Lezgin; and Barda was generalized as populated by "Barda Tiurks."[77] Some cities in "Tiurk regions" were also classified as non-Tiurk. Khachmaz, for example, was defined by its Russian inhabitants, while "Annenfal" and Elendorf were categorized according to the local German population.[78] This was a diverse Azerbaijan, complicating the plans of policymakers who opposed national minority autonomy and sought to build a centralized republic defined by and united through the Tiurk culture and language.

Unequal Change in National Minority Communities

From the late 1920s through 1937, the level of national-cultural support afforded to minority communities and cultures in Azerbaijan noticeably increased. The first Talysh schools were opened in 1929–1930. Just four years later, more than 17,000 students were studying in 137 schools with Talysh as an instructional language for grades one through seven.[79] State officials knew that to have a functioning educational system in all of these different languages, they had to create teaching materials and train native speakers to teach in those languages. Indeed, over the first half of the 1930s, the Talysh teaching cadre increased from 64 to 370.[80] With the help of minority intellectuals like Zulfugar Ahmedzade, Talysh print culture also started to come into its own with the publication of Talysh-language novels, poetry, and newspaper pages in the 1930s.

Yet, significant inadequacies continued to plague the system, making it difficult to ameliorate inequalities in the republic. A lack of comprehensible native-language materials and qualified teachers meant that schools designated as minority language schools often failed to fulfill their mission to teach in those languages. In a 1934 report that Ahmedzade sent to Azerbaijan's Minister of Enlightenment, for example, he noted that the percentage of teachers with a low-level of education in national minority regions far outpaced the average in the republic. If, in the average Azerbaijani rural region 36.2 percent of teachers lacked a higher education, this figure ranged from 44 to 85 percent in national minority areas. National minority educators were also less educated than their Tiurk peers. According to Ahmedzade, Zaqatala was a national minority region (with approximately 12,000 Avars, 8,000 Tsakhurs, 8,000 Tiurks, and 5,000 Ingilois), but out of 213 teachers in the region, only 15 Tiurk teachers (and no Ingilois, Avars, or Tsakhurs) had an advanced level of education. An additional 120 Tiurk teachers had a secondary school education, but only one Avar teacher matched this qualification. Students suffered as result of poor teacher preparedness in the republic. A visit to a school in Jewish slobodka, for example, revealed that Tat (Mountain Jew) students in a geography class there could not identify the Caucasus on a map and thought that Azerbaijan was in Africa and the Soviet Union in North America.[81]

Oral histories and archival documents show that state officials also faced myriad challenges trying to enroll children in these schools. I spoke with some people who attended Talysh and other minority-language schools when they started opening in the late 1920s and early 1930s. Many reflected on how lucky they were to attend school when they could learn in their native Talysh language, while other stories showed that language impediments were only one of many reasons why some families resisted state pressure to send their children to school. One Talysh woman born in 1928 explained that she attended school for only one year, when she was seven. She studied in the Talysh language, but her father did not allow her to return because he did not want his daughter studying alongside male students and teachers. When she left school, she started working in Lankaran's tea fields, where she remained until she married at the age of seventeen and her new mother-in-law forbade her from working outside the home. Soviet officials devised various measures to overcome conservative social mores undermining their policies. This was a particular problem in national minority regions. Across the republic, girls on average comprised 39.6 percent of students enrolled in primary schools, but these numbers significantly dropped in natsmen communities. In two Talysh regions bordering Lankaran, where this woman lived, primary school enrollments in 1933 were only 26 percent (Masallı) and 8 percent (Lerik) female. One solution was to train more minority and female teachers, but this presented its own challenges.[82]

Inadequate schools, delayed implementation of indigenization efforts, and problems distributing native-language materials hampered minority educational development throughout the school system, but with increased political will minority schools nonetheless started to proliferate in the 1930s. Take Lezgin schools, for example.[83] In the 1929–1930 school year, 80 percent of school-age Lezgin children studied in the Tiurk language, but by the 1931–1932 academic year, 4,967 of 9,464 Lezgin children (52 percent) between the ages of eight and eleven attended Lezgin schools. This number increased to 8,478 in the following year and to 9,186 primary school students (85 percent of students) in 1933–1934.[84] By the 1938–1939 school year, 48 schools aimed to educate 11,980 students in the Lezgin language through grade four. Lezgin students also studied in mixed schools that offered both Azerbaijani and Lezgin language instruction.[85]

Rapid Lezgin educational growth in Azerbaijan was enabled by the development of a Lezgin language Latin script in the late 1920s and access to Lezgin resources, including teachers, textbooks, and political materials, from

Table 1.1   Instructional languages in Azerbaijan SSR schools

	1914–1915[A]	1919–1920	1928–1929	1929–1930	1933–1934[B]
1.	Russian-Tatar	Tiurk	Tiurk	Tiurk	Tiurk
2.	Russian	Russian	Russian	Russian	Russian
3.	Armenian	Armenian	Armenian	Armenian	Armenian
4.	Russian-German	German	German	German	German
5.		Georgian	Georgian	Georgian	Georgian
6.			Volga Tatar	Volta Tatar	Volga Tatar
7.			Greek	Greek	Greek
8.			Mountain Jew	Mountain Jew	Tat
9.			Assyrian	Assyrian	Assyrian
10.			Persian	Persian	—
11.				Talysh	Talysh
12.				Lezgin	Lezgin
13.				Avar	Avar
14.					Kurdish
15.					Uzbek

[a]For data on 1914–1930, see ARDA 57.11.7.40.
[b]Gadzhieva, "Razvitie shkoly," 115.

neighboring Dagestan, where there were more than 90,000 Lezgins (in one count from 1930). There was no titular nationality of the Dagestan Autonomous Soviet Socialist Republic, a constituent part of the Russian Soviet Federated Socialist Republic (RSFSR), but several peoples were categorized as principal *narodnosti* in the territory, including Avars, Lezgins (11 percent of the population), Dargins, and others.[86] These groups shared the political representation and national cultural support extended—to varying degrees—to principal/titular populations in other republics.

But Dagestan wasn't entirely helpful to Azerbaijani officials. Some Azerbaijani Lezgins, inspired by Dagestani recognition of and support for Lezgins there, demanded similar rights in Azerbaijan. The Dagestani leadership also occasionally attempted to insert itself into Azerbaijan's political process on behalf of Avars, Lezgins, and other "Dagestani peoples" living there. In 1927, for example, the Dagestan Executive Committee formally requested to have their representatives join the Azerbaijani Executive Committee's Central Commission on National Minority Affairs. The Azerbaijani side rejected this proposition.[87]

The 1932 decree ordering the *korenizatsiia* of national minority regions in the South Caucasus ascribed equal rights to all minorities, but unequal resources, differentiated expectations, and development discourses shaped an informal hierarchy of rights, support, and recognition. In 1931, one government report identified sixteen native nationalities in Azerbaijan and divided the natsmen into three evolutionary levels. The first group included Armenians, Germans, Georgians, Greeks, and Volga Tatars. These nationalities all had developed literary canons, native-language school networks, and qualified native-language teachers. Although the report author sought to create cohesive categories according to levels of purported evolutionary development, national resources and support could vary widely within each grouping. Armenians enjoyed fairly widespread access to native-language instruction in schools and technical schools, but Georgians did not (the report noted their "cultural level was very low").[88] Indeed, throughout the 1920s, Narkompros investigators found that Georgian language and cultural opportunities in Azerbaijan were insufficient to meet the needs of its Georgian and Georgian-Ingiloi population.[89]

The report grouped Talyshes, Lezgins, Mountain Jews, Assyrians, and Uzbeks into the next level,[90] claiming that these nationalities had a lower level of cultural development in part because local educational authorities and Narkompros had done a poor job fostering their national advancement.[91] Other minorities—notably those termed "small peoples" (*melkie narodnosti*) such as Tsakhurs, Kaltakhs, Dzheks, Kryts, Budukhs, Khinaluqs, Udins, and others—were considered even more disadvantaged. According to the report, zero effort had been put into supporting their national cultural development (language development, native-language publications, teacher training, etc.) in Azerbaijan. Further, since all young children, half the women, and some of the men in these communities reportedly only knew their native language, it was proving difficult to integrate them into the Soviet system.[92] A 1937 study of the Qakh Tsakhur communities, for instance, claimed that Tsakhur children were still illiterate after reaching the fourth grade and could not continue their studies because they had to attend Azerbaijani language schools but did not know the Azerbaijani language.[93]

The absence of these "third-tier" minorities from table 1.2 indicates that *korenizatsiia* came even later, if at all, for them. Proposed policies for national advancement—including the development of written languages—remained largely unrealized. Only Udins had non-Tiurk educational accommodations before 1935 because some of them were considered Russian or Armenian native speakers and thus studied in those schools.[94] As is clear, the experience of minority-ness in Soviet republics was varied. What did it mean to be a national minority? Did the wide range of "minority experience" offer enough cohesiveness to justify categorizing all these disparate peoples as nontitular minorities

Table 1.2   Enrollment in Azerbaijan SSR native-language primary schools in the 1933–1934 school year

	NUMBER OF STUDENTS CLASSIFIED IN THIS NATIONALITY CATEGORY	STUDENTS STUDYING IN THE LANGUAGE OF THIS NATIONALITY	RATIO OF STUDENTS STUDYING IN THIS LANGUAGE TO NUMBER OF STUDENTS FROM THE CORRESPONDING NATIONALITY
Tiurks	249,251	265,337	106.5%
Russians	41,267	54,437	131.9%
Armenians	47,330	39,547	83.6%
Lezgins	10,821	9,186	84.9%
Talyshes	15,095	13,635	90.3%
Tats	7,317	5,491	75%
Germans	2,354	1,687	71.7%
Kurds	1,125	890	79.1%
Assyrians	206	204	99%
Greeks	83	53	63.9%
Georgians	1,062	893	84.1%
Volga Tatars	1,533	988	64.4%
Uzbeks	42	40	95.2%
Avars	2,269	1,133	49.9%

Source: Gadzhieva, "Razvitie shkoly," 115.

or did the hierarchy of "evolutionary progress" shape such divergent experiences that this category was meaningless? Government approaches to the nationality question in the late 1930s offer some answers to these questions.

The National Question in the Socialist Era

At a December 1935 meeting with Tajik and Turkmen *kolkhozniki* (collective farmers), Stalin declared that "the friendship between the peoples of the USSR is a great and serious victory. For while this friendship exists, the peoples of our country will be free and unconquerable. While this friendship lives and blossoms, we are afraid of no one, neither internal nor external enemies."[95] The Friendship of the Peoples campaign came amid mobilization for public debate about the upcoming Stalin Constitution of 1936. Minority residents across the Soviet Union interpreted the Kremlin's invitation for public participation as an opportunity to change their administrative status. In the Kyrgyz ASSR (now Kyrgyzstan), Dungans wrote to their "beloved father and leader (*vozhd'*) Comrade Stalin" to propose a Dungan district (*raion*) that would unite

Dungans split between the Kazakh and Kyrgyz ASSRs. Positioning themselves as a once-downtrodden people even more disadvantaged than other eastern nationalities and a "minority among minorities," they claimed that this would advance them economically and culturally, give meaning to their language, and help them overcome their minorityness.[96] A group of Lezgins in Azerbaijan similarly renewed interrepublic debates about Qusar's placement in Azerbaijan by writing to *Pravda* and proposing a constitutional amendment unifying Azerbaijani and Dagestani Lezgins.[97] The letter was forwarded to the Central Executive Committees of Azerbaijan and Dagestan who were asked to evaluate the merits of creating a Lezgin *okrug* or *oblast'*; however, nothing ultimately came of the proposal and the Lezgin population remained divided between the two republics.[98] While this request was rejected, other structural changes that altered the map of the South Caucasus did come to pass. Most significantly, the Transcaucasian Federation was dissolved, eliminating the middleman between the Transcaucasian SSRs and Moscow and elevating the status of the republics in the South Caucasus. This provided a new impetus for the state to recognize a titular Azerbaijani nation by transitioning from the old ethnonym—Tiurk—to a new one—Azerbaijani—in official documents and discourse.

The constitution also marked the Soviet Union's transition to the socialist phase of history. Francine Hirsch has argued that Stalin's declaration of socialist achievement in November 1936 "precipitated an all-out effort to further accelerate the revolution and its program of state-sponsored evolutionism." Ethnographers responded by facilitating "the rapid *completion* of the consolidation of clans, tribes, and nationalities into Soviet socialist nations."[99] Part of this effort can be tracked through changing census categorizations. The Second All-Union Census, conducted in January 1937, featured a list of 109 nationalities (*natsional'nosti*), a stark reduction from the 172 *narodnosti* enumerated in the list of nationalities for the 1926 census. The next All-Union Census—conducted a mere two years later in 1939—sought to demonstrate even greater ethnohistorical advancement, with only sixty-two nations, national groups, and *narodnosti* counted that year (national groups and *narodnosti* being defined as peoples who had national characteristics, but had not yet achieved the same phase of historical development as nations). This drastically smaller count of Soviet diversity required some sleight of hand: a number of peoples previously categorized as *narodnosti* were now deemed not advanced enough to warrant that designation and merged with others or shuffled to a separate list of ethnographic groups while dozens of diaspora nationalities (many of which supposedly had foreign homelands, such as Finns, Estonians, Germans, Latvians, Greeks) were also counted separately.[100]

The transition to socialism signifies a turning point in Soviet nationality policy, a moment when multiple minorities were declared assimilated in order to demonstrate Soviet evolutionary progress and when the system of national-cultural infrastructural support for nontitular minorities started to significantly contract. From this point on, extant historiography depicts an inexorable march toward assimilation and violated national rights for nontitular minorities in the Soviet Union. This viewpoint is mistaken, however. It took some time for this transition to happen, and when it did it was not final. As I show in later chapters, state officials and minorities themselves debated long past the 1930s what socialist progress should look like in minority communities. In some cases, these contestations even restored national rights circumscribed at the close of the 1930s.

At the start of this new "socialist phase," in 1937, stark contradictions emerged. For some national minorities, like Georgian-Ingilois and Tsakhurs, this was a year of national cultural growth and notable progress toward *korenizatsiia*. For others, such as Kurds and Talyshes, it marked a new era of national repression. Between 1933 and 1937, an estimated 260,000 people in the Soviet Union were internally deported to Siberia and Central Asia. For the first several years, these "frontier cleansings" targeted Koreans, Poles, Finns, and others in the western and eastern borderlands.[101] When the security regime was extended to the Iranian and Turkish borders, national deportations came to the South Caucasus as well.

At the close of 1936, the Sovnarkom ordered the "resettlement" (i.e., deportation) of 5,889 people from Azerbaijan and Armenia to Kazakhstan for counterrevolutionary crimes, contraband, banditry, and association with such activities. The decree broadly targeted multiple cross-border nationalities, including titular Armenians and Azerbaijani Tiurks, but it disproportionately affected local Kurds; though much smaller in total numbers, Kurds made up more than half of this number (3,101).[102] Confusion surrounding these unexpected deportations looms large in Kurdish retellings. Anvar Nadirov was a teenager studying at the Kurdish vocational school in Yerevan when he was deported in November 1937. Awakened by NKVD workers in the middle of the night, by morning he had been transported to a railway station in Azerbaijan's Nakhchıvan ASSR, where gathered Kurds found themselves surrounded by soldiers. Within days, he was part of a railway convoy packed with families who did not know why they had been rounded up or where they were going. Hundreds of miles later, they arrived in Kazakhstan.[103]

For a few years, mounting tensions with Turkey had been bleeding into cultural work in Soviet Kurdish communities. In March 1935, the Politburo started monitoring contacts between Soviet scholars of Kurdish studies and their foreign colleagues. It also banned the Kurdish language newspaper published in Armenia, *Ria Taza*, from publishing works by Kurds abroad, prohibited foreign export of both *Ria Taza* and Soviet Kurdish textbooks, and reorganized the Kurdish pedagogical vocational school into a "common party school" to train officials working in Kurdish areas. Although it initially retained a small Kurdish pedagogical department, this was eventually closed as well.[104]

The deportations were thus part of a broader disciplining of the Kurdish community and identification. At the same time that some Kurds were being deported from the republic, the Azerbaijan Sovnarkom resumed the practice of relocating migrant Kurds to interior areas of the republic. In the spring of 1937, the NKVD and the People's Commissariat of Agriculture (Narkomzem or NKZ) developed plans to relocate 400 Kurdish families—up to 2,000 people—who had migrated to Nakhchıvan from Iran. The area designated for their resettlement was hundreds of kilometers away from the Iranian border, close to Dzhafar-Abad (Cəfərabad) village on the road between Yevlakh and Nukha. As noted in a classified report sent to the Azerbaijan Central Executive Committee, this area was open for new settlement because Armenian villagers who lived there before had been "ravaged" during the Russian Civil War.[105]

Later that year, a new Politburo decree targeted nearly 6,000 Iranians for deportation from Azerbaijan. A few years prior, foreign nationals, including Iranian citizens, had been forced to assume Soviet citizenship or leave the country, but as these Iranians and others later came to learn, they remained vulnerable. Tens of thousands of Iranians had migrated north to Azerbaijan since the late nineteenth century, with many finding work in Baku-area oil fields. They came from a variety of ethnic backgrounds, including mostly Azeris and Persians, but also Armenians, Kurds, Shahsevans, Talyshes, and others.

The targeting of Iranians, and people thought to be connected to Iran, appears to have been broadly defined in practice. Oral history interviews indicate that many Talyshes living in settlements near the Iranian border were also forcibly removed from their homes at this time.[106] Government officials had long been anxious that Talyshes, whom some officials characterized as the "most backward people," had deep cultural and personal ties to Iran.[107] Slow "progress" in these communities exacerbated concerns that they were untrustworthy borderland inhabitants too isolated from the Soviet system and culture.[108] Indeed, report after report in these early decades document the border's porousness and resulting concerns about Iranian influences.[109] In his 1931 memorandum about work among Azerbaijani national minorities, Alimadatov devoted significant attention to border issues and Iranian influences in Talysh areas. He noted that their lifestyle was closer to that found in Iran than in the rest of Azerbaijan, and that Soviet Talyshes retained close kinship ties with Talyshes in Iran, including the "khans and beks" who fled there after the Sovietization of Azerbaijan, reestablished themselves along the border, and maintained contact with relatives on the Soviet side. Recent uprisings in the area had intersected Iran and Azerbaijan and were supposedly provoking both local anxieties and new waves of emigration to Iran.[110] Soviet officials were upset about demographic losses but also about resource flight, as migrants tended to take moveable property with them.[111] Alimadatov concluded that the sensitivity of these key border regions populated by culturally backward "little children" (*malyshi*), demanded prompt attention to the cultural and economic development of the Talysh *narodnost'*.[112]

Talysh culture in Azerbaijan had started to flourish around the time of Alimadatov's report, but by the late 1930s some officials had clearly decided that the best way to counter concerns about unstable borders and suspicious inhabitants was to physically remove people characterized as untrustworthy from those areas. Some Talyshes were deported to Central Asia, while others were compelled to leave their villages and move into towns like Astara and Lankaran where they could presumably be better monitored.[113] As I discuss in chapter 2, another wave of forced resettlement hit borderland Talysh communities after the Soviet occupation of northern Iran during World War II.

While some state officials were busy deporting and resettling these Kurds, Talyshes, Iranians, Tiurks, and Armenians, others were simultaneously ramping up the *korenizatsiia* of different national minority regions. A simple glance through the ambitious plans developed by the National Minority Council (Natsmensovet) for the republic in 1933–1934 clearly shows that they ultimately achieved little on their wish list.[114] In 1937, A. Isazanian, head of the Azerbaijan Executive Committee's Department of Nationalities, decided to tackle some of those deficiencies with renewed vigor.

Examining the implementation of the 1932 decree to indigenize national minority regions, he identified successes and failures in Qakh region's Georgian-Ingiloi and Tsakhur communities. Some "economic-cultural" achievements had come to pass: Georgian schools now had qualified teachers and Georgian-language textbooks, collectivization was going well in minority villages (thus bringing minorities into the broader Soviet system), and village and *kolkhoz* (collective farm) leaderships had been indigenized (*korenizirovany*). The Qakh region was still lacking Tsakhur, Avar, Lezgin, and Qakh Ingiloi party members, however, and a serious linguistic gap had developed between minority villages and the regional executive committee. Since the committee was made up of Azerbaijani-language speakers, village soviets had to communicate with the committee in Azerbaijani even if they conducted their own work in another language. This served the interests of the regional executive committee in Qakh but meant that village soviet members sometimes could not read the reports they submitted to that body. Isazanian suggested that adding Georgian-language speakers to the regional executive committee would allow Georgian-Ingiloi villages to submit reports in their native language.[115] He also recommended a series of educational reforms to better accommodate minority student learning. This was of particular concern in Tsakhur villages, which still lacked Tsakhur-language schools.

Baku officials intervened to try and fully indigenize the region in the summer of 1937. First, in July, the Central Executive Committee decreed that record-keeping in the Alibayli and Qakh Ingilo soviets would now be done in the Georgian language. They also mandated Georgian language newspaper reporting, the development of Georgian-Ingiloi clubs and other cultural resources, and the introduction of Tsakhur-language instruction.[116] Then, in November 1937, the committee issued an extended decree requiring the regional executive committees of Qakh, Balakan, and Zaqatala to ensure that Georgian-Ingiloi villages could work in the "native language of the Ingilo" by January 1, 1938.[117] This was accompanied a month later by an order to create Georgian-language classes in Georgian-Ingiloi villages in these three regions.[118] Available sources do not tell us whether these administrative structures were successfully indigenized, but school records show that Georgian-language sectors existed in both Muslim and Christian Georgian-Ingiloi villages into the early 1940s.[119]

These examples demonstrate divergent nontitular experiences in 1937, but more coherence started to emerge toward the end of the year. From the end of 1937 through 1938, one central nationalities institution after another— Komzet; nationalities departments at the central, *krai*, *oblast'*, and republic levels; special representatives of the autonomous oblasts and republics attached to the all-Russian Central Executive Committee; periodicals dealing with nationality issues; the Soviet of Nationalities; and others—closed or effectively ceased operations. The victory of socialism and amelioration of core inequalities meant that they were no longer needed. The educational infrastructure was one of the first targets. By the end of January 1938, Moscow had handed down orders to dismantle the Soviet Union's intricately constructed network of national minority classrooms. They started with schools, national soviets, and cultural institutions for diaspora nationalities, before quickly moving onto the entire system of national minority education, declaring the existence of special national schools and departments harmful to ordinary Soviet schools.[120]

While many of these changes targeted the Soviet Union's nontitular national cultural infrastructure, a March 1938 decree from the Sovnarkom and

Central Committee mandating Russian-language instruction in Soviet schools affected all non-Russian nationalities—both titular and nontitular.[121] Terry Martin has referred to this decree—alongside coeval decrees reducing national minority infrastructure—as evidence of the Russification of the RSFSR and the elevation more generally of the Russian nation in the USSR, but others have downplayed its Russifying intent.[122] Peter Blitstein, for example, has pointed out that Stalin rejected more radical drafts of the decree: the final version required all students to study Russian as a subject but did not require schools to use only the Russian language for instructional purposes.[123]

The decree nonetheless had a Russifying effect, injecting Russian-language instruction into non-Russian schools and undercutting efforts to increase the visibility and prestige of non-Russian languages like Azerbaijani. But this overhaul of the educational system was also experienced differently in nontitular communities, where, in Azerbaijan, it mostly had an Azerbaijanifying effect rather than a Russifying one. Students in Azerbaijani-language schools now had to study Russian as a subject in school, but students in natsmen schools found that their native language schools were replaced by Azerbaijani rather than Russian schools. This meant that minority students now had to study Russian as a subject *and* switch to full-time Azerbaijani-language instruction. There were a few exceptions. German schools were converted to Russian-language instruction because the students already knew Russian well, while Georgian- and Armenian-language schools and sectors stayed open due to the middle ground these nationalities occupied between titular and nontitular status.[124]

When these schooling decrees were enforced in 1938, the national minority school network in the republic was still expanding.[125] At the time, 38,061 students in Azerbaijan were studying in their native language in 386 national minority schools and mixed-language schools. Of the single-language schools, one was Volga Tatar (383 students), one was Udin (50 students), two were Tsakhur (88 students), 12 were Kurdish (808 students), 25 were Avar (2,087 students), 47 were Lezgin (4,668 students), 52 were Tat (3,575 students), and 124 were Talysh (9,746 students). An additional 2,048 students were studying in German schools, which were now classed separately as "foreign schools" given recent policies demonizing this so-called diaspora nationality.[126] Some national minority schools offered instruction in the native language through the fourth grade, while others switched to Azerbaijani- or, less commonly, Russian-language instruction after grade three.[127]

Some local officials may have been caught off guard by this drastic policy change, but new national minority school inspections were swiftly commissioned to justify these school closures. Inspectors in the early 1930s had lamented the failures of local officials to implement indigenization efforts, but these evaluators targeted the consequences of educational insufficiencies rather than their causes. The reports claimed that deep infrastructural problems in minority communities were exacerbated by insufficient supplies of native-language written materials, by Dagestan-provided textbooks that were unintelligible to Avars, Lezgins, and other Dagestani peoples in Azerbaijan, by untrained native-language teachers, and by the lack of native-language inspectors who could monitor and improve minority schools. These failings, the inspectors suggested, left minority students unprepared for the inevitable transition to Russian- or Azerbaijani-language learning, with some having to start their studies over again.[128] Furthermore, the weak and resource-draining minority school system required investments that would be even harder to make given the financial and technical demands of the new Russian-language learning decree.[129]

There were also ideological justifications for closing minority schools. Previous inspectors had determined that the native-language educational network needed to be expanded to increase literacy and prepare minority students for post-primary study, but inspectors in 1938 determined that native-language schools were fundamentally incapable of providing students with the skills needed to prosper in Azerbaijani society. This accusation was paired with the assertion that minority student success was dependent on students assimilating into Azerbaijani-language instruction from the very start rather than in grade four or five. They also concluded that the minority schooling system needed to be reformed to protect minorities from "enemies of the people," who had perverted cultural development in the republic. For instance, Kurdish language reformers were accused of sabotaging Kurds by giving their alphabet 38 letters, when "the alphabet of the richest language—Russian—only had 32 letters." These same "enemies" had also reportedly harmed some minority students by forcing them to study in their "native language" even though they were actually native Azerbaijani speakers.[130]

Given these financial, practical, and conceptual problems, the minister of Azerbaijan's Narkompros, M. Mamedov, declared in the summer of 1938 that the network was unfixable and the idea of national minority education fatally flawed. He substantiated this conclusion by pointing to meetings with teachers, parents, students, kolkhoz members, and others that had resulted in *unanimous* requests for native-language schools to be transferred to the Azerbaijani language in the 1938–1939 school year (except in Vartashen, where Assyrians were said to prefer Russian schools).[131] Some people undoubtedly agreed with his conclusions, but these meetings were also carefully orchestrated to justify the closure of minority schools.

Documents from the state archive in Shaki, the regional archive for the territories of the former Zaqatala *okrug* (Qakh, Balakan, and Zaqatala), show
how this process played out. In late July, several months after the decision had
been made to close national minority schools, a ritualized series of meetings
was held in Avar and Tsakhur communities in northwestern Azerbaijan. Typically, a state representative started the meeting by detailing the poor condition of minority schools in the community. Then, one after another, members
of the gathered collective testified about their preference for Azerbaijani-
language learning.

Nearly 300 men and women attended one of these meetings supervised by
a Narkompros representative at a kolkhoz in Yukharı Chardakhlar (Yuxarı
Çardaxlar). The general consensus among the eight documented speakers, including a local Avar teacher and an education department inspector, was,
first, that Avar-language learning was poorly executed because Dagestan-
provided books were locally incomprehensible, and, second, that the native-
language system held Avar students back by making it difficult for them to
transition to Azerbaijani-language learning in higher grades and isolating them
from the Azerbaijani-language government. The meeting ended with the decision to transition Avar-language classrooms to Azerbaijani. The head of the
Zaqatala region public relations department attended a similar meeting in the
Kalal Miqoyan kolkhoz a week later. There, the school principal explained to
the gathered attendees that Tsakhur-language learning was untenable because
teachers were untrained and there were too few Tsakhur writers to produce
Tsakhur-language written materials and literature. Concluding that the value
of Tsakhur learning was low (*dəyəri az olmuşdur*), the Kalal Miqoyan kolkhoz
similarly authorized the transition of native-language classrooms to the Azerbaijani language.[132]

Many of the complaints voiced at these meetings were legitimate and in
fact echoed those of national minority officials who had long criticized shortcomings in the system. In 1934, for example, Ahmedzade excoriated the Azerbaijan People's Commissariat of Enlightenment for failing to develop its own
educational materials and relying on Lezgin and Avar resources from Dagestan, Kurdish and Armenian texts from Armenia, as well as Tat materials from
Moscow that featured dialects of those languages that Azerbaijani Lezgins,
Avars, Kurds, Armenians, and Tats did not necessarily understand.[133] Yet,
time had now run out to fully develop local networks and realize the promise
of the 1932 decree to indigenize national minority areas. Unanimous decisions
like those made in Yukharı Chardakhlar and the Kalal Miqoyan kolkhoz
were documented throughout minority collectives in the region with nary

a voice of dissent recorded. In this way, native-language school closures were portrayed as a response to popular demand rather than as the inevitable outcome of decisions already made in Moscow and Baku.

In the summer of 1938, the conversation expanded to a condemnation of minority nationalisms. No longer would enemies of the people and bourgeois nationalists isolate Azerbaijan's minorities from the cultural riches of Soviet Azerbaijan.[134] During a plenum of the Communist Party of Azerbaijan on June 6, 1938—one month before meetings were held with Avars, Tsakhurs, and others to justify minority school closures—the issue of "cleansing" Arabic, Persian, and Ottoman influences from the Azerbaijani language was addressed. When someone asked whether they would also "cleanse" the Tat language, Bagirov responded that it was time to move away from the Tat, Kurdish, and Talysh languages and toward the Azerbaijani language. His reasoning? They were all Azerbaijanis, but enemies (presumably those who, like Ahmedzade, encouraged minority national consciousness) had obstructed "Bolshevik control" over the development of these "backward nationalities" (*otstalye natsional'nosti*) and prevented their assimilation into the Azerbaijani nation. There was thus no need to develop these languages further.[135] As historian El'dar Ismailov has observed, Bagirov made it clear in this moment that the language of the titular nation of Azerbaijan was Azerbaijani, not Tiurk, and that "there is one indigenous people [*korennoi narod*] of Azerbaijan and they are Azerbaijanis."[136]

Soviet officials had started embracing the concept of natural (as opposed to forced) assimilation in the mid-1930s, but the approach that emerged at this time was more aggressive.[137] Bagirov was not speaking about a gradual process through which minorities would voluntarily and naturally become Azerbaijani; rather, he was rejecting the notion that peoples conceptualized as minorities could and should continue to exist separate from the Azerbaijani nation in Azerbaijan. He imbued this with the discourse of the terror, of enemies and wreckers that trickled down into national minority reports produced later that summer. Assimilation, once a process that was acknowledged to take time, was now an imperative.

As national minority offices started closing across the Soviet Union in the late 1930s, the natsmen category lost much of its meaning and its definition changed. The process of minoritization and othering began in the 1920s when national minorities were, in practice, marginalized from *korenizatsiia* and cast as even more backward than their backward titular neighbors. National deportations accelerated the transformation of this category, and widespread erasure in the 1939 census completed this process. In Azerbaijan alone, Kurds, Laks, Tats, and Tsakhurs were assimilated into the titular nationality or otherwise lost their "named" status in public reporting for this final Stalin-era population count. More significantly, the 1939 census used the phrase "national minority" to refer specifically to diaspora nationalities, equating national minorityness with the nationalities that had been most intensely demonized and repressed in recent years. As Francine Hirsch has observed, "'national groups' and 'national minorities' were no longer synonyms. 'National groups,' like *narodnosti*, were peoples that might evolve into Soviet nations. 'National minorities,' on the other hand, were the diasporas of foreign nations whose allegiance lay elsewhere."[138]

Once regarded as backward peoples whose ethnohistorical transformation could illustrate socialist progress, those who had once been classified as national minorities were now considered potential enemies requiring threat mitigation. They were vulnerable to deportation and forced assimilation because their existence potentially undermined the territory and sovereignty of both the Soviet Union and the titular nations in the republics where they lived. Indeed, the bureaucratic and physical erasure of many national minorities played a key role in titular nation-building at a time when national affiliation began to supplant class as the most significant social marker in the USSR.

Bülbüləm nəğməmə gülşən dilərəm,	I am the nightingale, I long for a field of flowers for my song—
Qəm deyil, dərd deyil, şən dilərəm.	no sadness, no sorrow—I need joy.
Yolumu gözlər o zümrüd Qafqaz,	That emerald Caucasus awaits me—
Orda daim gülüşür nəşəli yaz.	where merry spring is ever laughing,
Rəqs edir il boyu hər dürlü çiçək,	where varied flowers dance year round—
Məni yalnız o mudafa edəcək.	only she can offer my sanctuary.
Dahinin doğma cocuqluq vətəni,	True motherland of the genius' childhood,
Bəsləyib qırx sənə köksündə məni.	for forty years you suckled me at your breast.
Oraya olsa əgər balü-pərim,	As on fairy-wings, may my sweet songs
Sorar afaqı fəsih nəğmələrim.	seek you at the world's edge.

—Poem that Zulfugar Ahmedzade sent to Moscow as he petitioned for his release from Siblag in 1939 (translated by Alison Mandaville)

Jörg Baberowski has characterized 1937 as a year of horror in Azerbaijan; Audrey Altstadt portrays it as a "year of blood;" and El'dar Ismailov describes it as "one of the worst pages in Soviet history," but the terror did not end when the year did. As Ismailov notes, executions, arrests, torture, deportations, denouncements, and other forms of violence extended from the summer of 1936 through the fall of 1938.[139] The effects of this violence lasted much longer, particularly for those who lost family members and friends or were themselves repressed.

Scholars have interpreted the national-cultural element of the terror in Azerbaijan differently. For Altstadt, this wave of purges was "an attack on Azerbaijani national culture" and confirms that the Soviet Union was a destroyer rather than a builder of nations.[140] Isabelle Kaplan and Jörg Baberowski take a different approach, identifying significant moments of nation-building amid the violence and destruction of the terror. Kaplan describes the Azerbaijani *dekada* of 1938 as a powerful "vehicle of nation-building within Azerbaijan" that shielded some vulnerable cultural producers from the terror, "consolidate[d] national identity at home," and generated national pride at a key moment of definition for the Soviet Azerbaijani nation. Baberowski, meanwhile, contextualizes the repression of Azerbaijan's cultural, intellectual, and political urban elite with widespread violence in rural areas and views the terror as evidence of the periphery terrorizing itself rather than as a top-down story of Moscow-directed cruelty. He further argues that since the nation continued to function as an organizing principle in the republic, the repression of Azerbaijan's titular elite was neither an attack on Azerbaijani national self-determination nor an attempt to Russify the periphery. Rather, the terror deepened the *korenizatsiia* of Soviet Azerbaijan by promoting *vydvizhentsy*, workers and peasants who were loyal to the party that had provided them with a path toward advancement and who brought conservative and traditional values with them to their new jobs, intensifying the Tiurkicization of the party and state administration in the republic.[141]

These are contradictory interpretations, but what they share is a focus on how the terror affected titular national development in Azerbaijan. Just as the purges could be destructive, they could also be productive. Ahmedzade's repression is representative of the broad violence the party enacted in the republic and its scapegoating of people, including its own members, for hindering desired cultural, social, economic, and political transformations. He was also likely targeted, however, because of the work he did, the nationality he promoted, and the perceived threat that nation posed to the titular nation. In other words, titular nationhoods and national actors were not the only targets of state repression. Concern about disloyalty extended to nontitular minorities and coincided with Moscow's desire to demonstrate both socialist progress and ethnohistorical advancement.

FIGURE 3.   Zulfugar Ahmedzade shortly before his arrest. Photo from private collection.

Zulfugar Ahmedzade's entry into the Gulag system was swift. While imprisoned in Siblag, he busied himself writing letters home and to Moscow, updating his family on his increasingly poor health and appealing for his release. Although he frequently reassured his family that these bad days would soon pass (*yaman günün ömrü az olar*), his letters reveal his struggles in the prison-camp system as well as why he thought he had ended up there. Perhaps revealing an awareness of the many hands through which his letters would pass, Ahmedzade strategically switched between the Azerbaijani and Talysh languages to obscure more sensitive messages. In one letter, he told his son how to circumvent a new restriction on sending money to prisoners in the camp. To an Azerbaijani reader, the message read, "Don't send money in the package. Now money is banned," but a Talysh word inserted into the middle of the first sentence changed its meaning to say that Ayyub should send money but hide it so as to circumvent the restriction.

The limits on political prisoners like Ahmedzade were numerous and constantly changing. Sometimes he could not receive packages, at other times he was unable to send or receive letters and telegrams. He turned to his fellow prisoners for support, including some from Azerbaijan who, he noted in the summer of 1939, were increasingly arriving in Siblag. They helped Ahmedzade circumvent mail limitations by passing letters to him from his children. They also helped him when he was sick. During a lengthy hospital stay, for example, a fellow patient from Azerbaijan nursed him back to health, helping him evade what he thought was certain death. Suspecting that the illnesses that repeatedly hospitalized him were caused by punishments but also by malnutrition and cold weather, Ahmedzade also relied on communication with his family to secure necessary parcels of food and clothing, as well as notebooks and envelopes.

Worried about his family and his fate, he revealed his fears, anxieties, and pain to his family, but he also sent them advice, warning them not to gossip, not to trust anyone, to be careful, disciplined, principled, respectful, honest, and wise. He admonished his children to continue their studies and professional training, to read literature and newspapers, to care for their health with rest and cold showers, and, after the Azerbaijani Latin alphabet was displaced by a Cyrillic one in 1939, to learn and use this new script. With people being released from the camps every day, he assured them that he had sent appeals and poetry to Moscow officials, including Stalin, and that he would soon return home and enjoy with them a "happy life in our socialist homeland."

In the fall of 1939, about a year after entering the camp system, Ahmedzade was informed by the prosecutor in Moscow that his case had been sent back to Baku for investigation. He was convinced that Moscow knew he was innocent and that this was why his sentence was shorter than the ten to fifteen years given to others with similar charges. But Ahmedzade still tried to influence the outcome of the investigation. Switching from Azerbaijani to Talysh in a letter to his son Ayyub, he implored him to visit an acquaintance on his behalf because "things are now happening through personal networks" (Isət koon de oşnoəti dəvardedən).

Why had Ahmedzade been repressed? He was initially charged with Article 64 of the Soviet criminal code (treason) after a certain Shirali Akhundov

claimed that Ahmedzade had entered a conspiracy with him in 1936 to separate the Talysh region from Azerbaijan. In essence, Ahmedzade was arrested
as a Talysh separatist after years of debate between centralizers in the republic's
government and proponents of Lezgin, Kurdish, and Talysh autonomy. It
also coincided with Bagirov's declaration that Azerbaijan's minorities were
not distinct peoples at all but Azerbaijani. Ahmedzade apparently managed
to fight off this original charge while detained in Baku, but instead of being
released was then accused of counterrevolutionary activity. According to
Ahmedzade, this new charge came with a five-year sentence but no description of his purportedly criminal activities.[142] As for the investigation that Moscow ordered while he was in Siblag, months went by with no results and
eventually Ahmedzade's fate was sealed: in June 1942, aged 43 and nearing the
end of his sentence, he died in Mariinsk.

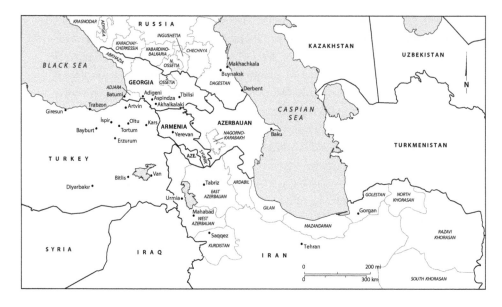

Map 2. Contemporary regional map.

CHAPTER 2

Territory, War, and Nation-Building in the South Caucasus

World War II brought immense devastation to the Soviet Union, but it also presented new opportunities to remake the country's borders and expand its geopolitical reach. Preexisting republics like Ukraine, Russia, and Belarus expanded westward; Soviet republics were established in Estonia, Latvia, Lithuania, and Moldova; and new socialist states oriented toward the Soviet Union emerged in Europe. Meanwhile, in the Far East, the USSR seized the Kuril Islands and southern Sakhalin from Japan and helped secure Mongolian independence, in part by withdrawing support for the East Turkestan Republic (ETR) in Xinjiang.[1]

Stalin also pursued extraterritorial maneuvers along the Soviet Union's southern border with Iran and Turkey. The Axis invasion of the USSR precipitated the August 1941 Anglo-Soviet invasion of Iran that gave the Allies access to Iran's oil fields, allowed them to run supplies to Soviet forces, and undermined German influence in Iran at a time when Moscow was gravely concerned about German encirclement.[2] The invasion led to Reza Shah's abdication (replacing him with his Swiss-educated son Mohammad Reza Pahlavi) and divided Iran into spheres of influence with the British moving into southwest Iran and the Soviet Union occupying the northern provinces. In January 1942, Iran, the Soviet Union, and Great Britain signed the Tripartite Treaty of Alliance, solidifying the Persian Corridor for Soviet-bound Allied resources and setting a date for Soviet and British troop withdrawal—within six months of the war's end.

The Iranian government pushed for withdrawal after German troops surrendered in May 1945 and intensified this demand after Japan's capitulation that September. Tehran was right to worry. There was a long-established precedent of British and Russian/Soviet meddling in Iranian affairs, and both sides treated wartime occupation as an opportunity to fortify lasting influence in Iran. In the south, Britain allied with conservative elements like tribal leaders, landlords, and religious elites to secure and extend British influence. They were particularly concerned with maintaining a foothold for the Anglo-Iranian Oil Company, which had held concessions in Iran since the early twentieth century. Meanwhile, in the north, the USSR reinforced—rather than reduced—its presence as the war came to a close. A well-known anecdote in Viacheslav Molotov's memoirs has Stalin expressing satisfaction with new Soviet borders in the north, west, and east on a map produced for Soviet schools in 1945. Turning to the South Caucasus, however, he reportedly took his pipe out of his mouth, used it to circle the Soviet-Iran border, and mumbled, "But I don't like our border here."[3] Indeed, that summer the Politburo instructed Mir Jafar Bagirov, the head of the Soviet Azerbaijan Communist Party, to organize separatist movements in Gilan, Mazandaran, Gorgan, Khorasan, and Iranian Azerbaijan, and to extend support to Kurdish elites seeking autonomy there as well. By December 1945 and January 1946, respectively, the Azerbaijan People's Government based in Tabriz and the Kurdish Republic of Mahabad had declared autonomy from Tehran.[4]

The Soviet Union also cultivated claims to Turkish territory. In the spring of 1945, Moscow, frustrated with its lack of control over the Turkish Straits and Turkey's Western alliances, decided to renegotiate, rather than renew, the expiring Soviet-Turkish neutrality pact. Soviet Minister of Foreign Affairs Molotov notified Turkish ambassador Selim Sarper of Soviet claims to eastern Turkish territories that challenged the territorial settlement in the 1921 Treaty of Kars and of plans to establish a Soviet presence in the straits connecting the Black and Aegean Seas. As relations declined with Ankara, the Soviet leadership also encouraged Kurdish, Georgian, and Armenian irredentist claims to Turkish territory and sanctioned the repatriation of diaspora Armenians to Soviet Armenia. Stalin approved repatriation in part to reinvigorate postwar Soviet Armenian society but also to define the Soviet Union as a guarantor of Armenian rights at a time when diaspora Armenians were injecting themselves into global debates about the postwar apportioning of territories and balancing of allied powers.[5]

Stalin's machinations in Iran and Turkey were ultimately unsuccessful. The Soviet government forged an agreement with Iran in the spring of 1946 that exchanged Soviet troop withdrawal for a joint Iran-Soviet oil company and agreement that Tehran would negotiate with Tabriz in good faith (notably not specifying the same for Mahabad), but Tehran reneged on its promises after Soviet troops returned home.[6] By December 1946, it had violently reasserted control over both Tabriz and Mahabad. Not long after, the Iranian Parliament rejected the promised oil concession.[7] Moscow also ultimately walked back its claims to Turkish territory and control over the straits.[8] Not only did the Soviet Union fail to acquire new territories or satellite states in Iran and Turkey, its new rival, the United States, used these confrontations to justify the Truman Doctrine and alliances with both countries.

Historians have cynically attributed Stalin's wartime support for foreign national movements and irredentist land claims to broader geostrategic aims. V. A. Barmin and David Wolff, for example, interpret his backing of national liberation movements in Xinjiang and Mongolia as ploys for greater strategic influence in China.[9] Fernande Raine and Natalia Yegorova similarly argue that Stalin "activated" Azeri and Kurdish national liberation movements in Iran to achieve vital oil concessions and form a pro-Soviet Majlis there.[10] Looking at the Turkish case, Ronald Suny cautions readers to be careful about too easily dismissing Soviet support for small nations, but nonetheless finds that Stalin was more interested in pulling Turkey out of the Western orbit and into an alliance with the USSR than in territorial gains.[11]

Geostrategic considerations are a legitimate part of state concerns, but by no means tell the whole story and do not rule out genuine interest in national causes. Furthermore, despite the overwhelming historiographical emphasis on Stalin's role in these foreign intrigues, he did not act alone. He partnered with and engaged colleagues in Moscow as well as myriad national actors to design and execute Soviet policies toward Iran and Turkey. Thus, even if his national intentions were insincere, there were plenty of others, including the first secretaries of the Armenian, Azerbaijani, and Georgian SSRs, who were able to develop and enact their national desires—at home and abroad—thanks to the evolving geopolitical situation he enabled.

This chapter is concerned with the question of how Soviet wartime interventions in Iran and Turkey intersected with nation-building agendas in the South Caucasus and influenced national relations there. In principle, Stalin's definition of the nation rejected national extraterritoriality, but the Bolsheviks repeatedly created exceptions to this rule by using *korenizatsiia* policies to exploit cross-border ethnic ties and expand Soviet influence abroad.[12] Terry Martin has argued that in the late 1930s this approach was replaced by a more defensive foreign policy that aimed to turn the Soviet Union into a "'fortress' against all foreign influence."[13] National deportations did become a hallmark practice as the state sought to physically separate targeted nationalities including Kurds, Iranians, and Poles from co-ethnics abroad, but Soviet elites continued to cultivate and enable geopolitically expedient transborder ethnic ties. In other words, national deportations (as well as repatriations and territorial annexations) emerged as technologies of population management and titular nation-building without entirely displacing other practices already in force.

Rather than focus only on whether Stalin succeeded in gaining territory, it is important to also examine how foreign interventions affected national relations in the Soviet Union. The Soviet occupation of northern Iran and claims to Turkish territory legitimized discourses of national extraterritoriality that Azeri, Armenian, Georgian, Kurdish, and other national advocates eagerly engaged and sometimes used against one another. This component of wartime nation-building, in concert with ongoing practices of minority assimilation and national deportation, altered the demographic and conceptual landscape in the South Caucasus. The contrasting experiences of various national elites and activists fighting for their national dreams amid Stalin's engagement with Turkey and Iran ultimately reinforced links between titularity and power in the region and contributed to the evolving divergence between empowered and disempowered nations in the Soviet Union.

Invasions, Irredentism, and Wartime Nation-Building

Azeri and Kurdish National Movements during the Soviet Occupation of Iran

Bagirov—and Soviet Azerbaijan—played a pivotal role in the Soviet occupation of northern Iran. Tapped by Stalin to micromanage Soviet interests there, Bagirov exerted significant influence over the goals, methods, and structures of the Soviet occupation and linked Azeri nation-building to Soviet wartime expansion. In many ways, it was natural for Stalin to rely on him. First secretary of the Azerbaijan Communist Party since 1933, Bagirov could speak to the large Azeri population in northern Iran, had extensive power and influence in the Azerbaijan SSR, enjoyed a close relationship with both Stalin and the then-head of the NKVD, Lavrentiy Beria, and had experience with Soviet-Iranian border issues. Although some scholars have dated Stalin's intervention in Iran to the 1939 German-Soviet partnership, northern Iran had long been a target of Soviet efforts to export socialist modernity.[14] Bagirov monitored these programs and other interwar policies concerning Iran, including the securitization of the Soviet-Iranian border and deportations of Iranians from Soviet Azerbaijan. In fact, prior to the invasion, Stalin turned to Bagirov for help evaluating his prospects in Iran. Bagirov, demonstrating his familiarity with the region, replied that "Southern Azerbaijan" (the irredentist term that many Azeris use to describe Iran's Azerbaijan provinces) harbored a wealth of natural resources, a disgruntled population primed for political agitation, and the networks and infrastructure necessary for Soviet penetration of the region.

Soon after the invasion of Iran in August 1941, the Soviet government dedicated itself to a course of cultural diplomacy, using humanitarian aid, basic consumer goods, and transborder co-ethnic ties to increase support for the USSR in northern Iran.[15] Bagirov quickly developed plans to dispatch medical, cultural, economic, security, and political emissaries from Soviet Azerbaijan to provide medical care, perform Azerbaijani-language operas and plays, screen Azerbaijani-language films, distribute basic supplies like sugar and kerosene, evaluate oil resources, conduct intelligence work, suppress opposition to the Red Army, and perform other tasks in Soviet-occupied northern Iran. Azerbaijan SSR Communist Party Third Secretary Aziz Aliyev (Əziz Əliyev), the republic's Commissar of the Interior Agasalim Atakishiyev (Ağasəlim Atakişiyev), and Mirza Ibragimov, a playwright, author, and future head of the Azerbaijan SSR's Narkompros and Supreme Soviet, coordinated these programs on the ground in Iran and reported back to Bagirov. One of Ibragimov's primary tasks at this time was to create an Azerbaijani-language army newspaper, *Vatan Yolunda* (*Vətən Yolunda*), that would counter pro-German and other anti-Soviet influences by explaining why the Soviets were there and advertising the achievements of Soviet Azerbaijan. Bagirov soon reported to Stalin that *Vatan Yolunda* had quickly gained wide popularity and sparked a "feeling of limitless satisfaction and national pride" among Iranian Azeris, who for a long time had not had a publication in their native language.[16]

The Azerbaijan SSR was now a primary site of Soviet interventionism, sending aid to northern Iran, sharing its political infrastructure and resources with the occupied zone, developing Azeri national cultural resources, and hosting Azeri, Shahsevan, and Kurdish elites whom the Soviets were courting.[17] It was a good base for these activities. All of the teams that Bagirov sent to Iranian Azerbaijan were led and mostly staffed by Azeris, but, as Bagirov explained to Stalin, he also sent "comrades who know the Farsi and Kurdish languages, as well as Armenians." Indeed, although Kurds in Soviet Azerbaijan had recently faced assimilation and had never achieved autonomy, Bagirov clearly recognized that the cultural infrastructure that Soviet Kurds had recently lost could prove useful for courting Kurds in Iran.[18]

As they had done elsewhere, Soviet officials related to the population of northern Iran through a discourse of national equality and liberation. Various segments of society contested the Soviet occupation, but others looked to see what it could offer them. The broader region harbored radical political traditions, economic inequalities, and resentment toward Reza Shah's centralizing government in Tehran. People were angry about disparities between what they paid in taxes and the benefits they received, strict restrictions on native-language use in the public sphere, closures of non-Persian publishing houses, and Persian dominance in local government apparatuses. The sense that the central government was attempting to Persianize minorities was exacerbated by economic and administrative reforms that had forcibly sedentarized tens of thousands of nomads, disrupting tribal confederations and moving Kurds to Mazandaran, Khorasan, Isfahan, and Yazd; Azeris to Kurdistan; and Bakhtiyaris and Lors to central and southern Iran.[19]

The Red Army in northern Iran encountered, as some internal reports put it, "anti-Soviet provocations" attributed to nefarious class interests, nationalist groups such as Dashnaks and Musavatists, people who had earlier fled or been deported from the USSR, and external influences (i.e., Germany, Britain, Tehran, and Turkey), but also an economic underclass that was thought to be hostile not only to the central government but to local "khans and beks" as well. According to the Azerbaijan NKVD, people in some villages greeted the arrival of Red Army troops by seizing resources and land from local landowners. In borderland areas, residents requested help acquiring Soviet citizenship and establishing Soviet power in their villages.[20] Some minorities also started to settle scores with Tehran. Kurds and Shahsevans swiftly disarmed local garrisons of the Iranian army and seized their weapons. Thousands of others who had been forcibly moved to inner Iran also returned to their villages in the Iranian-Turkish-Soviet borderlands.

Yet, while the Red Army disrupted Iranian sovereignty, it did not necessarily control what happened from that point forward. Although beyond the scope of this book, it is clear that there was a range of support and opposition to the Soviet cause in northern Iran. In the case of returning Kurds, many came with nothing and found their homes occupied or in disrepair. When the Soviet government did not provide aid as quickly as they expected, discontent grew. Kurds in Iran courted Soviet support, but they also looked to Turkey—where many had relatives—and Britain. Further, although Soviet officials noted that Kurds maintained good relations with their Armenian and Assyrian neighbors, they expressed concern about confrontations between Kurds and Azeris as well as between Kurds and Persians.[21]

This early intervention in northern Iran was curtailed in the summer of 1942 after Moscow negotiated the Tripartite Treaty of Alliance. Bagirov defended the need to maintain a strong presence on the ground to counter anti-Soviet agitation in northern Iran, but, with Moscow's direction, withdrew nearly all of these emissaries from the occupied zone. Nearly two years later, when Stalin instructed him to re-commit resources to Iranian Azerbaijan, Bagirov essentially grafted Soviet Azerbaijan's political and economic infrastructure onto the region. He also turned once again to classic techniques of Soviet cultural diplomacy to exploit local tensions with Tehran and foster support for the USSR, promoting minority-language political representation, cultural resources, and schools, and mobilizing intellectuals, artists, doctors, engineers, workers, politicians, and others in the Azerbaijan SSR to support their co-ethnics and the Soviet cause.[22] Soviet Azerbaijan established a dominant presence in Iranian Azerbaijan, but other republics also used this opportunity to engage with co-ethnics in Iran. The Georgian SSR, for example, sent its own cultural and political representatives, Georgian-language reading materials, cultural resources, and missions of brotherly help via doctors, teachers, historians, and linguists to Iran's Fereydan Georgians, whose Iranian origins are often traced to Shah Abbas's seventeenth-century military campaigns in Georgia.[23]

As became increasingly clear over the course of 1945, Bagirov's efforts advanced both Moscow's interests and Azeri irredentist aspirations. That April, as he charted a potential path forward in Iran, he outlined three possible goals: unifying "Southern Azerbaijan" with the Azerbaijan SSR, forming an independent Azerbaijan People's Republic, or, at a minimum, establishing "an independent bourgeois-democratic system" or cultural autonomy within Iran. He noted that Kurdish autonomy also needed to be supported.[24] In late June, not long after the German surrender, the State Defense Committee directed the Soviet Azerbaijan Oil Association (Azneft) to supervise geological prospecting for oil in northern Iran.[25] Then, on July 6, the Politburo endorsed one of the scenarios that Bagirov had previously outlined. They ordered Bagirov to help create a national autonomous Azerbaijan province in Iran governed by a new party, the Azerbaijan Democratic Party (ADP), that would increase Soviet control by coopting other leftist centers of power like the Tabriz branch of the communist Tudeh Party of Iran; develop a separatist movement in the Gilan, Mazandaran, Gorgan, and Khorasan provinces; form a Kurdish national autonomous district; create and arm "self-defense" groups to support Soviet efforts and the separatist movement; establish a Society of Friends of Soviet Azerbaijan network in Gilan and Iranian Azerbaijan to build support for separatism; and work with Ibragimov to make sure pro-separatist delegates from "Southern Azerbaijan" would be elected to the Iranian Majlis, among other measures. They even outlined the platform for the Majlis election, including promises to distribute land to peasants, eliminate unemployment, improve public health services, spend more tax revenue locally, and establish equal cultural and political rights for national minorities and tribes.[26]

The Azerbaijan SSR team coordinating matters on the ground in Tabriz—Atakishiyev, Azerbaijan Communist Party Secretary Hasan Hasanov, and Ibragimov, who had recently become Soviet Azerbaijan's Commissar of Narkompros—picked the ADP's leader, Ja'far Pishevari (Mir Ja'far Javadzadeh), and worked with him and his chosen associates to draft its bylaws and programs.[27] Pishevari's long history of involvement with the Bolshevik Party and critical relationship with the Tudeh Party made him an attractive option for Baku. Born in Iran in 1893, he migrated to Baku at a young age, attended school there, became a teacher, and joined the revolutionary movement. In the heady months after the February Revolution, Pishevari served on the executive committee that edited the newspaper of the first Iranian communist organization, the 'Adalat (Justice) committee, which formed among the thousands of Iranian workers in Baku's oil fields and related industries. When 'Adalat evolved into the Communist Party of Iran, he was one of its founding secretaries. Pishevari was also a government commissar in the short-lived Soviet Socialist Republic of Gilan, but after Tehran defeated the Republic and banned the Communist Party in 1921, he spent the next several years moving between the Soviet Union and Iran. The Comintern sent Pishevari to work in Iran in 1927,[28] but after a politically motivated arrest in 1930, he spent more than a decade in prison and secured release only after the arrival of the Red Army in 1941.[29]

Although the Politburo directed Bagirov to organize separatist movements in a number of northern Iranian provinces, he put most of his energy into exploring oil prospects and working with the Azeri and Kurdish autonomy movements.[30] With Pishevari already on board and ADP organizing underway, Bagirov brought Qazi Muhammad and other Kurdish elites from Mahabad, Bukan, Miandoab, Mamash, and Begzadeh to Baku in September 1945.[31] He offered to provide practical assistance, to help open and equip both a Kurdish school and hospital in Mahabad, and to enroll select Kurds in Soviet Azerbaijani military schools, secondary schools, and universities,[32] but he also tried to convince his Kurdish counterparts that they could achieve what they were looking for within the bounds of an autonomous Azerbaijan and to delay their demands for a separate state until after the Azeris succeeded in establishing autonomy in Tabriz. When these proposals met opposition, Bagirov switched tactics and assured his guests that Moscow would support their independent aspirations as well. Bagirov subsequently instructed Qazi Muhammad to form a new party, the Democratic Party of Kurdistan (which came to be known as the PDKI), and to assert control over all competing political parties and movements, including *Komalay Ziyanaway Kurd* (the Society for Kurdish Resurrection). As they had done with the ADP, officials from Soviet Azerbaijan shaped the PDKI's political program, making sure that it, like the ADP, promised equal rights for and fraternity with other national minorities in Iranian Azerbaijan.[33]

For a long time, historians did not know about the leading role that Soviet officials played in creating the ADP and PDKI, but it has been clear for some time now that the Soviet leadership initiated, named, defined, and supported these political parties and the autonomous governments established in Tabriz and Mahabad.[34] At the same time, Bagirov and his collaborators understood that their legitimacy required the concealment of this fact. As ADP and PDKI claims against Tehran escalated in late 1945, the Soviet government vociferously denied that they played any role in these movements while Bagirov quietly funneled munitions of non-Soviet manufacture to the region—first to Tabriz and then to the Kurds.[35] By the end of December 1945, the ADP—in line with its demands for autonomy and unfettered national cultural and political development—had taken control of the government and garrisons in Tabriz and established the Azerbaijan People's Government (APG).

Their success emboldened Kurdish demands. Though there is still much to be learned about the relationship between Kurdish autonomy and the Soviet side, it is clear that Bagirov prioritized Azerbaijani autonomy. Yet, there were also strategic reasons to back the Kurds, even if they wanted autonomy from both the APG in Tabriz and Tehran. Kurdish separatism had always been a complicated issue given the many tribes involved and the complex regional relations forged with Turkey, Iran, Iraq, and—under these conditions—Britain. But the situation also shifted in the fall of 1945 with the arrival of Mustafa Barzani, his brother Sheikh Ahmed, the spiritual leader of the Barzani Kurds, and several thousand Barzani fighters and allies who had been forced to flee after rising in revolt against the Iraqi government earlier that year. Having met with Qazi Muhammad and the Soviet military commander based in Nairgei, Mustafa Barzani pledged his support to the Kurdish cause and 1,500 Kurds from his contingent were subsequently organized into three regiments and armed to support the Kurdish movement in Iran. An additional 700 Barzanis created a reserve force. Bagirov initially cautioned Qazi Muhammad that Barzani might be a British agent, but his arrival undisputedly bolstered the Kurdish cause.[36] Plus, as Bagirov argued in late December 1945, "providing assistance" to Kurds in Northern Kurdistan could help form a buffer between the Soviet zone and the Iranian troops and tribes armed by the British in the south.[37]

On January 22, 1946, Qazi Muhammad stepped onto a platform in the central square of Mahabad and declared Kurdish autonomy in Iran. With this announcement, he became president of the Kurdish Republic of Mahabad, which reached from Urmia to Saqqez (including Bukan, Naqadeh, and Oshnaviya), but excluded economically powerful Kurdish territories further south

FIGURE 4.   Qazi Muhammad in his office in Mahabad 1946. A map of Kurdistan hangs on the wall behind him. Photo courtesy of the Archives of Chris Kutschera in the Photolibrary of Kurdistan.

and in neighboring Iraq and Turkey. Following the Soviet model, the autonomous governments in Tabriz and Mahabad immediately introduced Azerbaijani and Kurdish language learning, respectively, to local schools and developed native-language print cultures, including newspapers and books.

The Azerbaijan People's Government and Republic of Mahabad drew legitimacy from the long-standing grievances their constituencies held with central authorities, but they also faced internal divisions and depended on Soviet support for their survival.[38] Not long after Soviet troop withdrawal in 1946, negotiations started to break down between the autonomous governments and Tehran. Iranian forces defeated the Soviet-backed partisans and retook Tabriz that December, prompting many Kurdish tribal chiefs to pledge loyalty to Tehran. This sealed the Kurdish republic's fate. As Tehran reasserted control over the autonomous territories, it repressed thousands of autonomy leaders, members, and sympathizers, and suppressed the flourishing Azerbaijani and Kurdish cultural scenes, closing the new native-language schools, newspapers, and publishers, and demonstratively destroying Kurdish and Azerbaijani books and other publications.[39]

ADP leaders begged Baku and Moscow for support in their negotiations with Tehran over the course of 1946, and Bagirov lobbied Moscow on behalf of Azeri autonomy into the spring of 1947, but the Kremlin ultimately offered little more than sanctuary to some of its former allies.[40] More than 9,000 emigrants from northern Iran fled to the Soviet Union, mostly to Soviet Azerbaijan. Many of those who remained behind—particularly among the APG and Mahabad leaderships—were shot, imprisoned, or exiled to southern Iran.[41] Pishevari was among those who made their way north, but he died soon after, with some historians suggesting that Soviet authorities helped this along. Pishevari and many of his compatriots arrived in Soviet Azerbaijan full of resentment about the circumstances of their defeat: keeping the Soviet Socialist Republic of Gilan in mind, this was the second time Pishevari participated in a revolutionary movement in Iran that was abandoned by its Soviet benefactors.[42] In Baku, he had an openly contentious relationship with Bagirov and, as he lay dying, reportedly complained about Soviet treason, muttering, "I stayed eleven years in solitary confinement in Iran. Neither Reza Shah nor [Iranian Prime Minister Ahmad] Qavam could destroy me. Now, those people got me for their own ends."[43]

Qazi Muhammad, meanwhile, had stayed behind in Mahabad to meet the approaching Iranian troops. On March 31, 1947, Qazi Muhammad; his brother, Sadr Qazi, a deputy in the Tehran Majlis and envoy between Mahabad and Tehran; and his cousin and minister of war, Seif Qazi, were hanged in Mahabad's central square, where Qazi Muhammad had proclaimed Kurdish autonomy just fourteen months earlier. The executions were performed at night, but the bodies were pointedly left hanging throughout the next day.[44] More hangings followed in April. In the meantime, the Barzanis formed a line of defense west of the city, waiting for the snow to melt. After a tenuous period of clashes with Iranian armed forces, Sheikh Ahmed reentered Iraq in mid-April 1947 with most of the Barzani contingent. Sheikh Ahmed and many of his compatriots were imprisoned until the Hashemite monarchy in Iraq was overthrown eleven years later. Mulla Mustafa and 499 elite Barzani fighters took a different path, illegally entering Iraq further north to try and negotiate an unconditional return to Iraq. Unable to find a solution with Baghdad, they fled, making their way through Turkey and Iran with the help of other Kurdish tribes. Finally, in late spring 1947, Barzani and his followers crossed the Aras River and entered the Soviet Union, initiating a new phase of Soviet engagement with Kurdish national aspirations.[45]

Soviet troops had physically retreated from Iran, but the government did not completely sever the relationships it had formed there. In December 1947, Soviet authorities created a Barzani military regiment outside Baku. Although Kurdish instruction was no longer available to local Kurds, Barzani and his followers were offered Kurdish language lessons alongside military training. The next month, Baku also hosted a conference of Iranian and Iraqi Kurdish

FIGURE 5. In 1946, Qazi Muhammad, saluting in the center, proclaimed the creation of an autonomous Kurdish republic in the same central square of Mahabad where he would be hanged the next year. Mustafa Barzani stands in front of him. Photo courtesy of the Eagleton Archives in the Photolibrary of Kurdistan.

leaders. Speaking to the gathered crowd, Barzani denounced British and American imperialist support of Turkish, Iranian, and Iraqi efforts to violently crush the "Kurdish struggle for freedom and independence" in exchange for oil (a fairly awkward denunciation given Stalin's recent prioritization of oil over Azeri and Kurdish autonomy in Iran). Calling for the liberation of Kurdish Iran and the restoration of the democratic republic there, Barzani described a domino effect wherein Kurdish autonomy in Iran would spread to Iraqi and Turkish Kurds, freeing them from the "chains of slavery and foreign influence."[46]

Barzani and his national ambitions were only briefly accommodated in Soviet Azerbaijan. In August 1948, the Council of Ministers ordered the relocation of the Barzanis to a former MVD camp in Uzbekistan. There are disputes over the facts here: Mustafa Barzani's son Massoud (president of Iraqi Kurdistan from 2005 to 2017) claims that his father requested the transfer because he suspected that Bagirov aspired to "obliterate . . . the identity of the Kurdish people" by subjugating them to Azeris.[47] Soviet Minister of Internal Affairs Sergei Kruglov's version is different. In a report to Stalin in 1949, Kruglov wrote that Bagirov recommended that the government move the Barzanis away from the Iranian border because Mustafa Barzani was "politically illiterate" and wanted to organize and lead a Kurdish tribal principality (*kniazhestvo*).[48]

Barzani may well have replicated traditional (i.e., non-Soviet) power relations with the fighters who followed him to the Soviet Union, but he almost certainly also clashed with Bagirov by suggesting that a Kurdish autonomous region could be created in the Norashen area of Azerbaijan's Nakhchıvan ASSR near the nexus of the USSR, Iran, and Turkey.[49]

In late 1948, Barzani reportedly demanded a meeting with Stalin. According to Kruglov, he threatened to kill himself if his request was denied. Whether or not this is true, Kruglov used this situation to justify proposing—with Molotov and Uzbek Party First Secretary Usman Yusupovich Yusupov's support—that the MVD disband the brigade and divide the community to disrupt Barzani's authority over his followers.[50] Massoud Barzani blames Bagirov and Yusupov for his father's struggles in Uzbekistan, claiming that Moscow intervened in 1951 and reunited the community in Tashkent after extended protests and acts of resistance, but Soviet archival documents show that Stalin worked with the MVD from the start to manage this community. After Stalin died and Bagirov was arrested in 1953, Malenkov further eased restrictions and Barzani subsequently enrolled in the Higher Party School in Moscow. Yevgeny Primakov reports that Barzani took credit for these changes: "I went up to the Spassky Gate of the Kremlin and started knocking. An officer came running out . . . and asked, 'What are you knocking for?' I told him that this wasn't Barzani knocking at the gates of the Kremlin, it was the Kurdish revolution."[51]

Barzani returned to Iraq after the coup against the British-backed Hashemite monarchy in 1958. The rest of his community, which by this time had grown from 500 men to 851 people—456 men, 141 women, and more than 250 children—returned to Iraq the following year, sailing from Odessa to Basra, where they were met by gathered crowds, Iraqi government officials, members of the Iraqi Communist Party, representatives from the Soviet embassy, and journalists, including some from TASS and *Pravda*.[52] The Iraqi government issued a general amnesty for Barzani Kurds like Sheikh Ahmed who had been imprisoned in Iraq and rehabilitated those who had been sentenced to death. His exile over, Barzani took control of the Kurdish Democratic Party (KDP) in Iraq, which he had helped establish in 1946, and initiated a new era in the battle for Kurdish autonomy there. Soviet Kurds, meanwhile, did not regain the national rights they lost in the late 1930s. Marked as potentially traitorous, many of the tens of thousands of Kurds deported from the South Caucasus in the 1930s and mid-1940s never returned home and most of those who remained in Azerbaijan were mostly assimilated into the Azerbaijani nationality. Barzani's call for Kurdish autonomy meant that he had only a

FIGURE 6. Mustafa Barzani sits with his brother, Sheikh Ahmed, in Iraq after returning from the USSR in 1958. Photo courtesy of the Archives of Sheikh Adham in the Photolibrary of Kurdistan.

brief sojourn in Soviet Azerbaijan, but the dream stayed alive and, as I explore later in the book, was renewed once again in the waning years of the Soviet experiment.

It is important to underscore the fundamental role that the Azerbaijan SSR, leadership, and population played in the Soviet occupation of Iranian Azerbaijan. Soviet Azerbaijan was a staging ground for the Soviet intervention in Iran and was increasingly enmeshed with the occupied territory. Soviet funds for the state-building project in Tabriz were funneled through the Azerbaijan branch of the state bank and managed by the Azerbaijan Communist Party. Thousands of workers, artists, politicians, and others from Soviet Azerbaijan were the face of this intervention. When the APG opened the Azerbaijani State University in Tabriz in January 1946, for example, its staff was largely comprised of Soviet Azerbaijani academics and experts. Soviet troops also used the SSR as an entry point to northern Iran.[53] The military side of the intervention was so prominent that residents from the Astara region on the Azerbaijan side of the Azerbaijan-Iran border still remember watching Red Army troops moving down the main road from Baku and hosting army divisions in and around area villages.[54]

Iranian Azeris, Kurds, and others also moved in and out of Soviet Azerbaijan at this time. During the war, students, soldiers, and others received training and support there. Later on, the republic absorbed those who fled north to escape Tehran's reassertion of control in northern Iran.[55] Although Stalin and other members of the Soviet leadership in Moscow might not have been as committed as Bagirov, Pishevari, and other Azeri political leaders to Iranian Azerbaijani autonomy (or, indeed, to Bagirov's dream of unifying Soviet and Iranian Azerbaijan), they could not control the expectations that their show of support generated. This was true not just for Azeris but for Kurds and others in the Caucasus, some of whom saw Azerbaijan's brief expansion into Iran and Moscow's fleeting support of Azeri irredentism as an opportunity to redraw the political map of the South Caucasus as well.

The Geopolitics of Armenian and Georgian Foreign Land Claims

Soviet geostrategic interests in Turkey provoked and legitimized nationalizing discourses in Armenia and Georgia similar to those unfolding in Azerbaijan, where the general population was drawn into the issue of Iranian Azerbaijan either as active participants in the Soviet intervention or in more indirect ways. Soviet troops never occupied Turkish territory, but the Kremlin partnered with Yerevan and Tbilisi to develop ethnohistorical land claims that would put pressure on Ankara. Armenian and Georgian elites needed little encouragement to invest in this projection of power: they had been urging the Kremlin to move in this direction for some time.[56]

Soviet Armenian claims to eastern Turkey were bolstered by diaspora petitioners who wrote to world leaders at a succession of international conferences in the 1940s to proclaim support for Soviet annexation of historically Armenian regions in Turkey and to express interest in diaspora repatriation to an Armenian SSR that they hoped would soon expand westward. Their demands were backed by Soviet Armenian officials. In May 1945, the Armenian People's Commissariat for Foreign Affairs (Narkomindel), responding to a request for information from colleagues in Moscow, supported the idea of Armenian repatriation and outlined three annexation options. The first called for the restoration of the 1914 border between Turkey and Russia and transfer of the Ardahan and Surmalin regions to the USSR, while the second endorsed the borders delimited by the San Stefano treaty of 1878. The third and most ambitious proposal called for the annexation of Kars, Surmali, the Alashkert (Eleşkirt) valley, and "three of six Armenian vilayets," namely Erzurum, Van, and Bitlis.[57]

In contrast with Iranian Azerbaijan, where Bagirov carved out a monopoly over Soviet territorial pretensions, Soviet land claims against Turkey set two republics against one another, with Armenian and Georgian elites competing for some of the same Turkish regions. In fall 1945, Giorgi Kiknadze, the Commissar of Foreign Affairs for the Georgian SSR, petitioned Beria to protest an Armenian proposal endorsed by Soviet Deputy Commissar of Foreign Affairs S. I. Kavtaradze. It suggested transferring 26,000 square kilometers of Turkish territory to the Soviet Union, with 20,500 adjoined to Armenia and 5,500 to Georgia. Kiknadze insisted that ancient Georgian provinces comprised 13,190 square kilometers of this area, including the southern parts of Batumi *okrug* and all of the former Artvin, Ardahan, and Olti (Oltu) *okrugs*. Kavtaradze had hypothetically apportioned Ardahan and Olti to Armenia, but Kiknadze contended that Armenia was only entitled to lands corresponding to the former Kars and Kaghızman (Kağızman) *okrugs*, the Surmali *uezd*, and Erivan *guberniia*.[58]

The debate over these irredentist claims extended to the public sphere. As in Soviet Azerbaijan, where newspaper articles and books celebrated Soviet and Iranian Azeri ties and condemned Tehran's treatment of Iranian Azerbaijan, newspaper articles and books about ancient Armenian kingdoms in Turkey also appeared in the mid-1940s, reinforcing the evolving Soviet Armenian sense of self and granting historical legitimacy to Moscow's territorial pretensions.[59] State media in Soviet Georgia also took up these conversations. Prior to the Moscow Conference with the foreign ministers of the USSR, Britain, and the United States in December 1945, two Georgian historians, Simon Dzhanashia and Nikolai Berdzenishvili, published "On Our Lawful Claims toward Turkey," condemning Turkey's friendly relations with Germany and asserting Georgian rights to Ardahan, Artvin, Olti, Tortum, İspir, Bayburt, Gümüshkhane (Gümüşhane), eastern Lazistan, Trabzon, and Giresun. Initially published in Georgia's *komunisti* newspaper (the Georgian-language *Pravda*), the article was swiftly broadcast on radio stations throughout the USSR and published in *Zaria Vostoka* (a Russian-language Georgian newspaper), *Pravda*, *Izvestiia*, and elsewhere. This indicates a coordinated effort to advertise Georgian land claims to a broader Soviet and foreign audience.[60] Discussions continued in Georgian newspapers, with Georgian scholars and religious figures from both the Transcaucasian Muslim Ecclesiastical Authority and the Georgian Orthodox church publishing articles about Georgian claims to Turkish territories in both *komunisti* and *Zaria Vostoka*.[61]

Repatriation schemes also engaged the public. They supported the idea that the Georgian and Armenian nations extended beyond the borders of the respective SSRs and sometimes even the notion that borders should change to accommodate this fact. As the Armenian Narkomindel contended in a communication with Kavtaradze in May 1945, repatriation was "intimately and inextricably intertwined with the question about the return to the USSR of formerly Armenian territories that have been ceded to Turkey."[62] Georgian proposals for Fereydan Georgian repatriation were not very successful,[63] but

Armenian repatriation brought around 95,000 Armenians to Soviet Armenia from the Middle East, the United States, and Europe between 1946 and 1948.[64]

While some planners assumed that Armenia would expand into eastern Turkey and thus have more land for repatriate settlement, when this did not occur officials devised other living arrangements for repatriates within the boundaries of the Armenian SSR. The Armenian and Azerbaijani leaderships developed one solution to this problem that purportedly benefited both sides, though not necessarily the everyday people caught up in their plans. Between 1948 and 1953, Bagirov and his counterpart in Yerevan, Armenian First Party Secretary Grigor Arutiunov, coordinated with resettlement officials in Moscow, Yerevan, and Baku to relocate approximately 45,000 Azeris from Armenia to Azerbaijan.

One of the justifications for Azeri resettlement was that it would "facilitate conditions for the reception and establishment [*ustroistvo*] of Armenians returning to their homeland from foreign countries."[65] What was the benefit for Azerbaijan? It needed more laborers. The Mingachevir dam and hydroelectric station under construction there made it possible to expand the republic's irrigation infrastructure and cotton economy into the sparsely inhabited Kura-Araks lowlands, but a new labor pool was required for it to become an agriculturally productive region. Officials had struggled to staff infrastructure development jobs there and previous resettlement proposals were unsuccessful, including an earlier one that anticipated moving Dagestani collective farmers (*kolkhozniks*) to the Kura-Araks region.[66]

From an all-Union perspective, the resettlement made economic sense. Azerbaijan was an essential part of the Soviet cotton harvest, which Stalin considered one of four key components (along with metals, fuels, and grains) of Soviet postwar economic recovery.[67] In order to rebuild the postwar economy, Soviet policies focused on building new dams and irrigation systems and moving people to places where they could be economically productive, whether in the forestry and paper industries in Arkhangelsk and Karelia, fisheries in Sakhalin, or lowland areas cultivating valuable crops like cotton.[68] Azeri resettlement from Armenia to the Kura-Araks zone had an unmistakable ethnic element, but Moscow also bound this migration to economic planning, insisting these Azeris be resettled only in the Kura-Araks region.

Today it may seem counterintuitive that Bagirov helped to formulate a proposal that aimed to remove Azeris from Armenia. Without access to backroom conversations among Bagirov, Arutiunov, and Stalin as they formulated this plan, it is difficult to know what exactly motivated his participation in this migration scheme and associated plans to reduce Azeri national cultural infrastructure in Armenia. This would be accomplished by merging Azerbaijani sectors of pedagogy institutes there with their Azerbaijan SSR equivalents and moving the Azerbaijani pedagogical training school from Armenia to Khan-lar, Azerbaijan.[69] What is clear from available documents is that officials in the Azerbaijan SSR, for the most part, willingly participated in the resettle-ment and even pushed for its fulfillment at times accusing Armenian officials of sabotaging the migration by blocking some Azeris from leaving Armenia and failing to return Azeris to Azerbaijan when they abandoned the Kura-Araks region and returned to Armenia.[70]

The resettlement of Azeris to Azerbaijan indeed had myriad failings. The Council of Ministers decree characterized it as voluntary, but many Azeris felt that they were forced out of Armenia—sometimes by local Armenians and other times by Armenian and Azerbaijani resettlement officials. Some targeted Azeris in Armenia compared themselves to other Muslims and "Turks" who had recently been deported from the Caucasus or saw themselves as victims of Armenian repatriation. They protested resettlement plans by destroying their orchards and properties to keep them out of repatriate hands, sending complaint letters and petitions objecting to the migration plan, refusing to move, and, finally, returning to Armenia when they found conditions in the Kura-Araks zone disagreeable.[71] As the migration wore on, Armenian offi-cials, who were increasingly loath to lose productive Azeri kolkhozniks, also started sabotaging the migration by preventing some Azeris who wanted to move from leaving and helping others return.[72] As a result, by January 1952, resettlement authorities had only fulfilled about 40 percent of the resettle-ment target of 100,000 Azeri kolkhoznik migrants laid out in a Council of Ministers decree signed by Stalin and dated December 23, 1947. This was a high failure rate compared to contemporaneous resettlements elsewhere in the USSR.[73] Resettlement officials eventually responded by finding other re-settlement candidates. That year, Baku's plans shifted to accommodate more internal migrants to the Kura-Araks region rather than rely on interrepublic plans. These new resettlers, who also experienced varying levels of force in their migration, originated from two primary places: villages in the Mingache-vir Dam's flood zone and the Talysh-dominated Soviet Azerbaijan-Iran borderlands.[74]

Although Bagirov and Arutiunov linked Armenian repatriation to Azeri re-settlement in their proposal to Stalin in late 1947, the repatriation plan was already starting to fall apart by this point. Soviet Armenia was often depicted as a repatriation utopia in propaganda photos like the one shown in Figure 7, but many repatriates were shocked by their transport experiences and, after their arrival, by the low quality of life in a republic scarred by postwar short-ages of food, utilities, and housing. Migrants also struggled to integrate into

FIGURE 7. "Armenian repatriates settle down in their homeland [Soviet Armenia]." Soviet Information Bureau Photograph Collection, Box 2, Davis Center for Russian and Eurasian Studies Collection, H. C. Fung Library, Harvard University.

and be accepted by the Soviet Armenian culture, economy, and society, leading to growing discontentment among repatriates.[75]

Some disgruntled repatriates tried to escape to Iran or Turkey. This was a significant problem for state officials, particularly since repatriation had been implemented in part to put pressure on Turkey. The number of border guards in Armenia was increased to halt repatriate defections, but repatriates found new routes out through Georgia and Azerbaijan. It was a risky journey: many were captured at the border and some were even shot by border guards trying to keep repatriates from absconding from their Soviet "homeland."[76] State authorities in Yerevan and Moscow first tried to appease repatriates by improving their quality of life. They moved those settled at high elevations to more desirable lowland villages (sometimes ones previously occupied by now-resettled Azeris) and increased state investment in new home construction, resources, and cultural programming. When these efforts fell short, they turned to a tried-and-true method: forced resettlement, pushing repatriates who exhibited a "re-immigration" mood in border villages to interior areas of the republic before escalating to deportation from the republic.[77] In 1949, the Ministry of State Security (MGB) expelled (*vyselit'*) more than 43,000 so-called Dashnak Armenians, Greek and Turkish subjects, stateless Greeks and Turks, and former Greek and Turkish citizens to Central Asia and Siberia in Operation Volna. Most of the deportees came from Georgia, but Azerbaijan and Armenia contributed numbers as well, including thousands of repatriates.[78] In brief, the short-lived Armenian repatriation scheme, which like Bagirov's work in Iran was linked to irredentism, fell far short of migration targets, but nonetheless

FIGURE 8. "Russians [Soviet Troops] stand guard on the Turkish border." Soviet Information Bureau Photograph Collection, Box 19, Davis Center for Russian and Eurasian Studies Collection, H. C. Fung Library, Harvard University.

strained regional resources and increased national tensions in the South Caucasus by intertwining Azeri resettlement with Armenian repatriation.

The Soviet Union ultimately failed to gain territory in the Middle East as it had in Europe and the Far East, but wartime pretensions to Iranian and Turkish regions nonetheless justified a variety of population management, cultural diplomacy, and nation-building policies in the South Caucasus. The willingness of the Soviet leadership to use expansive definitions of Armenian, Azeri, and Georgian nationhoods and national territories to legitimize Soviet claims to foreign "historical lands" encouraged republican leaders to look beyond their own republics to build and consolidate their nations. It did not take long for them to link external claims to internal ones, setting a new course for intra- and inter-republic national relations during and after the war.

What's Yours Is Mine: Nation-Building and Extraterritorial Nationhood Inside the South Caucasus

The wartime legitimation of transborder nationhoods breathed new life into territorial and national disputes in the South Caucasus. Whether Stalin thought he had a real chance at adding Iranian or Turkish territory to the USSR or merely participated in these high-stakes maneuvers to achieve a greater sphere of influence and key economic goals, many of his partners in the South Caucasus were sincerely committed to Soviet southward expansion. As geopolitical tensions intensified between Moscow and its rivals in Tehran and Ankara, and while Bagirov managed Soviet operations in Iranian Azerbaijan, Armenian and Georgian elites turned their gaze inward and devised plans to alter the map of the Soviet South Caucasus.

Arutiunov renewed contestation over Azerbaijan's Nagorno-Karabakh Autonomous Oblast' in November 1945. Petitioning Moscow to adjoin the territory to Armenia on the basis of economic, ethnographic, and political claims, he invoked arguments similar to those developed for aspirations to Turkish territory. That same month, Georgian First Secretary Kandid Charkviani rekindled Georgia's long-standing claim to the three regions of Azerbaijan—Balakan, Zaqatala, and Qakh—that were home to Georgian-Ingilois (as well as Avars, Lezgins, Mugals, Tsakhurs, Laks, Azeris, and others). Georgians and Georgian-Ingilois called this area Saingilo, or land of the Ingilo. Bagirov vigorously rejected Armenian and Georgian pretensions to Soviet Azerbaijani territory, asserting that if the transfer of Azerbaijani territories to Georgia and Armenia was under serious consideration, then Azerbaijan had claims of its own—to the Azizbekov (Azizbeyov), Vedi, and Garabaglar regions of Armenia, the Borchali region of Georgia, and the Derbent and Kasumkent areas of the Dagestan ASSR in Russia.[79]

Charkviani explicitly linked the Soviet occupation of northern Iran—and the potential for Soviet Azerbaijani territorial expansion there—to his own plans to annex Azerbaijani territory. Stalin had previously denied Charkviani's requests to renegotiate Saingilo's status out of concern that it would set a dangerous precedent, but Charkviani apparently felt that wartime developments like the Soviet occupation of Iran and Georgia's acquisition of some Chechen, Ingush, and Balkar territories after their respective deportations during the war had vitiated this concern.[80] According to Charkviani's memoir, when he reignited the issue in 1945, Stalin told him that, if "Southern Azerbaijan" was resolved in the USSR's favor, then "the issue of your Saingilo will also be resolved." As Charkviani later concluded, "Saingilo's destiny remained unchanged" because the Soviet Union had lost its contest for Iran.[81]

M. G. Seidov, an Azerbaijani CP secretary in the 1940s, also coupled geopolitics with internal territorial disputes in his memoir. Recounting a conversation among Bagirov, Beria, and Anastas Mikoyan in the Kremlin in 1945, Seidov reported that Beria and Mikoyan told Bagirov that the unification of Iranian Azerbaijan and Soviet Azerbaijan was nearly complete and jokingly asked whether it would now be possible to transfer Nagorno-Karabakh and Saingilo from Azerbaijan to Armenia and Georgia, respectively.[82] Beria and Mikoyan's role in Seidov's recollection underscore that Charkviani and Arutiunov likely drafted their proposals after conversations with—and endorsements from—central party leaders.

Kremlin-backed irredentism brought opportunities to reshape republican power, resources, and demographics but also reinforced other impulses among Soviet republican nation-builders seeking to advance the assimilatory policies that came into force at the close of the 1930s. Let us take Georgia as our primary example. Georgian pretensions to historic lands in Turkey and Azerbaijan are best understood when contextualized with other policies—namely, national deportations and assimilatory practices—that often expanded titular footprints at the expense of nontitular minority communities in the Soviet Union. While these practices were implemented across the USSR with Kremlin sanction or direction, Moscow's role should not overshadow the agency of local political actors and national community leaders.

Charkviani and Beria were at the center of nation-building efforts in Georgia. Beria, who preceded Charkviani as Georgian first secretary, had since risen through the ranks to become head of the NKVD and deputy chairman of the Sovnarkom, but he was still deeply involved in the region, exerting significant influence over the first secretaries of the three republics—who were all connected to his extensive patronage network.[83] Throughout the 1920s and 1930s, the Georgian leadership agitated to categorize Mingrelians, Adjarans, Laz, and Svans as Georgians rather than as separate peoples in Soviet censuses. With the all-Union contraction of Soviet nationality categories in the 1939 census, this goal was achieved, increasing the purported percentage of Georgians in Georgia by reducing the number of documented national minorities.

Two minority populations—Ossetians and Abkhazians—were perhaps shielded from bureaucratic erasure by their territorial autonomies in Georgia, but Beria and Charkviani still sought to subordinate them to the Georgian nation. Consider Abkhazia and Abkhazians. In 1931, Abkhazia's political status was downgraded. It had been categorized as a treaty republic (SSR) associated with Georgia (itself an unusual arrangement), but, in 1931, was converted into an Autonomous Soviet Socialist Republic (ASSR) and made a constituent part of Georgia. As first secretary in Georgia in the 1930s, Beria used the terror to remake Abkhazia, first eliminating his political competition, Chairman of Abkhazia's Central Executive Committee Nestor Apollonovich Lakoba, then dismantling Lakoba's mostly Abkhazian political network and stacking the political apparatus with people loyal to him instead. He also initiated resettlement policies that brought tens of thousands of Georgians and Mingrelians to Abkhazia, replaced and translated Abkhazian and Russian place names with Georgian ones, and swapped out the Latin-based script of the Abkhazian language with one based on Georgian.[84] This shift to a Georgian script in 1937 was a unique assertion of titular influence given the broader Soviet trend of replacing Latin scripts for Avar, Azerbaijani, Tajik, Uzbek, and other languages with Cyrillic in the late 1930s. Unlike these other languages, which had initially shifted from Arabic to Latin scripts in the 1920s, Abkhazian had transitioned from a Cyrillic alphabet instituted in the late nineteenth century to Latin and then Georgian over the course of the 1920s and 1930s (a Cyrillic alphabet was reintroduced in 1954).

As first secretary of the Georgian Communist Party from 1938 to 1952, Charkviani continued earlier efforts to assimilate Abkhazians into the Georgian nation and marginalize them in the ASSR. In the 1945–1946 school year, Charkviani and First Secretary of Abkhazia Akaki Mgeladze transformed Abkhazian-language schools into Georgian schools where Abkhazian, like Russian, would be a subject of study rather than the instructional language.[85] Up to this point, more than 9,000 students in 81 schools studied in Abkhazian language before transitioning to Russian in the fifth grade.[86] The political leadership justified the switch to Georgian as a fix for students who struggled when changing languages in fifth grade and portrayed the Georgian language as an ethnohistorical advancement for Abkhazians who were supposedly already accustomed to it thanks to centuries of "idyllic" exposure to the Georgian cultural milieu (*v krug gruzinskoi kul'tury*).[87] Charkviani and Mgeladze continued and intensified Beria's efforts to place trusted colleagues in power positions in Abkhazia, move Georgians to the territory, and replace Abkhazian toponyms with Georgian ones.[88]

Working with Beria and other party leaders in Moscow, the Georgian leadership also cleansed Georgia's diverse population by deporting targeted nationalities to Central Asia, Kazakhstan, and Siberia. There were two main waves of deportation. In July 1944, Stalin, as head of the State Defense Committee (GKO), approved the deportation of 86,000 Turks, Kurds, and Khemshins (also known as Khemshils) from Georgian regions (Akhaltsikhe, Adigeni, Aspindza, Akhalkalaki, Bogdanov, and the Adjar ASSR) bordering Turkey to Kazakhstan, Uzbekistan, and Kyrgyzstan.[89] The deportation was swift: before the end of the first day more than 26,000 people had been loaded into eastbound trains.[90] Approximately 95,000 "special settlers" were deported from Georgia at this time.[91] Brutal conditions on the trains and in the special settlements contributed to significant death rates among deportees.[92] In 1949, Operation Volna brought another wave of expulsions to the South Caucasus, with the majority of deportees (43,344) coming from Georgia.[93]

On the one hand, these deportations can be understood as part of a broader impulse in the Soviet Union to defend geopolitically vulnerable borderlands by targeting and ultimately punishing nationalities constructed as untrustworthy and accused of misbehavior, poor acculturation to the Soviet system, wartime deeds, or dangerous foreign ties. In this context, deportees from Georgia comprised a small percentage of the 2,562,830 "deportees and special settlers" under the control of the Ministry of Internal Affairs in the summer of 1949.[94] On the other hand, the population of Georgia made up just 2 percent of the Soviet population but was proportionally overrepresented in the special settlement system. This imbalance grew over time; Claire Kaiser has calculated that Georgia accounted for 14 percent of postwar deportations.[95]

What can explain these robust national expulsions from Georgia? Decrees ultimately came from Moscow, but expulsion plans were formulated in conversation with republican officials who exerted significant influence over deportation operations and the reshaping of emptied minority settlements. In the case of Georgia, Communist Party documents show that Georgian Kurds, Turks (*turki*), and Khemshins were deported for "national characteristics" (*po natsional'nym priznakam*), but the evolution of migration plans over the summer of 1944 reveals how Georgian officials molded the deportation conversation, as well as the fairly spontaneous way that Kurds were swept into these plans.[96] In a letter Charkviani and Valerian Bakradze, the head of Georgia's Sovnarkom, sent to Beria in May 1944, they discussed moving the Turkish (*turetskii*) population from the Georgian-Turkish border zone to eastern (i.e., internal) areas of the Georgian republic. Claiming that it would be difficult to find room for these deportees in eastern Georgia, they agreed to do so since there was "no other option." At this point, they declared that Kurdish relocation was unnecessary.[97]

In June, however, Charkviani, Bakradze, and Avksentii Narikievich Rapava, the People's Commissar for State Security in Georgia, reported to Beria that, since there was now an option to resettle people outside of Georgia, it was "also necessary to evict" more Turks (*turki*), 1,030 Kurdish households from the Akhaltsikhe, Aspindza, and Adigeni regions, and Kurds and Khemshins from Adjara. No explanation was provided for the deportation of the 1,030 Kurdish households and Turks, but Charkviani et al. framed the Adjara deportations in essentializing language reminiscent of recent deportation orders issued for Chechens, Ingushes, and Balkars in the North Caucasus: the Kurds and Khemshins in Adjara avoided participation in collective farms (*kolkhozes*), their cattle roamed in border regions, and they had been implicated in spying.[98] Archival documents show that, at the same time, the republican leadership was developing plans to resettle Georgians from other areas of Georgia in these soon-to-be-emptied borderlands. Some of these settlers would be used to develop the resort network in Borjomi.[99] It is clear that republican officials expanded deportation plans once it was possible to send deportees out of the republic.[100] Both Beria, with his dual power base in Moscow and the Caucasus, and republican leaders such as Charkviani and Bakradze share responsibility for these deportations with Stalin, who signed expulsion orders as chairman of the Council of Ministers.

The Soviet Georgian leadership's enthusiasm for deportations continued after the war. During Operation Volna, they targeted communities outside the geographic areas specified in the deportation order.[101] Then, a few months after Volna, Charkviani wrote to Stalin proposing to deport 4,500 of the 5,600 people in Georgia with a history of Iranian citizenship. Although these deportation orders were again framed in the language of state security, many deportees, recognizing that their expulsion bolstered titular nation-building, considered themselves to be victims of "Georgification."[102] Following these postwar deportations, Greeks, Iranians, "Turks," and others who could somehow be linked to Greece, Iran, and Turkey—the countries linked to the Truman Doctrine—had been cleansed from Georgia.

There is a clear titular nation-building component embedded in these deportations. Georgian resettlement to areas like Abkhazia had been going on for years, and many of the regions targeted for deportation were demographically dominated by minorities considered unassimilable into the Georgian nation. According to the 1939 census, Georgians made up less than 14 percent of the population in the Adigeni, Aspindza, and Akhalkalaki regions. They were significantly outnumbered locally by "Azerbaijanis" (most Meskhetians later recategorized in the catch-all "Turk" category), at almost 64 percent of the regional population, and Armenians, who made up a little more than 15 percent.[103]

Why is it important to understand how the Georgian leadership—Beria included—"managed" minority regions and communities before, during, and after the war? Charkviani's intervention on behalf of the Georgian-Ingiloi in Azerbaijan and complaints about Azerbaijani chauvinism must be contextualized as part of this broader story. His proposal to annex Azerbaijan's Balakan, Qakh, and Zaqatala regions was about more than taking land from Soviet Azerbaijan or offense at minority assimilation there. It was part of a larger process of nation-building enhanced by wartime exigencies and, more important, possibilities. Georgian claims on Azerbaijani territory overlapped with Bagirov's push to integrate Iranian Azerbaijan with the Azerbaijan SSR, but also with Charkviani, Beria, and Bakradze's deportation plans for Georgia's "Turks," Kurds, and Khemshins; overtures toward Fereydan Georgians in Iran; and Charkviani and Mgeladze's efforts to "Georgianize" Abkhazia. In other words, many of the things that Charkviani complained about in the Azerbaijani context mirrored his own oppressive treatment of Abkhazians and other minorities in Georgia. After all, who better to protect their "own" people than those who are using similar tactics?

The Case of Saingilo

As with Nagorno-Karabakh, control over Zaqatala, Qakh, and Balakan was disputed from the very start of the Soviet project. In the late Russian Empire, the region was part of the Zaqatala *okrug*, which was a separate administrative territory bordering the Elizavetpol *guberniia* (governorate), the Tiflis *guberniia*, and Dagestan *oblast'*. After the Russian Revolution, three inchoate states—the Mountainous Republic of the North Caucasus based in Temir-Khan-Shura, which is now Buynaksk (Dagestan); the Azerbaijan Democratic Republic (ADR) centered in Baku; and the Georgian Democratic Republic with its capital in Tiflis, which later became Tbilisi—laid claim to the territory.[104]

The Zaqatala National Council negotiated autonomous provincial status with the ADR in summer 1918, but Baku exerted only nominal control over the region and the local population harbored multiple belongings and self-understandings. Many in the area, including Avars, Laks, and others had long been oriented toward Dagestan, in part because of the many Dagestani peoples who had migrated to the area but continued to travel back and forth across mountain paths. Others, meanwhile, had co-ethnic bonds and a general alignment with Georgia and Georgians. There is evidence of this, for instance, in a 1921 appeal from the Ingiloi Georgian Organization of the Communist Party to the "workers, peasants, and soldiers of Georgia," entreating them to abandon their defense of the Georgian Democratic Government and establish the power of the workers and peasants once and for all.[105]

About a week after the Red Army took control of the ADR in late April, the Soviet government signed the Treaty of Moscow with Georgia on May 7, 1920, recognizing Georgia's sovereignty and establishing peaceful relations. The treaty, signed by Grigorii Illarionovich Uratadze (Georgia) and Lev Mikhailovich Karakhan (Soviet Russia), defined the Zaqatala *okrug* as part of Georgia, but a supplement created five days later—with Baku and Ordzhonikidze's urging—acknowledged the dispute between Georgia and the new Azerbaijan Soviet Republic over the region and established a joint commission to determine its status.[106] The subsequent period was tumultuous, with both Georgia and Azerbaijan claiming control over the region. Within a month, the Red Army used the excuse of local uprisings to occupy Zaqatala. By the following spring, the Georgian Democratic Republic had been overthrown and Georgia integrated into the Soviet system. Not long after that, a conference was held in Tiflis to regularize the borders between Soviet Azerbaijan and Georgia, and on July 5, 1921, the Georgian Socialist Soviet Republic officially "renounced all pretensions to the Zaqatala *okrug*."[107]

Although the decision was made to adjoin Zaqatala to Azerbaijan rather than Georgia, the region—like so many others in the Soviet Union—was populated by a multiethnic population that did not fit neatly into any one national box or orientation. Its placement in Soviet Azerbaijan did not sit well with many Georgians and Georgian-Ingilois, for example, who continuously agitated for Georgian annexation of the region. Their alignment toward Georgia was in line with decades of Russian imperial ethnographic texts that positioned Saingilo as a historical part of the Georgian Kakheti region and defined Georgians and "Engilos"—Christian and Muslim alike—as part of the same national community.[108] In these texts, Georgian-Ingilois were described as indigenous to the region and juxtaposed with other nationalities that were often portrayed as interlopers who had historically abused them. Further, it was implied that these "late arrivals" had less right to the territory.

In 1870, for instance, the ethnographer Aleksandr Ivanovich von Plotto explained that, when the Zaqatala *okrug* formed the eastern edge of the Kakhetian kingdom, Georgians made up the dominant population but had been joined by Mugals (Mongols) during the Timurid-era "great migration of peoples" and Lezgins who arrived from Dagestan to take advantage of Shah Abbas's attack on Kakhetia in the seventeenth century. According to von Plotto, local Georgians, now known as "ingelo" because of their history of Islamic conversion used the Georgian language at home and were increasingly exposed to Christianity by missionaries.[109] Indeed, Russian incorporation of the region enabled intensive Christian missionary work that returned many Georgian-Ingilois to the Christian faith in the late nineteenth century.[110]

These characterizations of Georgian-Ingilois and the region persisted after Zaqatala was adjoined to Soviet Azerbaijan in 1921. Ethnographic and political reports continued to emphasize Georgian-Ingiloi "Georgianness," providing additional fodder for Georgians and Georgian-Ingilois aggrieved by Azerbaijan's claims to the region. In 1924, for example, the ethnographer and Caucasus specialist Grigorii Filippovich Chursin determined that the estimated 15,000 Ingiloi in the Aliabad, Qakh, and Jar-Mukhakh districts of the Zaqatala region were part of the Kartvelian ethnographic group. Chursin further explained that they knew the Azerbaijani dialect or language (*azerbaidzhanskoe narechie*) for intertribal communication, but their native language was of Georgian extraction.[111] An Azerbaijani state report from the mid-1920s, meanwhile, disaggregated the community into two groups: (1) "ingiloitsy (*engiol'tsy*)" Georgian Muslims in the Zaqatala region, and (2) "gruziny (*kakhetichnskie*)" (*sic*) in Zaqatala and Baku, but also categorized both the Muslim Ingilois and Christian Georgians as "*Kartavel'tsy*," or Georgians (Kartvelians is the basis for the Georgian word for Georgia, Sakartvelo).[112]

Although the divide between Christian and Muslim Georgian-Ingilois is frequently elided in these texts by an emphasis on their shared Georgianness, the differing religious identifications are key to understanding how the population has been contested, claimed, and policed by competing actors (local and otherwise) seeking to mobilize cultural and political resources and power. Not unlike in Kemalist Turkey, from Baku's perspective the most meaningful marker of identity in this community was often religion rather than nationality. Differentiated national policies and practices applied to Christian and Muslim Georgian-Ingiloi settlements demonstrate that Azerbaijani officials considered Muslim Georgian-Ingiloi to be more assimilable than their Christian Georgian-Ingiloi neighbors and proceeded from this assumption.[113]

In this regard, the experience of Christian Georgian-Ingilois in Qakh closely resembled that of titular diasporas in the Soviet Union, like the Armenians in Azerbaijan. In the Soviet period, Christian Georgian-Ingilois were counted as Georgian in censuses and registered as such in their passports. Compared to their Muslim counterparts, they had fairly consistent access to Georgian-language schools, kolkhozes, and cultural resources in Azerbaijan's Qakh region. Nonetheless, Azerbaijani nation-building practices carried out in Muslim Georgian-Ingiloi communities meant that Christians also worried that their Georgian identification and cultural resources were at risk.[114]

This was for good reason. Muslim Georgian-Ingilois in Soviet Azerbaijan experienced significant pressure to identify as part of the titular Azerbaijani nation. Although most ethnographers continued to categorize Christian Georgian-Ingilois as Georgian, Muslim Georgian-Ingilois at best were considered an ethnographic group of the Georgian nation and registered as Azerbaijani in Soviet passports and censuses. They were also more integrated into Azerbaijani educational and political spheres than their Christian counterparts. Georgian-language schools and sectors in Muslim communities opened later than in Christian settlements and often lasted for only a few years before being transformed back into the Azerbaijani language. In this regard, Azerbaijani authorities treated Muslim Georgian-Ingilois much as they did other nontitular peoples like Talyshes. Thus, although the Saingilo dispute was fed by Georgian accusations of discrimination against all Georgian-Ingilois in Azerbaijan, the most pitched identity battles centered on the orientation of Muslim villages, including Aliabad (Əliabad), Yengiyan, and Mosul in Zaqatala region, İtitala in Balakan region, and Zayam (Zəyəm), Qoraghan (Qorağan), and Tasmalı in Qakh.

The first Georgian-language schools were opened in Christian communities in Qakh after Sovietization in 1920, but *korenizatsiia* generally came late to area minorities. It was only in 1937 that an Azerbaijani Narkompros decree ordered regional executive committees to switch local schools and governmental affairs from Azerbaijani to the "native language of ingilois" in Qakh, Balakan, and Zaqatala.[115] Due to the titular status of Georgians in neighboring Georgia, Georgian-language schools survived the purge of native-language schooling at the close of the 1930s. Over the next couple of years, the Georgian-language educational network even expanded from Qakh into Zaqatala and Balakan.[116] At some point in 1943, however, Georgian-language schools in Muslim communities like Zayam, Tasmalı, and İtitala were switched back to Azerbaijani-language instruction, prompting protests from some residents.

The school closures motivated Qakh-born, Tbilisi-based academic Georgii Gamkharashvili to intensify his activism for Georgian-Ingiloi national rights in Azerbaijan. Over the course of the 1940s, he established a relationship with Charkviani, but in a letter sent to Charkviani and Bakradze in 1943, he still found it necessary to validate his claims by referencing his history of agitation for Georgian-Ingiloi rights and his acquaintanceship with Comrade S. Khoshtaria.[117] This connection would prove key, as it was Khoshtaria who appears to have brought the letter to Charkviani's desk. In this letter, Gamkharashvili argued that Georgian-language school closures in Marsan, İtitala, Aliabad, and other Muslim villages proved that republic officials were trying to "Tiurkify" ("*tiurki-fitsiruetsia*") Georgian-Ingilois: "As in the past with the mullahs, now some employees of AzNarkompros exaggerate the question of Georgian-Muslim belonging to Tiurks and argue that there is no reason why Georgian schools should exist." He closed by offering to supply Charkviani with informational reports about Saingilo's ethnography, history, economy, and culture that would explain why the region belonged to Georgia and the injustice of Azerbaijani control there. Gamkharashvili clearly considered Saingilo to be a natural part of the Georgian SSR and believed that all Georgian-Ingilois—regardless of religious orientation—were part of the Georgian nation.[118]

By 1944, Gamkharashvili and another Tbilisi-based academic from Qakh, Archil Dzhanashvili, had established a relationship with Soviet leaders in both Moscow and Tbilisi. Indeed, in addition to continuously petitioning Georgian and Azerbaijani officials, Gamkharashvili traveled to Moscow several times to try to meet with Stalin, succeeding on at least one occasion.[119] Gamkharashvili and Dzhanashvili's letters also reveal an intensified level of ease and engagement over time. As their familiarity with the leadership grew and reports about Georgian claims to Turkish territories spread in the newspapers, their writing remained deferential but their demands expanded. They eventually started submitting lengthy memorandums about Saingilo to the Georgian Communist Party.[120] While they were still interested in ending national discrimination against Georgian-Ingilois in Azerbaijan, they also started requesting the transfer of the region from Azerbaijan to Georgia. As Gamkharashvili put it, only then would the population truly reap the benefits and justice of Stalin's socialism.[121] By 1946—after Charkviani's annexation overture—Gamkharashvili was opening and closing his letters with statements supporting the Georgian annexation of Saingilo. In one letter to Stalin, for instance, he wrote that, in order "to eradicate abnormalities [mentioned earlier in the letter], the Qakh, Zaqatala, and Balakan regions must immediately be transferred to the Georgian SSR."[122]

In March 1944, objections to the Georgian-Ingiloi situation also reached Charkviani from the Georgian NKVD after Major Isashvili, head of NKVD operations in Akhaltsikhe, a major site of Meskhetian Turk deportation a few months later, reported on a recent trip home to Qakh. Over several pages, Isashvili described Georgian-Ingilois' marginalization in Azerbaijan. Employing dramatic anecdotes about their alienation from rich kolkhoz lands, Azeri men assaulting Georgian-Ingiloi female kolkhozniks, Azeris calling Georgian-Ingilois degrading names, Azerbaijan's educational authorities exhorting "Ingilois-Azerbaijanis" to study in Azerbaijani because they are Muslim, and Georgian-Ingilois lacking telephones, lights, radios, and other resources, Isashvili built a case to prove the oppression of Georgian-Ingiloi in Azerbaijan.[123]

In a sign that Georgian-Ingiloi petitions and complaints were hitting the right desks, in the spring of 1944 Stalin instructed Charkviani and Bagirov to arrange a fact-finding trip to Qakh, Balakan, and Zaqatala. In their post-trip report to Stalin, they acknowledged that local officials, "motivated, allegedly, by the wishes of the population, and also by inadequate numbers of Georgian teachers in connection with mobilization for the army, incorrectly transferred instruction in schools from Georgian to the Azerbaijani language" in Aliabad, İtitala, and Mosul during the war. They further agreed that, starting with the 1944–1945 school year, all schools in Ingiloi villages would be renovated, switched to the Georgian language, and provided appropriate instructional resources and qualified teachers.[124] Charkviani also promised to enroll forty Ingiloi students in Tbilisi higher education institutions every year, further strengthening Georgian-Ingiloi ties to the Georgian republic.[125] This agreement remained the status quo until 1954, when, as is discussed in chapter 3, Georgian schools were closed once again in Georgian-Ingiloi Muslim communities.

The "Saingilo expedition" represented a remarkable case of interrepublican interference. Officials from Soviet Azerbaijan were understandably frustrated, but Georgians were also discontented. Drafts of the report provide some insight into their differing interests, conclusions, and motivations. Charkviani, for example, edited a draft to emphasize that Georgian schools were incorrectly switched to the Azerbaijani language during the war and to downplay excuses for the closures. He also inflated the number of Georgian-Ingilois in Azerbaijan from 8,147 to 9,000 and emphasized that Ingilois are Georgians: the opening line of Bagirov's draft discussed schools "in Ingiloi villages," but Charkviani's version addressed schools in "Georgian (Ingiloi) villages."[126]

Charkviani also bitterly complained to Beria—his partner in reshaping Georgia's demographics—about the trip and his displeasure with his Azerbaijani counterparts. He explained that he followed instructions and came to an agreement with Bagirov, but "everything that was written in complaint letters about national education in Saingilo was completely proven. From 17 schools functioning in 1937 (3 of them existing since 1920), only 7 are left." He continued, "It is significant to note that Georgian schools were liquidated in all Mohammedan Ingilo villages, although the latter speak Georgian."[127] Although the investigatory report from Georgian and Azerbaijani education officials, including Ibragimov as Azerbaijani Commissar of Enlightenment, claimed that school closures were implemented without approval from Baku,[128] Charkviani informed Beria that the closures could not have happened without "silent agreement and support from the center, at least from the national enlightenment organs. Teachers at Azerbaijani schools and local workers carry out intense propaganda in favor of Azerbaijanization [*azerbaidzhanizatsiia*] among Muslim-Georgians; they hammer into their heads that they are 'Tatars' and not Georgians."[129]

The 1944 agreement formalized Georgian involvement in educational, cultural, and economic affairs in Qakh, Zaqatala, and Balakan, but reports from Georgian workers indicate that local officials were more likely to greet them with hostility rather than brotherly Soviet warmth. In December 1945, an artistic brigade from Georgia attempted to organize twelve free concerts in the region but only gave six concerts in Zaqatala, Qakh, and Balakan before local officials disrupted their shows, claiming they lacked authorization from Azerbaijan's Sovnarkom.[130] Grigorii Kutubidze, a teacher from Georgia who taught in Qakh and edited a Georgian-language newspaper there from 1944 to 1946, similarly complained to Charkviani about local authorities obstructing his work. Reiterating many of Gamkharashvili and Isashvili's points about discrimination against Georgian-Ingilois, Kutubidze also criticized Lezgin and Mugal mistreatment of Georgian-Ingilois. If we take Kutubidze's report at face value, it would appear that Georgian-Ingilois (whom he alternately refers to as "Georgian-Muslims" and "Georgians") were under assault from all sides in this "ancient corner" of Georgia.[131]

Officials in Azerbaijan were similarly frustrated. In a draft Sovmin and party decree from August 1946 about work among Georgian-Ingilois, they complained about Georgian SSR interference in the three regions.[132] The section was ultimately crossed out, but they were less circumspect elsewhere. In multiple MVD and party reports, and in at least one Azerbaijan Communist Party bureau meeting, Baku officials denounced the negative influence that Georgians were having on the local "Ingilo" population, blaming these outsiders for fostering a rise in nationalism within the republic.[133] They also went on the attack, showing their Georgian colleagues that two could play at this game. In December 1947, Azerbaijan's Ministry of Enlightenment sent a group of inspectors, including Deputy Minister D. A. Aleskerov, to Georgia to investigate Georgia's many Azerbaijani-language schools. Returning with a report full of instructional and material shortcomings and insufficiencies, Azerbaijan's Ministry of Enlightenment crafted a decree outlining Azerbaijani assistance plans for Azerbaijani schools in Georgia and forwarded it to Georgia's Minister of Education.[134]

Why did Charkviani get involved in Saingilo and stoke tensions with his neighboring republic? His pitch for Georgian-Ingiloi rights and attempt to expand Georgia's footprint complemented other efforts he was making in Abkhazia and the Georgian-Turkish borderlands, but nationalizing elites were not the only political actors who recognized local political opportunities in Soviet territorial pretensions abroad. Public discussions of Southern Azerbaijan and ancient Armenian and Georgian lands in Turkey encouraged everyday people to take up these discourses and express their own nation-building desires to republic leaders like Bagirov, Arutiunov, and Charkviani. The inspiration could work both ways: Gamkharashvili was encouraged by Stalin and Charkviani's engagement with Saingilo, but Charkviani also drew inspiration from Gamkharashvili's activism, describing him as having "worked all his life to have his native region returned to Georgia" and crediting him with inspiring Stalin to order Charkviani and Bagirov to meet in Saingilo and devise a plan for its Georgian schools.[135]

Further, while Azerbaijani officials blamed Georgia for a perceived rise in nationalism among Georgian-Ingilois, myriad forces were in play. World War II was incredibly destructive for the Soviet Union, but it was also productive in that it created opportunities—good and bad—for republican elites across the Soviet Union to advance the nationalizing, consolidating, and modernizing trends already underway when the war started. In the South Caucasus, Stalin's geopolitical maneuvers in Iran and Turkey emboldened regional leaders on the national front and created opportunities for them to renew land claims, as seen in Bagirov's power play in Iran, Arutiunov's pretensions toward Nagorno-Karabakh, and Charkviani's push to annex Qakh, Balakan, and Zaqatala. Indeed, the entanglement of Azeris, Armenians, Kurds, Shahsevans, Georgians, Khemshins, Greeks, Meskhetian Turks, and others in the Kremlin's interventions in Iran and Turkey paint a picture of a regional world that transcended the political borders dividing the Soviet Caucasus from its international neighbors. It also documents a circularity of influence wherein developments in one place inevitably affected others and the fungibility of wartime borders legitimized not only claims against foreign countries but against Soviet brothers and sisters as well.

Moving into the post-Stalinist period, the range of possibilities continued to evolve. Extreme tools of nationality politics such as mass deportations lost favor as the liberalizing tendencies of de-Stalinization generated new political avenues and sociopolitical behaviors. Despite these changes, the formative wartime period continued to shape South Caucasus political elites and national activists as they worked toward consolidating their nations and republics. Tactics and discourses evolved and expanded, but experiences were not forgotten.

After Stalin: Reform and Revenge

When Stalin died on March 5, 1953, Soviet society plunged into an existential crisis. As Jan Plamper has noted, "With the passing of the leader, the force that held their lives together suddenly was no more . . . His cult and its alchemy of power had made him seem larger than life."[1] What was the Soviet Union without the leader who had just led the Soviet people to a glorious victory over fascism? News of his passing was met with shock. When Lamara Akhvlediani, a university student in Moscow, heard the news, she felt the bottom fall out: "We were very worried that he died. We thought the world was over, that definitely something terrible would happen, that all of us would be completely destroyed. We thought Stalin was the savior of our country and an extraordinary leader."[2] The fear and anxiety that many in the general public like Akhvlediani felt was shared at the top of the Communist Party and government, where political elites also experienced insecurity, suspicion, and doubt about how they would rule and what the future would hold. For three days, people streamed into the center of Moscow to view Stalin's embalmed corpse; so great were the crowds pressing toward the House of Unions' Hall of Columns that more than a hundred people died in the crush. Akhvlediani was among those trying to see the *vozhd'* one last time: she snuck into the front of the line by climbing over a truck parked outside the building. After a night of waiting, she entered the building to find a "grief-stricken" Moscow.[3]

Yet this reaction to Stalin's passing was not universal. For decades, his poli-cies of dekulakization, collectivization, terror, and national deportations had caused immense suffering. An uptick in arrests for "anti-Soviet agitation" after Stalin's death suggest that there were many who were celebrating—rather than mourning—a death they had long awaited.[4] He had also dominated and ter-rorized those closest to him; indeed, his colleagues were apparently so wor-ried about disturbing him if nothing was amiss, they left him alone and without treatment for hours after his cerebral hemorrhage.

Some of them also saw some promise in his passing, however. Beria's voice reportedly rang out with "a note of triumph" as he called for a car to rush him from Stalin's deathbed to the Kremlin, where new prospects awaited him and others able to step into the void.[5] People like Beria, who had governed alongside Stalin, were best positioned to take advantage of this new situation. In the last years of his life, as his health declined, Stalin had delegated more authority to bureaus in the Council of Ministers and groups of Politburo mem-bers, allowing the bureaucratic apparatus to evolve toward an oligarchy with elements of collective leadership.[6] It is perhaps not surprising, then, that a new government took shape even as he lay dying, with Georgii Maksimilianovich Malenkov, Molotov, and Beria, the heads of the Council of Ministers, Minis-try of Foreign Affairs, and Ministry of Internal Affairs (MVD), forming a rul-ing *troika* alongside Khrushchev, who soon after emerged at the head of the party.[7]

As much as Stalin's closest colleagues had been shaped by him and the sys-tem they helped to create, their first moves after his death indicate that they also recognized his mixed legacy and the uncertainty into which they had been launched. In a memoir written in 1971, Nikita Sergeevich Khrushchev ad-dressed this dynamic, testifying to the fragility of the regime in March 1953:

> What we inherited after Stalin's death was painful and difficult. Our country was in disarray. Its leadership, which had taken shape under Sta-lin, was not a good one, if I may put it that way. An ill-assorted group of people had been lumped together . . . Ten million people were in prison camps. The prisons were overflowing. There was even a special prison for party activists . . . In the international situation there was no light at the end of the tunnel; the Cold War was in full swing. The bur-den on the Soviet people from the priority given to war production was unbelievable.[8]

Substantive reform was needed and significant changes were introduced almost immediately, but it was Beria, Stalin's longtime secret police chief and super-visor of the Soviet atomic project, who initially pursued the most aggressive reforms and, it seemed, most obviously sought to be at the top of this ruling team. Amy Knight argues that Beria understood that there was "an urgent need to back away from rigid Stalinism," but he also likely recognized that if he wanted to unseat other presumed heirs like Malenkov, he needed to remake his own reputation.[9] Less than two weeks after Stalin's death, Beria initiated a major shakeup of the Gulag and justice system that reduced the MVD's power and scope. More knowledgeable than most in this domain, he broke the economic ties binding the penal system to labor extraction, transferred the Gulag from the MVD to the Ministry of Justice (special camps for political prisoners were excluded from this deal), reformed the penal code, ordered an end to torture, and initiated what came to be known as "Beria's amnesty," during which nearly 50 percent of the Gulag's criminal (not political) population was released.[10]

His reforms extended beyond his portfolio in the security and penal services. Elena Zubkova argues that 1953 marked the start of a Soviet New Deal, because the post-Stalin leadership in Moscow understood that national resentments and imbalances needed to be addressed to preserve the USSR.[11] To this end, Beria moved toward national liberalization by tying up both the anti-Semitic "Doctor's Plot," which seemed to presage a return to the purges and show trials of the 1930s, and the Mingrelian Affair of 1951–1952, which targeted Georgian Party members for allegedly conspiring to collaborate with Western powers. The latter, of course, also had some elements of revenge. The purge targeted Beria's home region in Georgia and many of the accused were his clients, including Charkviani and Aleksandr Mirtskhulava, one-time head of the Georgian Komsomol, second secretary of the Abkhaz Communist Party, and chairman of the Council of Ministers of Abkhazia. Personally invested in the Mingrelian case, Beria remade the Georgian government and party in his name and hunted down those who had collaborated with this purge of his network in 1952.[12]

Beria wanted to do more than reestablish his network in Georgia; his broader goal was to resurrect the prewar discourse of "Great Russian chauvinism" and strengthen the titular identities of the republics by promoting titular political cadres and the use of titular languages in state business.[13] Sheila Fitzpatrick argues that de-Russification was in fact a policy of the leadership team, not just of Beria, but the furious pace with which he sought to implement these reforms, particularly in the western border republics of Belarus, Ukraine, Lithuania, and Estonia, provoked "a reactive surge of nationalism." His "contemptuous," "bullying," and "arrogant" behavior also triggered animosities—and concern—among his Moscow colleagues.[14] During debates over the path forward with East Germany, for example, a collective agreement emerged that they would advise the East German leaders to ease their policy of forced socialist construction, but Beria wanted to push even further, dismissing the need to encourage socialism at all in East Germany and emphasizing instead the importance of working toward a united and democratic Germany.[15]

In the first 112 days after Stalin's death, Beria implemented sweeping reforms. The next day, June 26, 1953, he was arrested. His unique ties to the security services and aggressive efforts to reshape his image (and that of the Soviet Union) were threatening both to the stability of collective governance and to colleagues who were also eyeing the power vacuum caused by Stalin's death. Khrushchev, who, unlike Beria, seems to have cried real tears at Stalin's bedside, had recovered enough by now to secure support from key colleagues—including Malenkov, Molotov, Chairman of the Presidium of the Supreme Soviet Kliment Efremovich Voroshilov, and First Deputy Chairman of the Council of Ministers Lazar Moiseevich Kaganovich—for a risky military takedown of Beria and his associates in the security services. The charges were clarified a few months after his arrest—treason, terrorism, and counterrevolutionary activity in Azerbaijan during the Russian Civil War. The trial itself, held on December 23, 1953, focused on Beria's role in the terror of the late 1930s. Along with six of his closest associates, he was found guilty and summarily executed. His affiliation with the MVD made him an easy scapegoat for Stalinist excesses, allowing his colleagues to mask their own culpability while simultaneously stopping Beria's furious efforts to rewrite his legacy.[16]

Although Beria was arrested only months after Stalin's death, his reforms had long-lasting effects. After his execution, the Politburo extended most of his policies, including those concerning Soviet national relations. Most notably, in 1954 it introduced the gradual rehabilitation of some repressed peoples languishing in the special settlement regime in Central Asia and Siberia. But it quickly became apparent that reversing problematic national policies could engender new complications. For example, tens of thousands of accused nationalists and their families returned to the Baltic republics, Belarus, Moldova, and Ukraine after a series of Gulag amnesties enabled their release between the mid-1950s and early 1960s. Their return proved disruptive, enabling anti-Soviet agitation, creating conflicts over confiscated property, and "reopen[ing] the scars of the post–Second World War civil war" in Ukraine. The spillover effect of uprisings in Hungary and Poland in 1956 only exacerbated these tensions. Amir Weiner has argued that these amnesties reflected Moscow's sense of stability and self-confidence at the time, but the disorder these returns engendered alarmed and frustrated republic officials who often opposed the amnesties and pushed to limit where returnees could settle after their release.[17]

Similar troubles accompanied the return of exiled nationalities to the Caucasus. Settlers had occupied many of the deportees' homes in their absence, leading to overpopulation, housing and resource shortages, and local disturbances when deportees started to return home in large numbers (with and without authorization) in the mid-1950s. In Dagestan, local officials in the early 1960s were still struggling to provide needed resources (houses, schools, work sites, stores, hospitals, cafeterias, etc.) and manage intercommunal conflicts between settlers, the more than 5,000 Chechen families that had since returned to Dagestan, and the rest of the local population. As in the western borderlands of the Soviet Union, local officials sought to restrict where rehabilitated deportees settled once they returned to Dagestan, sometimes depriving them of the ability to actually return home.[18]

Beria's downfall also altered the political landscape in the South Caucasus, where so many state and party officials were tied to him. In the Armenian SSR, First Secretary Arutiunov tried to separate himself from Beria at a plenum of the Armenian Communist Party after Beria's execution.[19] Although he downplayed his connection to Beria in public as well as in a personal plea to Molotov—claiming he had met with Beria only three or four times after becoming first secretary sixteen years prior—Arutiunov was unable to shake accusations that he was close to this "enemy of the people"; that Beria nominated him for his appointment as first secretary; that he built a cult of Beria in Armenia; that he replicated Beria's style of rule, cultivating flattery and ignoring self-criticism; and that his knowledge of the Armenian language was insufficient (though Armenian by nationality, Arutiunov was from Georgia).[20] After being pulled from the first secretary post, he later resurfaced as head of an Armenian kolkhoz.

In Georgia, Beria had rewarded his close ally Mirtskhulava for his loyalty by first releasing him from prison (he was imprisoned in 1952 during Stalin's purge of Beria's network) and then, on April 14, 1953, elevating him to first secretary of the Georgian Communist Party. Who did he replace? Akaki Mgeladze, whom Stalin had promoted from first secretary of the Abkhazian Obkom (regional committee) to first secretary of the Georgian Communist Party a year earlier during the Mingrelian Affair that landed Mirtskhulava and others in prison. After Beria was arrested, however, Georgian political elites scrambled to disassociate themselves from him. On July 15, an article in the newspaper of the Georgian Communist Party, *Zaria Vostoka*, denounced Beria and his malignant effect on the Georgian SSR. It also singled out Charkviani and Mgeladze—Mirtskhulava's first secretary predecessors—as Beria's "protégés" (*stavlennik*) and enablers.

Upon reading this denunciation, Mgeladze panicked. Suspecting Mirtskh-ulava and chairman of the Georgian Council of Ministers Valerian Bakradze of planting the accusation to detract from their own culpability and to settle personal scores with him, Mgeladze immediately wrote to Khrushchev, down-playing the significance of his tenure as first secretary (basically describing it as a non-event) and pointing the finger instead at Bakradze, Mirtskhulava, and Charkviani. In closing, Mgeladze complained that the leadership of Georgia was interfering with his life, leaving him unable to work and reducing him to selling personal goods to get by. He would, he said, move anywhere for work—even to the Far North—if Khrushchev was willing to intervene on his be-half.[21] Like Arutiunov, Mgeladze landed in the farm system after his political downfall, taking over a Georgian farm.

In September 1953, Khrushchev replaced Mirtskhulava as first secretary of the Georgian Communist Party with his own client—Vasil Mzhvanadze, a Georgian who previously served under him in the Ukrainian Communist Party. Concurrent with his appointment, the party leadership in Moscow reversed many of the Georgification measures that Beria, Charkviani, Mirtskhulava, Mgeladze, and others had implemented in Abkhazia and South Ossetia, dis-placing Georgian influences with Russian ones. In October 1953, Russian lan-guage instruction was reintroduced to Abkhazian schools. Soon after, the Georgian script for both the Abkhaz and Ossetian languages was dropped in favor of Cyrillic, more than a decade after Cyrillic became the primary script for most languages in the region (Armenian and Georgian were notable ex-ceptions to this rule). Political changes accompanied these education and lan-guage policy reversals, fostering the gradual reemergence of titular influence in Abkhazia after more than a decade of elite purges, migratory practices, and assimilatory politics implemented to build Georgian hegemony and cement Tbilisi's control there.[22]

As a political outsider in Georgia, Mzhvanadze was the perfect choice for Khrushchev, who faced the near impossible task of finding an ethnic Georgian leader outside Beria's deep political networks. Yet, although Mzhvanadze en-joyed Khrushchev's support, he faced a complicated situation in Georgia, where the leadership had long enjoyed and benefited from their proximity to Georgia's native sons, Stalin and Beria, but more recently suffered through years of elite purges. Indeed, Charkviani and Mirtskhulava got off easy in com-parison with what happened to others tied to Beria in Georgia. Some of Be-ria's closest associates in the Georgian security services were accused of treason, terror, and conspiracy for aiding him and prosecuted in a public trial held in Tbilisi in September 1955. Six of the eight men put on trial were condemned to death and executed, including Avksentii Narikievich Rapava, who had last served as the Georgian Minister of State Control, and Nikolai Maksimovich Rukhadze, the one-time Minister for State Security in the republic.

The political fallout from Stalin's death also manifested in the public sphere. On the last day of the Twentieth Party Congress—February 25, 1956—Khrushchev took the podium at a closed meeting of elite party delegates. Over the next several hours, he denounced Stalin and the excesses of his regime in his report titled "On the Cult of Personality and its Consequences." Only top party elites were initially privy to the full content of his speech, but this changed in early March when an abridged version of his report was distributed and discussed in workplace, party, and trade union meetings. Word spread quickly about its contents, provoking reactive anger and humiliation in Georgia, where criticisms of Stalin and his cult of personality were interpreted as a condemnation not only of a still-beloved *vozhd'* but, more broadly, of a Georgian nation that claimed him as their own. Indeed, in his speech, Khrushchev openly mocked the relationship between Stalin and the Georgian people while criticizing the Mingrelian Affair: "There was no nationalistic [Mingrelian] organization in Georgia. Thousands of innocent people fell victim to willfulness and lawlessness. All of this happened under the 'genius' leadership of Stalin, 'the great son of the Georgian nation,' as Georgians like to refer to him."[23]

Rumors about Khrushchev's report overlapped in Georgia with the annual commemoration of Stalin's death on March 5. This had become an unofficial tradition over the last couple of years, but in 1956 the spontaneous memorial gatherings that started at a monument to Stalin escalated into widespread demonstrations. These protests climaxed four days later on March 9, when soldiers shot at demonstrators trying to forcibly enter the Ministry of Communications in Tbilisi after false reports about arrests there. After several more hours of clashes, the military and police finally broke up the demonstrations in the middle of the night. Levan Avalishvili has shown that these protests initially began as a defense of Stalin but evolved into an "anti-government movement with strong nationalist undertones."[24] According to state records, twenty-one people were killed (some by bayonets and gunfire) and fifty-five were injured during these demonstrations in March 1956, but it is likely that many others avoided necessary medical care out of fear of persecution. While the police and military ultimately were able to end these public demonstrations, their decision to open fire on the protestors and then suppress information about casualties was a fateful one that led to exaggerated rumors

FIGURE 9.   Mir Jafar Bagirov (center) and Lavrentiy Beria (right) in 1935. Source: Wikimedia Commons.

about the events. Ultimately, the conflict that Khrushchev sparked in Georgia aggravated nationalist and anti-Russian sentiments and generated a new national-independence movement there.[25]

The leaderships of Georgia and Armenia faced party expulsion, demotions, and executions for their connections to Beria, and the consequences of his arrest were equally severe in Azerbaijan, not least because of Beria and Bagirov's close relationship. On the day of Stalin's death, Beria helped his confidant, Bagirov, become a candidate member of the Politburo in Moscow. The next month, Bagirov stepped down as first secretary of Azerbaijan's Communist Party, a position he had held with an iron grip for twenty years and briefly became head of the Council of Ministers of Azerbaijan. His willingness to forfeit the first secretary role signaled Bagirov's trust that he could maintain control in Azerbaijan without this title, and the shifting role of the party in these first months after Stalin's passing.

When Beria fell, however, Bagirov went down too: first expelled from the party, then arrested in March 1954 and accused of supporting anti-Soviet elements. As he had done with Beria, Khrushchev methodically dismantled Bagirov's extensive political network. Bagirov's close colleagues—Mir Teymur Mir

Teymur Yaqubov and Teymur Quliyev—had been leading the party and Council of Ministers in Azerbaijan, but in spring 1954 Khrushchev established a new leadership team in the republic, appointing İmam Dashdamir oglu Mustafayev (İmam Daşdəmir oğlu Mustafayev) first secretary of the Azerbaijan Communist Party, Sadıq Hajıyarali oglu Ragimov (Sadıq Hacıyarəli oğlu Rəhimov) head of the Azerbaijan Council of Ministers, and Mirza Ibragimov chairman of the republic's Supreme Soviet. It was a difficult transition, however. Mustafayev soon found himself in conflict with the republic's KGB leadership, prompting a party investigation of Mustafayev and the party bureau in 1955. Mustafayev retained his position, but the Central Committee of the CPSU censured the Communist Party of Azerbaijan that fall and appointed a new second secretary from Moscow to keep an eye on the party leadership in Baku.[26]

When Bagirov finally came to trial in 1956, not long after Khrushchev's Secret Speech, he was prosecuted alongside five of his colleagues—Agasalim Ibragim oglu Atakishiyev, Timofei Mikhailovich Borshchev, Stepan Fedorovich Emel'ianov, Khoren Ivanovich Grigoryan, and Ruben Ambartsumovich Markaryan. Atakishiev and Emel'ianov had been part of Bagirov's inner circle during the Soviet occupation of northern Iran. In what became known as the Bagirov affair (delo Bagirova), Bagirov and his coconspirators were accused of having terrorized Azerbaijan in the late 1930s. Theirs was the third trial in what Samuel Casper has termed a "slow-moving purge" of Beria's networks in Moscow and his home region of the South Caucasus.[27] In Baku, all six defendants were found guilty: four were executed, including Bagirov, and two were sentenced to twenty-five years of forced labor, five years of lost rights, and property confiscation.

Key differences between the Beria trial in 1953 and the Caucasus trials of 1955 and 1956 illustrate variance in this transitional period. Like their peers in Tbilisi, Bagirov and his codefendants were tried publicly in an open courtroom and granted access to defense lawyers. Hundreds of people, carefully cultivated for this signal event, witnessed the proceedings. And Bagirov and his cohort were not summarily executed; rather, they and their families went through a formal appeal process. Bagirov denied the counterrevolutionary intent of his actions, defended his loyalty to the Communist Party and Soviet people, and sought to separate himself from Beria and his crimes, but he did not appeal his sentence, writing, "I would have to be incredibly low and vile to ask to save my life. Even a part of my crimes is enough to subject me to the highest degree of punishment."[28] He was only fifty-nine at his death, but his shaky signature on the appeal petition looked like that of someone far beyond his years.[29]

His codefendants did contest their sentences, however, and, along with their wives and children, scapegoated Bagirov in their petitions, arguing they would have been in danger had they resisted his orders. Borshchev, for example, had enjoyed a long career in the security services of Azerbaijan, Turkmenistan, and Russia. Along with his codefendants, he was accused of falsifying criminal cases, carrying out illegal methods of investigation, and directing the mass arrest of prominent Bolsheviks for Bagirov's personal gain, including former chairman of the TSFSR Sovnarkom Gazanfar Mahmud oglu Musabekov (Qəzənfər Mahmud oğlu Musabəyov), former chairman of the Azerbaijan Sovnarkom Dadash Khoja oglu Bünyadzada (Dadaş Xoca oğlu Bünyadzadə), and hundreds of other innocent citizens—many of whom were shot.[30] In the course of the investigation and trial, he admitted to participation in these activities and detailed some of the ways he abused people who were repressed

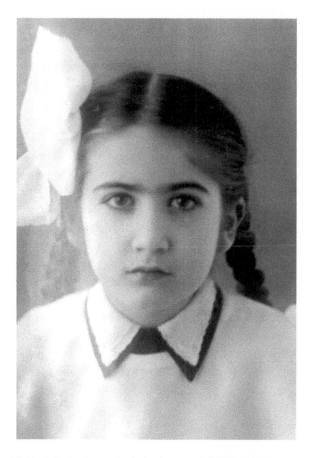

FIGURE 10.   Alla Borshchev's picture attached to her appeal. GARF R-7523.89a.8444.59.

during the terror.[31] In his appeal petition, however, he blamed Bagirov and others for his crimes, claiming that he was so fearful of Bagirov he secured a transfer to the NKVD of Turkmenistan in 1938.[32]

In a heart-wrenchingly innocent letter sent to Khrushchev, Borshchev's young daughter, Alla, also begged for his life, writing that she loved her father and was afraid to live without him. In careful, childish cursive writing she elaborated, "I am in the fifth grade in the music school and we begin our exams soon. All of the girls are preparing for exams and for the summer holiday, but I think about my father all the time. I beg you, please save my father's life." She signed off "with pioneer greetings."[33] Alla's school photo was attached to her letter, perhaps by an adult who recognized that her mournful gaze might do the work of a dozen written appeals. The defendants—intimately familiar with the darker impulses of the system—surely knew, however, that the appeal procedure was unlikely to go their way. And what happened to Alla's father, Timofei Borshchev? He was executed alongside his onetime boss for treason and terrorizing "honest Soviet people."

Jörg Baberowski has argued that Azerbaijan occupied a special place in the Stalinist system because Stalin and Beria leveraged their close relationship with Bagirov to use his republic as a testing ground for Bolshevik policies.[34] Historians of other republics in the Soviet Union could arguably make the same type of argument about the places that they study, identifying specificities that made each republic a testing ground for some policy or practice. Yet, in these early post-Stalin years, Bagirov's connections to Beria and Stalin meant that Azerbaijan did stand out in the post-Stalinist order: it was the only republic that witnessed the performative purge and execution of someone with Bagirov's profile—long-time first secretary of a SSR and recent candidate member of the Politburo—making it a laboratory in which Stalin's successors tested the political limits of their transition.

State surveillance reports (*svodki*) have been analyzed as a problematic type of evidence, but they are a valuable source of information about the state, its concerns, and the shaping of policy.[35] Reports from this period in Azerbaijan demonstrate the difficult and unpredictable nature of de-Stalinization there. They detail widespread sympathy for both Beria and Bagirov, coupled with public skepticism about the official reasons they were repressed. The security agents who produced these reports focused in particular on people who were interpreting the change of power through a national or anti-Russian lens. For example, a mechanic from Qazakh was reportedly convinced that Beria was arrested because he was Georgian and the Russians in the Politburo wanted to seize control. Similarly, a store manager in Khudat allegedly speculated that the Russians who came to power had destroyed Bagirov because he was a Muslim who had worked closely with Beria. Finally, an Armenian from Nagorno-Karabakh purportedly praised Bagirov's arrest, believing that it was punishment for removing influential Armenians from their jobs and closing the Armenian Drama Theater in Baku.[36]

Khrushchev's not-so-secret speech has been enshrined in popular memory and historiography as the first major step toward de-Stalinization and the Thaw, but this process started years earlier, perhaps with Beria's first reforms and certainly by the time of his arrest a few months later. Yet Khrushchev's denunciation of Stalin and the violent excesses of the previous decades is still a watershed moment. Like Beria, Khrushchev used reform and the politics of de-Stalinization to separate himself from his rivals, emboldening political processes already underway and launching them into the public sphere. As he quickly discovered, however, he could neither predict nor control the ways political elites and others took up the mantle of reform, pushing him to define the boundaries of post-Stalinist reforms. This is the story to which our attention now turns.

CHAPTER 3

Defining the Azerbaijan Soviet Socialist Republic

A duality was embedded in wartime nationality practices. The simultaneous promotion of Soviet and republican identities to rally support for wartime imperatives largely served this purpose but also generated a range of unintended side effects. In many republics, wartime experiences empowered local leaders and emboldened national particularism. Beria's reforms in 1953 and the loosening of the special settlement regime in 1954 indicated Moscow's awareness of this widening contradiction, and early moves by some national-minded elites reinforced this evolving environment. It was only after Khrushchev's Secret Speech in 1956, however, that a cluster of elite-driven nationalizing politics and popular nationalisms entered the public sphere, blurring the line between acceptably communist national behaviors and inappropriately nationalist ideas and identifications.

Azerbaijan was one of the republics where the republican leadership tested—and found—the limits of Moscow's willingness to let republics chart their own path. At the close of the decade, the top leadership in the republic was ousted amid allegations of nationalist deviations. Mirza Ibragimov, head of the presidium of the Azerbaijan Supreme Soviet, was the first to fall in 1958, followed not long after by the head of Azerbaijan's Council of Ministers, Sadıq Ragimov. While Ibragimov and Ragimov's dismissals were handled fairly quietly so it looked like they were voluntarily transitioning out of their high-level offices, the party's censure of first secretary of the Azerbaijan

Communist Party İmam Mustafayev was a public affair in the summer of 1959.[1]

The stage was set in a closed-door meeting of the CPSU Central Committee in Moscow, where Khrushchev attacked Mustafayev with language reminiscent of earlier hunts for spies, saboteurs, and national deviationists in the party ranks. Accusing Mustafayev of harboring and empowering Ibragimov, Khrushchev declared, "This [Ibragimov] is not a Leninist, not a Communist, this is a nationalist, an enemy who scaled the leadership . . . You [Mustafayev] are a questionable person yourself, you have a party card, but you are not a Communist."[2] Not long after this meeting, Nuritdin Mukhitdinov, a member of the Presidium of the Central Committee of the CPSU, and Iosif Shikin, the first deputy chairman of the CPSU Department of Party Organs, flew to Baku to meet with the Azerbaijan Communist Party Central Committee Bureau, investigated its mistakes, and discussed how to frame these inadequacies in writing. Despite serious concerns about Ibragimov and Ragimov's nationalist missteps, as well as fears that mishandling them might provoke other nationalists, the focus remained on Mustafayev and the Bureau's shortcomings.[3] Five days later, on July 11, 1959, a front-page article in the Russophone newspaper of the Azerbaijan Communist Party—*Bakinskii rabochii* (Baku Worker)—declared that the Bureau was guilty of serious economic, political, and ideological failings, including localism, and that Mustafayev, a poor leader, had been sacked as first secretary and removed from the Bureau.[4] Six months later, Ibragimov had his own public moment: in the December 11, 1956 edition of *Bakinskii rabochii*, he confessed to "several mistakes in the language field." Yet, he never faced the same level of public censure as Mustafayev.[5]

These dismissals highlighted the fact that double assimilation, a guiding principle of Soviet nationality theorizing and policymaking, aimed to ameliorate the national question but could also generate national tensions. Double assimilation refers to efforts the state made to mold the Soviet population into coherent, republic-based nationalities that would then merge into a Soviet nation bound by the "international" Russian language.[6] The *korenizatsiia* practices that were a key part of this process privileged titular populations within the boundaries of "their" republics, yet members of those national communities—including Ibragimov, Ragimov, and Mustafayev—often felt that this first step had not gone far enough, preserving the hegemony and prestige of the Kremlin leadership and the Russian nation in non-Russian republics like Azerbaijan. They also chafed at the second part of this assimilatory process, the one that aimed to merge these socialist nations into a supranational (but in many ways Russian-defined) Soviet nation, because they recognized ways in which it compromised non-Russian national identifications, cultures, and sovereignties. Clashes between the Kremlin and republic leaderships in Azerbaijan, Latvia, and elsewhere became a critical part of negotiating these policies; between 1959 and 1961, Moscow accused the leaderships of Azerbaijan, Kyrgyzstan, Latvia, Moldova, Tajikistan, Turkmenistan, and Uzbekistan of nationalist behaviors.[7]

This purge of Azerbaijan's leadership—the second in less than five years—has long been contextualized as fallout from a struggle between the center (Moscow) and the periphery (the non-Russian republics). In 1962, for example, Yaroslav Bilinsky invoked the example of Azerbaijan and other republics to argue that de-Stalinization enabled the rejection of Soviet nationhood (i.e., Russification) in favor of national loyalties.[8] More recently, Jeremy Smith declared that Azerbaijan was the most "flagrant" example of republican elite nationalism at a time when nationalism was on the rise in the Soviet Union and Eastern Bloc.[9] In making this argument, Smith underscored a structural contradiction in the Soviet system: republican elites simultaneously represented Moscow and led titular national communities in the republics, but the interests of these two parties sometimes diverged.[10]

Some historians from Azerbaijan likewise have employed a center-periphery framework to explain the politically tumultuous Azerbaijan of the 1950s. Viewing Moscow as a colonial power—and Bagirov as Moscow's agent in Baku—they take seriously the accomplishments of this brief leadership cohort and portray Ibragimov, Ragimov, and Mustafayev as heroes who stood up to Moscow and Russian hegemony in defense of an oppressed Azeri nation. Ismailov describes the post-Stalin 1950s as a sea change for Azeris.[11] Jamil Hasanli, meanwhile, has invoked the language of national liberation to argue that in this period the Azeri nation, "long under the pressure of national discrimination, felt itself master of its own house."[12]

Although it certainly was expedient for republic politicians to distance themselves from Bagirov after his arrest (and contemporary Azerbaijani historians have continued to divorce the condemned Bagirov from his more popular successors), it is a mistake to draw a hard line between the nationalizing politics of the Bagirov and post-Bagirov eras. The post-Stalin leader of the republic in the 1950s did not necessarily share the language and tactics of their predecessors, but the policies and practices they pursued were not entirely new. In some ways, they represented a continuation of earlier efforts to build the titular nation of the republic and align it with the territory of the Azerbaijan SSR. In other ways, they developed new strategies for building and defining that nation and place. One key difference, of course, was the independence that this leadership cohort occasionally asserted from Moscow when crafting its vision of Soviet Azerbaijan.

Finally, while center-periphery conflicts produced important political flash-points in the 1950s, disputes among top-level actors only tell part of the story of how Azerbaijan "became Azerbaijani" over the midcentury decades of the twentieth century. The post-Stalin republican leadership clashed with Moscow over policies that challenged the authority of the Russian language in Azerbaijan, but this was only one part of a broader effort to consolidate the national identity of the republic by defining the contours of the Azerbaijani nation and assimilating others into it. Nontitular minorities played a key role in this process because they were considered potential rivals for dominance in the republic, and additionally were more assimilable than Russians, who occupied a unique position of privilege in the Soviet Union.

Prioritizing titular hegemony in their territorial domain, governing elites in Azerbaijan worked toward the discursive, linguistic, and demographic assimilation of the republic's nontitular minorities as a way of building the titular nation in the Azerbaijan Soviet Socialist Republic. Lest one go too far with the center-periphery conflict model, it is important to recognize that long-running central policies that supported titular nation-building and minority assimilation in the republics complemented these efforts. Azerbaijan's post-Stalin leadership in the 1950s thus worked within the system of which it was a part, both embracing opportunities to advance the Azeri nationality at the expense of nontitular minorities and resisting impulses from higher up that promoted Russian influences at the expense of the Azerbaijani language and culture.

Ethnogenesis and the Discursive Remaking of the Nation and the Republic

The Soviet Union had fifteen constituent Soviet Socialist Republics, each named after a titular nationality that was considered the "main" nationality of its eponymous territory. As the use of their names for the whole republic suggests, these nationalities were the primary focus of *korenizatsiia* policies that promoted, to some extent, the indigenization of Soviet republics through the linguistic, cultural, and political development of these major constituent nationalities. These policies were first developed in the early years of Bolshevik power to counter the imperial legacy of the Russian Empire, but they eventually became a defining feature of the new Soviet system.

Titular nationalities derived their authority at least partially from claims to indigeneity, heightening their need to prove that they were the true inheritors of "their" republics. In the Soviet Union, the study of ethnogenesis played an essential role in this process by providing "evidence" that anchored titular peoples in the ancient history of their republics. These historical narratives also legitimized the ethnoterritorial structure of the Soviet Union by undercutting competing claims to primacy in those spaces.[13] In this way, the field of ethnogenesis helped to naturalize the institutionalized power of titular nations over nontitular peoples in the USSR.

Ethnogenesis emerged as a major field of study in the USSR around the same time that Stalin's constitution divided the Transcaucasian Soviet Federated Socialist Republic into the Armenian, Georgian, and Azerbaijani Soviet Socialist Republics. The SSRs needed corresponding titular nationalities, but up until this point Azeris were more often designated as Türk (Tiurk) in official Soviet records such as state censuses and passports. Various competing ethnonyms were employed in the public sphere.[14] In the early years of the Soviet Union, Russians and state officials tended to call them Tiurks but also used other terms, including Muslim, Azerbaijani Tatar, Caucasian Tatar, and Azerbaijani Tiurk. Some of these terms were indiscriminately used to refer to a range of Muslim peoples in the former Russian Empire. Azeris, meanwhile, often identified themselves by their place of origin or as Muslims or Türks. In state terms, this confusion was cleared up in 1936. Those who had once been Tiurks were now officially Azerbaijanis, and the Tiurk language became the Azerbaijani language in official parlance, giving the Azerbaijan SSR, at least nominally, its titular nationality.[15] Similar processes of standardization were underway elsewhere in the Soviet Union.

Although the state attempted in this way to recognize and establish a titular nationality in the Azerbaijan SSR, more was required to "root" the Azeri nation in its Soviet homeland. Azeris were commonly branded as outsiders in a region where other titular nationalities—including Georgians and Armenians—traded on their widely accepted status as inheritors of the ancient heritage of the Caucasus. Azeris, in contrast—like many other Turkic peoples of the Soviet Union—were frequently categorized as descendants of "late" Turkic mass migrations in the eleventh through thirteenth centuries. For example, in his 1924 ethnography of Caucasus peoples, Grigorii Filippovich Chursin explained that,

> Azerbaijani Tiurks are the descendants of Turkish tribes that at different times penetrated the Caucasus and settled there: a large part of them settled in Transcaucasia in the 13th century, after the great Mongol-

Turkish invasion. In 1258, Hulagu-Khan sent to Transcaucasia more than 150,000 families of Turkish *narodnosti* from Asia. The name "Azerbaijani Tiurks" refers to the fact that most of the Tiurks in Transcaucasia passed through the neighboring Persian province of Azerbaijan, where they even now comprise the bulk of the population.[16]

Characterizations like this conflated Azeris with "outsider" Turkic peoples or constructed them as derivative of other nations rather than portraying them as an independent people with an ancient local history that could justify their claim to primacy in Soviet Azerbaijan.

Ethnogenesis theories developed across the Soviet Union both in defense of titular dominance in Soviet republics and in reaction to deteriorating international politics.[17] As relations with Iran and Turkey became more fraught, Moscow increasingly worried about the loyalty of borderland nationalities. In the Caucasus, some peoples—Greeks, Meskhetian Turks, and others—were en masse deported from their homes near the Turkish and Iranian borders to Central Asia and Siberia. With others, like Azeris, state officials took a different approach: pursuing targeted deportations but also redefining those nationalities in an effort to transform them from points of vulnerability to bulwarks of security.

As first secretary of the Azerbaijan Communist Party in the 1930s, Bagirov played an integral role in transforming the history of the Azeri people to delimit them from their Turkic and Iranian pasts. Early in this process, Bagirov oversaw the purge of established and influential historians in Azerbaijan who promoted a Turkic ethnolinguistic explanation of Azeri identity, history, and origins. The elimination of these history producers made it easier to create and promote revisionist narratives that helped the Soviet Azerbaijani nation conform to the evolving domestic and geopolitical environment. At the close of the 1930s, Bagirov directed historians to write a narrative of Azerbaijani history that, as Victor Shnirelman has put it, "would represent the Azeri people as the true indigenous population and break them off from any Turkic roots."[18] Published as a student textbook in 1939, a 1941 revision produced a significantly more developed explanation of Azeris' ancient roots. This book, *Istoriia Azerbaidzhana (kratkii ocherk)*, emphasized the autochthonous origins of Azeris in the AzSSR, distanced them from Turkic migration narratives like the one Chursin and others promoted, complicated their historical relationship to Islamic and Persian history, and established ancient Azeri traditions of statehood and literary heritage.[19]

Inspired by the Soviet occupation of northern Iran a few years later, historians writing in the mid-1940s and later supported Baku's irredentist desires by emphasizing the "early and continuous unity" of northern (Soviet) and southern (Iranian) Azeris and portraying them as ancient people of Atropatene in northern Iran.[20] Early texts that replicated this theme emphasized transspatial Azeri unity, but still downplayed modern relations with Iran and Turkey by highlighting the ways in which Russian exposure and the Soviet system elevated Soviet Azeris over their foreign neighbors who had been "the cruelest assimilators." As Adil' Nadzhafov wrote in his 1955 book, *The Formation and Development of the Azerbaijani Socialist Nation*, "Turkish and Iranian oppressors sought to assimilate the Azerbaijani *narod*, to destroy its rich and distinct culture," but the unification of Azerbaijan and Russia freed Azeris from their historical tormentors and enabled their economic, political, and cultural advancement beyond that offered by those states to their own citizens.[21]

In the midcentury decades, republican officials and scholars developed evidence of Azeri indigeneity in conversation with one another. Throughout this process, party and state officials helped to define the boundaries of acceptable scholarly discourse. Specialists at the Institute of History of the Academy of Sciences in Baku produced another significant publication, the first volume of the *History of Azerbaijan*, with Mustafayev's stewardship in 1958.[22] In this iteration of Azerbaijan's past, the territory of Soviet Azerbaijan was lauded as one of the world's earliest civilizational centers, with a lineage of political traditions traceable through Media Atropatene and Caucasian Albania, ancient states in the territory that Soviet Azeris called their own. The population of Media Atropatene, an ancient kingdom located in the Azerbaijani region of Iran and a small piece of Soviet Azerbaijan, was portrayed as the foundation of the future Azeri people. Regarding Caucasian Albania—an ancient federation of more than two dozen tribes that stretched across much of northern and central Soviet Azerbaijan, as well as parts of Dagestan, Georgia, and Armenia—the book enhanced Khazar, or Turkic, tribal elements in the federation while downplaying Armenian ties to it. This contradicted Armenian scholars who claimed Caucasian Albania as part of their historical heritage, a clear threat to Azerbaijan's territorial sovereignty.[23] By connecting Azeris to these ancient states, neither of which were clearly defined by Turkic-speaking peoples, this version of Azerbaijan's history transgressed Soviet national-theoretical norms by privileging primordial territorial bonds over linguistic affiliations.[24]

The 1958 history of Azerbaijan is also noteworthy because, to a certain extent, it rehabilitated Azeris' Turkic heritage. The Turkic Seljuqs were still portrayed as a disruptive force in terms of Azeri statehood, but they were also partially redeemed for linguistically consolidating the northern and southern Azeri people and thus precipitating their national formation. This ambivalence marked a significant change from earlier revisionist histories that offered no redemption for the Turkic elements of Azeri history. The genesis of Soviet Azerbaijan's titular nation now included a combination of Media Atropatene (Iranian), Albanian (Caucasian), and Turkic (Oghuz) heritage, coopting all of the major elements of Soviet Azerbaijan's ethnohistory and firmly anchoring Azeris in their eponymous Soviet territory. This new history of Azerbaijan shaped standard narratives in textbooks, encyclopedias, and popular histories from this point forward, facilitating the transmission of these ideas to the masses.[25] A few years later, in the early 1960s, some historians, including Ziya Bünyadov and Makhmud Ismailov, pushed the limits of the permissible even further by challenging the "voluntary" nature of Azerbaijan's initial union with Russia amid celebrations to commemorate the 150th anniversary of Azerbaijan's unification with Russia. The party subsequently censured them for this transgressive line of historical inquiry.[26]

Aliagha Mammadli has argued that challenges to prevailing ideological frameworks at this time demonstrate the extent to which Soviet republics were breaking free of central control, and that attempts "to make the histories of the titular ethnic groups more ancient and heroic . . . were a kind of latent protest against Communist ideology," but the intensifying Cold War and shifting geopolitical relationships were in fact also altering the landscape of ethnogenesis studies.[27] Throughout the Soviet Union, a spate of new academic institutions were established in the 1950s to generate knowledge that would help the state respond to external threats and court new friends in the decolonizing world. In Azerbaijan, a Department of the History of Foreign Eastern Countries was established within the Institute of History in Baku in 1954. Four years later, a separate Institute of Oriental Studies was created. The revitalization of Persian, Arabic, and Turkish studies in the republic advanced the examination of Azerbaijan's past and matured the field of ethnogenesis. Local scholars were also supported by a contemporaneous call from the Azerbaijan Communist Party to restore sites of "Azerbaijani ancient heritage," deepening material evidence of Azeri roots in the Caucasus.[28] It is unsurprising that some of Azerbaijan's preeminent scholars of ethnogenesis like Ziya Bünyadov emerged in this period.

Scholars of the subaltern have documented how native peoples seeking to define themselves in a system of external or foreign domination have used ethnogenesis as a positive tool of resistance. Ethnogenesis certainly played this role in Azerbaijan, where many view their Soviet past through a lens of foreign control and colonial domination. Russians play a central role in these narratives of Azeri subjugation, but many Azeris also view Armenians and other nationalities in the Caucasus as competitors angling for control over the territory and people of Azerbaijan. The idea that Azeris are latecomers to or interlopers in the Caucasus region has proved remarkably resilient, causing many Azeris to worry that they are susceptible to the loss of their territory and sovereignty because their nationality and national history are not respected or valued by Armenians, Georgians, and others whose rival claims to indigeneity have more often been taken for granted in a region where indigeneity continues to legitimate and validate power.[29]

In fact, minorities who complained about Azeri chauvinism in Soviet Azerbaijan sometimes did couch their complaints in accusations of Azeri "foreignness" (in contrast with their own indigeneity, of course) and interpreted Azeri ethnogenesis as a form of historical-cultural appropriation. Take Gamkharashvili, for example. In one of the letters he sent to Charkviani, Gamkharashvili undercut Azeri claims to indigeneity to support his argument that the Azerbaijan SSR regions of Qakh, Balakan, and Zaqatala should be reassigned to the Georgian Soviet Socialist Republic. He complained that Lezgins, Georgians, and Mugals made up 95 percent of the population in these areas but were officially underrepresented because Azerbaijan SSR officials recorded "Georgian Muslims" and other minorities as Tiurks in the census. He further emphasized that "Azerbaijani Tiurks" were not indigenous to this region and—linking them to foreign enemy others—argued that for these reasons their claim to power was illegitimate: "This is not Soviet politics, this is old Iranian-Turkish politics to Tiurkify the Georgian population . . . Azerbaijanis do not have any rights to this territory and this population. There is no Azerbaijani Tiurk population there, except for abominable functionaries (*chinovniks*) sent from other regions of Azerbaijan."[30]

Ethnogenesis has played a vital role in attempts to strengthen Azerbaijan's titular nation and defend it from attacks like Gamkharashvili's, but, as Barbara Voss has noted, neoteric social identities rooted in ethnogenesis can also be "deployed in the exertion of power over others." That is, marginalized peoples can reproduce systems of dominance and oppression while attempting to improve their own situation.[31] This happened throughout the Soviet Union, particularly in places where multiple national populations competed for territorial control and authority. In Central Asia, for example, titular authorities and scholars often undercut one another as they battled for recognition of their autochthony and control over the ancient heritage of "their" republics. During a heated dispute in the early 1970s, a well-known Tajik ethnogenesis scholar, Bobodzhan Gafurov, sparked Uzbek outrage by incorporating historical figures claimed by the Uzbeks—including al-Khorezmi, al-Farabi, and al-Biruni—into Tajik history and declaring that Tajiks' regional lineage was more ancient than that of their Uzbek "migrant" neighbors. Gafurov's work was particularly provocative given long-standing Tajik claims to Uzbek territories and accusations that Uzbeks discriminated against Tajiks in the Uzbek SSR.[32]

In Soviet Azerbaijan, some republic officials felt subjugated by the Russian-dominated Soviet state but replicated these unequal power dynamics when dealing with minorities under their control. They wanted the official narrative of Azeri ethnogenesis to be respected and upheld, but in turn sometimes discounted the ways in which other peoples of Azerbaijan understood themselves and their histories. In the 1950s, local officials and scientists increasingly invoked the purportedly ancient, local origins of the Azeri nation to naturalize assimilatory practices in nontitular communities and subsume restless minorities into the history of the titular nation. In an ethnohistorical report produced for the Azerbaijan Communist Party in its battle with Georgian-Ingiloi national rights activists, the author wrote the titular nation into the history of nontitular minorities, emphasizing that Talyshes, Tats, Kurds, Lezgins, Avars, Ingilois, and other peoples of Azerbaijan descended from the same ancient population as Azeris. Writing about Lezgins, for example, the author noted that they were "known by this name in the territory of Azerbaijan, together with ancient Azerbaijanis, around 2,000 years ago."[33]

Although the report was about the ethnohistory of various minorities, the author took care to insert the titular nation into each minority story. By ensuring that Azeris played a role in the ancient history of Soviet Azerbaijan's various minority communities, he provided evidence for a broader argument that Bagirov articulated decades earlier: the titular nation of the republic included most of the republic's minorities as well. In other words, the formation of the Azeri-defined Soviet Azerbaijani people was a natural, centuries-long process rather than the result of forced assimilation, as some minorities claimed.[34]

Revisionist histories of nontitular populations also undercut any claims those populations or their co-ethnics might have to Azerbaijani territory. In the above report submitted to the Azerbaijan Communist Party, for example, the author explained that Ingilois descended from ancient Albanian tribes that were later "Georgianized." That is, Ingilois were not originally Georgian but had been alienated from their Albanian roots by Georgians who assimilated them (conveniently casting Georgians as aggressive assimilators at a time when some Ingilois were accusing Azeris of the same). It also specified that, although the Ingiloi language is part of the Southern-Kartvelian (Georgian) branch of the Caucasus language group—and thus deemed by linguists to be a Georgian language—it is distinct from Georgian. This narrative discounted the authenticity of Georgian-Ingiloi claims to Georgian heritage and, by emphasizing a shared Albanian heritage, again attempted to draw Georgian-Ingilois closer to Azeris.[35]

Regarding Azerbaijan's Armenian population, in the Soviet Azerbaijan Encyclopedia that Mustafayev shepherded through Azerbaijan Communist Party Central Committee approval in 1958, the entry for "Albania" declared that the Armenians of the Nagorno-Karabakh region in Azerbaijan were actually Armenianized Albanians. As such, these so-called Armenians had a stronger ancient connection to Azeris than to the Armenian nation that claimed them and agitated on their behalf.[36] Ziya Bünyadov further developed this argument in 1965 with his monograph *Azerbaijan in the Seventh–Ninth Centuries*, where he erased Armenians from the history of ancient Azerbaijan and replaced them with the Caucasian Albanians, the claimed ancestors of Soviet Azerbaijan's titular nation.[37]

The desire to undercut Armenian ethnohistorical ties to Azerbaijan correlated with the perception that Armenians substantially threatened Azerbaijani nationhood and territorial integrity. One part of this was the recent history of ethnic violence between Armenians and Azeris in the Caucasus. The Armeno-Tatar War in 1905–1906 resulted in as many as 10,000 deaths.[38] Later, during the independence period following the Russian Revolution, another wave of interethnic violence (exacerbated by Turkish, British, and Russian military interventions) claimed the lives of thousands more and was not limited to only Armenians and Azeris; Kurds also participated in some attacks on Armenian communities resisting incorporation into independent Azerbaijan.[39] Disputed territories like Zangezur, Nakhchıvan, and Karabakh were at the center of these conflicts, but the violence extended throughout the territories of contemporary Azerbaijan and Armenia.

The Red Army takeover of the Azerbaijan Democratic Republic and its Armenian counterpart, the Democratic Republic of Armenia, in 1920 did not quell these territorial disagreements. It took some time for the Bolsheviks to establish meaningful authority in the region and violence continued throughout this rebellious period. The status of Nagorno-Karabakh was a central point of contestation for both national and economic reasons (on the latter point, there were concerns about disrupting connections between highland and lowland areas of Karabakh).[40] The Bolsheviks had agreed to include Nagorno-Karabakh in the Armenian SSR, but Arsène Saparov notes that this conciliation was made to generate support among Armenians and strike a blow against anti-Bolshevik Armenian rebels who had seized control of Zangezur (now Syunik). Once the rebels had been defeated, it was no longer necessary to placate the Armenians. The Kavburo reversed its decision during a meeting in July 1921, placing Nagorno-Karabakh in Azerbaijan.[41] According to Grigory Lezhava, Georgian Bolsheviks are responsible for this final decision about Nagorno-Karabakh's placement. At the Kavburo meeting, they pushed to include Nagorno-Karabakh in Azerbaijan out of concern that granting it to Armenia would empower Abkhazian, Ossetian, Adjaran, and Armenian attempts to renegotiate control over parts of Georgia.[42] Although it was determined that Nagorno-Karabakh would be a constituent part of Soviet Azerbaijan, its actual status within the republic remained uncertain. Finally, after a long period of negotiation, and under pressure from the Zakkraikom, the Azerbaijan Central Executive Committee created an autonomous *oblast'* for Karabakh in 1923.

Although Karabakh now had a low level of autonomy (*oblast'*-level rather than republic-level) within Azerbaijan, Armenians continued to dispute its inclusion in Azerbaijan. Arutiunov tried to annex Karabakh in 1945 around the same time that Charkviani proposed attaching Balakan, Qakh, and Zaqatala to Georgia, but this was not the only time the leadership of Soviet Armenia formally attempted to renegotiate the status of this autonomous region. Rumors also spread in 1960, that they had tried—and failed—once again to acquire Karabakh. Annexation proposals were submitted confidentially, but they were an open secret in the region and, as in the case of Georgia and Georgian-Ingilois, garnered popular support both in the contested *oblast'* and in the Armenian Soviet Socialist Republic.

In a classified report from 1967, the Azerbaijan KGB reported that "unhealthy" nationalist behaviors and provocations had started to escalate in Nagorno-Karabakh in 1962. They documented support for Armenian annexation among both residents of Soviet Armenia and Nagorno-Karabakh, and showed how rumors about Armenian annexation fed disruptive activities.[43] Thousands of Karabakh Armenians signed petitions requesting the region's transfer to Armenia, complaining about reduced recognition of Armenian cultural and political rights in Azerbaijan and Azeri displacement of Armenians in Nagorno-Karabakh. Moscow's repeated failure to answer these demands only fed nationalist tensions in the region. Unauthorized demonstrations in Yerevan connected to the fiftieth anniversary of the Armenian Genocide in 1965 further escalated nationalist sentiment among some Armenians, who openly expressed a desire to reclaim lost Armenian territories in both Turkey and Azerbaijan. Interethnic violence also broke out in Nagorno-Karabakh at multiple points in the 1960s.[44] It was in this charged atmosphere that Bünyadov and other ethnogenesis scholars in Azerbaijan ramped up historical debates with their Armenian counterparts over claims to the territory of Azerbaijan and the legacy of Caucasian Albania.[45]

Territorial debates also played out in toponymic disputes. Sometimes scholars in Azerbaijan dismissed minority claims to toponyms in Azerbaijan in favor of Turkic etymological explanations for names of cities, geographical features, and historical sites in Azerbaijan. In other cases, officials renamed sites to alienate minorities from potential territorial claims. For example, at some point in this period, the Georgian-Ingiloi village Qakh-Gürcü (Qakh-Georgian) was renamed Qakh-Ingilo (Qakhingiloy). Why was the name changed? In part to eliminate the reference to Georgia and reinforce the point that Ingilois were derived from Albanians rather than Georgians (and thus a natural part of the Azeri nation).

Toponymic debates may seem benign, but they are not. As Rashid Khalidi has explained, the "process of naming [places] is an attempt to privilege one dimension of a complex reality at the expense of others, with the ultimate aim of blotting out or decisively subordinating them."[46] No less happened in Azerbaijan—and other republics of the Soviet Union—where the agents of titular nation-building time and again have rewritten the history of nontitular minorities while crafting narratives rooting titular peoples in the ancient past of their eponymous republics. In so doing, these scholars enact discursive practices of dominance that downplay minority histories and subordinate them to the narratives of the titular group. By considering many nontitular peoples to be a threat to the titular nation, this form of memory politics obscures and discounts the stories that many minorities tell about themselves as well as their national self-identifications.

"Enemies Scaling the Leadership": Language Politics in the Late 1950s

Ethnogenesis bolstered the Azeri claim to titularity by defining the territory of Soviet Azerbaijan as the ancient heritage of the Azeri people, but language use superseded most other quotidian markers of identification in Soviet national contests. Myriad social structures reinforced linkages between language and the long-term development of any given nationality, and changes in language policies inevitably altered daily routines and experiences. Efforts to redefine the prominence and status of the Azerbaijani language vis-à-vis Russian (and other languages) in the latter half of the 1950s thus radically transformed national relations and the space for minority cultures in Azerbaijan. These language reforms also piqued the interest—and concern—of officials in Moscow who were sensitive to the role of the Russian language in building a *sovetskii narod*.

Structural factors such as the evolution of Soviet governance in the 1950s are key to understanding the political environment in which Ragimov, Mustafayev, and Ibragimov operated, but it is also worth considering why Soviet

Azerbaijan's leadership pushed to improve the reputation and importance of the Azerbaijani language at this time. Discussions and debates about the role of the titular language in Azerbaijan indicate that its leadership was concerned about more than a simple desire to control the republic. Rather, the elites and masses who supported Azerbaijani language development in the 1950s were motivated by deep-rooted insecurities, as well as by frustration that rhetoric about the rights of titular populations did not match their lived experience of Russian hegemony.

The governing cohort that came to power in the post-Stalin 1950s was deeply affected by its experiences in Iran during World War II, and particularly by Stalin's abandonment of the Azerbaijan People's Government there. In this, Azerbaijan's history reminds us of the local contexts that must be folded into general discussions about how the Soviet victory over fascism influenced Soviet nation-building. World War II was transformative because it gave new meaning to the Soviet nation, helping to bind the population and bring people into the Soviet project who previously resisted or felt victimized by it.[47] This dynamic also played out in Azerbaijan, but, as elsewhere, it intermixed with a localized narrative that competed with the centrality of the All-Union experience. Most of the people in Azerbaijan celebrated Soviet victory in the Great Patriotic War, but many also mourned their losses in the Iranian region of Azerbaijan, which they called Southern Azerbaijan.

Hasanli has described this generation as one whose political consciousness was forged by their passage "through the school of patriotism in Southern Azerbaijan" during World War II.[48] Indeed, both Mustafayev and Ibragimov—and many others from Azerbaijan—distinguished themselves while working in Iran during the war and were inspired by these wartime experiences. Mustafayev headed Soviet agriculture projects in Soviet-occupied Iran, and the Iranian-born Ibragimov was one of the top-ranked Soviet officials there, implementing the Soviet agenda and helping to define the identity and contours of the Southern Azerbaijan national movement. Reflecting later on his editorial work in Tabriz with the controversial Red Army newspaper *Vətən Yolunda*, Ibragimov revealed just how central he felt his work was to the Southern Azerbaijani cause:

> For southern Azeris for whom schools, the press and literature in the mother tongue was banned, and who had been exposed to oppression and persecution through the denial of their identity, nationality, history, culture, and language under the severe social and national tyranny of Reza Shah's despotism for many years, *Vətən Yolunda* shone like a light in the darkness.[49]

Mustafayev and Ibragimov's work among Iranian Azeris reinforced not only the connection that Soviet Azeris felt to their "southern half," but also to their own nascent Soviet Azerbaijani identification and its various components.

For them and many others, Stalin's decision to pull out of Iranian Azerbaijan during the Iranian Crisis was painful because it imperiled their co-ethnics in Iran and disrupted irredentist dreams of adjoining Iranian Azerbaijan to Soviet Azerbaijan. This disappointing end to their wartime operations, however, did not undo the connection that Soviet Azeris had forged with Iranian Azerbaijan. Their service in Iran changed them, and many maintained a connection to it long after they retreated to Baku. This was helped along by the state's continued engagement with the question of Southern Azerbaijan. In the late 1940s, for example, a Soviet radio station broadcasting from the South Caucasus encouraged Iranian Azeris to "revolt against the Shah."[50] In August 1953, Soviet Minister of Culture Panteleimon Kondrat'evich Ponomarenko enhanced engagement with Iranian Azeris, directing the Ministry of Culture in the Azerbaijan SSR to transmit daily Azerbaijani language radio broadcasts to listeners in Iran. Broadcasts usually touched on global, Soviet, and Soviet Azerbaijani news based on material sent from Moscow for broadcasts to Iran and Turkey plus information generated locally. These dispatches aimed to show Iranian Azeris how the Soviet system enriched the Soviet Azerbaijani nation: Soviet Azerbaijani students talked about their summer breaks, broadcasters reported on increased purchasing power among workers in the Azerbaijan SSR, and musicians performed pieces composed by well-known Soviet artists such as Rashid Behbudov (Rəşid Behbudov) and Bülbül.[51]

Thus, even at the height of xenophobic Zhdanovism, Southern Azerbaijan remained a sensitive, yet sanctioned, cultural theme in Soviet Azerbaijan, generating some of the cultural works that were later transmitted to Iranian Azeris over the radio. Ibragimov was one of many writers and artists who cultivated a literary movement called the "literature of longing" (hasrət ədəbiyyatı), which nurtured sympathy for Soviet claims to Iranian territory and Azeri national rights. In the late 1940's, he published the novel Galajak Gün (Gələcək Gün, The Day Will Come), which described Azeris' struggle for national liberation from despotic Iranian overlords and Anglo-American capitalists. After the book was translated into Russian as "Nastupit Den'," Ibragimov was awarded a Lenin Prize. The poet Süleyman Rüstam (Rüstəm) was similarly celebrated for his contributions to the genre. He received a State Prize in 1947 for a book of poetry titled İki Sahil, or Two Shores (referring to the Iranian and Soviet banks of the Aras River), and, in 1949, Ogonek named his poem "Tabrizda Qısh" ("Təbrizdə Qış"), or "Winter in Tebriz," one of the best poems of the year.[52]

Having spent years promoting the Azeri movement for sovereignty and national rights in Iran, it is perhaps understandable that people who supported the Soviet project there would turn their gaze inward and focus on their own national rights. In this, they at times clashed with Bagirov and his vision for the republic. Many of Azerbaijan's cultural and intellectual leaders had a complicated relationship with Bagirov. He oversaw significant advancements in Azerbaijani nation-building, literacy, and cultural development during his tenure as first secretary of the Azerbaijan Communist Party—and advocated for Azeris in Iran—but many elites disagreed with his subordination of republic interests to Moscow demands, the way in which he defined the titular nation and its interests, and the violence he employed to achieve his goals and purge those with whom he disagreed.

His approach to Soviet Azeri nation-building is thus both significant and controversial. Having eliminated a significant amount of Azerbaijan's cultural and intellectual elite, including perhaps as many as one-third of its poets and playwrights, during the purges in the late 1930s, Bagirov continued to coercively sway cultural and national development through the early 1950s.[53] At one meeting of the Baku intelligentsia in 1950, for example, he criticized several cultural elites—Mirza Ibragimov included—for pan-Turkism and pan-Islamism, once again delimiting the acceptable boundaries of the Soviet Republic's titular identity. One of the men Bagirov targeted at the meeting, Heydar Hüseynov (Heydər Hüseynov), a noted philosopher and linguist, was also punished at work and, fearing arrest, committed suicide soon afterward.[54]

Given their complicated relationship with Bagirov—and his increasingly toxic status post-arrest—it is perhaps not surprising that Mustafayev, Ibragimov, and others publicly distanced themselves from Bagirov upon their ascension to power. In the spirit of Khrushchevism, they accused Bagirov of hindering Azerbaijan's titular development by destroying its cultural and political heritage during the purges of the 1930s. This new governing cohort fixated in particular on allegations that Bagirov subordinated the Azerbaijani language to Russian in the Azerbaijan SSR, a battle they had fought recently vis-à-vis the Azerbaijani and Iranian languages in Iran.

Amid the shifting political climate after Stalin's death and Khrushchev's Secret Speech, policymakers in Baku began to treat language policies emanating from Moscow more as suggestions than declarations as they explored different ways of elevating and refining their mother tongue (that is, the Azerbaijani language) through a stream of new decrees, orders, constitutional amendments, and informal practices. They were particularly focused on increasing its use in non-Azerbaijani-language schools. Up until about 1952, students in these schools usually studied the Azerbaijani language for two to three hours per week from the third to the tenth grade. Time spent on Azerbaijani-language learning started to decline, however, as concerns about overloaded schedules in these schools took over. By the 1954–1955 school year, Azerbaijani was taught for only two hours per week in Russian-language schools after the third grade and had been eliminated entirely in Armenian- and Georgian-language schools, where students still studied three other mandated languages—their native language, Russian, and a foreign language.[55] This trend toward simplified language requirements was reinforced in May 1955 by a Soviet Council of Ministers All-Union decree exempting students from the compulsory study of a non-Russian language that was not their native language.

The Azerbaijan Council of Ministers initially adopted Moscow's decree and mandated that students who continued to study Azerbaijani in non-Azerbaijani-language schools (such as Azeri students in Russian-language schools) would begin those classes in the fifth grade to ease the academic burden on younger students. This decree provoked an angry response from some officials, however. In the spring of 1956, Azerbaijan's Minister of Education, Mirza Mamedov (Mirzə Məmmədov), complained that it prevented Azerbaijani students from acquiring a deep knowledge of their mother tongue. Mamedov, like Ibragimov and many others, spent years working with the Soviet government in Iran during World War II. The ministry received Azerbaijani party approval to investigate the effects of the decree and, along with party investigators, held a series of meetings with select teachers and directors at Russian and Armenian schools in Baku.[56] Their investigation concluded that the decree caused a precipitous decline in the quality of Azerbaijani-language instruction and suppressed interest in native-language learning among Azeri students, who were increasingly unprepared for class and resented staying longer at school to study it, and in Russian-speaking Azeri households, where parents already tended to be more critical of mandated Azerbaijani-language learning.

The Ministry of Enlightenment and Azerbaijan Communist Party investigators recommended that the Azerbaijan Communist Party Central Committee mandate Azerbaijani-language learning for all students, regardless of national orientation, in order to preserve the status and vitality of the Azerbaijani language in the republic.[57] Debates about overturning the 1955 Soviet Council of Ministers decree shifted to the Azerbaijan Council of Ministers over the summer.[58] On August 9, 1956, after months of investigations, discussions, and planning, Ragimov, as head of the Azerbaijan Council of Ministers, allocated nearly five million rubles to reincorporate two hours of required Azerbaijani-language classes in Russian, Armenian, and Georgian schools starting from the third grade.[59] The Azerbaijan CP Central Committee quickly confirmed this proposal, setting the stage for renewed mandatory Azerbaijani-language learning in the 1956–1957 school year.[60] The decision to disregard Moscow's guidance on this issue could not have been taken lightly.

While Mustafayev and Ragimov coordinated to expand Azerbaijani-language learning in the republic, Ibragimov spearheaded his most significant language reform—a constitutional amendment designating Azerbaijani as the republic's official language.[61] Constitutional amendments guaranteeing the titular language as the state language of the republic were unusual in the Soviet Union but not in the South Caucasus, where both Georgia and Armenia already had similar stipulations in their republican constitutions.[62] Ibragimov brought the issue to Mustafayev, who subsequently presented a draft of the amendment to the Central Committee Bureau in Baku in July 1956. With their approval, Ibragimov set off to discuss the matter with Chairman of the Presidium of the Supreme Soviet Kliment Voroshilov in Moscow. Upon his return to Baku, Ibragimov informed the Azerbaijan Central Committee that he received Voroshilov's support.[63] The committee accepted Ibragimov's draft amendment, which he strategically introduced to the presidium of the Azerbaijan SSR Supreme Soviet alongside a policy package corresponding with Khrushchev's call to transfer more power to the republics.[64]

In his speech to the third session of Azerbaijan's Supreme Soviet that August, Ibragimov invoked the spirit of Khrushchev's Secret Speech and stridently defended the amendment as the fulfillment of *korenizatsiia* in Azerbaijan, stating:

> It is impossible to tolerate an indifferent attitude to the Azerbaijani language in any state, public or other type of organization, nor in any company. But unfortunately this ugly fact exists . . . The conducting of affairs in the native language of the republic follows from principles of Leninist nationalities policy. All of us, every responsible worker must perfectly know his own native language. Shame on those of us who don't know the Azerbaijani language.[65]

He avoided direct criticism of the Russian language and closed his speech with stock phrases about this language of "brotherly communion in the USSR," but Russian was clearly the foil against which he was promoting this change. The amendment was approved and, as of August 20, 1956, Azerbaijani became the official language of the Azerbaijan Soviet Socialist Republic.

A few months later, in October, Ibragimov reinforced the amendment by declaring that Azerbaijani should be used for all state business.[66] No longer masking his frustration with Russian-language hegemony in the republic, he couched this announcement in a proxy criticism of colonialism and national discrimination in the Russian Empire, writing that "Any pressure from the ruling nation, the so called 'great nation,' causes hatred and compels the oppressed people to wait for revenge." Then, taking an explicit dig at the significant Russian population in Baku, he continued, "With the purpose of oppressing and exterminating peoples and dissolving them inside the Empire, tsarism sought to fill the outskirts of the country with Russian migrants."[67] Internal investigations of Azerbaijani language use in republic ministries subsequently unfolded, each one reinforcing the idea that too few Azerbaijani speakers worked in government offices and too much state business was being conducted in the Russian language. As a result, the presidium of Azerbaijan's Supreme Soviet directed republic ministries to increase Azerbaijani language use among employees and to train non-Azerbaijani speakers in the language. Presidium members once again strategically contextualized this policy with familiar party language, arguing that it would reinforce both Lenin's nationality policy and "the brotherhood of nations."[68]

Moscow party officials repeatedly intervened to police this evolving situation in Baku. The August 14, 1956, Azerbaijan Communist Party decree mandating Azerbaijani-language learning in non-Azerbaijani-language schools lasted only two months. Party member G. B. Antelepyan was one of the complainants who petitioned against the decree. Tackling the issue from the Armenian perspective, he pointed out that, because students in Armenian-language schools were now required to study four different languages, the decree compromised their ability to achieve fluency in their native language—Armenian. Antelepyan proposed delaying Azerbaijani-language learning to later grades or making it optional.[69] The archival file on this matter in Baku does not preserve the details of Moscow's intervention in this instance, but, on October 16, the Azerbaijan Central Committee, citing the same reason as Antelepyan— overloaded school schedules in Armenian, Georgian, and Russian schools— once again made Azerbaijani optional in these schools.[70]

Although Voroshilov reportedly gave Ibragimov his blessing for the language amendment, the party took a different view from the Supreme Soviet on this issue. In November 1956, M. Lebedev and Evgenii Gromov (who headed the CPSU Central Committee organization for party organizations in the republics) complained that the CPSU had not been consulted about the amendment, which they believed fostered nationalism and needlessly alienated a significant proportion of the population. Lebedev and Gromov based this conclusion in part on a wave of complaints they received from Azerbaijan SSR residents, as well as on their belief that Azerbaijani was already widely used in Azerbaijan's governmental affairs.[71] In December 1956,

Mustafayev was brought to Moscow to answer for the amendment at the plenum of the Central Committee of the CPSU. Citing local objections to the amendment, First Deputy Head of the Department for Party Organs Iosif Shikin instructed Mustafayev to revisit the matter with the Central Committee Bureau in Baku.

Mustafayev adroitly avoided the issue until March 1957, when two comrades from Moscow arrived in Baku to force his hand. During a subsequent meeting with Azerbaijani Central Committee Bureau members and Ibragimov, the amendment—and related disturbances—were discussed at length. The meeting exposed deep divisions within the ruling leadership in the republic. Some bureau members turned against Ibragimov (and Mustafayev), blaming them for the controversial amendment, while others argued that it didn't go far enough. Ibragimov remained unrepentant. Despite Moscow's concern about rising nationalism in the republic and worry about the precedent that the amendment set for other republics, the amendment stood.[72]

Ibragimov was removed from power early in January 1958, but language reforms—as well as this oppositional cycle with Moscow—continued through Mustafayev's dismissal in the summer of 1959. Azerbaijani orthography emerged as another site of contention. Since at least the publication of *The Orthography of the Azerbaijani Language* in 1954, the Cyrillic version of the Azerbaijani alphabet and its effect on Azerbaijani grammar had been a matter of public discussion and debate. In 1955, a commission at the Nizami Institute of Language and Literature was formed to investigate possible paths of revision. The commission's proposals generated significant debate across the Supreme Soviet, Party Central Committee, and Council of Ministers in Baku, resulting in new orthographic rules that purged the Cyrillic letters "Ю" and "Я" from the Azerbaijani alphabet, replaced "Й" with the Latin letter "J," altered the role of "E," and introduced "Ə" in place of "Э" in June 1958.[73] Although these changes were implemented to improve the correlation between spoken and written Azerbaijani, Moscow-based officials viewed them through the lens of recent language battles and worried that they signified a broader shift in Azerbaijan away from Russia and toward Turkey.[74] Around the same time, Ragimov was removed from office, in part because of personality conflicts with counterparts at the Azerbaijan Central Committee but also because of political decisions that led to accusations of localism. One well-known case in particular was his decision to prioritize ore, electric power, and gas deliveries to Azerbaijani regions over shipments to Armenia and Georgia, triggering supply shortages in these neighboring republics.

Like Ibragimov, Mustafayev's decisive clash with his Moscow overseers was connected to his involvement in a new language decree, highlighting once

FIGURE 11. İmam Mustafayev, standing at the podium, addresses the Supreme Soviet of the Azerbaijan SSR on June 5, 1957. ARDKFSA 0-8161.

FIGURE 12. İmam Mustafayev, far left, speaking with comrades at a factory in Azerbaijan on March 23, 1959. ARDKFSA 4-1645.

again the high stakes of language politics and clarifying the limits of republican independence from Moscow. At the close of 1958, Soviet republics were provided with Nikita Khrushchev's theses "on the strengthening of the relationship of the school with life and on the further development of the system of public education in the country." One of articles of this document, Article 19, gave parents the right to choose the language of education for their children, whether it be Russian, their native language (in Azerbaijan this was limited to Georgian, Russian, Armenian, and Azerbaijani), or the titular language of the republic in which they lived. Part of the motive behind this proposal was to tackle ongoing debates about uneven language burdens that created inequalities across schools and took time away from other subjects like science, economics, and history. Up to this point, students in Russian-language schools and sectors were only required to study Russian and a foreign language, but students in non-Russian schools had to study three languages—Russian, a foreign language, and their primary language of instruction. In republics like Azerbaijan where there was interest in mandating titular language learning as well, some students were facing a situation where they might have to study as many as four languages.

Politicians, scholars, educators, and parents throughout the USSR expressed concern that the new guidance from Moscow discouraged titular language learning. Public discussions held in the summer of 1958 about restructuring education in the Soviet Union revealed that in many republics the preference was to extend the number of years students spent in school or to drop the requirement to study a non-Soviet foreign language. Khrushchev's solution—making titular language learning optional—only found demonstrable support at this time in Uzbekistan.[75] As the republics formulated their versions of this policy several republic leaderships looked for a way to preserve the titular language learning requirement. Ukraine and Estonia devised counterproposals for Moscow to review that accommodated Estonian- and Ukrainian-language learning in nontitular schools, but both ultimately adopted the principle of parental control over language instruction after Moscow rejected these propositions.

The political leaderships in Riga and Baku took a different approach, creating education laws for their republics that clearly deviated from the CPSU's guidance. In Riga, the Latvian education law did not give parents the right to choose the language of education for their children and left open the option of extending the number of years students spent in school. This decree lasted for only two months before it was amended to fall in line with Khrushchev's theses in late May 1959, but Azerbaijani's officials in the meantime looked to Riga for inspiration in crafting a version of the law that would be acceptable for their republic.[76] Party officials in Baku saw this as another opportunity to secure Azerbaijani-language learning less than three years after having revoked the earlier decree mandating it in the republic. Thus, in Azerbaijan, the CPSU guidance was adopted with a significant modification requiring both Russian- *and* Azerbaijani-language learning in all schools. As in the Riga case, this provoked a swift and definitive response from Moscow: Khrushchev censured the leaderships of both republics that July. The deputy head of the Latvian Council of Ministers Eduards Berklāvs and first secretary of the Azerbaijan Communist Party Mustafayev were dismissed and the Azerbaijani education law was revised to correspond with the Moscow text.

As these clashes with Moscow indicate, the language issue was at the forefront of political change and national politics in Soviet republics at this time. When Azerbaijan SSR officials in and around governing circles in the 1950s spoke about the need to defend and promote the Azerbaijani language, they invoked the discourse of Leninist nationality policy, emphasized the importance of native-language knowledge, and criticized Azeris who lacked knowledge of their mother tongue. At a meeting of the Azerbaijan Supreme Soviet in August 1956 about the constitutional amendment, Ibragimov argued that "measures are being taken in our republic to remove nihilism and cosmopolitanism and thus implement Lenin's national policy . . . All of us should be proficient in our native language; it's shameful not to know the mother tongue."[77] There is no question that Ibragimov was referring here to Azerbaijani-language knowledge rather than to the right and desire of nontitular minorities to be proficient in their native languages, whether Lezgin, Tat, Talysh, Kurdish, or something else. Similarly, at a plenum of the Union of Writers of Azerbaijan in May 1958, influential Azerbaijani writer Rasul Rza (Rəsul İbrahim oğlu Rzayev) declared:

> The use of this [Azerbaijani] language as the state one in all parts of Azerbaijan is a natural phenomenon. Though there are still elements of resistance or indifference in some places, it is because of misunderstanding of the national policy of the Party and the Soviet State . . . in turning away from the mother tongue, speaking an unintelligible language, the sons treat their native mother cruelly. Every people values its native language. He who tries "to study" a language of another people at the expense of his native language shall obtain nothing but the hatred of his own people.[78]

Rza's argument that the Azerbaijani language was the natural language of Soviet Azerbaijan calls to mind ethnogenesis narratives that portrayed Azeris as the natural inheritors of Soviet Azerbaijan's ancient heritage. What would

Rza have said to minorities who sent their children to Azerbaijani schools? Were they also "treating their native mother cruelly" and "obtaining the hatred of their own people"? Or did Rza believe, like Bagirov, that they were all Azerbaijanis and thus there was no need to develop and teach anything other than the Azerbaijani language?

Similar to Georgian and Armenian constitutional amendments on state language, the Azerbaijani amendment declared the titular language to be the state language of the republic *and* guaranteed national minorities in the territory of the Azerbaijan SSR the right to freely develop and use their native language in cultural and state matters.[79] This was broadly in line with constitutional guarantees of equality for Soviet citizens irrespective of their nationality or race and provisions protecting citizens from national or racial exclusiveness. Yet, the officials who shaped Azerbaijani language policies in the 1950s consistently viewed national minority languages as an impediment to Azerbaijani language proficiency, rather than as native languages that deserved developmental support and protection equal to that of the titular Azerbaijani language. This is still a common perspective in Azerbaijan. For example, historian Jamil Hasanli laments that "the status of the Azerbaijani language faced great difficulties in the mid-1950s" because Armenian, Georgian, and Russian schools hampered efforts to transform Azerbaijani (which he also refers to as the "mother tongue" without acknowledging there are many different "mother tongues" in Azerbaijan) into "the means of communication of the local population."[80]

Indeed, rather than work to improve the status of all native languages in Azerbaijan, state and party officials in Azerbaijan regularly subordinated national minority languages to promote and expand the Azerbaijani language. When these officials appealed to Leninist national rights, they were speaking about *titular* national rights, fully embracing the notion that the titular nation should be the dominant nation in its republic. From this perspective, if it was supposedly shameful for Azeris to not know Azerbaijani, the same could not be said about minorities and their native languages. Rather, these nationbuilders expected that minorities would attend Azerbaijani schools because it would help them assimilate into the titular nation, which, thanks to ethnogenesis, was increasingly asserting itself as the true representative of Azerbaijan's ancient and multinational heritage.

Thus, native-language learning in Azerbaijan was basically a proxy for Azerbaijani-language learning and republic officials championed it not to support all national cultures in Azerbaijan but to criticize the role of the Russian language vis-à-vis Azerbaijani in the republic. They were reacting in part to Moscow deprioritizing titular language learning in nontitular schools, but also to a broader short-term trend pointing toward increased Russian-language learning in the republic. As of 1959, Russians made up 13.6 percent of the Azerbaijan SSR population, but Russian language sector enrollment fluctuated between approximately 22 percent and 24 percent between 1953 and 1963, indicating that many non-Russian students (Azeris, but also Armenians, Georgians, Lezgins, and others) were choosing to study in Russian rather than in the native languages of their ascribed nationalities.

Yet, despite a decline in Azerbaijani-language sector enrollment relative to Russian in the 1950s, the vitality of the Azerbaijani language was not seriously threatened in the republic as a whole. Officials were reacting to pressure from Moscow to improve Russian language learning as well as frustration that Russian language use continued to be perceived as more prestigious than Azerbaijani in Soviet Azerbaijan. Indeed, there were many incentives to study Russian, and it was a popular choice, including among Azeris in Baku. Nonetheless, as table 3.1 shows, declines in Azerbaijani-language learning vis-à-vis Russian in the 1950s were short-lived, perhaps due in part to the nationalizing policies and practices that promoted Azerbaijani-language learning at that time. Even when Azerbaijani-language learning mildly declined in the 1950s, enrollments in these schools and sectors (ranging from 68 percent of students to slightly more than 70 percent between 1955 and 1963) was still outsized relative to the number of Azeris in the republic. In 1959, for example, 67.5 percent of people in the Azerbaijan SSR were categorized as Azerbaijani, but this in itself was an exaggeration because tens of thousands of nontitular peoples were categorized as such when their own national identifications were excluded from census recognition.

The real crisis at this time was thus not in Azerbaijani-language learning but in the remnants of minority-language education, where the gap between the recognized size of minority populations and the number of students being

Table 3.1   Percentage of Azerbaijan SSR students enrolled in different language schools and sectors by year

	1953–1954	1955–1956	1956–1957	1958–1959	1959–1960	1961–1962	1962–1963	1964–1965	1965–1966
Azerbaijani	69.44	68.84	68.25	68.46	68.63	68.67	70.03	72.68	73.61
Russian	21.77	23.15	23.98	24.61	24.85	25.38	24.22	21.95	21.33
Armenian	8.42	7.92	7.52	6.70	7.95	5.91	5.57	5.14	4.82
Georgian	0.37	0.28	0.26	0.23	0.19	0.13	0.18	0.23	0.24

Source: This chart is drawn from the following archival files: ARDA 57.11.1868, 57.11.2040, 57.11.2140, 57.11.2326, 57.11.2419, 57.11.2499, 57.11.2670, 57.11.3084, 57.11.3213.

educated in those languages rapidly increased. The minority schools and sectors that outlasted declines in minority education at the close of the 1930s continued to face myriad pressures and challenges. Armenian schools, for example, experienced a wave of closures and diminishing matriculation that resulted in a more than 3 percent decline in enrollment relative to population size between 1953 and 1966. Although Armenians made up 12 percent of the Azerbaijan SSR population in the 1959 census, Armenian schools enrolled less than 8 percent of students in Azerbaijan in the 1959–1960 academic year and steadily decreased thereafter.

Armenian students sometimes enrolled in Azerbaijani-language schools, but often chose Russian-language schools when Armenian ones were not available or they did not want to study in that language. This made sense for the large Armenian population in Baku with its diverse population and strong Russian influence, but some rural Armenians also thought that Russian schools were the most strategic option. As one Armenian woman from Khanlar explained to me, her parents sent their children to Russian schools because they could learn Armenian at home, didn't see much of a future for Armenians in Azerbaijan, and the Russian language opened the rest of the Soviet Union to them. When they later fled to Armenia in 1988 amid escalating interethnic violence between Armenians and Azerbaijanis in the region, they suffered some consequences from this earlier schooling decision. Although they could speak Armenian, they were illiterate in that language and thus experienced economic and social discrimination in their supposed Armenian homeland. With fellow Armenians calling them "Black Armenians" and telling them to go back to Azerbaijan, her family ultimately ended up in Russia, hoping their Russian skills would help them carve out a better future there.[81]

As I discuss in chapter 5, Georgian schools experienced a similar decline between 1954 and 1962. Until that point, the percentage of students enrolled in the Georgian-language school network roughly matched the percentage of people recognized as Georgians in the republic.[82] Unlike the Armenian example, however, the vast majority of Georgian-Ingiloi students affected by school and sector closures switched to Azerbaijani-language instruction rather than Russian. For example, Georgian-language schools were converted to Azerbaijani-language schools in the Muslim Georgian-Ingiloi Qakh region villages of Tasmalı and Zayam in 1954, in 1957 in the neighboring region of Zaqatala (Aliabad village), and in 1958 in Balakan (İtitala village).[83] As I discuss in chapter 5, this decline reversed in 1962 thanks in large part to Georgian-Ingiloi activism but also because more favorable policy changes emerged in line with Mustafayev's dismissal in 1959.

The nationalizing atmosphere in the republic pushed nontitular students toward Azerbaijani-language learning, but a number of specific policies and practices that targeted these communities also suppressed Armenian and Georgian school enrollment in the 1950s. Most obviously, school closures like those that happened in Muslim Georgian-Ingiloi communities made it difficult, if not impossible, for these students to enroll in native-language schools. Successive decrees mandating Azerbaijani-language classes in Armenian and Georgian schools also made these schools and sectors less attractive to students and parents. Why? When Azerbaijani was compulsorily added to student schedules in Armenian and Georgian schools, students went from studying three mandated languages to four, resulting in overburdened schedules that made it difficult for them to learn any single language well and limited the range of subjects they had time to study.

Other decrees also encouraged minority parents to reconsider the educational choices they were making for their children. In 1958, the Communist Party of the Azerbaijan SSR ordered that Azerbaijani-language preparatory classes be created for preschool aged children in Avar, Lezgin, Tat, Talysh, and other nontitular communities. Without the program, students were enrolling in school without any Azerbaijani-language knowledge, setting them back from their peers who were exposed to Azerbaijani at home.[84] From the perspective of many nontitular parents, however, this was not a practical measure but an assimilatory attack on the sustainability of their native cultures and communities. These parents believed that by taking their children out of the home at an early age to expose them to the Azerbaijani language, republic officials were attempting to transform their children from the inside out. This program was closed after Mustafayev's dismissal, but with the Azerbaijani language given new life in state and party fora, it was increasingly difficult to get by in Soviet Azerbaijan without the Azerbaijani language.

Consolidating Republican Populations: Demography in Soviet Azerbaijan

Soviet censuses were integral to the power dynamic in republics because, like ethnogenesis, they were a tool of governance and power. By providing data about the linguistic and national composition of the republics, censuses documented Soviet ethnohistorical advancement.[85] The growth of the titular nationality in any given republic illustrated progress toward the erasure of national differences and set the stage for the future amalgamation of all Soviet nations into one communist people. Census data was also strategically

Table 3.2   Azerbaijanis and Russians as percentage
of population in the Azerbaijan SSR

	1939	1959	1970
Azerbaijani	58	67.5	73.8
Russian	16.5	13.6	10

significant because the ethnoterritorial structure of the USSR incentivized linkages between nationality and territorial rights and, in turn, titular statistical majorities in the republics.[86]

Azerbaijan was demographically remade in the midcentury decades. In the 1939 All-Union Soviet census, 1,870,471 Azeris made up 58 percent of Soviet Azerbaijan's population.[87] By 1970, this figure had grown to 3,776,778 persons, or 73.8 percent of the population—significantly increasing Azeri demographic dominance in the SSR.[88] The capital city, Baku, replicated these changes, with the gap between Russians, the city's largest national population, and Azeris shrinking to just 12,000 persons between 1939 and 1959. As of 1959, Azeris outnumbered Russians in the broader metropolitan area of the Baku city soviet.[89] This trend accelerated over time. By 1979, the city was majority Azeri, partly because of the urbanization of the Azeri population but also because of Russian out-migration due to economic concerns and the evolving attitude toward the Russian language and culture there.[90]

A variety of artificial and so-called natural processes—emanating from both Moscow and the republic—boosted titular representation in the 1959 census. Historian El'dar Ismailov attributes demographic change to rising titular birthrates, reduced migration of non-Azeris to the republic, and amplified rural to urban migration after Khrushchev granted peasants internal passports that allowed them to leave their villages. He portrays Ibragimov and Mustafayev as passive players whose nationalizing politics merely responded to the strengthened titular national consciousness that accompanied the "Azerbaijanization" of the urban population and intelligentsia.[91] Süha Bölükbaşı, however, argues that Azeri urban migration resulted from Mustafayev "catering to native interests" and "tipping the ethnic balance in favor of the natives."[92]

Although his category of "native" is both simplistic and problematic, Bölükbaşı is right that Azerbaijan's state and party officials helped increase the actual and perceived homogeneity of the republic. He is mistaken, however, in solely crediting Mustafayev with the demographic consolidation of Azerbaijan's titular nationality. In fact, the statistical growth of the Azeri population was the result of long- and short-term, central and local policies. The republic's leadership differentiated itself from the Bagirov era, and Musta-fayev denounced his predecessor at the Twentieth Party Congress in Moscow, but Azerbaijan's demographic consolidation started in the Bagirov era. Local impulses to standardize and homogenize the population were also complemented by central policies that enabled minority assimilation and national deportations.

As elsewhere, state violence played an essential role in Soviet nation-making.[93] Censuses paint a picture of consolidating titular socialist nations in the South Caucasus in the 1950s but mask the practices that contributed to this "evolutionary progress": economic resettlements, national deportations, and forced assimilations were among the "technologies of population policies" that contributed—intentionally or not—to these results.[94] Take Azerbaijan as one example. One of the largest resettlements was the one I discussed in chapter 2, the relocation of approximately 45,000 Azeris from Armenia to the Kura-Araks region of Azerbaijan between 1948 and 1953.[95] It is widely believed in Azerbaijan that this migration was one of several acts of genocide against Azeris by Armenians in the twentieth century and was a national deportation worse than (or at least comparable to) the deportation of Chechens, Ingushes, and others.[96]

As I have shown elsewhere, however, it more closely resembled other Stalin-era economic migrations than national deportations, and the Azerbaijani leadership took an active role in moving these Azeris. It had a clear ethnic component, and many people felt compelled to move, but both of these characteristics were also present in other Stalin-era economic resettlements.[97] Motives aside, the migration had demographic consequences for both Armenia and Azerbaijan. Several thousand of these Azeri settlers ultimately returned to Armenia, but Azerbaijan nonetheless gained tens of thousands of Azeris through this resettlement.[98] The migration also changed the national composition of Soviet Armenia; the number of Azeris there declined from 130,896 (about 10 percent) in the 1939 census to 107,748 (just over 6 percent) in 1959.

Like many other Soviet republics, Azerbaijan also lost national communities as a result of national deportations in the 1930s and 1940s. Soviet historians studying these deportations have focused largely on the operations themselves and how they affected people targeted for deportation. Less attention has been paid to the ways in which deportations altered the local sites that experienced these cleansings. In republics where the titular population experienced mass deportation, like Chechnya, deportations grossly changed the national character of those spaces. In others, like Azerbaijan and Georgia, where the titular population was not expelled en masse, national deportations helped to homogenize republic populations and reinforce the visibility of the titular nation.

Little is known about Kurdish deportations in the 1930s. There are few available documents, and those that are accessible mostly provide information about deportations from the Transcaucasian Federation as a whole rather than on a republic-by-republic basis. For example, in late 1936, the Sovnarkom ordered the "resettlement," or deportation, of 3,101 Kurds from Armenia and Azerbaijan to Kazakahstan.[99] It is not clear how many came from each republic, but we do know that Kurdish population figures in Azerbaijan drastically declined over a short period of time and not just through deportation. In 1931, state officials claimed that there were more than 46,000 Kurds in Soviet Azerbaijan, but by the 1937 census this figure had declined to 10,878. Two years later, in the 1939 census, the state only recognized 6,005 Kurds in the republic. When the next census was taken twenty years later in 1959, only 1,500 Kurds reportedly remained in Soviet Azerbaijan.[100] Most of this decline seems to have been caused by Kurds being recategorized as Azerbaijanis, but deportation also played a role in this story.

Both deportations and assimilations generated cloaks of silence in the Soviet Union that can be hard to overcome. According to Daniel Müller, after this period "the very existence of Kurds in Azerbaijan was often deemed unmentionable" and very little research was conducted in Azerbaijan's Kurdish communities.[101] Kurds who had been expelled from the South Caucasus, as well as those who remained, mostly failed in later attempts to rebuild their national-cultural infrastructure and revisit the question of Kurdish autonomy in Azerbaijan. It was only in 1989 that Kurds regained native-language radio broadcasts (three times a week for fifteen minutes) and classes at the elementary school level in the republic.[102]

Not long after some Kurds were expelled from the Azerbaijan SSR, the Politburo also ordered the deportation of 6,000 Iranians from Azerbaijan to Kazakhstan. Oral history interviews indicate that some Talyshes were also deported at this time either because they were folded into the Iranian category or because they lived along the Iranian border in Soviet Azerbaijan.[103] Three years later, approximately 31,000 Germans were deported en masse to Kazakhstan and Novosibirsk from Armenia, Georgia, and, mostly, Azerbaijan, where 23,133 people were registered as German in the 1939 census.[104] Finally, during Operation Volna in 1949, 3,058 people (323 Greeks, 1,045 Armenians, and 1,690 Turks) were deported from Azerbaijan; purported Armenian Dashnaks as well as stateless Greeks and Turks or those who once held Greek or Turkish citizenship were targeted in this case.[105]

Even though some deported people were rehabilitated and allowed to return home in the 1950s, many could not reclaim their national categorization because their national populations had since been assimilated into the

Azerbaijani nationality category. Returned members of those communities were thus integrated into the titular census category. Similarly, when some of the Meskhetians deported as "Turks" from Georgia in the 1940s were freed from the special settlement regime in 1957, they were resettled in Azerbaijan rather than in Georgia, reclassified as Azerbaijanis, and included in that category in the 1959 census. By 1958, 2,150 of these "Turk" households had moved to Azerbaijan from Uzbekistan.[106]

Indeed, nationality erasure through census reclassification was one of the main ways that titular majorities increased in Soviet republics. Some minorities were recategorized by the ethnographers who consulted on census design, others by census workers, and some chose to reclassify themselves either because they considered themselves to be part of the titular nationality (however defined) or because of the benefits that accompanied membership in the titular nation (and the discrimination with which they might otherwise contend). Take Talyshes in Azerbaijan as one example. According to the 1939 census, Talyshes comprised the fifth largest national community in Azerbaijan—after Azeris, Russians, Armenians, and Lezgins—and were the largest minority lacking co-ethnic ties to a titular or principal (in the case of Lezgins in Dagestan) population of a neighboring republic. Between the 1939 and 1959 censuses, however, the documented Talysh population declined from 87,510 to 85.[107]

The official explanation was that the Talysh nationality category was eliminated from the Azerbaijani census in 1959 because Talyshes voluntarily and en masse self-identified as Azeri to census workers.[108] Yet some Moscow ethnographers and cartographers argued that Azerbaijani census authorities artificially assimilated Talyshes to "portray their region as more ethnically homogeneous and their *natsiia* or *narodnost'* more consolidated" than it was in reality.[109] Indeed, as I discuss in chapter 4, the documentary record clearly shows that the Central Statistical Administration in Moscow planned to include the Talysh nationality category in the 1959 census, but it was eliminated through the process of census collection and reporting in Azerbaijan.

In oral history interviews, Talyshes discussed some of the ways that census workers helped to sustain their official assimilation in subsequent decades. As one Talysh man reported, "During these censuses [from 1959 to 1979] no one asked us about our nationality or self-identification. The census workers sat in the regional or village office and filled in the national composition of the population ahead of time based on orders from above. Then they asked us to fill in the other lines."[110] In other interviews, respondents recounted stories of census workers denying the existence of a Talysh nationality, recording them as Azerbaijani when they identified themselves as Talysh, and avoiding the nationality and native language categories altogether while collecting census data.[111]

Members of other minority communities in Azerbaijan have reported similar experiences. For example, Muslim Georgian-Ingilois in both archived complaint letters and conversations with me described the challenges they experienced when they tried to register as Georgian or Ingiloi in Soviet Azerbaijani censuses and passports. The informal policy at the time was to categorize Muslim Georgian-Ingilois as Azerbaijani and Christians as Georgian. One way that Muslim Georgian-Ingilois tried to circumvent this practice was by traveling to Georgia and re-registering themselves as Georgian while there, sometimes with Georgianized names disallowed in their home communities.[112]

Forced assimilation was also a hot topic among Lezgins in the 1950s and 1960s, and the 1959 census offers some clues as to why. That year, census records for the Lezgin population recorded zero natural population growth. In fact, the population was shown to have declined from 111,666 in 1939 to 98,211 in 1959.[113] Lezgins were not deported from Soviet Azerbaijan like some other national communities, so where did they go? While it is difficult to know exactly what happened when the census information was collected, Lezgin activists in the 1960s detailed the many cultural, economic, and political pressures that encouraged Lezgins to assimilate into the Azerbaijani nation. For one thing, in the late 1930s, Lezgin-language schools and sectors—as well as other nontitular schools and sectors—were closed in Azerbaijan, which diminished the value of learning the Lezgin language and identifying oneself as such.

Myriad informal practices also encouraged minorities to assimilate into the Azerbaijani nation. One well-known method was to charge minority students an informal fee for educational access. A Lak woman explained to me that when she was a student in Zaqatala in the 1940s, nontitular minority students could attend Azerbaijani-language schools for free but were charged an informal fee if they attended the Russian-language school. On more than one occasion, students were sent home when they were unable to pay the fee.[114] In the Lezgin community, informal taxes like these were commonly referred to as "Lezgi pulu":

They assimilated us like this: from us they collected "Lezgi pulu"— money for study from Lezgins, you understand? . . . my older brother paid "Lezgi pulu" . . . Look, Lezgins paid in school 250 rubles, and in technical schools 400 rubles. In order not to pay, many Lezgins registered under different nationalities in passports, you understand?[115]

"Lezgi pulu" was also a key point of contention in a complaint letter that Lez-gin rights activists wrote in the early 1960s. The complainants—perhaps stra-tegically given Bagirov's fairly recent execution—blamed him for this policy, claiming that when Lezgins complained to Bagirov about these fees he made it known that Lezgins could avoid them by changing their passport national-ity to Azerbaijani.[116]

The demographic consolidation of the republic occurred over a long pe-riod and reflected the results of varied population movements and assimila-tory practices, but the nationalizing politics of the 1950s also left a distinct mark. Some scholars have argued that Ibragimov, Mustafayev, and other elites were responding to popular demand when they pursued nationalizing lan-guage policies in the early post-Stalinist years, but sources about non-elite popular opinion are elusive, and it is difficult to establish a flow of political influence from the masses to the elites on the basis of what is available.[117] Nonetheless, it is clear that the rhetoric of the republic's top leadership was well received by like-minded residents, which in turn increased assimilatory pressure on others.

Indeed, archived complaint letters and petitions document a burgeoning na-tional consciousness (and nationalism) in Azerbaijan, as well as a growing willingness to openly articulate the ways in which Russian language hegemony in the Soviet Union disadvantaged titular populations in "their" republics.[118] For example, Ia. A. Madat, who self-identified as Azeri, sent a letter to Khrush-chev to explain both his support for the Azerbaijani language constitutional amendment and his frustration with the status quo. He wrote,

> All affairs, correspondence in institutions, and even all gatherings, meet-ings, and conferences are conducted solely in Russian language. But in Armenia, Georgia, Ukraine, Belarus and the Baltic Soviet republics [they are conducted] in their own languages. By the way, the national cadre in Azerbaijan in relative numbers is much larger than in Armenia and Georgia. And Azerbaijani language, literature, and culture are higher [more significant] than them.
>
> In 1936, 90 out of 100 schools in Baku were Azerbaijani. And now in Baku only 3–4 schools are Azerbaijani schools. All the rest are Russian . . . What kind of politics is this if not chauvinist? Of course, Russian lan-guage is necessary to know . . . but does this [have to] mean the burial of the Azerbaijani language . . . [119]

While the school statistics Madat references are inaccurate, his perception of anti-Azeri bias in the Azerbaijan SSR (and apparently in the Soviet Union more generally) is important and tracks with the rhetoric expressed by elites like Ibragimov, who publicly complained about disrespect shown to the Azerbaijani language and connected its low status vis-à-vis Russian to various social ills, including Azeri youth underemployment.[120]

We can also find evidence of popular support for the language amendment by carefully reading protests against the measure. For example, R. Bagdasarov, a student at the music conservatory in Baku, complained to Khrushchev that non-Azeri speakers were becoming uncomfortable in Soviet Azerbaijan because there was "a notable 'flourishing' of nationalism" in connection with the constitutional amendment.[121] Bagdasarov referenced preferential treatment for Azeris in employment, university admissions, and party organizations, and argued that nationalism had taken off among the intelligentsia. As evidence for this, he described instances in which Azeri composers refused to accommodate non-Azeri speakers, even when they were visitors from other republics.[122]

In a letter that some factory workers sent to Khrushchev, Voroshilov, and the head of the Soviet Trade Unions, Viktor Grishin, the petitioners complained about being forcibly taught the "Tatar" language. Their claims track with other sources that document hardening attitudes toward Russian-speaking Azeris and reduced accommodations for non-Azerbaijani speakers in workplaces after the constitutional amendment. At a university event in Baku for the Turkish writer Nazım Hikmet in the mid-1950s, Ibragimov declared that intellectuals who did not know the Azerbaijani language, or who knew it but could not speak it, were scoundrels and traitors. The crowd reportedly reacted with wild applause.[123] During another meeting in late 1956—this time among state ministers and representatives—Ibragimov told the Minister of Culture, M. Kurbanov, that Russian speakers who did not like being interrupted in meetings were "free to go away."[124] Indeed, Hasanli notes that after the constitutional amendment, "panic reigned among the non-Azerbaijani population of Baku" as workplaces switched to the Azerbaijani language and some "Tatars" told "foreigners" (i.e., Russians, Georgians, Armenians, Ukrainians, and others) to "go home," reinforcing the idea that Azerbaijan was for Azeris.[125]

To be sure, nationalism was also flourishing elsewhere in the USSR. Soon after Beria pushed for rapid de-Russification of the Baltic republics in 1953, the first secretary of the Latvian Communist Party detailed how many Latvians had been killed or exiled since the Soviet Union's annexation of the territory in a party plenum speech. As if the subject was not provocative enough (or perhaps precisely because of its inflammatory content), he spoke only in Latvian, providing no translation for non-Latvian speakers in the audience.[126] Nationalists in the western borderlands were also emboldened in the mid-1950s with the return of accused nationalists from the camp system and news of unrest in Poland and Hungary. In Estonia in October 1956, disgruntled residents celebrated these uprisings by toasting Hungary and singing "Poland Has Not Perished Yet." In Lithuania that November, tens of thousands of people gathered for All Souls' Day, but soon started praising Hungary and Poland, singing patriotic songs to honor dead Lithuanian soldiers, and chanting "Russians out of Lithuania!" as they marched through the streets in Vilnius and Kaunas.[127] Similar anti-Russian sentiments and nationalist slogans were heard earlier that year on the streets of Tbilisi.

The Soviet leadership in Moscow carefully tracked this rise in popular nationalism—and grew increasingly concerned about it—over the course of the 1950s. This factored into the way they handled the situation in Azerbaijan. When Mukhitdinov and Shikin flew to Baku in the summer of 1959 to investigate the Bureau of the Azerbaijan Communist Party's Central Committee and prepare for the public announcement of Mustafayev's dismissal, they had heated conversations with convened members. One of the Azerbaijan party secretaries acknowledged that they all were guilty, but that Mustafayev should bear the consequences because, as first secretary, he had to take responsibility not just for his own mistakes but for theirs as well.[128] Vali Akhundov, Mustafayev's successor as first secretary of the Azerbaijan Communist Party, and Mukhitdinov both emphasized that they had to manage the situation carefully to avoid stirring up nationalism or thoughts of revenge in the republic.[129] Akhundov clarified a strategy to emphasize economic problems rather than national issues in an attempt to avoid many of the bigger conflicts that had developed in republic governance. In his view, accentuating the national question in reports would merely encourage the proliferation of nationalist sentiment in Azerbaijan.[130]

Recognizing that titular peoples were relatively advantaged in Azerbaijan, many minorities embraced opportunities to change their passport nationality and census designation. They understood that Azerbaijani or Russian language fluency alone was insufficient to overcome lingering *korenizatsiia* practices that meant people categorized as part of the titular nationality experienced some preferential treatment, including in employment decisions. As one Lak woman reminisced:

> Sometimes you could change your nationality in your passport if you gave money or you knew somebody very well and he could do you a favor . . . I remember that . . . the head of the international department of the Central Committee of the Azerbaijan Communist Party was Lak, but for his promotion, to work in the Central Committee, he needed to write in his passport Azerbaijani, and he did that . . . and my sister was Lak and her husband was Kazan Tatar, and probably they gave money

or they knew somebody . . . because how was it possible that the father is Kazan Tatar, the mother is Lak, and the son is Azerbaijani? It was important for jobs, mainly for jobs, and to become a member of the party . . . you know, as for me, I never felt that I was treated like the *other* nationality, but again the first positions were never occupied by minorities—maybe the second, but never the first.[131]

A Lezgin man similarly argued that nationality was often unimportant for ordinary people, but it was important to "be Azerbaijani" if you were involved in the party, or if you wanted an important position like the directorship of a large factory.[132]

Although Talyshes did not have a choice about whether or not to "become Azerbaijani" in 1959, the varied way they now talk about their assimilation reveals many of the pressures they felt at the time. Les Field has argued that non-recognition "is not merely a denial or repression of recognition . . . [it] is a powerful discourse that produces knowledge and is sustained by entrenched discursive practices built into the cultural, ideological, political, ecological, and spatial/geographic environments."[133] Indeed, while some Talyshes petitioned state, party, and census elites for the right to identify themselves as such in state records (these requests were denied until 1989), many others explained in interviews that they accepted an Azerbaijani identification either because they did not recognize any other choice or because it made life easier. For example, in 2011 a Talysh man from Masallı recalled, "In the Azerbaijani encyclopedia and in the Great Soviet Encyclopedia, they wrote that we were all one nation [*natsiia*], one people [*narod*], and that the Talysh had merged with the Azerbaijanis. They wrote this because they had to, because Stalin had said that we were building socialist nations, but we believed what we read back then about ourselves."[134] In 2008, another man explained that he would have chosen to be classified this way even if he had been given a choice:

> I wanted to be Azerbaijani, not Talysh . . . Nobody said that they were Talysh or Lezgin at that time. If I had said, "I am Talysh," I would have been punished for this . . . I lived in that period and if somebody told me that I was Talysh I felt bad . . . We were brought up this way. The Talysh people did not have a developed culture and their customs were not promoted either. The Talysh were not a developed nation . . . at that time it was forbidden.

Although Talysh was his native language, he worried about the stigmatization of the Talysh nationality and feared that his children would experience discrimination if they spoke Azerbaijani with a Talysh accent. Raised in a Talysh-speaking home by parents who received a partial education in the Talysh language in the 1930s, he had had no personal memory of Talysh national cultural support, refused to teach his children Talysh, and as an adult only spoke Azerbaijani at home.[135]

Another Talysh man revealed similar instrumental motivations for preferring an Azerbaijani nationality: "If I went to the local authorities and said 'I'm Talysh, write Talysh in my passport'—had it even been possible—I wouldn't have had any opportunities in Azerbaijan. I had to work and there was nothing to being Talysh then—no schools, no alphabet, no books, no jobs."[136] A woman similarly argued that there was no point to teaching her children the Talysh language because Talyshes had no national infrastructure or future in Azerbaijan. In their stories, they neatly summarized the way that institutionalized accoutrements of nationhood came to define what it meant to be a nation in the Soviet context. If a nationality lacked access to the institutions and practices promoted through *korenizatsiia* (native-language schools, cultural development, cadre promotion, and other preferential benefits) and was unable to perform the instrumental work done by other nationalities, was it a nation?

Zubkova invokes the example of Kazakhstan to argue that targeted efforts to pacify restive nationalities in the western republics had the unintended effect of renewing *korenizatsiia* politics elsewhere in the USSR.[137] The case of Azerbaijan, meanwhile, shows some of the ways in which attempts to satisfy titular demands in the republics disrupted registers of national relations and belonging. Rogers Brubaker has observed that in East Central Europe "structurally similar conflicts were reproduced at successively lower levels of political space."[138] Something similar happened in the Soviet Union, where structural oppositions cultivated nested nationalisms within the republics. Like other Soviet republics, Azerbaijan in the 1950s increasingly looked and acted like a homogenizing nation-state under the shadow of a communist government.

If we incorporate the experiences of minorities into the midcentury consolidation of the Azeri nationality, we gain a clearer understanding of the recursive relationship between majority-minority nationalisms in the Soviet Union. On the All-Union scale, titular nationalities were minorities, but in the republics they were often in a position of power over nontitular populations. At the same time that Azerbaijani elites and others complained about their handicapped national rights, their own nation-building policies infringed on the national rights of minorities sharing the republic of Azerbaijan.

The ethnoterritorial structure of the USSR sanctioned uneven rights fulfillment that fed conflicts among different national communities. Trigger points for problems with Moscow were policies that encroached on the roles of the Russian language and Russian-speakers in the republics. Nationalizing politics that infringed on the rights of nontitular communities, meanwhile, met with a more unpredictable response and indeed at times were bolstered by Moscow policies such as national deportations. Some minority communities, namely Georgian-Ingilois and Lezgins, produced activists who went to great lengths to agitate for recognition of their national rights and sometimes found success in the face of rising Azeri national consciousness. Other nontitular populations, such as Talyshes, were swept en masse into the expanding titular nationality. We have seen to some extent that the local fate of minorities hinged not only on the plans and intentions of the republic leadership but on Moscow as well. What happened when Moscow and Baku's interests did not align regarding a specific population? How did co-ethnic relationships influence nontitular trajectories? The reasons that responses varied across the republic and what they symbolized about social and political relations in the post-Stalin decades are the focus of the next two chapters.

CHAPTER 4

Scholars, Politicians, and the Production of Soviet Assimilation Narratives

> They organized one census of the population, then another. No one remembered about the Talysh. "They existed some time ago, but not now," one Bakinets . . . told me. "Why?"—"They dissolved"—he answered without joking. And this was the totally official story!
>
> . . . Can it be that really and truly there is nothing to talk about? Or, rather, no one? Can it be that the entire people [*narod*] actually dissolved?
>
> —Murad Adzhiev, "Skazhi Svoe Imia, Talysh," *Vokrug sveta* 7 (1989): 13

In 1978, some Talyshes sent collective complaint letters to the Central Statistical Administration in Moscow and to the newspaper *Pravda* about census workers denying their request to register as Talysh in the upcoming census.[1] A. A. Isupov, the head of the Administration's Department of the All-Union Census, replied via letter that they, of course, were free to register as part of any nation, *narodnost'*, or ethnographic group they preferred, but reiterated that the Talysh category would not be included in the census. How did Isupov justify this decision? He invoked an ethnographer's account of Talysh assimilation to explain to these Talysh men that they were in fact not Talysh at all but Azerbaijani.[2]

Censuses have constitutive power and in the Soviet Union played an important role in naturalizing discourses of minority assimilation. In a practical sense, denying a people categorization was meaningful because census recognition was intimately intertwined with national rights fulfillment and recognition. This, in turn, affected communal vitality. Yet the assimilatory theories and interconnected narrative strategies that ethnographers, historians, philosophers, linguists, ideologists, political officials, and others generated and invoked to justify minority assimilation were equally important. They explained the inexplicable and contributed to the culture of secrecy that helped sustain these erasures.

Consider the Talysh case. Between the 1939 and 1959 Soviet censuses, the recognized number of Talyshes in Soviet Azerbaijan declined from 87,510 to 85. Having survived the great purge of peoples in the 1939 census, Talyshes thus earned the distinction of being the only nonforeign, nondiaspora nationality erased from Soviet census categorization for the first time in 1959.[3] These census data were used to support subsequent claims that Talyshes had voluntarily and completely become Azerbaijani and that this occurred naturally over time rather than from artificial manipulations of minority communities and identifications.

This interpretation of Talysh assimilation was disseminated through census reports, encyclopedias, ethnographic maps, books, and articles produced for popular and specialist audiences. It was reinforced in daily experiences when, for example, parents were unable to enroll their children in native-language schools or were denied the ability to register as members of their preferred national community in censuses and passports. These discourses of assimilation had powerful effects that reverberated not only in broader society but in targeted communities where minorities often internalized the narratives they were told and read about themselves. In this way, these stories of assimilation contributed to social, political, and economic pressures that incentivized nontitular peoples to merge with titular nations termed "socialist nations," in part to justify their continued visibility and relevance as the Soviet Union progressed toward communism.

The narrative of voluntary and natural Talysh assimilation eventually became hegemonic, masking both critiques of Talysh assimilation and the efforts that were made to assimilate them. To understand the complex history of Talysh erasure, it is helpful to start in the early years after Stalin's death, the time that set the stage for the 1959 census and its aftermath. Many Caucasus specialists saw 1956 as a moment of rebirth for their field. Some of their number had been swept up in the Stalinist purges with other Eastern specialists. In Azerbaijan, the repression of intellectuals who promoted national minority cultures and who wrote about national minorities, including Zulfugar Ahmedzade and Kurdish specialist A. Bukshpan, had a chilling effect.[4] Colleagues in Moscow were also repressed, including prominent ethnographer Anatolii Nestorovich Genko. In 1938 he was arrested with other scholars accused of anti-Soviet propaganda and chauvinism. Released after more than a year in custody, Genko was rearrested in 1941. His professional activities were once again used as evidence against him. This time, he was charged with "anti-Soviet activity, libelous fabrications regarding the activities of the All-Soviet Communist Party (Bolsheviks) and the Soviet government and actions by bodies of the NKVD."[5] One of the witnesses reported that, after a trip to the

Caucasus, Genko blamed Soviet policies like collectivization for worsening already poor living conditions in the region. He was also accused of claiming that Soviet nationality policies fostered "an intolerable situation for minorities, who suffered from the great-power chauvinism of Georgians and Azeris," an idea that might have been acceptable a few years earlier but had now fallen out of favor. After a few months in detention, Genko died in solitary confinement in an internal prison of the NKVD Directorate on December 25, 1941. The Caucasus specialists who remained watched as many of the populations they studied—including Germans, Chechens, Ingushes, Balkars, Karachays, Kalmyks, Khemshils, Meskhetian Turks, Kurds, Iranians, and others—were labeled traitors, forcibly loaded into trains, and exiled to lives bounded by special settlement regimes in Siberia and Central Asia. Others specialists no doubt participated—intentionally or not—in government planning and execution of these deportations.

By 1956, many of the people who had left the Caucasus were making their way back to the region.[6] Some of the experts who helped design the 1959 census thus viewed it as an opportunity both to reincorporate national populations they thought had been wrongly expunged from the 1939 census and to evaluate assimilatory processes in the Soviet Union more critically.[7] Convinced that artificial assimilations fostered dangerous and unstable falsifications disruptive to Soviet society, these experts believed that a more cautious approach would create a solid foundation for the impending Soviet transition from socialism to communism.

There were competing impulses, however. Other scholars interpreted Khrushchev's challenge to build communism in the USSR at the 1956 Twentieth Party Congress as a call to find more evidence of Soviet ethnohistorical achievement—that is, more examples of successful assimilations.[8] As philosopher Ivan Petrovich Tsameryan argued at a 1959 conference about theoretical issues related to building communism, "There can be no transition to communism in the presence of small *narodnosti*. The process of consolidation, it would seem, must be completed in the period of building communism."[9] For Tsameryan, that time was now, and he and his intellectual allies searched anxiously for signs that the Soviet peoples were coming together and socialism was conquering petty national differences.

Myths of nontitular assimilation were formed and reinforced through these scholarly debates, but that cannot entirely explain why some narratives triumphed over others. Many social scientists and humanists helped to guide the assimilation process and to justify it after the fact, but other actors were also involved. State officials in Moscow and the republics played a key—if at times more opaque—role in deciding which nationalities and *narodnosti* would remain in the Soviet brotherhood of nations and which would be judged relics and merged into the titular nationality of the republic in which they resided. A host of variables, including local preferences and security concerns, ultimately guided these decisions. Only by considering all of these factors can we explain how Talyshes were made to disappear in a census that was designed, in part, to undo the injustices of the past.

Ethnography and Assimilation
Nationality Theories under Khrushchev, or Building Communism at the Height of the Cold War

Nicholas Dirks has argued that "Colonial knowledge both enabled conquest and was produced by it; in certain important ways, knowledge was what colonialism was all about."[10] This was no less the case for the Russian Empire and the Soviet Union, where languages, borders, maps, censuses, the arts, museums, and other forms of informational and bureaucratic knowledge were used to make sense of, reorder, and rule the diverse population. For Dirks, these technologies sustained colonialism in British India by creating and perpetuating oppositions between colonizers and the colonized;[11] Francine Hirsch argues that in the Soviet Union these technologies were used to produce the opposite effect, that is, "to 'modernize' and transform all the lands and peoples of the former Russian Empire and bring them into the Soviet whole."[12]

The erasure of difference plays an important role in this process of unification. Soviet ethnographers who documented national assimilations and Soviet ethnohistorical progress emphasized commonalities in the culture and daily life of Soviet peoples.[13] Their evidence was increasingly filtered through the theoretical concepts of *sblizhenie*, the rapprochement of smaller nationalities and larger ones, and *sliianie*—a more advanced "fusing" of nations—which were central to Leninist theorizing; Lenin had identified these assimilatory processes as key components of socialist progress.[14] In a meeting of the Institute of Ethnography after the Twenty-First Congress of the CPSU in 1959, V. K. Gardanov, B. O. Dolgikh, and T. A. Zhdanko thus applauded evidence that small peoples were merging with titular socialist nations:

> Up until the October Revolution, small, isolated, and insular ethnographic groups—the remains [*ostatki*] of ancient and medieval tribes—existed within the majority of *narodnosti* of Tsarist Russia. Now, a number of peoples [*narod*] no longer have these isolated groups; for others, the process of their gradual rapprochement [*sblizhenie*] with large nations

[*natsiia*] has significantly progressed. Different parts of various *narodnosti* and ethnographic groups of the RSFSR, being among the masses of the Russian population, are gradually merging with it. In the union republics of Central Asia and the Caucasus, most of the small ethnographic groups are merging [*sliianie*] with the principal nation [*natsiia*] of the republic.

They celebrated the shared "traditions and features" of everyday life (including the Russian language) that were uniting these disparate Soviet peoples and helping to build a united Soviet community.

Certain regions were of particular interest to Soviet theorists of assimilation and ethnohistorical evolution.[15] The remarkable diversity of the Dagestan ASSR's population made it, along with Kabardino-Balkaria and the Far North, a central site of Soviet assimilation studies. From 1950 to 1960, scholars in the Caucasus sector at the Academy of Science's Institute of Ethnography in Moscow concentrated on two main projects—publishing a comprehensive ethnographic study of all peoples in the Caucasus, *Narody Kavkaza*, and studying national consolidation in Dagestan.[16] In this period, most academic expeditions to Dagestan—whether of ethnographers, economists, cartographers, artists, or photographers—studied the national evolution of nations, *narodnosti*, and ethnographic groups there.[17]

Ethnographers and politicians alike celebrated Dagestan as a renowned example of how the Russian language and shared Soviet culture were helping diverse populations advance along the ethnohistorical path of progress. As Comrade A. D. Danialov from Dagestan declared at the Twentieth Party Congress in 1956,

> The most noteworthy result of Soviet rule in Dagestan is the process of consolidation of tribes and ethnic groups . . . On the basis of the growth of the national economy and culture the small ethnic groups are consolidating around the larger nationalities of Avars, Dargins, Kumyks, Lezgians and Laks. In turn the process of increasing rapprochement of these peoples is going forward. They now form a single fraternal family of Dagestanians, builders of a communist society.[18]

Dagestan was particularly interesting because, unlike most other Soviet republics, it had no titular nationality. Instead, select principal *narody*, including Avars, Lezgins, and Dargins, shared privileged political representation and national cultural support in the republic. Smaller "ethnographic groups" were said to be converging with these main nationalities—Andis, Akhvakhs, Bagulals, Botlikhs, Godoberins, Karatins, Tindis, Chamalals, Bezhtas, Tsezs, Khvarshins, and others with Avars; Aghuls, Rutuls, Tabasarans, and Tsakhurs with Lezgins; and so on—which were, in turn, merging into a unified Soviet socialist Dagestani nation.

Dagestani ethnographer Mikhail Matatovich Ikhilov directed his readers to examine Soviet censuses, treating them as irrefutable evidence of how Soviet rule had transformed the ethnohistorical landscape of this complex and diverse region.[19] He particularly liked the example of the Kubachis and Kaitags, who were ethnographically related to Dargins, but counted separately in 1926. By 1959, ethnographers decided that their differences had been conquered, allowing them to merge into the Dargin category.[20] For Ikhilov, this was something to celebrate and confirmed that Kubachis and Kaitags had become more similar to Dargins, a sign of advancement toward a united communist future. These processes were, of course, said to be occurring elsewhere in the Soviet Union, including in Azerbaijan, where Talyshes, Georgian-Ingilois, Tats, and others were supposedly blending into the Azerbaijani socialist nation. According to the theory of double assimilation, this titular nation would eventually merge with Georgians, Armenians, and other socialist nations to create a supranational Soviet people.

Dagestan is also a helpful case study for understanding the challenges that ethnographers encountered as they tried to integrate their field work into dominant theories of ethnohistorical progress. The field notes of Leonid Ivanovich Lavrov, an ethnographer who headed the Caucasus sector at the Academy of Sciences from 1957 to 1961, show how ethnographers sometimes struggled to map Soviet categorizations and theories onto the complicated reality of everyday life in Dagestan. For example, he recounted this anecdote in his notes from a 1952 research trip:

> In Akhty, waiting for a lift to Rutul, I spoke with a teacher from the Rutul village Khnov. From him I heard that Khnovtsy use the bazaar more in Nukha [Shaki] than in Akhty, which is 50 kilometers from them on a difficult pack trail [v'iuchnaia tropa].[21] 90–95 percent of the population in Khnov knows the Azerbaijani language, around 30 percent—Lezgin, and no more than 20 percent—Russian. Although it is written in passports that Khnovtsy are Lezgins, upon meeting with a real Lezgin they converse, as a rule, in Azerbaijani. Khnov belongs to the Akhty region which is populated almost entirely by Lezgins, and therefore Lezgins from the regional center often speak at meetings in Khnov. In these situations their speech is translated into the Rutul language. Only a few in Khnov can read the regional newspaper, which is issued from Akhty.[22]

Rutuls were recorded as Lezgins in their passports because the Rutul language is part of the Lezgic group of the North Caucasus languages, and because they were said to be blending ethnographically with Lezgins (that is, becoming Lezgin). But as Lavrov indicates here, and as other ethnographers, including Ikhilov, made clear in later studies, the "Lezgin group" was one of many *narodnosti* in the Soviet Union more successfully merged in theory than in practice.[23]

Soviet nationality theorists separated the merging of peoples into two distinct phenomena: consolidation (*konsolidatsiia*) and assimilation (*assimiliatsiia*). In 1961, Viktor Ivanovich Kozlov, a prominent Soviet ethnographer and demographer who consulted on censuses, described consolidation as "the process of the *sliianie* of several *narody* (or significant parts of *narody*) into one *narod*."[24] The ethnohistorical progress that Ikhilov described in Dagestan was consolidation; groups susceptible to consolidation shared territorial, economic, linguistic, cultural, and origin commonalities. Assimilation, in contrast, was understood to arise from the "ethnic interaction of population groups, [that were] usually very different in their origin, language, and culture."[25] As such, assimilation—which the Iranian-speaking Talyshes were said to experience with their Turkic-speaking Azeri neighbors—was rarer, more difficult, and thus a more impressive achievement for the Soviet state.

Two political developments during the Khrushchev years encouraged ethnographers to find more evidence of Soviet ethnohistorical advancement— that is, of consolidation and assimilation. First, at the Twentieth Party Congress in 1956, Khrushchev announced that the Soviet Union was in an advanced state of socialism and called for the Soviet people to move toward the ultimate goal of the Russian Revolution and the highest stage of evolutionary development— communism. He expanded on this call to action at other venues including the Twenty-Second Congress in 1961, where he identified nations and national identifications as a potential roadblock in this all-important process. Linking the attainment of communism to necessary ethnohistorical change, Khrushchev declared "people are to be encountered, of course, who complain about the effacement of national distinctions. Our answer to them is that communists are not going to freeze or perpetuate national distinctions. With uncompromising Bolshevik implacability we must eradicate even the slightest manifestation of nationalist survivals." His speech was more strident than what was printed in the Congress program, but there, too, advancement toward communism was linked to a "new stage in the development of national relations in the USSR . . . the further *sblizhenie* of nations and the achievement of their complete unity."[26] This provoked more studies of double assimilation, including the "higher-level" *sblizhenie* of socialist (titular) nations and "lower-level" merging of subrepublic minorities into these titular nations.

Khrushchev's call to build communism came at the same time as an intensifying Cold War that generated numerous scholarly initiatives to advance the party's ideological mandates at home and abroad. The People's Friendship University was founded in 1960 to demonstrate the Soviet Union's commitment to decolonization by providing a university education to thousands of international students from Africa, Asia, Latin America, and elsewhere.[27] The expectation, of course, was that these students would advocate for the Soviet model when they returned home. The Academy of Sciences also opened new institutes for the study of Africa and Latin America (in 1959 and 1961, respectively), and Soviet intelligence bodies were reorganized to help Soviet leaders get to "know" these contested parts of the Cold War map.[28] Soviet ethnographers, with their expertise in foreign cultures, economies, societies, and so on assumed leadership roles in friendship and cultural relations societies that sponsored visits between the USSR and other countries to build global networks and promote Soviet ideals. Many of them also advised the government on foreign policy matters at a time of growing global competition for power—a competition, it should be noted, that existed not just between the socialist and capitalist powers but within the socialist world, as China, Cuba, and other socialist states increasingly pursued their own interests in Southeast Asia, Africa, Eastern Europe, Latin America, and elsewhere.

As the Soviet leadership tried to connect to the decolonizing world through the language of national liberation, equality, and advancement, Soviet ethnographers helped strengthen the case against the capitalist alternative by detailing the exploitation of minorities in capitalist countries, such as African Americans and Indigenous peoples in the United States.[29] Some of this scholarship argued that racism and discrimination prevented the United States from embarking on the "path of progress."[30] In other publications, Soviet scholars explained how capitalist colonization destroyed "aboriginal peoples" by disrupting their self-sustaining "native economies," spreading disease, and supplanting healthy diets and sturdy clothing with cheap imports.[31]

Ethnographies of non-Russian peoples in the Soviet Union, meanwhile, formed an implicit contrast to these examples of capitalist exploitation. Changes in diet, clothing, and housing in the USSR were praised for helping its indigenous peoples (e.g., Talyshes) overcome past inequalities and reap the benefits of socialism. This was the future that awaited newly liberated peoples in the decolonizing world if they adopted the Soviet model and vanquished the inequalities generated by Western capitalist imperialism.[32] Both goals—building communism and increasing foreign outreach—thus encouraged ethnographers, linguists and other scholars to underwrite and justify Soviet ethnohistorical "progress" rooted in nontitular minority assimilation.

The Design and Implementation of the 1959 Census

Over the course of 1957 and 1958, experts at the Institutes of Ethnography and Linguistics at the Academy of Sciences worked with the Central Statistical Administration to correct the assimilatory excesses of 1939 by compiling an expanded list of nationalities for the upcoming census. This list was then sent to republican, *krai*, and *oblast'* Communist Party Central Committees for their approval. In some cases, these officials disagreed with the scholars' recommendations. The Mordovia regional committee, for example, wanted higher disaggregation of the Mordvin nationality and specifically requested that Erzas and Mokshas—who had not been enumerated in the 1926 and 1939 censuses—be counted separately.[33] In Stavropol, the regional committee thought that they should collect data for all nationalities, regardless of their size. Officials from Uzbekistan, Tajikistan, Georgia, and Azerbaijan also rejected the Administration's proposals for their republics, but they wanted *fewer* nationalities counted. They opposed reintroducing nationalities that had already been assimilated into titular categories and protested the disaggregation of Adjarans, Lazs, Mingrelians, Svans, and Tsova-Tushes in Georgia; Airums, Karapapakhs, Padars, and Shahsevans in Azerbaijan; Kypchaks, Kurams, and Tiurks in Uzbekistan; and Pamiri peoples in Tajikistan. From the perspective of these Central Committees in the republics, these were not nationalities but ethnographic groups that should not be resurrected as they had become—or always had been—indivisible parts of the respective titular nationalities and would identify as such if given the chance. Talyshes were not included in this discussion.

In a cautionary letter sent to Secretary Brezhnev, Africanist Ivan Izosimovich Potekhin and ethnographer of Soviet nationalities Liudmila Nikolaevna Terent'eva argued against the republican position, asserting that the artificial consolidation and assimilation of population groups could damage interethnic relations.[34] They advised Brezhnev that the party needed accurate information about the population (i.e., a truthful and accurate All-Union census) to craft evidence-based interventions and policies that would shape ethnohistorical processes in the USSR without provoking unintended consequences.[35] Eminent ethnographer and director of the Institute of Ethnography Sergei Pavlovich Tolstov supported this position, individually lobbying census authorities to disaggregate the Pamiri category in the census. He also wanted it labeled Pamir *narody* rather than Pamir Tajiks, as he worried that the latter term would suggest to Pamiris that they should identify themselves as Tajiks, thus biasing the results.[36]

Despite the strenuous objections of these renowned Moscow ethnographers, republican leaders largely succeeded in their appeals. At the end of 1958, the

Table 4.1   Nationalities included in the Azerbaijan SSR 1959 census

	NUMBER OF PEOPLE	PERCENTAGE OF NATIONALITY AS PORTION OF SSR POPULATION	PERCENTAGE OF PEOPLE WHO CONSIDER THE LANGUAGE ASCRIBED TO THEIR NATIONAL-ITY TO BE THEIR NATIVE LANGUAGE
Entire population of the Azerbaijan SSR	**3,697,700**	**100**	**94.6**
Azerbaijanis	2,494,400	67.5	98.1
Russians	501,300	13.5	99.9
Armenians	442,100	11.9	85.3
Peoples of Dagestan	121,400	3.3	88.6
Lezgins (as part of the Dagestani category)	98,200	2.7	89.9
Avars (as part of the Dagestani category)	17,300	0.5	79.8
Jews	40,200	1.1	17.1
Mountain Jews (as part of the Jewish category)	10,300	0.3	10.4
Tatars	29,500	0.8	78.6
Ukrainians	25,800	0.7	42.6
Georgians	9,500	0.3	78.3
Tats	5,900	0.2	63.1
Belarusians	4,300	0.1	44.3
Udins	3,200	0.09	92.8
Ossetians	2,100	0.06	51.7
Mordvins	1,800	0.05	46.4
Moldavans	1,500	0.04	62
Kurds	1,500	0.04	84.7
Germans	1,500	0.04	28.9
Poles	1,500	0.04	16.7
Assyrians	1,400	0.04	69.7
Other nationalities	8,800	0.2	59.9

head of the Statistical Administration, Vladimir Nikonovich Starovskii, endorsed the republican perspective by submitting to the CPSU Central Committee a revised list of primary nationalities and *narodnosti* as well as a secondary list of ethnographic groups and "small-numbered peoples." In comparison with 1939, the primary list contained a larger number of disaggregated categories, particularly in Crimea, Dagestan, and the Far North. Starovskii proposed that groups consigned to the secondary list of ethnographic groups and "small-numbered peoples," including most of the contested populations mentioned above, should be counted only in areas where there were concentrated communities. This was a victory for the republic leaderships. In Baku, Airums, Karapapakhs, Padars, and Shahsevans—many of whom had been counted in the 1926 census—never reappeared in Soviet Azerbaijan's public census reporting.

Starovskii did take issue with republic guidance concerning Adjarans in Georgia, however. Tbilisi wanted the category eliminated entirely, but he kept Adjarans on the primary list of nationalities due to Adjara's autonomous status in Georgia, reinforcing linkages between territorial status and national recognition that had been murky up to this point. In the 1939 census, when Ossetians and Abkhazians—who also had autonomous status in Georgia— were categorized separately in the census, Adjarans were merged into the Georgian nation, reflecting perhaps a differentiated appraisal of religious and linguistic differences in the republic and, more broadly, in Soviet definitions of nationhood.[37] By taking this stand, Starovskii thus proposed to reintroduce a separate Adjaran category to Georgian census reporting. As is discussed in more detail later, Starovskii's decision was overturned in practice, with officials reporting after the 1959 census that Adjarans had once again been counted as part the Georgian nation.

There is no comparable debate about Talysh categorization in available archival records in Moscow and Baku. Archival records from the Academy of Sciences and the Central Statistical Administration in Moscow show that the Talysh category was included on all draft lists of nationalities in 1957 and 1958, as well as in the official pamphlet that the Administration produced in 1959 to guide the processing of census materials.[38] That is, all indications from Moscow were that Talyshes would be counted and enumerated separately in the census. This makes sense: pre-census disputes revolved around the reintroduction of nationalities eliminated in the 1939 census, but Talyshes had been tallied in every census to this point.

The Talysh category, then, appears to have been expunged after ethnographers drafted the list of official nationalities, most likely when the census was underway in Azerbaijan. This is consistent with the claim of republican officials that Talyshes all self-identified as Azerbaijanis, thus rendering their separate categorization irrelevant.[39] As evidence, Azerbaijan SSR census officials produced records showing that all residents—old and young, male and female, literate and illiterate—in places with well-known Talysh communities were Azerbaijani by nationality and, for the most part, native speakers of the Azerbaijani language.[40] In a sample household from Kargalan, for example, a 76-year-old literate man, his illiterate wife, aged 55, and their 29-year-old son, who had not advanced beyond a secondary school education, were all identified as Azerbaijani-speaking Azerbaijanis. All of their neighbors were characterized in the same way. The various shades of ink and writing styles on this census form and many others reinforce the stories that people tell about their experiences with census-takers: different census workers and officials filled out different sections of this form, possibly at different times and in different locations.[41]

Census records can never capture all the nuances of personal identity, including in the USSR where factors of language, ethnicity, and regional identification were so complex, yet, read critically, they help explain how the state used bureaucratic procedures to delimit Soviet diversity. Census officials' claim that all but eighty-five Talyshes stopped identifying as such in the span of twenty years is not surprising in and of itself. As discussed previously, minorities from many communities have detailed the ways that census workers refused minority self-identifications in favor of titular categorizations. Official lists of nationalities meant little when census workers came knocking on the doors—if they came at all—as it was believed local officials had long since decided which national designations were and were not allowed in each community. The Talyshes who were recorded that year in Azerbaijan appear to have been registered mostly in settlements far away from the southern regions that had concentrated Talysh communities. Five Talyshes, for example, were counted in Khachmaz and Qusar, northern areas of the republic bordering Dagestan.[42] Maybe the decision that Talyshes no longer existed did not make it to census workers there, or perhaps Talyshes were perceived as less threatening in small numbers.

Talyshes: Survivals in Soviet Modernity

There were different components of national erasure in the Soviet Union. After the Talysh nationality category was excluded from census reporting, scholars who played an important part in explaining ethnohistorical change in the USSR sought to understand and justify what had happened. The work that some of them produced on the subject of Talysh assimilation was ultimately used to substantiate Talyshes' remarkable transformation and communicated to the public through a variety of means, including encyclopedias, textbooks, and maps. This was not a smooth or uncontested process, however. For some time, there had been a difference of opinion in the scholarly community about the relationship between Talyshes and their Turkic neighbors. These conversations shifted after the Bolshevik Revolution and again after the 1959 census, but ethnographers and others continued to debate the meaning and significance of Talysh census data long after Talyshes were assimilated into the Azerbaijani nation.

Imperial Russian Ethnographic Categorizations of Talyshes

As the Russian Empire expanded to the south, the South Caucasus increasingly hosted specialists who were affiliated with the Russian Academy of Sciences and had been instructed to gather statistical, ethnographic, linguistic, geographic, political, cultural, social, and economic data about the places and peoples in this region. This interest grew over the late eighteenth century, but significantly increased after the 1813 Treaty of Gulistan and the 1828 Treaty of Turkmenchay which ended the Russo-Persian wars of the early nineteenth century and brought much of contemporary Armenia and Azerbaijan into the Russian Empire. Another significant shift in activity followed the establishment of a regional branch of the newly formed Imperial Russian Geographical Society in Tiflis (now Tbilisi) in the 1850s. Scholars who studied the area generated knowledge, stereotypes, and assumptions about the people who inhabited Russia's new territorial acquisitions. Along with information produced by locals, their publications helped shape state policies and practices as bureaucrats in this ever-expanding empire fumbled their way toward familiarity with newly conquered places and populations.[43]

Ethnographers affiliated with the Academy of Sciences and Geographical Society consistently described Talyshes as part of the Persian world. The 1888 *Caucasus Calendar*, for example, emphasized that the Talysh language was a dialect of Persian and classified Talyshes as part of the Indo-European (Aryan) family of the white race. The *Caucasus Calendar* was the Russian Empire's first ethnographic, statistical, and historical serial about the region and, while read locally, was also used by visitors to plan their trips to the region.[44] At the turn of the twentieth century, geographer and ethnographer Petr Petrovich Nadezhdin similarly noted that the 88,449 Persian-speaking Talyshes in the Baku province of the Russian Empire were closely related to inhabitants of the Gilan and Mazandaran regions of Iran.[45] On the one hand, these classifications make sense given the long history of Persian rule over Talysh communities, Talysh proximity to the Persian Empire, and the inclusion of the Talysh language in the Iranic language family. On the other, this latter point is particularly significant as it tells us something about the way in which dominant paradigms within Caucasus studies came to define how people in the empire and elsewhere understood, classified, and ordered the peoples who lived in this region. As Florian Mühlfried pointed out, philology played an oversized role in Caucasus studies at the time and forged enduring patterns in representations of the peoples who lived there, namely by linking ethnicity to language and propagating the notion that peoples speaking languages classified as part of language families indigenous to the Caucasus (i.e., Georgian, Avar, Lezgin, Abkhazian) had a greater claim to the region and "are more 'Caucasian' than others."[46]

Early Soviet Classifications of Talyshes

The 1920s brought another spate of ethnographic studies, undoubtedly inspired by the Bolshevik leadership's desire to know more about the people populating the porous border tenuously separating Azerbaijan from Gilan, where the Bolshevik–backed Soviet Socialist Republic of Gilan had just been overthrown.[47] Between 1920 and 1926, philologist and Eastern specialist (*vostokoved*) Nikolai Iakovlevich Marr, ethnographer Grigorii Filippovich Chursin, and philologist Boris Vsevolodovich Miller all published reports about Talyshes and the Talysh language. Their narratives differ in a number of ways from earlier reports. For one thing, these scholars addressed the question of whether Talyshes constituted their own nationality (that is, were they not only a distinct ethnic population but a people with their own national consciousness?). Second, their studies were overlaid with theorizing about Talysh ethnohistory and questions about Talyshes' relationship with their Turkic neighbors. Were similarities between them positive symbols of ethnohistorical development and cooperative relations or representative of Azeri chauvinism?

Georgian-born Marr's studies were published in 1920 and 1922, which was a time of transition for Azerbaijan. The Red Army invaded the Azerbaijan Democratic Republic (ADR) in April 1920, just before its second anniversary.[48] Although the ADR government claimed sovereignty over much of contemporary Azerbaijan, it contested the border claims of its neighbors and had a number of competitors for control of its own declared territory. It lost control of Baku for a while, plus governments based in Georgia and Dagestan disputed territories in the north, including the region stretching from Balakan to Qakh and northeastern areas around Qusar; Armenia claimed parts of Azerbaijan's west, including Karabakh; and the ADR's southern border with Iran was also in question. Lankaran and its surrounding regions hosted multiple ephemeral and fragile regimes during the ADR period, including the Provisional Military Dictatorship of Mughan, the Mughan Regional Administration, and an equally short-lived Mughan Soviet Republic. Socialist revolutionaries, Bolsheviks, Mensheviks, British soldiers led by General Lionel Dunsterville, ADR representatives, Russian and Ukrainian colonists, Turkish troops, General Denikin's Volunteer Army, Dashnak Armenians, and others pursued competing agendas in this chaotic time. In short, although the Red Army's defeat of the ADR brought Azerbaijan under Bolshevik influence, it remained a contested region and continued to absorb competing power plays.

It was in this turbulent moment that Marr released successive ethnographic publications. In 1920, he published a report on the Caucasus, and, in 1922, a study of Talyshes. The first one displayed significant continuity with imperial-era narratives, classified Talyshes as one of the indigenous Japhetic/Indo-European populations in the region, and emphasized their high level of "Iranization." This categorization also corresponded with his evolving Japhetic Theory on the origins of Indo-European languages.[49] In the 1922 publication, he again stressed that the Lankaran region was oriented more toward Iran than the Caucasus but also began to "root" Talyshes on the Soviet side of the border by identifying them as a part of the Soviet family of nationalities and

FIGURE 13. "Talysh woman in national costume," Khamosham (Xamoşam), Lankaran (Lənkəran) region, 1920s. Courtesy of the Archive of Atiga Izmailova.

speculating about their national psychological orientation toward the Caucasus.[50] To support this theory, he emphasized Talysh relations with local "Azerbaijani-Turks" (conjecturing that Talyshes had perhaps experienced some degree of "Turkification") and discussed traits Talyshes shared with other Japhetic peoples in the Caucasus.[51]

Chursin and Miller engaged more explicitly with the prospect of Talysh nationhood. In a general study of the Caucasus published in 1924, Chursin included a short section on Talyshes based on notes from a 1916 research trip. Like Marr, he classified Armenians, Kurds, Tats, Persians, and Talyshes as part of the Japhetic/Indo-European group. Estimating that 70,000 Talyshes lived in the "Talysh *krai*" of Azerbaijan, he identified them as the area's oldest inhabitants. Picking up where Marr left off in 1922, Chursin posited that Talyshes were gradually assimilating with "Azerbaijani Tiurks" due to their close proximity and the prominence of the "Azerbaijani dialect of the Turkish language" in intertribal dialogue.[52]

Similar to Marr, Chursin published a focused study of Talyshes shortly after releasing his general overview of the Caucasus region. This second piece, from 1926, sharply contradicted his first publication and its sanguine analysis of "Turkification." He had earlier discussed assimilatory processes in fairly neutral terms, but now attacked the "Turkification" of Talysh areas and blamed repressive practices for growing "Tiurk" influences there. Chursin also emphasized that Talyshes were indigenous to this area, unlike their Turkic neighbors who arrived through the Seljuk migrations of the twelfth century.[53] It was precisely this idea—that Azeris were disruptive and illegitimate outsiders displacing Azerbaijan's true indigenous cultures and communities—that Azerbaijani ethnogenesis scholars worked to discredit a few decades later.

Chursin also criticized decades of Talysh population statistics as "inaccurate and unreliable" and labeled the fluctuating number of Talyshes over time a "strange phenomenon."[54] Claiming that only mass death or dislocation could realistically cause such extreme demographic changes, he ruled out these explanations for this case. Noting instead that declines in Talysh population figures consistently correlated with increased numbers of "Tatars" or "Azerbaijani Tiurks" in population counts, he raised the issue of assimilatory pressures in this community. In an indication that Miller may have had something to do with his change of heart, Chursin endorsed Miller's estimate that 80,000 Talyshes lived in Soviet Azerbaijan.[55]

Why did Miller's opinion carry so much weight? Miller, a linguist from the Academy of Sciences who specialized in the northwestern branch of the Iranian language family (e.g., Talysh, Tat, and Kurdish), began his field research among Talyshes around the turn of the twentieth century and participated in the development of Soviet Talysh education and literary culture. When republic officials started supporting Talysh national cultural development in the late 1920s and 1930s, he helped craft a Talysh grammar book and dictionary and reviewed other publications, including a Talysh language textbook that Ahmedzade co-authored.[56] From this period until shortly before his death in 1956, however, he was critical of developments in Talysh regions and repeatedly denounced manipulated census surveys of Talysh communities. In 1926, for example, he labeled pre- and post-revolutionary statistics (in particular a 1921 Azerbaijan Central Statistical Administration report) "extremely imperfect," arguing that Tiurks were overrepresented in these surveys because Talysh villages were left out of the census or mislabeled as Tiurk when lowland Talyshes living along trade routes knew the Tiurk language.

Suspecting that state officials suppressed Talysh numbers to justify Tiurk power in the region, Miller further added that Talyshes were subjected to "involuntary Tiurkification" because they did not yet have a written language and thus had to use the Tiurk language in school and administrative contexts.[57] These criticisms clearly influenced Chursin, but they were also echoed in some state analyses of Talysh national cultural development. A 1931 Zakkraikom evaluation of national minority development in Azerbaijan similarly criticized the national cultural conditions in Talysh communities and concluded that their lack of an alphabet forced them to study in Tiurk-language schools, which, ultimately, "compelled [zastavilo] them to assimilate."[58]

Miller's 1953 publication Talyshskii iazyk (Talysh language) was the last substantive study of Talyshes prior to the 1959 census, and its themes were consistent with his previous works. He classified Talyshes' as an Iranian narodnost' and again disparaged census reports, this time singling out the 1931 Soviet Azerbaijan census. It registered 89,398 Talyshes in the republic but, according to Miller, was still inaccurate because the 11,688 residents of Lankaran city were all listed as Azerbaijani.[59] Miller acknowledged that many Talyshes (especially men) knew the Azerbaijani language and shared some cultural practices with them because of the "intensive process of socialist construction" underway in the republic, but he also clearly portrayed Talyshes and Azerbaijanis as distinct national communities. In other words, in his evaluation, language use was not the prevailing determinant of ethnic orientation.[60]

Prior to 1959, then, ethnographers and philologists studying Talyshes in the Soviet Union often noted shared linguistic and cultural practices among Talyshes and "Tiurks," but had differing opinions about what this signified. Did inconsistent census reporting mean that Talyshes were being suppressed to feed Azerbaijani chauvinism? Could Turkic influences in Talysh communities be explained as a natural development among neighboring peoples or were they evidence of "involuntary Tiurkification"? After the 1959 census, more scholars embraced the concept of Talysh *sliianie* with Azerbaijanis, but some continued to ask questions about what assimilation meant in the Soviet Union and how it could be measured.

The Discursive Erasure of Talyshes

After the 1959 census, a new scientific description of Talysh assimilation started to coalesce. This new narrative justified the disappearance of this large population, which, unlike some other Soviet nations, had not been denounced as an enemy nation or sent into mass exile.[61] The explanation had two main parts. First, although ethnographers and others identified the process that Talyshes were experiencing as assimilation, they rarely used the term. Instead, Talyshes were described as having merged or fused with the Azerbaijani nation (*sblizhenie* or *sliianie*). Second, when scholars or officials mentioned the census, they reproduced the stock explanation that census officials stopped categorizing and counting Talyshes because all Talyshes self-identified as Azerbaijani. For example, in a 1970 publication touting the diversity of languages spoken in the USSR, the linguist Magomed Izmailovich Isaev included Talyshes in the Iranian language section, but also clarified that "Talyshes consolidated with the Azerbaijanis into one socialist nation (*natsiia*). They are entirely bilingual and at the time of the census in 1959 called themselves Azerbaijani."[62]

Transcripts of Azerbaijani ethnographer Atiga Izmailova's discussions with her supervisors about her 1964 dissertation, "The Socialist Transformation of the Economy, Culture, and Way of Life of the Talysh," shed light on how the narrative of Talysh assimilation was crafted and the instrumental uses of Soviet ethnographers and their publications in this process. Izmailova's project is a rare example of substantive research and writing about Talyshes after 1959. In a March 1964 meeting of the Caucasus sector at the Institute of Ethnography in Moscow about Izmailova's upcoming dissertation defense, the ethnographer Veniamin Pavlovich Kobychev, who specialized in ethnogenesis and ethnic history in the Caucasus, advised Izmailova to strengthen her theoretical discussion of Talysh *sliianie* with Azerbaijanis in the final version of her thesis.[63] Valentin Konstantinovich Gardanov, who led the Caucasus sector at the Institute of Ethnography in Moscow from 1961 to 1985, similarly emphasized to Izmailova that the main thrust of the dissertation should be the *sliianie* of a small *narod* with a big one and that she needed to show how "the process of the *sliianie* of the Talysh with the Azerbaijanis began before the revolution and continued more intensively in the Soviet period."[64] An extended timeline was necessary to make Talysh assimilation resemble a natural phenomenon rather than a manufactured or forced process of ethnohistorical change. At the meeting's end, the members of the Caucasus sector decided that Izmailova could proceed to her defense after she had incorporated revisions that clearly demarcated the historical periods of the *sliianie* of Talyshes and Azerbaijanis.[65]

Eight months later at her *kandidatskaia* defense in Moscow, Izmailova's examiners enthusiastically received her revised ethnography. Aleksandra Grigor'evna Trofimova, an ethnographer who specialized in Azerbaijan and had worked out of the Institute of History in Baku in the mid-1950s before moving to the Caucasus Sector at the Institute of Ethnography in Moscow, excitedly noted that the dissertation illustrated how the "very interesting process of the peaceful, voluntary, and quite natural" *sliianie* of the small Talysh *narodnost'* (which she describes elsewhere at the defense as "a backward and ignorant *narod* lost in a forgotten corner of Tsarist Russia") and the great neighboring Azerbaijani nation was occurring "literally before our very eyes."[66] Izmailova, meanwhile, noted that, although many people in the region still spoke Talysh and thus were bilingual, "they [nonetheless] consider themselves to be part of the Azerbaijani *narod*."[67]

Talysh bilingualism was one of the primary reasons why scholars at Izmailova's defense were so intrigued by the Talysh case. Gardanov commented that the Talysh region was one of the most interesting and important research sites in the Soviet Union because the ethnohistorical evolution of this population involved the *sliianie* of *narody* belonging to completely different language families: Turkic and Iranian.[68] This was a tremendous accomplishment, especially since Talyshes were constructed as a backward people, while Azerbaijanis were by now considered an advanced socialist nation. It was an example not just of two groups merging together but of assimilation (*assimiliatsiia*), that far rarer and more complicated process of ethnohistorical change. In fact, Gardanov argued that researchers like Izmailova had to carefully explain the rapidity with which Talyshes "completely disappeared" between the 1930s and 1959 because observers might otherwise be confused by what had happened.[69]

Azerbaijani historian and one-time director of the Institute of History at the Academy of Sciences in Baku Aliovsat Guliev stepped in to answer Gardanov's directive to Izmailova. Invoking Azerbaijani ethnogenesis theories that rooted the Azerbaijani nation in the ancient history of Soviet Azerbaijan and sought to create natural connections between the titular Azerbaijani nation and the many indigenous populations of the republic, Guliev explained to his Moscow-based colleagues that the ancient southern core of the Azerbaijani nation had spoken Azari (*Azəri*), a northwest Iranian language similar to the Talysh language. Then, after the Seljuk migrations, Turkic language influences began to spread in Talysh communities, drawing Talyshes and Azerbaijanis closer together. Thus, according to Guliev, Talysh assimilation into the Azerbaijani nation was both possible and natural because it started long before the Bolshevik Revolution (although he also credited the onset of Soviet power with speeding up the process).[70]

At several points in her dissertation defense, Izmailova discussed ethnographic specificities that continued to distinguish Talyshes from Azerbaijanis. *Assimiliatsiia* did not require Talyshes to abandon all Talysh particularities. The idea of Talysh assimilation meant that Talyshes had been subsumed by the modern Azerbaijani socialist nation and thus did not constitute a separate nationality, but an Azerbaijani person could still have Talysh ethnic origins. Talysh language and culture were thus portrayed as being on the cusp of fading away but still valuable. They spoke to the complexity of Talysh-Azerbaijani *sliianie* and could be invoked as evidence of the advantages Soviet modernization had bestowed on the Talysh people.

As Izmailova asserted toward the end of her defense, "They absolutely voluntarily called themselves Azerbaijani in the census. They consider themselves to be part of the Azerbaijani *narod*. Members of the younger generation even call themselves Azerbaijani." She pointed out that the older generation—those who still called themselves Talysh—were perhaps confused about their national consciousness and just as likely to claim that their national identity was Muslim. This explanation was no doubt meant to delegitimate the older generation by casting Talysh elders as so ignorant and backward that they identified themselves in pre-national religious terms. Here we get a sense of the way in which "Talyshes" who were not fully modern could be contrasted with progressive Azerbaijanis of Talysh descent who were integrated into present-day Soviet culture.[71]

Ethnographers also juxtaposed the characteristics of nontitular peoples with those of the titular nationalities with which they were merging. There was, for example, the question of "survivals" in nontitular communities. Survivals were remnants of the past (i.e., anti-social behaviors or practices like theft, hooliganism, cosmopolitanism, nationalism, polygamy, and religious superstition) that persisted despite the victory of socialism in the USSR. According to ethnographer Sergei Alymov, the concept of survivals in Khrushchev-era ideological discourse could be used in a critical way to ask difficult questions about ongoing problems in contemporary Soviet life. Ethnographers, however, were also charged with studying these survivals and helping to eradicate them.[72]

Ethnographic discussions about "survivals" were not confined to descriptions of nontitular communities, but by this period there were variations in the way the concept was applied to nontitular and titular peoples.[73] National customs and traditions deemed "survivals" were valuable because Soviet policies could vanquish them and this, in turn, documented Soviet ethnohistorical progress.[74] Yet, while titular peoples could exhibit "backward" behaviors or practices, ethnographers termed those nationalities "modern" and "socialist," while portraying some nontitular *narody*—the people themselves, not just their customs or cultural characteristics—as isolated remnants of the past. The act of merging with the modern socialist titular nations in the republics where they lived supposedly broke these nontitular populations out of the harmful, dark seclusion that previously defined their existence. In this way, titular communities served as a bridge between these "backward" peoples and a brighter Soviet future.[75] Thus, although some Talysh customs were considered outdated, cultural change was not thought to be normative for them. Talyshes who adopted modern dress and other new cultural forms were exalted as modern and progressive Azerbaijanis and contrasted with relatives and neighbors who still clung to outdated ways.[76]

Indeed, the concept of a modern Talysh person does not seem to exist in Soviet scientific and popular literature. A 1964 article by Izmailova on Talysh national dress is an example of this discourse. In the body of the article, Izmailova examined pre- and early-Soviet dress habits among Talysh women, men, and children, and contrasted these customs with the dress practices she observed several decades later during her fieldwork in Talysh communities. Subtle statements of ethnohistorical theory in the introduction and conclusion bookend this detailed description of Talysh dress culture. In the introduction, Izmailova explained that she studied old and modern clothes and observed how Soviet influences changed Talysh dress practices.[77] At the end, she argued that the principal elements of Talysh national dress resembled those found elsewhere in Azerbaijan and thus illustrated the close ties and mutual influences of Talyshes and Azerbaijanis. In this way, she subtly integrated Talysh dress culture into the narrative of Talysh-Azerbaijani *sblizhenie* that Guliev and others instructed her to develop in her dissertation. The Talysh adoption of modern dress forms thus became representative not of a modern Talysh Soviet culture or Talysh cultural change on its own but of Talyshes becoming Azerbaijanis, of their *sblizhenie* and movement toward a modern Azerbaijani community, culture, and identification under the auspices of the Soviet system.

The Soviet communist and U.S. capitalist models were diametrically opposed during the Cold War, but the Talysh case shows how a shared discourse of modernity could transcend political polarizations. As Bruno Latour argues, "'modern' is . . . doubly asymmetrical: it designates a break in the regular passage of time, and it designates a combat in which there are victors and van-

FIGURES 14 AND 15.   Much of Izmailova's ethnographic work explored national dress cultures in Azerbaijan, as well as labor and housing specificities. Her photographs depict similarities in modern dress practices across the republic, but also document traditional forms of national dress. The photo on the left shows a woman in national dress from the Astara village of Palikash (Pəlikəş) in the 1950s. The photo on the right, from the 1960s, shows women in modern dress from Kholmili (Xolmili) village in the Lankaran region. Courtesy of the Archive of Atiga Izmailova.

quished."[78] Some ethnographers, politicians, and ideologists insisted that the USSR managed its ethnic minorities fundamentally different from how the United States treated its indigenous populations, for example, but Talyshes, Pamiris, and other assimilated populations can also be seen as having been vanquished in a war the two nations fought, not with each other, but with pasts they saw as burdensome.

In her study of Indians in New England, Jean O'Brien shows how locally produced histories helped convince New Englanders that New England Indians had become extinct when they had not. She argues that narrative strategies used in these texts constructed Indians as unchanging symbols of the past that could not evolve into the modern present: "Even though non-Indians had Indian neighbors throughout the region, and even when they acknowledged that these neighbors were of Indian *descent*, they still denied that they were authentic Indians. A toxic brew of racial thinking—steeped in their understanding of history and culture—led them to deny the Indianness of Indians."[79] The 1959 disappearance of the Talysh nationality had its own particularities but was similarly understood and explained through a complex web of theories about ethnohistorical progress and modernity. Just as many New Englanders thought that Indians could only be ancient, in the Soviet imagination the modern Talysh person was Azerbaijani, the modern Pamiri was Tajik, and so on.[80]

In a model of ethnohistorical development reproduced throughout the Soviet Union, nontitular peoples were destined to merge into socialist titular nations, naturally or through the efforts of people and policies dedicated to effecting socialist progress. In this way, nontitular identifications were constructed as impediments to the modernity of the Soviet Union and its socialist nations. As one Talysh man explained, "They could never *see* us. When ethnographers came to Lankaran they had to say that we all called ourselves Azerbaijanis, but they never looked beyond that. They said that we had passed through one era and all that remained was to Russianize us. If everyone called himself or herself Azerbaijani then that meant that we were on the right path. There was no other way for us to be back then."[81]

The Debate about Nontitular Assimilation

Assimilation narratives were crafted around the erasure of minorities like Talyshes, but they emerged from contestation rather than from consensus. These debates show that the theory or policy of double assimilation could be invoked to support policies and arguments both for and against narratives of nontitular assimilation. A number of scholars challenged the notion that stark population declines in minority communities accurately documented historical progress among Soviet peoples. At a 1959 conference on building communism, ethnographer and statistician P. E. Terletskii took aim at republican officials over this issue. He was particularly frustrated that Pamiri peoples had been grouped with Tajiks and Mingrelians with Georgians in the 1959 census against the recommendation of ethnographers. Speaking directly to Tolstov, who was in the audience and had lobbied for a separate Pamiri category in the census, Terletskii ridiculed the idea that all Pamiris identified themselves as Tajiks and implied that local officials falsified these census results. As for the Georgian case, he argued that the Mingrelian population had declined drastically between the 1920s and 1959 (they were not delineated in the 1939 census) because of "high powered pressure" placed on statistical bodies, and concluded by saying: "I, as a statistician and ethnographer, ask myself this question: what sort of process is occurring, can this process be subsumed under the concept of the assimilation of Mingrelians with Georgians or under the concept of the consolidation of the Georgian nation? It seems to me that this process is non-existent . . . I cannot imagine that the number of Mingrelians has declined like this."[82]

Terletskii, Tolstov, and others who lodged complaints about the census and the assimilation narratives that started to coalesce after its completion were equally committed to the idea of ethnohistorical advancement but disagreed about what it looked like, the pace at which it was proceeding, and how it could be measured. Although most of Izmailova's examiners pressured her to deepen the case for Talysh assimilation, one of the ethnographers at the defense, Iakov Romanovich Vinnikov, who specialized in Turkmen studies, challenged Izmailova's observation that Talyshes had merged with Turkic Azerbaijanis despite still being oriented toward the Iranian language group.[83] Gardanov, who was fascinated by exactly this aspect of Izmailova's work, rebuked Vinnikov's criticism. Echoing Guliev's earlier point about Azerbaijani ethnogenesis, Gardanov reiterated that some ancient Azerbaijanis were also Iranian-speaking (the Media-Atropatene theory of Azerbaijani ethnogenesis) so ongoing Talysh language use in Talysh communities did not undermine the case for their assimilation into the Turkic Azerbaijani nationality.[84]

While Vinnikov was something of an outlier at Izmailova's defense, some of his other colleagues were also skeptical about the narratives coalescing around the Talysh case. Solomon Il'ich Bruk and Viktor Ivanovich Kozlov raised similar theoretical concerns a few years later when they criticized Talysh assimilation in a 1967 article in *Sovetskaia etnografiia* (*Soviet Ethnography*) about the upcoming 1970 census. Bruk and Kozlov regularly consulted with the Central Statistical Administration on census design and the national composition of the Soviet Union. Just after Bruk became the deputy director of the Institute of Ethnography in 1966, they published this article detailing several ways to improve the census. As part of this discussion, they denounced the disappearance of the Talysh nationality in Azerbaijan and the Pamiri peoples in Tajikistan, arguing that Talysh and Pamiri erasure displayed little coherence with Soviet theories of ethnohistorical evolution and that neither consolidation nor assimilation were viable explanations for what had happened to these national communities.

Bruk and Kozlov pointed out that assimilation should start with linguistic assimilation, but the 1959 census recorded more than 10,000 Talysh-language speakers and more than 40,000 Pamiri-language speakers. Consolidation, the other model, was also the wrong paradigm for the Talysh case because the Iranian Talysh language and Turkic Azerbaijani language were in different language families.[85] They concluded that the Talysh and Pamiri categories had been erased from census categorization by census workers who interfered in the collection and reporting of population data. They attributed some of these workers' errors to innocent terminological and instructional misunderstandings and mistakes, but Bruk and Kozlov also determined that some census workers purposefully assimilated distinct *narodnosti* into titular nationalities in order to "portray their region as more ethnically homogenous, and their *natsiia* or *narodnost'* [as] more consolidated than it actually is."[86]

Debates about census assimilations and ethnohistorical change also played out in ethnographic maps produced at this time. At Izmailova's defense in 1964, Trofimova discussed the erasure of Talyshes from Soviet ethnographic maps in a matter of fact manner, as though this would certainly happen, given the 1959 census findings and Izmailova's detailed explanation of their assimilation.[87] Talysh visibility in Soviet ethnographic maps did progressively diminish after the census, but they did not entirely disappear as Trofimova predicted. Bruk led a team (including Vinnikov, Kozlov, and V. V. Andrianov) to design one of the first post-census ethnographic maps. These scholars linked their 1962 map to 1959 census data, but also challenged this source by including a large area of Talysh settlement in southeastern Azerbaijan. This meant that their map more closely resembled maps produced prior to the census than those that would follow it. Yet this map, like many other ethnographic maps, in claiming to represent the diversity of the Soviet Union flattened the communities that lay within its borders; these ethnocartographers carefully included Russian communities located in the Talysh zone, but left out numerous Azeri settlements in the area.[88]

Was this a type of countermapping? Did Bruk and his colleagues consciously demarcate a dominant Talysh space to subvert the emerging Talysh assimilation narrative? Soviet ethnographic maps were often based on census data, but they should be analyzed as argumentative sites rather than as illustrations of statistical data. Indeed, Bruk and Kozlov asserted as much in a 1963 article they coauthored with M. G. Levin. In this piece, they defined the discursive value of ethnographic mapping and proposed to create a new field of interrelated study: ethnogeography (*etnogeografiia*).[89]

Subsequent mapmakers either reduced the area demarcated as a homogeneous Talysh zone or entirely erased Talyshes from their ethnographic maps. This variance suggests that there was some room for cartographers to interpret census data and use maps to make their own arguments about Soviet ethnohistorical progress. For example, in the 1964 *Atlas of the Peoples of the World*, the Institute of Ethnography published a map that included a newly reimagined Talysh region that was split into two, with one half attributed solely to Talyshes and the other to a mixture of Talyshes, Azeris, and Russians. The Talysh presence was minimized, but they were still differentiated from their Turkic neighbors.[90] This split zone model persisted in cartographic representations of the region and is also found, for example, in a 1977 ethnographic map produced for the *Great Soviet Encyclopedia*. Bruk was again lead cartographer for this project.[91]

There were also cases, however, where mapmakers depicted Soviet republics—not just areas of those republics—as nearly homogeneous ethnographic spaces, a choice that necessitated more heavy-handed minority erasure. This was more common with small-scale maps that showed less detail in broad depictions of the entire Soviet Union, but was sometimes also the case for large-scale maps of smaller regions like the Caucasus. On a 1983 map, for example, the southeastern corner of Azerbaijan was portrayed as an area of Azerbaijani and Russian settlement with no Talyshes in sight.[92] Why did it matter that Talyshes, who once dominated ethnographic representations of this space, were left off of some maps after the 1959 census? Ethnographic maps were important not only for state officials and scholars engaged in mapmaking, ethnohistorical theorizing, and policymaking, but for everyday people as well. They were nuanced representations of Soviet ethnohistorical debates, but they were also visual sources more publicly accessible than articles published in academic journals. Maps like these tended to be printed in mediums designed for public consumption like school textbooks and encyclopedias.

Many Talyshes, Lezgins, Azeris, and others with whom I spoke specifically cited encyclopedias, maps, textbooks, newspapers, and other sources of public historical-ethnographic information as resources that bolstered or, alternately, undercut their self-identifications and sense of belonging in the republic where they lived. Talysh representation in maps was somewhat uneven after their 1959 census assimilation, thanks to the interventions of individual cartographers, but Talysh evolution was more linear in Soviet encyclopedias that were crafted according to directives from the highest levels of the Soviet state and Communist Party. In the 1926 publication of the *Granat Encyclopedic Dictionary*, Talyshes were described simply as an Iranian people living in the Talysh *oblast'* of the South Caucasus.[93] Twenty years later, the *Great Soviet Encyclopedia* similarly characterized them as members of the Iranian language family and indigenous inhabitants of northern Iran and the southeastern part of Azerbaijan alternately known as the Talysh region or the Lankaran region. This time, however, the encyclopedic entry had a slight modification, noting that Talysh communities also displayed clear Azerbaijani linguistic influences.[94] By the 1950s, their description was laden with ethnohistorical theorizing. According to the 1956 edition of the *Great Soviet Encyclopedia*, Talyshes were gradually fusing with Azerbaijanis and using the Azerbaijani language in schools, work, and literature. Although they had been an "oppressed national minority" in the Russian Empire, thanks to the Great October Socialist Revolution, they had sedentarized, undergone a socialist economic revolution, and developed a national intelligentsia. This last point was specifically juxtaposed with the condition of Talyshes in Iran, who, it was noted, still experienced feudal relations and preserved tribal "survivals."[95] By the 1976 version of this encyclopedia, the indigenous Talysh *narodnost'* had nearly completed its amalgamation (*slivat'sia*) with Azerbaijanis, with whom they now shared not only the Azerbaijani language, but also material and spiritual cultures. This, it was explained, was the reason why they were not included in the 1970 census.[96]

The erasure of the Talysh census category was a significant victory for proponents of assimilation and ethnohistorical progress in Azerbaijan and the Soviet Union more generally, but there were clearly differences of opinion about what this meant and how it happened. Bruk, Kozlov, Vinnikov, and some of their colleagues suspected that census officials manipulated data to achieve this drastic reduction in Talysh numbers. Ethnographers with whom I spoke echoed the sense that something was not quite right about narratives of natural assimilation in Azerbaijan's nontitular communities. When I first described my research about nationality practices and nontitular minorities in Soviet Azerbaijan to colleagues at the Institute of Ethnography in Moscow, one snorted with laughter while another, after shooting him a censuring look, sympathetically asked, "And how is that going for you?" In the subsequent discussion about ethnographic fieldwork, they described their own difficulties working in the Azerbaijan SSR and explained that since local officials frequently disrupted studies of minority communities there, they generally pursued other types of projects in the republic or relocated to other sites in the Caucasus. Lia Pireiko, a linguist from the Academy of Sciences who studied under Miller and began her academic career studying Talyshes in Astara, drew similar conclusions about national practices in the republic:

KG: After the 1959 census the Talysh population was listed as Azerbaijani.
PIREIKO: Well, so . . . yeah, they were assimilated. But there was always a policy there of assimilating the Talysh.
KG: Really?
PIREIKO: Well, yes.
KG: And you . . . what was it like?
PIREIKO: You felt it all the time. It just did not require any sort of special acknowledgment. Yes, all the time Azerbaijanis were inspired by this fixed idea that their *narod* was larger, that everyone was to assimilate . . .[97]

These questions were outside the scope of Pireiko's linguistic research, which culminated in the publication of a Talysh-Russian dictionary in the 1970s, but Moscow State University ethnographer Viktor Vladimirovich Karlov has clearly documented how local officials disrupted a survey project about ethnocultural and ethnosocial processes that he coordinated with the Institute of Ethnography in Baku in the mid-1980s.[98] In a 2010 interview, he offered the following anecdote about what happened when he tried to complete the survey in the Talysh area of the republic:

> We tried (although it was not always possible) to have interviewers of the same nationality as the respondents. And when we surveyed Talyshes, we involved the local intelligentsia—generally doctors and teachers. We had around ten to fifteen Talysh interviewers. At the briefing, when I explained how to fill out the survey, I suddenly was asked an unexpected question: "Here on the cover you have written nationality, and how should we write nationality? According to the passport, we are all Azerbaijanis, but in fact we are Talyshes, so are we a *narod* or not?" I answered, "Let's agree that when you approach someone, do not ask who he is according to documents, but rather which nationality he considers himself to belong to." The experiment failed miserably because in the end 100 percent of polled Talyshes identified as Azerbaijani on the questionnaire. But I attribute this to the fact that—and about this I am certain—after my briefing someone else instructed them how to answer. Because, from the side of the Azerbaijani authorities (*vlast'*), there was clearly a policy regarding the assimilation of the Talysh population.[99]

Many ethnographers who worked on the ground in Azerbaijan, as well as those observing it from afar, were familiar with—and at times cautiously critical of—assimilatory pressures in Talysh and other nontitular communities, but the Talysh category only returned to public census reporting in the midst of a broader political revolution in 1989. Some Moscow-based ethnographers like Kozlov exerted significant influence over census design, but their power also had clear limits. What else was going on? Given the debates that arose after the 1959 census, what tipped the scale in favor of narratives of Talysh assimilation?

Political Mechanisms Sustaining Assimilation?

Bruk, Kozlov, and others blamed republic officials for census manipulations, but is this explanation satisfactory? The homogenizing, nation-building impulses of the republic elite in the 1950s support accusations that they interfered in census outcomes, but it is doubtful that they could independently assimilate a large population without Kremlin approval. As we saw in the previous chapter, the leadership of the Azerbaijan SSR had the space to make bold political moves at this time, but they also faced repercussions when they made decisions that conflicted with Kremlin priorities. There is no evidence that this is what happened in this case. Mustafayev was dismissed in the summer of 1959, just after the census was conducted, but there is no mention of Talysh assimilation (or Talyshes for that matter) in available notes from the closed-door, frank discussions about his political errors. This suggests that someone in Moscow sanctioned Talysh assimilation either before or after the fact.[100]

The Talysh nationality category was the only one expunged for the first time in 1959, but comparing Talyshes with Adjarans and Pamiris offers some clues as to why Talyshes were assimilated. Consultants from the Institutes of Ethnography and Linguistics and the Central Statistical Administration planned for all three populations to be disaggregated in census reporting, but this did not happen because republic officials insisted that Talyshes identified as Azerbaijanis, Adjarans as Georgians, and Pamiris as Tajiks to census workers. Some Moscow-based ethnographers contested these assimilations, but did not find measurable success and all three populations were left out of public census reporting until 1989, when the Talysh category was reintroduced in Azerbaijan (Adjarans and Pamiris remained excluded).

What did these three national populations have in common? Talyshes, Adjarans, and Pamiris all lived along sensitive international borders and had co-ethnics across those borders. The Gorno-Badakhshan Autonomous Oblast', home to Pamiris in Tajikistan, bordered China and Afghanistan, and was narrowly separated from Pakistan by the Wakhan corridor. By the late 1950s, the Sino-Soviet divergence was intensifying, China still claimed parts of Gorno-Badakhshan, and Cold War competition was thriving in both Pakistan and Afghanistan. Because of strained Soviet-Turkish relations during World War II and Turkey's close postwar relationship with the United States, Adjarans experienced similar tensions in the border zone where they lived. The Turkish-Soviet border in Adjara was first sealed in the late 1930s; by the mid-1950s, it had been turned into an impermeable special border zone.[101]

Soviet Talyshes' ethnonational kin lived on the other side of an international border with Iran that long provoked concern among state leaders. Areas of the Azerbaijan SSR with large concentrations of Talyshes (Lankaran, Astara, Lerik, and Masallı) were also under a border security regime that was fortified by a *propusk* system requiring everyone entering and leaving the area to obtain advance permission. These types of surveillance practices developed deep cultures of control—and insecurity—that lingered long after they were formally ended. When I first arrived in Lankaran on an evening *marshrutka* from Baku in 2007, for example, I was walking toward the neighborhood where I planned to stay when a security official demanded that I show him my *propusk*. I eventually extracted myself from this situation, but this was only the first of many experiences there that recalled Soviet-era border security practices.

Talyshes also experienced waves of involuntary resettlement as state authorities sought to clear borderland areas of supposedly undesirable or untrustworthy persons. In the latter half of the 1930s, some Talyshes living along the border were deported from the republic or forcibly moved into cities.[102] Later, in the early 1950s, thousands of people in this area, mostly Talyshes, were involuntarily resettled to the Kura-Araks region of the AzSSR. In a "top secret" (*sov. sekretno*) document, Azerbaijan Minister of State Security S. Emel'ianov directed Chairman of the Azerbaijan Council of Ministers T. I. Kuliev to remove 165 families (409 people) who had moved to Masallı from Lerik and Yardımlı. Pursuant to an Azerbaijan SSR Sovmin decree from February 14, 1952, ordering the "Cleansing of border regions of the republic from antisocial, parasitic, and suspicious [*somnitel'nyi*] elements," he condemned these families for not having residence permits as well as for other faults such as unemployment and keeping their children home from school.

A few months later, in January 1953, Emel'ianov ordered another classified resettlement. This time, fifteen villages in the Bandasar sel'sovet (Astara region), including Unuz, Bandasar, Dilmadi, Armudi, and Vanabidzhar, were involuntarily incorporated into the Kura-Araks resettlement plan for that year.[103] The planned mass resettlement of Azeris from Armenia to the Kura-Araks region was clearly failing by this point so there was an economic need for new migrant pools, but Emel'ianov's request was rooted in security concerns rather than economic ones. In this document, also marked "top secret," he explained that they needed to transfer this population away from the border "primarily for operational reasons because many of the residents of these settlements have family ties in Iran, which greatly affects the protection of the state border." He later gave the same justification to Kuliev when he said that it was "essential" (*kraine neobkhodimo*) to resettle the inhabitants of the nearby Alasha, Qapıchımahalla, and Masjidmahalla villages (130 households in total) to "rear" areas of the Astara region (in military parlance "*tyl*" is commonly used to denote the rear as opposed to the frontline).[104] Emel'ianov's orders do

FIGURE 16. The Azerbaijan-Iran border area from which Talyshes were forcibly resettled. Author photo looking into Iran from Azerbaijan.

not specify the nationality of the people being moved, but he is singling out Talysh areas of rural Astara.

Had the assimilation of the Talysh border population simply been an example of republican overreach, it likely would have featured in Mustafayev's dismissal. Talyshes and other border communities like Adjarans and Pamiris also could have been easily reintroduced in subsequent censuses. The fact that it took Talyshes and their supporters decades of activism to bring the category back in the reform environment of 1989 encourages speculation. It seems likely that Khrushchev's administration sanctioned the assimilation of sensitive border minorities such as Talyshes to isolate them from their co-ethnics across the border and strengthen Soviet border security. In an era in which the violent excesses of the Stalin regime were no longer viable, this was a different way to pursue some of the same goals as earlier national deportations. But even if the impetus for border security ultimately came from Moscow or required Moscow's approval, minority assimilation was also in the interest of republic elites who bought into the idea of titular dominance in the republics and wanted to homogenize their populations. It seems quite likely then that Talysh assimilation represented the fulfillment of complementary objectives emanating from both Moscow and Baku.

The 1970s saw an increase in Talysh organizing around both the census question and cultural issues, such as the creation of Talysh folkloric ensembles. When I asked some of the people who participated in these activities what motivated their activism, they explicitly said that they were inspired by stories they had been told about Talysh books, schools, and passport designations. They also invoked the memory of Ahmedzade and other Talysh cultural figures who were repressed in the 1930s. This younger generation was thus shaped by those around them, as well as by a collective fear about Talysh organizing that grew out of the 1930s. For example, a woman from Astara explained that, "earlier there were Talysh classes and schools, but in 1937 they shot these teachers and poets. They shot them all as though they were nationalists, you understand. For this reason, everything was destroyed, everything!"[105] Ahmedzade's name in particular was passed down locally as an example of what had happened to "people who had been Talysh." One man recalled that in the 1990s he asked an elder who had known Ahmedzade why he opposed any sort of Talysh revival and the man replied: "They [the purges] scared me so much that I never again said the word 'Talysh.'"[106]

The fate of repressed cultural figures scared some Talyshes, but it inspired others. Long after Ahmedzade and other Talysh cultural figures were arrested and the Talysh language was removed from schools, some Talyshes drew on remembrances of the past to envision an alternate present.[107] Lacking state support for national cultural development, they protected the cultural markers of their own communities. They taught their children the Talysh language, singing songs and reciting Ahmedzade's poems when they were going to sleep or doing chores.[108] They shared old Talysh books with family, friends, and neighbors, and passed down stories. Some Talyshes, like those in the introduction to this chapter, wrote letters to state authorities, newspapers, and party officials requesting to be counted as Talysh and encouraged their family, friends, and neighbors to do the same.

It took years of protest—and the onset of *glasnost'*—for Talyshes to regain census recognition, but when it finally happened the people who had long waited for this change realized that it would only partially fulfill their dreams of rebuilding Talysh culture and community in Azerbaijan. On the cusp of the 1989 census, in the winter of 1988–1989, the journalist Murad Adzhiev traveled from Russia to the Talysh region of Azerbaijan for a piece he subsequently published in *Vokrug sveta* (*Around the World*)—a popular geographic magazine.

While there, he observed that Talyshes and Talysh culture were quite visible in Azerbaijan—his seatmates from Baku to Lankaran casually spoke Talysh on the train; he met people who identified as Azerbaijani but said their parents were Talysh; a group of Talyshes, afraid to speak openly with him during the day, snuck into his hotel one night to tell him about assimilatory pressures in their communities—but at the same time, he was repeatedly assured that Talyshes were "no more."[109]

In his article, he exhorted Talyshes to "say their name," but this was easier said than done. Now that the census category had been reintroduced, people who had agitated for this outcome realized that they still had to convince others to identify themselves to the state as Talysh. They discovered that many people were scared to register as such after decades of being told that it was not allowed and paralyzed by the uncertainty about potential consequences of going this route. Still others who possibly could register as Talysh, declined to do so because they considered themselves to be Azerbaijani, thought it was more advantageous to be registered as Azerbaijani, or at least saw no conflict with identifying themselves in this manner. Further, just because the category had been reintroduced, this did not mean that all relevant officials agreed with this decision. Conversations about this census, like previous censuses, generated stories about local officials categorizing people as Azerbaijani even though they identified themselves as something else.[110] Yet, even under these conditions, the 1989 all-Union Soviet census recorded 21,169 Talyshes in Azerbaijan—a steep increase from the eighty-five lonely Talyshes registered in 1959. State counts of Talyshes have increased since then; the 2009 census recogni.. Talyshes in Azerbaijan.[111]

Nonetheless, the myth of Talysh assimilation persists to this day. In 2012, for example, I gave a lecture at a university in the United States on the role of minorities in Azerbaijan's national imagination. Leading up to the event, the lecture announcement was circulated on a listserv for Azerbaijanis and Azerbaijani studies in which responding members missed my perhaps too subtle allusion to Benedict Anderson's imagined communities thesis and the broader point that all nations are constructed, instead interpreting the title of my talk to mean that I thought the Azerbaijani nation was somehow more artificial than other nations (which, no doubt, fed extant insecurities given the persistence of nationalist ethnogenesis battles in the Caucasus). They also concluded that, with my University of Michigan affiliation, I was likely from the Armenian Research Center in Dearborn or the "lion's den" of the University of Michigan's Armenian Program and thus could not possibly be "objective and neutral." I thus expected criticism at the event and, sure enough, a historian from Baku who attended let me know that I had gravely erred in my presentation. What was my mistake? I erroneously portrayed Talyshes as a separate people in Azerbaijan. According to her, Talyshes have never been developed enough to constitute their own nationality; they are Azerbaijanis and thus cannot be considered a minority or separate from the Azerbaijani nation.

While there are many other examples of this myth's persistence, James Minahan's 2004 book, *The Former Soviet Union's Diverse Peoples: A Reference Sourcebook*, is an illustrative one. Minahan explains the Talysh nationality category's reinstatement in the 1989 census this way:

> Soviet authorities, convinced that the Talysh in southern Azerbaijan had disappeared, did not try to count them in the censuses of 1970 or 1979 . . . in the late 1980s, during the liberalization of Soviet society, it became clear that at least a core of Talysh continued to cling to their ancient language and culture and refused to assimilate. The Gorbachev reforms allowed the Talysh to organize and recover their national identity . . . the local Soviet authorities, forced to count the Talysh as a separate ethnic group in the 1989 census, were surprised to find that 21,914 people in the region still stubbornly registered themselves as ethnic Talysh.[112]

My point in mentioning Minahan is not to analyze this "Sleeping Beauty" variant of Talysh nationalism. Others have convincingly critiqued that discourse in the Soviet context.[113] Minahan's argument that local officials were "convinced" that the Talysh had "disappeared" and thus were "surprised" to find them in 1989, instead illustrates the continuing relevance and power of old narratives developed to justify Talysh census erasure. He also frames the issue in familiar terms of modernity and survival; he notes that the Talyshes "clung" to their old ways, "refused" to assimilate, were "stubborn," and "forced" the hand of the Soviet authorities. Even after Talyshes regained census recognition, the old narratives attached to their "disappearance" did not go away.

The idea that Talyshes naturally, voluntarily, and completely assimilated into the Azerbaijani nationality became so hegemonic that it has obtained despite state-sanctioned data disproving it. What explains the power and persistence of this myth? Michael Taussig, drawing on Elias Canetti's assertion that "secrecy [is] the very core of power," writes that "Wherever there is power, there is secrecy, except it is not only secrecy that lies at the core of power, but public secrecy."[114] Though a public secret—*"that which is generally known, but cannot be articulated,"* as Taussig puts it—seems inherently paradoxical, these secrets bind together those who understand what is and is not to be known or spoken about.[115] Erasures of a people who never left like Talyshes functioned as a type of public secret in the Soviet Union. It was well known that censuses were manipulated and that Talyshes still existed, but the visibility of the state's narrative coupled with a pervasive fear of repression if one complained too loudly about assimilatory practices helped to sustain the official explanation of their disappearance.[116]

In Taussig's formulation, public secrets are reinforced by their visibility, which enables their use as a tool of social cohesiveness. In the fervor of *glasnost'*, Adzhiev used his platform at *Vokrug sveta* to amplify the voices of those Talyshes who snuck into his hotel room to unmask the public secret of Talysh assimilation. In a 1989 article and another published two years later, he exhorted Talyshes to embrace this identification and articulated how Soviet officials had used censuses, the school system, and media to manufacture the narrative of a completely voluntary and natural Talysh assimilation.[117] Given that so many people have disputed this myth of assimilation, why does it persist? Its exposure has not lead to its downfall because secrets like this are sustained by structural, symbolic, and everyday violence, as well as by the tension that is generated through a continuous cycle of suppression and revelation. Public secrets like Talysh assimilation are, after all, more pretense than secret, and revelations like Adzhiev's, Bruk's, and Kozlov's do not expose anything that is not already known.

CHAPTER 5

Minority Activism and Citizenship

> We love the languages of all the republics of our
> Soviet Union and their culture, why not love our
> language and our culture . . . Why with such
> bitterness do they forbid us from studying in our
> native language . . . Why do they close our schools
> and if someone dares to protect the native language or
> native school he suffers persecution and all sorts of
> coercion?
>
> —Anonymous Georgian-Ingiloi petitioner addressing
> Nikita Khrushchev in 1962[1]

During Khrushchev's term as first secretary, a
number of grassroots movements emerged, pressuring the party to honor
ascribed but long unfulfilled national rights. These movements, at times,
achieved some success. Chechens, Ingushes, and other deportees used letter
campaigns, work stoppages, demonstrations, and unauthorized migrations to
demand that they be allowed to leave their places of exile and return to their
homes in the Caucasus. By 1957, the CPSU had approved the repatriation of
exiled Chechens, Ingushes, Balkars, Karachays, and Kalmyks, and restored
their national autonomies.

Others met with a different response. Meskhetian Turks and Crimean Tatars, for example, also petitioned Khrushchev, his successors, and other high-
ranking officials for permission to return home and regain the rights that had
been stripped from them. After 1967, when Crimean Tatars' collective letters
with thousands of signatures helped achieve their rehabilitation but not the
right to obtain a *propiska* (residence permit), work, or purchase property in
Crimea, they continued their mobilizations and acts of protest, including unauthorized returns to Crimea (where they faced continuous harassment and
potential imprisonment for violating the passport regime), public demonstrations, and, in the case of Musa Mamut, self-immolation.[2] While these
acts raised their visibility, Crimean Tatars were only able to force the issue
when a general loosening of controls and reexamination of relevant policies

and practices in the late 1980s enabled their mass return, with or without permission.

While national movements linked to deportation cases have attracted some scholarly attention, nationality-based popular activism after Stalin's death extended beyond the exile paradigm.[3] Clearly factors other than the extreme conditions of deportation and the special settlement regime emboldened grassroots mobilization and national contention in the Soviet Union. A wide range of movements from Azerbaijan to Latvia and beyond embraced the flexibility of the Thaw to address both contravened national rights and the use of intimidation as a tool of social control. Political de-Stalinization and the Thaw affected how elites and everyday Soviet citizens conceptualized their rights, expressed demands, and engaged with the state. Elite voices were amplified and decisive in titular battles for greater power and prominence in the republics, but archived petitions and complaint letters from Azerbaijan indicate that these actors drew support from broad popular movements seeking to elevate titular nationalities and languages. It should be noted that these movements were comprised of a variety of people, not only those categorized as part of the titular nationality. There were also nontitular members of republic populations who considered the titular language to be their native language or supported it as a counterpoint to Russian dominance in the republics. Yet, while the titular identity of Azerbaijan consolidated in opposition to the perceived hegemony of the "Great Russian people," it also relied on the conceptual, linguistic, and demographic assimilation of peoples who had been demarcated as nontitular minorities in the early years of the Soviet Union.

The manufactured assimilation of Talyshes affirms historiographical assumptions that minority communities were inexorably in decline from the late 1930s onward, but the Talysh experience was not universal. Nearly simultaneous with Talysh erasure, other minority communities experienced new or renewed cultural investment and recognition in the Soviet Union. For example, after Stalin withdrew his support for the East Turkestan Republic, Soviet officials maintained interest in Uyghur and Kazakh affairs in China. Between 1954 and 1963, more than 100,000 Uyghurs and Kazakhs migrated from Xinjiang to Soviet Central Asia, attempting to evade violence and repressive policies linked to China's Great Leap Forward and efforts to populate Xinjiang with Han settlers.[4]

Their migration coincided with expanding Uyghur resources on the Soviet side. In 1949, the Kazakh Academy of Sciences in Almaty opened a Uyghur-Dungan cultural sector, which was soon renamed to encompass eastern studies more broadly. This was in line with contemporaneous efforts to expand area studies in other republics. Scholars affiliated with this sector studied

Uyghur and Dungan history and language, produced new native-language texts, and trained teachers to support the expansion of the Soviet Uyghur school network in the 1950s. If Uyghurs arriving from China stated a preference for Russian schools, Kazakh party officials pushed them toward these new Uyghur schools, mirroring earlier efforts to bind minorities to the schools matching their nationality and to create an image of Soviet national equality and development that could be geopolitically useful.[5]

Although one could argue that cases like this are unique because of their geopolitical and migratory contexts, they developed amidst ongoing conversations about what Leninist nationality ideals meant (and should mean) in everyday practice. In Azerbaijan, for example, some Lezgins and Georgian-Ingilois countered renewed titular nation-building efforts in the 1950s by fighting to expand their own national cultural resources. They couched their demands in the language of Leninist nationality politics, understanding it to represent the promise of national equality. At a time when some Azeris were complaining that Russian dominance constrained their national rights, these minority activists saw Azeri chauvinism as the greatest threat to the continuation of their own communities and identifications. Nontitular minorities who agitated for a restoration of lost national rights were motivated by the political opportunities offered by the Thaw, its renewal of the language of Leninism, and their experiences with the consolidation of titular cultural, social, and political authority—itself a product of this evolving political moment.

Moscow's changing attitude toward Baku at the close of the 1950s helped nontitular petitioners achieve rights gains, but these disgruntled minorities also drew support from kin republics that played an important role in their rights negotiations. Lezgins and Georgian-Ingilois in Azerbaijan were inspired and emboldened by the example of Lezgin rights in the Dagestan ASSR and Georgian national rights in the Georgian SSR. These republics also functioned as sites of national cultural incubation when support could not be found in Azerbaijan. Yet, these relationships were also complicated. Lezgins were one of several principal nationalities in Dagestan, generating a complex national-political landscape there. In the Georgian-Ingiloi case, meanwhile, their earlier conversion to Islam fostered ethnographic and political disputes that muddled relations between not only Christian and Muslim Georgian-Ingilois in Azerbaijan, but with the Georgian SSR as well.

Minorities in Azerbaijan lacking these Soviet kin republic ties generally experienced different national rights trajectories. In the case of minority peoples with international kin relations, these could be a significant hindrance rather than a help. For instance, Talysh and Kurdish connections to co-ethnics in Iran

and Turkey, combined with those states' physical proximity and Western part-
nerships, marked these minorities as potentially disloyal and were invoked to
justify their forced migration from border areas. This, along with the history
of Talysh and Kurdish efforts to achieve autonomy in Azerbaijan, negatively
affected their national cultural situation there. A movement for national recognition and rights expansion started in the 1950s among Kurds who had been
deported to Central Asia from the South Caucasus, but Talyshes and Kurds in
Azerbaijan struggled to regain recognition and form cohesive national movements like those that emerged among Georgian-Ingilois and Lezgins. Thus,
while some Talyshes, Kurds, and other minorities also pushed for recognition
of their national rights in the crucial decades after Stalin's death and concomi-
tant reforms, they found less traction than Georgian-Ingiloi and Lezgin
complainants.

This chapter draws heavily on oral history interviews I conducted as well
as complaint letters and petitions that were preserved and made available by
both people I interviewed and state archivists. Petitioning was commonplace
in Russian administrative and legal cultures before the Soviet period and has
long been a feature of historical analysis, but I use petitions differently than
many other Soviet scholars. In the imperial period, the differentiated-rights regime fostered a type of citizenship in which petitioning was a normal aspect
of the relationship between society and the state. A number of imperial historians have interpreted these petitions as evidence that individuals were entitled to negotiate with the state and empowered to help shape the meaning
of their rights.[6] Soviet historiography, however, is largely at odds with this approach. Because histories of Soviet citizenship focus mainly on the Stalin era,
historians have primarily explicated the many ways in which citizenship fell
short of universalized measures of citizenship and how its conferral or removal
functioned as tools of repression.[7] In this framework, Soviet-era petitions have
generally been read as evidence of nonviolent resistance to the Soviet regime
or of the failure of Soviet citizenship.[8]

In Azerbaijani historiography, meanwhile, historians frequently dismiss petitions and complaint letters from nontitular actors agitating for national
rights fulfillment as disingenuous or unreliable. For example, when Hasanli
writes about minority petitions, he either systematically discredits them (sometimes through misrepresentation of archival sources), dismisses them as un-
worthy of attention, "libelous," "cunning," and merely intended to "whip up
a ballyhoo," or ignores them entirely.[9] When he writes about Georgian schools
reopening in Georgian-Ingiloi communities, for instance, he replicates the arguments made by state officials in the 1950s that Georgian-Ingilois wanted to
study in Azerbaijani and that Ingilois and the Ingiloi language are ethnograph-

ically and linguistically more similar to Azeris and their language than to Georgians and the Georgian language. In so doing, Hasanli overlooks abundant archival evidence contradicting the state's position and flattens these communities, ignoring the range of opinions Georgian-Ingilois had about their relationship to Georgians and access to Georgian-language education.[10] In general, his handling of minority petitioners contrasts starkly with his portrayal of Azeri complainants, whom he consistently presents as sympathetic characters with justifiable grievances. This latter portrayal, notably, also reifies and essentializes Azeri groupness, equating it with a nationalist push to diminish Russian-as-Soviet influences in the republic.

Similarly, in the few weeks that I was allowed to work in the former party archive in Azerbaijan (I was denied access during later trips), the main archivist informed me that archived minority letters and petitions were proof of petitioners' and complainants' mental instability. As she repeatedly told me, my desire to view such documents was evidence that I was not a "real historian." Her subsequent actions highlighted the role that archivists can play in shaping historical narratives. At the end of my brief visit, when I submitted the list of documents that I hoped to copy, she expunged complaints, petitions, and letters from it, leaving me with mostly state-produced decrees and reports, as well as the notes that I had happened to take up to that point.

I take a different approach to these sources, finding that minority actors used petitions and other means of protest to challenge internal borders of citizenship and to gain (or regain) constitutionally guaranteed national rights that were violated by everyday practices. Although officials branded them as nationalists, hooligans, and mentally unstable, they displayed a contractual understanding of political life in the USSR and used sanctioned channels of protest to agitate for rights they theoretically already had but could not access.[11] For them, Soviet citizenship was not a zero-sum game in which rights were or were not fulfilled, but an open space that facilitated their demands. As Alexei Yurchak found for the Brezhnev period, "the fundamental values, ideals, and realities of socialist life . . . were of genuine importance [to many Soviet citizens], despite the fact that many of their everyday practices routinely transgressed, reinterpreted or refused certain norms and rules represented in the official ideology."[12] Acts that could be framed or understood as resistance by historians or, indeed, by state officials, were more often protests against specific experiences and practices than against the core ideals of the Soviet state.

Rather than measure Soviet citizenship as real, handicapped, or fictive in comparison to other models, I strive to judge it on its own merits.[13] Even when constitutional guarantees of economic, cultural, social, and political equality for all citizens, as well as affirmations of these rights in revered tracts by

Soviet leaders, were not upheld, their existence created possibilities for rights negotiation and contention. The disputes described in this chapter are testaments to nontitular investment in citizenship rights and to the promise of Leninist nationality politics. Their successes, meanwhile, affirm that national cultural investments were continuously evolving and being negotiated in both titular and minority communities, and that relations between Moscow and the republics and between minorities and co-ethnics were important variables in these negotiations.

Evolving Rights Debates

After the state dismantled much of the national cultural infrastructure in nontitular communities in the late 1930s, local residents, activists, academics, politicians, and others kept debating what these changes meant for these communities and contesting practices that violated their expectations of state-support for national rights and recognition. It often proved difficult, however, for people from minority communities to overturn official policies and informal practices that undercut their nontitular identifications. For example, some Lezgins in the Azerbaijan SSR in the late 1930s pushed for Lezgin autonomy and in the 1940s protested the practice of "Lezgi pulu," an informal tax levied against Lezgin students in Azerbaijan, but they were unable to leverage the relationships necessary to succeed in these low-level and sporadic rights negotiations.[14]

As the uneven contraction of resources in minority areas at the close of the 1930s showed, however, connections to elite networks and kin republics could bring greater resources to nontitular communities. Take Georgian-Ingilois as an example. When local officials closed Georgian-language schools and sectors in northern Azerbaijani villages during World War II, some Georgian-Ingilois protested. From his base in Tbilisi, Gamkharashvili sent letters to Stalin, Georgian Communist Party First Secretary Kandid Charkviani, and other Georgian politicians complaining about discriminatory practices in Azerbaijan and asking for the "Saingilo" region—Qakh, Balakan, and Zaqatala—to be transferred to the Georgian SSR. He even traveled to Moscow to petition Stalin in person.[15]

Charkviani, in turn, used the complaints that Gamkharashvili and other Georgian-Ingilois generated to justify his attempt to annex Azerbaijani territories. When this failed, he leveraged his relationships with Stalin and Beria to extract promises from Bagirov to improve living conditions and Georgian language and cultural resources in Georgian-Ingiloi villages.[16] Charkviani's in-

teractions with Gamkharashvili and successful interference in internal Azerbaijani affairs demonstrates the privileged relationship that Georgians and
Georgia had with the Kremlin during the Stalin years and the importance of
connections—whether laterally across republic borders or vertically to the
elite.

Stalin's attack on the Georgian leadership during the Mingrelian Affair of
1952, his death the following year, and the subsequent rise of new leaders in
the South Caucasus altered local power dynamics in the region. In his memoir, Charkviani alludes to dark times for Georgian-Ingilois after his removal
from power, perhaps referencing the closure of Georgian schools—in Tasmalı
and Zayam in 1954, in Aliabad in 1957, and in İtitala the following year—that
he had fought to open in Georgian-Ingiloi villages. It is certainly the case that
the dismantling of Beria's political network in the region broke some of the
links between Georgian-Ingiloi activists and sympathetic figures in the Georgian SSR government.

The party cadre who replaced them, including Khrushchev's client, Mzhvanadze, seems to have taken a different approach to the Georgian-Ingiloi issue. The party archive in Tbilisi is filled with Georgian-Ingiloi records from
the Charkviani era, but displays a precipitous decline in record-keeping from
1953 to 1972, when Mzhvanadze was first secretary of the Georgian Communist Party. This is not because letters stopped coming—Azerbaijani records
indicate that these school closures provoked a flurry of complaints to Tbilisi
and Baku in the 1950s and 1960s and that Tbilisi continued to participate in
some joint investigations of conditions in Georgian-Ingiloi villages—but perhaps reflects shifting priorities in Tbilisi that affected who engaged with these
complainants and what was preserved in the archives.[17] Generally speaking,
minority-authored letters and petitions were filed alongside state reports, decrees, and other paperwork that documented the state's response to petitioners. If Mzhvanadze employed different tactics to deal with Georgian-Ingiloi
complaints, this would have affected formal Georgian party engagement with
Georgian-Ingilois and their grievances.

In 1957, for example, an investigatory commission was sent to Aliabad after
people complained to the Council of Ministers in Baku and the Communist
Party Central Committees in both Baku and Tbilisi about the closure of the
Georgian secondary school there. Although representatives of Azerbaijan's
Central Committee, Council of Ministers, and Ministry of Enlightenment
(Minpros) all joined in this trip, the only participant from Tbilisi was the Georgian deputy minister of Minpros. A decade earlier Charkviani personally participated in investigatory trips to Saingilo, generating thick archival files full
of Georgian-Ingiloi complaints, his related communications with Moscow

(mostly with Beria) and his Azerbaijani counterparts, and reports on the situation in Georgian-Ingiloi areas of Azerbaijan. The Communist Party in Tbilisi, however, now took a different approach. No comparable file is available for this instance or for subsequent investigations carried out in Georgian-Ingiloi areas at this time. While the Georgian Minpros continued to document its engagement with Georgian educational initiatives and Georgian-Ingilois, it is clear that the Georgian Communist Party's relationships with Moscow, Baku, and Georgian-Ingilois had evolved and that Georgian-Ingiloi organizing had changed as well.

The Thaw created new opportunities for social organization and protest among dissatisfied nontitular minorities. In the 1950s, emboldened activists formed engaged grassroots movements that relied less on high-level connections to achieve results or shield members from local retribution. These movements took up many of the issues at the center of earlier battles, but also raised new ones and proposed specific demands suggesting how to improve the Georgian-Ingiloi situation in Azerbaijan. Preserved petitions and government reports not only document Georgian-Ingiloi frustration with the closure of their Georgian-language schools, but also a general perception that their communities were being discriminated against. They complained about a lack of Georgian radio broadcasts, newspapers, and movies in Azerbaijan; delayed electrification of Georgian-Ingiloi villages; poor employment opportunities for Georgian speakers; difficulty acquiring documents to pursue higher education opportunities in Georgia; limited access to butter, cheese, meat, sugar, and other food staples; poorly trained teachers in Georgian schools and sectors; and Georgian-Ingiloi underrepresentation in local government.[18] Even issues that were not strictly related to national rights, like economic concerns, were filtered through a national lens, with economic shortcomings clearly being interpreted as evidence of national bias or discrimination.

There is also a notable change in behavior among some complainants and activists who moved beyond letter writing to direct action. In one incident, Georgian-Ingiloi students who were enrolled in Georgian universities allegedly returned to Azerbaijan, entered a school in Aliabad, and tried to forcibly move Georgian-Ingiloi students in the Azerbaijani sector to the Georgian sector.[19] Petitioners were also bolder and more collectively organized. In contrast with the single-authored reports and letters from the previous decade, in the 1950s we start to see more communally produced documents originating from student dormitories in Tbilisi but also from Christian and Muslim Georgian-Ingiloi villages in Balakan, Zaqatala, and Qakh. In one collectively authored anonymous letter sent to Moscow from Zayam in the early 1960s, the authors noted that they were Muslim but considered themselves to be Georgians who had been deprived of access to Georgian-language resources and schools since 1944. Attacking government claims about the voluntary nature of Georgian school closures, they accused local officials of compelling Zayam villagers to sign letters requesting the conversion of their Georgian-language schools to Azerbaijani instruction.[20]

In oral history interviews, Georgian-Ingilois often praised Moscow for backing them and blamed republic and local officials for their travails. These interviewees agreed that there was support both for and against Azerbaijani-language learning in their communities, but they also detailed the ways that local officials pressured community members to support Georgian school closures. A man from Aliabad recalled:

> Azerbaijanis agitated among people in those villages [Zayam, Tasmalı, Marsan], saying: "Why do you study Georgian if you don't live in Georgia? You live in Azerbaijan and you have to become Tatars." One man who worked here [in Zaqatala region] came from Zayam and told us about what was happening in Zayam, Tasmalı, and Marsan . . . [The local officials] were afraid of Moscow and when [people] wrote something to Moscow they could be punished. If [people] hadn't written those letters no one [from our village] would speak Georgian now.[21]

Another interviewee from a Muslim village in the Qakh region argued that schools were closed in Zayam and Tasmalı right after Stalin's death because of pressure applied by both the Qakh regional committee and Baku. When asked if school closures were voluntary, he said, "That's a lie, it all came from above. İmam Mustafayev was the secretary of the Communist Party and he was from Qakh. He fought so that Georgian schools would close. It wasn't hard for him to find facilitators who would create petitions, collect signatures from a few people, and maybe then some would themselves write that they wanted Azerbaijani schools instead of Georgian ones. That's it."

Mustafayev's name came up in several conversations. Some Georgian-Ingilois believe that he focused on closing Georgian schools because he was from the Qakh region. This echoes similar claims from Lezgins in Qusar that Bagirov had a particular interest in assimilating them because he was from neighboring Quba. Mustafayev was a particularly sensitive topic among some Georgian-Ingilois, however. For example, in one long conversation, a man I spoke with claimed that Mustafayev was just an agronomist and had no involvement or interest in Georgian-language schooling matters. More than an hour later, when the conversation cycled back to school closures, I asked whether he thought it was a local initiative or an order from Baku. He answered, "I do not want to return to this question, you said the surname . . .

he knew, he was aware that all this was done, he led, in the truest sense, he led all of these issues. You know, right, who this was? The surname?"[22]

Petitioners agitating for Georgian schooling in Azerbaijan encountered resistance from local and republic officials but also from some of their neighbors. Many nontitular people in the republic supported, or at least did not object to, enrolling their children in Azerbaijani-language schools.[23] Preference among minorities for titular or Russian-language learning existed throughout the Soviet Union. In some cases, people categorized by the state or by others as part of a minority community identified more strongly with the titular nation or the Russian-language-defined Soviet community. Quite often, a person's preferred language or first language was not the one associated with their nationality. There were many Talyshes, for example, who were raised in Azerbaijani-speaking homes, Azeris in Russian-speaking homes, and so on. Indeed, just as these Georgian-Ingiloi petitioners agitated for greater disaggregation and more recognition of their national identification, there were others at this time who favored more unity among Soviet citizens and wanted to eliminate those categories and practices that preserved differences and ethnic particularism—including the nationality category that identified people as Jews, Russians, Ukrainians, Azerbaijanis, Uzbeks, Lezgins, and so on in Soviet passports.[24]

Many minorities also preferred titular or Russian-language schools because minority-language education could make it difficult for them to integrate into broader social contexts and because titular language knowledge was often linked to higher social status. As one Georgian-Ingiloi woman reminisced, "Every population has an elite group. My father's family was considered among this group and they always spoke Azerbaijani even though they were natives of Aliabad. I thus was sent to Azerbaijani school, although I learned Ingilo too because my mother would use it when she was upset with us kids."[25] Other interviewees explained that Azerbaijani-language knowledge was necessary to counter discriminatory practices. One woman described events such as local government meetings where the lack of accommodations for Georgian-speakers made it difficult to understand what was going on or participate. Several people referenced the limited employment opportunities for non-Azerbaijani-speakers.[26] Both of these issues grew more salient after the Baku leadership formalized Azerbaijani as the official language of the republic, increasing its use in official business and public spaces.

Through most of the 1950s, republic officials claimed that the local population overwhelmingly supported the closure of Georgian-language schools in their communities, not unlike Georgian officials in the 1940s who claimed the impetus to Georgianize schools in Abkhazia originated with Abkhazians themselves.[27] For example, in March 1959, the secretary of the Balakan Regional Committee, A. Mansurov, told Baku that residents and teachers from İtitala had demanded "the unmasking and punishing" of people who had signed a letter claiming that schools there were switched to Azerbaijani instruction against the will of the local population.[28] A few months later, when Azerbaijan Communist Party Secretary Bairamov responded to a Moscow query about school closures and Georgian-Ingiloi unrest, he similarly informed them that Georgian-Ingilois who objected to Azerbaijani-language schools were outliers and that the local community was "outraged" that these petitioners had "positioned themselves as 'defenders of their interests'" in complaint letters.[29]

The state's response to the Georgian-Ingiloi situation drastically changed after Khrushchev replaced Mustafayev as Azerbaijan's first party secretary in the summer of 1959. A recent decision to introduce mandatory Azerbaijani-language instruction to Georgian classrooms in Qakh-gürcü (Qakh-Georgian) village was immediately revoked. To justify this policy reversal, the now-chastened Azerbaijan Central Committee in Baku denounced the Qakh decision as "incorrect both in form and substance" and censured the local secretary for his "irresponsible" decision.[30] State and party inspectors subsequently began to produce more nuanced reports about national relations in the region and to take minority complaints more seriously, rather than automatically deny and downplay them.

An investigatory brigade—comprised of an Azerbaijan Communist Party secretary, the editor of *Bakinskii rabochii*, the head of the Azerbaijan Statistical Administration, and others from the republic's Ministries of Culture, Education, and Agriculture (but no one from the Georgian SSR)—arrived in the region that summer to scrutinize complaints about assimilatory pressures. The trip was clearly prompted by allegations of abuses of power and economic, political, social, and cultural discrimination against Georgian speakers in these communities, including an order banning Christian Georgian-Ingilois from pig farming. As seen in box 1, brigade members were tasked, among other duties, with verifying the national belonging of the Georgian-Ingiloi community (amid debates about whether they were Georgianized descendants of Albanians—and thus historically related to Azeris—or an ethnographic part of the Georgian nation), and evaluating the condition of monuments that could potentially root the Georgian-Ingiloi community in this territory.[31]

Over the next several years, officials repeatedly noted widespread agitation in Georgian-Ingiloi communities dating back to the 1954 decision to close Georgian schools in Muslim villages and acknowledged shortcomings in Georgian-language schools and sectors. In 1961, for example, Azerbaijan's Minister of Education M. Mexti-zade and R. Balayan from the republic's

Box 1: List of questions for the investigation of Qakh, Balakan, and Zaqatala Georgian-Ingiloi communities

1. Are Georgian collective farms and collective farmers in Kakhi [Qakh] having the best-cultivated lands for perennials such as vineyards, orchards, and hazelnuts taken away from them, and are these areas being settled by people who come from other regions and do not work in the collective farms?

2. Did the regional executive committee in Qakh take land away from Georgian collective farms in 1957 and 1958, and was it suggested that Georgians move to other regions?

3. Is it true that executive committees in these regions do not allow Ingilo [Ingilo is often used interchangeably with Ingiloi] to be nominated to leadership positions in regional organizations?

4. When the local population was banned from breeding pigs, were "surplus" pigs confiscated without the collective farmers being paid in 1958 upon the order of Shikhi Mamedov, head of the Qakh regional executive committee?

5. Is it true that when the new highway was built from the Qakh bazaar to İlisu village, collective farmers' fruit trees and vineyards were cut down and they were not paid?

6. Under what circumstances were eight Georgian schools in Balakan, Zaqatala, and Qakh regions closed and transferred to the Azerbaijani language of instruction over the past five years?

7. Is it true that local authorities in these regions campaign among Ingiloi and forcibly closed Georgian schools in villages where the native language is Georgian?

8. Are bookstores in Qakh and Aliabad banned from selling schoolbooks in the Georgian language?

9. What is the situation regarding radio broadcasts in Georgian in these regions, are there lectures and concerts in the Georgian language, are there Georgian-language books, magazines, and newspapers in libraries and reading rooms?

10. What is the condition of historical monuments in these regions?

11. Have mistakes been made in the determination of Ingiloi national belonging [nationality]?

12. Clarify a few issues connected with the history and ethnography of the regions.

Communist Party confirmed that a school director in Aliabad had underreported the number of Georgian students at his school and, as a result, it did not have enough teachers. They also implicated local officials in this director's "inappropriate proposals" to close the Georgian sector at his school.[32] Other reports referenced similar issues while corroborating parent interest in reopening Georgian schools. In a further indication of widespread discontent among Georgian-Ingilois, commissions were formed in both Azerbaijan and Georgia to inspect the schools and "remove existing resentment" in the area.[33]

After his visit in February 1961, Mexti-zade declared that real change was necessary. He proposed opening a Georgian sector in the Zaqatala boarding school (*internat*), offering parallel Azerbaijani and Georgian classes in İtitala, and closing Azerbaijani preparatory courses for children preparing to enter İtitala's school. His final recommendation was that an authoritative and productive commission might finally put an end to "unhealthy conversations on this issue."[34] That same year, a new Azerbaijan Communist Party decree— "About measures to improve the work regarding the coverage of schools of children of Ingilois in the Zaqatala, Belokan, and Qakh regions"—reversed formal efforts to close Georgian schools. The decree provided support for Georgian-language education and assured Georgian-Ingiloi parents of their right to choose the language of instruction for their children. By the 1962–1963 academic year, Azerbaijan's Minpros had opened new Georgian sectors in Muslim Georgian-Ingiloi villages, increased access to Georgian-language teachers, and sponsored Georgian cultural events such as movie screenings.[35] Indeed, a letter from Minpros to the Azerbaijan Central Committee in 1962 optimistically declared that, "inadequacies in the work of local organs on the question of the allocation of cadres, creation of groups and schools in the Georgian language, provision of teaching aids, etc., have been liquidated."[36]

Minpros school enrollment records are available in the Azerbaijan State Archive through the mid-1960s and indicate that declining enrollments in Georgian schools and sectors reversed after the 1961 decree. Yet archival sources also show that the Central Committee of the CPSU and the Azerbaijan

Table 5.1   Number of students enrolled in Georgian-language schools and sectors in Azerbaijan by academic year

YEAR	1953–1954	1955–1956	1956–1957	1958–1959	1959–1960	1960–1961	1961–1962	1962–1963	1964–1965	1965–1966
NO. OF STUDENTS	2,149	1,647	1,516	1,342	1,194	1,113	1,319	1,441	2,222	2,479

Source: ARPİİSSA 1.53.36.115 and ARDA 57.11.1868.1; 57.11.2140.1; 57.11.2326.1; 57.11.2419; 57.11.2499.1; 57.11.2670.1; 57.11.3084.1; 57.11.2040.2.

Communist Party continued to receive requests from Georgian-Ingilois for expanded business and trade opportunities, village electrification, kolkhoz assistance, and improved access to Georgian-language radio transmissions. As before, these petitioners argued that official decrees and policies were short-lived or undermined in practice. Letter writers claimed that Muslim Georgian-Ingilois were blocked from enrolling in Georgian schools in the Zaqatala region, that "wandering groups of fanatically minded Muslims" were disrupting the re-Georgianization of schools, and that Zaqatala and Balakan party and government officials were compelling villagers to enroll their children in Azerbaijani-language school sectors.[37]

The letters largely track with what I heard in interviews, where people often described feeling pressured to send their children to Azerbaijani-language schools and complained about Georgian cultural resources being underfunded and undersupplied. Kolkhoz brigade leaders, for example, were told that their jobs were contingent on sending their children to the Azerbaijani-language sector and making sure that other kolkhozniks followed suit.[38] Education officials also discouraged parents from enrolling their children in Georgian-language schools by denigrating those schools or emphasizing how important it was to know Azerbaijani. I had a lengthy conversation, for example, with a school inspector who had worked since the Soviet period in some of these Georgian-Ingiloi communities. The inspector detailed myriad ways in which parents were—subtly or not—"encouraged" to enroll their students in Azerbaijani-language sectors and schools, alleging that Georgian schools were purposefully kept understaffed, undersupplied, and poorly maintained so they would be less appealing.

In yet another sign of how sensitive this topic remains in contemporary Azerbaijan, particularly in minority areas, when I returned the next day to continue the conversation and collect promised information about other people with whom I could speak, the inspector, in a demonstrably loud voice (we were in a public space), greeted me as though we had never met and politely but firmly rebuffed my tentative attempt to resume our previous conversation. Someone had clearly intervened to stop further disclosures. This happened on a number of occasions. One day I would visit someone—sometimes just to socialize—and the next day they would find a way to tell me that they or their families had been threatened (usually via an anonymous phone call, sometimes through an unsigned note) and that they were sorry, but I should probably not visit them again.

In response to ongoing disquiet among Georgian-Ingilois, the Central Committee in Baku issued a follow-up decree in 1966 reaffirming the party's commitment to improving the material conditions of Georgian-language classrooms; acquiring textbooks and other literature from Georgia; providing opportunities for Georgian-Ingiloi students to enroll in post-secondary educational institutions outside the normal competition structures (in part to offset language issues during exams); and increasing ideological-political education to preclude future problems.[39] While officials clearly understood that there were ongoing problems in the region, state documents also show that they frequently blamed outside forces rather than themselves for these issues. In a report sent to the Central Committee in Baku in February 1966, for example, state officials linked a rise in complaint letters to visits from the "Shefskaia" commission, which was comprised of intellectuals from various institutes at the Georgian Academy of Sciences who sought to enhance Georgian-Ingiloi identification with the Georgian nation by distributing notebooks, textbooks, and other Georgian cultural materials in Azerbaijan's Georgian-Ingiloi villages and towns.[40] The officials also alleged that many of the Georgian-Ingiloi complaints were sent by the same people, implying they had a low level of support in their communities. In another state report on problems among Georgian-Ingilois, the author blamed "an insignificant group of Ingiloi students studying . . . in the Georgian SSR" and their Georgian "enablers" for stirring up nationalism in Georgian-Ingiloi communities.[41]

Azerbaijani officials were right that Georgian-Ingiloi students in Tbilisi played a conspicuous role in national rights agitation in the 1960s, but they were part of a broader grassroots movement that included people still living in Azerbaijan, and thus were not merely outsiders who had been radicalized in Georgian universities. It would also be a mistake to dismiss these university students as agents of Georgian nationalists just because they had connections to the Georgian SSR. To be sure, Georgian-Ingilois who studied in Tbilisi in the late 1950s and 1960s were living in a city that had just witnessed mass nationalist protests against Khrushchev's denunciation of Stalin. They were also steeped in an environment rich in Georgian cultural resources and found people there who supported their activism, including Gamkharashvili and others.[42] When I brought up the issue of Tbilisi-based activists directing Georgian-Ingiloi students in oral history interviews, one of the Muslim Georgian-Ingiloi petitioners lowered his voice and responded, "That big man, you know, he was the main organizer of all these things there."[43] Many of these students clearly knew Gamkharashvili and others, yet even this "big man" that my interviewee mentioned was, like Gamkharashvili, not a Georgian from Georgia, but a fellow villager who had made his way to Tbilisi and was involved in a range of Georgian diaspora affairs, including efforts to extend Georgian cultural resources to Fereydan Georgians in Iran. Further, university students weren't the only ones with connections to Georgia and Georgians. Georgian-Ingilois traveled to the neighboring republic for a variety of reasons, sometimes simply because it was the most convenient place to go shopping, to visit Tbilisi (which was significantly closer than Baku), to attend residential schools when Georgian was not taught in their home village, to see friends and family, to visit holy places, and, even, to work in *kolkhozes*.[44]

Georgia may have provided some Georgian-Ingilois with an environment in which they could envision an alternate reality for themselves, gather, and organize, but they were not mere puppets. As one petitioner recounted in an interview, he sincerely believed in the ascribed national rights articulated in *Marxism and the National Question* and the Soviet constitution. Indeed, he quoted freely from this text and from Soviet constitutional articles guaranteeing national equality. According to him, he expressed his own beliefs by rooting them in a language of legality and rights borrowed from the Soviet constitution, "Leninist nationality policy," and Khrushchev's call for a "return to socialist legality" in 1956.[45] Displaying reverence for the center and engagement with Soviet ideology, he blamed local officials for contravened national rights and was convinced that Moscow officials would intervene as soon as they found out what was happening in his community.[46] Routine transgressions of his national rights—and the fact that his situation remains precarious in post-Soviet Azerbaijan—have not destroyed his belief in Soviet ideals and his understanding of how things should work. We only managed to meet twice before he received an anonymous, threatening phone call that ended my visits to his home.

Georgian-Ingiloi grassroots activism bears a striking resemblance to what developed among Lezgins in the late 1950s. In the fall of 1959, Zabit Rizvanov, a Lezgin poet and native of the Qusar region, helped organize a movement there called Rik'in Gaf (Рикӏин Гаф), known as Serdechnoe Slovo (A Heartfelt Word) in Russian.[47] It was comprised mainly of writers, poets, musicians, and teachers who initially started meeting to discuss one another's creative works. Their circle quickly grew from nine to sixty-four members, and by the following year they had expanded the scope of their activities. They continued to develop their cultural works, but also now turned their attention to rehabilitating the Lezgin language and culture in Azerbaijan more broadly.[48] As one former participant recalled, they had decided that it was "necessary to re-establish their forfeited national rights."[49] Like Gamkharashvili, they petitioned local and republic-level officials, but also traveled to Moscow to present their demands to central authorities.

A year after the decree on Georgian-language schools in May 1961, the Azerbaijan Communist Party Central Committee adopted a parallel but scaled down decree for Lezgins, titled "About the improvement of cultural and everyday conditions for the population of Lezgin nationality, living in the Qusar region of the Azerbaijan SSR." The decree required the Azerbaijan Ministry of Enlightenment to organize Lezgin-language sectors in Qusar for grades one through four by September 1, 1962 and ordered the Ministry of Culture and publication agency to print pages of local newspapers in the Lezgin language, provide Lezgin newspapers from Dagestan, and create Lezgin ensembles and a theater in Qusar.[50] Given that previous Lezgin-language schools had closed more than two decades earlier, Minpros faced several logistical problems, not least of which was finding Lezgin-language textbooks and instructors who were qualified to teach in the Lezgin language. They initially acquired materials from Dagestan, but Rik'in Gaf members later helped produce local Lezgin educational resources, including the primary school text, *Lezgin Language* (Лезги чlал).[51] Another problem was fitting new class hours and another language into an already overloaded school curriculum. According to the schedules drawn up after the decree, language learning now took up so much time that mathematics and negligible amounts of arts and physical education provided the only variation in the academic week of young students.[52]

Lezgins also gained cultural capital in Azerbaijan from the rights campaign. Two months after the decree was signed in 1962, the first secretary of the Azerbaijan Writers' Union informed the Central Committee of the Azerbaijan Communist Party that he would incorporate Lezgin writers into the Union, open a branch in Qusar, and support the publication of poems, prose, and stories by Lezgins (publication language unspecified).[53] After several years' delay—and a rough start with the Dagestan Writers' Union, which scolded its Azerbaijani counterpart for lacking "elementary courtesy" (the Azerbaijan Union apparently sent the Lezgin files without any accompanying explanation)—A. Abu-Bakar from the Dagestan Writers' Union led a review in Makhachkala of Lezgin writers potentially qualified to join Azerbaijan's Writers' Union. The Dagestani union had to be involved in this process because it lacked the linguistic resources to evaluate Lezgin-language materials.

The February 1965 discussion in Makhachkala revealed that some Rik'in Gaf leaders, although marginalized in Azerbaijan, were already well known in Dagestan. Their work had been available there on radio and in print, including in the Dagestani newspaper *Kommunist*. Reviews of all but one writer were glowing. Izzet Sharifov, for example, was praised for his "sharp eye, observation, and the ability to distinguish between the beautiful and the ordinary."[54] Dagestani Writers' Union representatives ultimately recommended that the Azerbaijani Writers' Union admit Zabit Rizvanov, Iadullakh Shaidaev,

Niiamet Mamedaliev, and Sharifov and start publishing their poems, satires, stories, plays, and other works in Azerbaijan.[55]

As in the Georgian-Ingiloi case, the 1962 decree did not quell frustration among Lezgins in Azerbaijan who wanted even more national cultural support. After its adoption, Lezgins throughout the republic submitted requests to expand the scope of the decree beyond the Qusar region so they could also access Lezgin-language newspapers, radio, literature, theater, and schools in their communities. For example, in a handwritten note from Siyazan, a town roughly equidistant from Baku and the Dagestan border, a Siazanneft worker wrote, in Azerbaijani, that he could receive radio transmissions in Russian, Armenian, and Azerbaijani. He continued, "This is very good and makes us happy, but we would like it if it was possible to listen to transmissions in our native Lezgin language as well, and to read newspapers [in Lezgin], which would be printed in Baku."[56] In February 1963, a new commission visited Qusar to investigate ongoing Lezgin claims and ordered local party officials to conduct more political work among Lezgins and improve their cultural and economic life.

Frustrations persisted in these communities in part because the decrees of the 1960s expanded Lezgin and Georgian-Ingiloi national cultural infrastructure in the republic, which incidentally afforded them some recognition in the public sphere, but local officials easily found ways to undermine these new provisions. Both Lezgins and Georgian-Ingilois continued to protest their treatment in Azerbaijan in the years and decades after these decrees were implemented. In 1987, for instance, Moscow ordered the Azerbaijan Communist Party to investigate complaints from Lezgins in Qusar and Sumqayıt who wanted to unite with Lezgins in Dagestan and claimed that they were living in the territory of Lezgistan, which Azerbaijan unjustly controlled. The Lezgins in Qusar claimed that they were being neglected economically and had been prevented from enrolling their children in Russian and Lezgin schools. They also wanted to listen to Lezgin music on the radio and receive Lezgin newspapers. The Sumqayıt Lezgins, meanwhile, referenced constitutional rights guarantees before asking why Lezgins had to study in Azerbaijani and lacked cultural, artistic, educational, and literary support in the republic.[57]

The Azerbaijani officials who investigated these complaints for Moscow downplayed Lezgin grievances, but their responses indicate that the provisions created in the 1962 decree still dictated Lezgin rights in the republic, on paper if not in practice. Lezgins in Qusar (where Lezgins made up 87.8 percent of the population) reportedly could access once daily Lezgin radio broadcasts, one Lezgin-language page in the local newspaper, a Lezgin national theater, folkloric ensembles, and Lezgin-language classes in fifty-eight out of eighty-two local schools. Lezgins also made up 90 percent of the regional committee's no-menklatura. Even if Lezgin rights were supported and upheld in Qusar (which at least one of these letters indicates was not the case), in keeping with the regionally restricted nature of the decrees in the 1960s, significant Lezgin populations outside Qusar still lacked access Lezgin radio shows, schools, newspapers, and publications.[58]

Party officials in Moscow also investigated complaints about violated Georgian-Ingiloi rights in early 1987, but this time they sent one of their own rather than an Azerbaijani counterpart. Party secretary and then-candidate member of the Politburo (he became a full member a few months later) Alexander Nikolaevich Yakovlev ordered an inspector from the party's propaganda department, V. Iashin, to determine what was happening in these communities. Perhaps not surprisingly, the precipitating factor was letters of complaint sent from Georgia and, more specifically, from well-known Georgian writer Akaki Gelovani, who claimed that, as a Soviet writer, he could not stay silent about violations of both the socialist ethos and the brotherhood of nations. Gelovani's lengthy letter detailed a myriad of discriminatory acts against Georgian-Ingilois in Azerbaijan, but was also riddled with its own nationalist bias. Invoking the ethnogenesis battles so popular in the region, he explained to his intended CPSU Central Committee audience that Azeris were treating Georgian-Ingilois so poorly because they were jealous of Georgians' ancient culture—implying, of course, that Azeri culture was a more recent import.[59] In a later letter, he more explicitly exposed his own intolerance, complaining that Georgia was being overrun by Azeris, Armenians, Kurds, and Ossetians, as well as "Soviet Turks" from Central Asia. Accusing these "others" of raping Georgian girls and children, flooding into the republic, and harming ancient Georgia, he demanded, "Georgia needs to be saved."[60] In his mind, Georgia clearly belonged to Georgians.

Iashin nonetheless set off to investigate the Georgian-Ingiloi situation and confirmed many of Gelovani's claims. The Georgian-language school network established in the 1960s was still largely intact but undermined by schools in gross disrepair with unsanitary conditions, broken windows, no heating or sewer systems, rotten floors, no visual aids or provisions for receiving Georgian educational materials, and no support for teaching development. In Aliabad village, a significant Georgian-Ingiloi settlement in the Zaqatala region, only 200 out of 9,363 books in the local library were in Georgian and local government affairs were conducted only in Russian or Azerbaijani despite most people claiming to speak Georgian at home.

Concluding that local officials at best were uninterested in meeting the needs of Georgians and at worst had "rudely violated their legitimate interests,"

Iashin also criticized these officials for lying to him and for ignoring their responsibility to foster a "healthy internationalist atmosphere." What were some of his other discoveries? For one, local census figures were being manipulated. He estimated that there were more than 7,000 Ingilois in the area, but the census only registered 1,785 in 1970 and 224 in 1979. In Zaqatala, teachers told him that their settlement had more than 6,500 residents—the majority of them Georgian-Ingilois—but their census responses had been falsified. In by now familiar language, the region's first secretary claimed that low counts could be explained away by Georgian-Ingilois themselves demanding to be counted as Azerbaijanis. Qakh officials were also reportedly trying to merge Qakh-Ingilo village with Qakh city to dilute Georgian-Ingiloi demographic dominance there and close Georgian-language kolkhozes. In terms of political representation, Georgians in Qakh made up 17.2 percent of the local population but only 12 percent of the regional party organization. There were additionally only two Georgian members (out of fifty-four) of the police, one Georgian worker (out of eighteen) in the *raikom* (regional committee) party apparatus, and no Georgians heading administrative units of the regional executive committee.[61] In short, the decrees from the 1960s were still in force in Georgian-Ingiloi communities, but, as with the Lezgin example, this was not stopping local attempts to undercut them in practice. Speaking to this dynamic in the Soviet Union, one Talysh man reminded me, "Leninist nationality politics . . . there was such a thing, but what they said and what they did, it was not the same."[62]

It is productive to contrast the Lezgin experience with that of Georgian-Ingilois because viewing them alongside one another complicates charges of exceptionalism. Together, the two nearly simultaneous, separate movements illustrate how new forms of social organization gained currency in the Khrushchev era. The differences between the two are also informative, however. For example, although Lezgins far outnumbered Georgian-Ingilois in Azerbaijan, their activism achieved more limited results. One key explanatory variable is the kin-republic factor. Lezgin activists sometimes relocated to Dagestan for political or other reasons, but they never cultivated the level of political clout that Georgian benefactors brought to the Georgian-Ingiloi case early on.[63]

The Language of Dissent

The shift from fairly autonomous individual efforts to popular movements in the 1950s is one indication of how minority activism changed over time. Another is the language activists invoked in their petitions. I am not suggesting that there was a linear progression of writing styles or a sharp break between

Stalin- and post-Stalin-era petitions. Styles carried over, and contemporaneous petitioners often used overlapping strategies.[64] Nonetheless, there are some marked differences between available examples from the late-Stalin era and the Khrushchev and Brezhnev years. Letters written by Gamkharashvili and his contemporaries reflect many of the pre-Soviet tropes that scholars have identified in supplicant letters from the 1930s. Although their language was often submissive, a supplicant's relationship to power also implied the expectation of a social contract. Golfo Alexopoulos argues that there was a clear formula for rehabilitation at this time—demonstrate one's dedication and usefulness to the regime—but many ignored it in favor of a non-Soviet lamentation style of the "pathetic self," which also met with success.[65] Sheila Fitzpatrick has similarly analyzed 1930s letter writing to define what it meant to be a supplicant rather than a citizen. She contends that supplicants performed as subjects, construed authority figures as beloved fathers, and appealed for justice rather than rights.[66] Another tendency was for the writer to emphasize his or her "Soviet credentials" through an expository biography.

Gamkharashvili's numerous examples from the 1940s closely follow this supplicant pattern. His primary goal was to convince Moscow- and Georgia-based officials, particularly Stalin, that Azerbaijan unjustly controlled Georgian-Ingiloi territories and discriminated against that population. However, rather than invoke specific laws to argue that Georgian schools should be opened, Georgian-Ingiloi kolkhoz lands kept separate from Azerbaijani kolkhozes, or territories transferred between republics, Gamkharashvili made vague pronouncements about "injustice" and "prejudice" directed toward Georgian-Ingilois and the "rightness" of Georgian territorial annexation of Azerbaijani lands.[67] He occasionally referenced "Soviet law," the spirit of "Lenin and Stalin's teachings," and the "foundations of the Soviet constitution," but did not point to specific policies or laws.[68]

Further, he positioned himself—and his former neighbors—as supplicants begging for merciful help from the guardians of Georgian justice. In one passage he wrote: "Only my sincere desire to help my suffering countrymen, and to fulfill my duty to them, makes me again raise this tragic question of Georgians, who have mistakenly and wrongly found themselves outside Georgian Soviet control."[69] He pressed Charkviani and others for assistance by appealing to them as people "leading the lives of the Georgian tribe [plemen]."[70] His letters to Stalin reinforced this approach:

Knowing the exceptional burden of your varied and difficult government affairs, and given your extreme lack of free time, nevertheless please allow me to appeal to you with the request to set aside 20 minutes to acquaint you with the accompanying memorandum . . . The memorandum concerns the extremely abnormal and difficult life of Azerbaijani Georgians (Ingilo). The intolerableness of their situation deserves your attention . . . In the present historical period, only your personal intervention can correct their fate.[71]

Gamkharashvili also frequently described his biographical appropriateness for the task at hand, explaining that he was from Qakh, graduated from an institute in Moscow, and had since worked as an agronomist and university lecturer in Georgia.[72]

His style was echoed in contemporaneous Georgian-Ingiloi letters preserved in Georgian archives. Archil Dzhanashvili, for instance, also presented his biography and justified his qualifications as a petitioner—he was an "Ingiloi" from Qakh who worked as an academic in Tbilisi, but he regularly visited Saingilo for research and personal reasons. Praising the Stalin constitution and the successes of Soviet power, he assumed a deferential attitude in his lengthy appeals to Charkviani and other Georgian officials. For example, in one letter to Charkviani, he wrote,

> In the past I wanted to raise the question of the difficult life of the Ingilois to you, but I thought that maybe it was just my opinion and I was mistaken . . . but [given the situation] I decided to bring to your attention the factual material that I have in my possession and personal observations in the hope that this material would attract the attention of the heads of government organs to the intolerable situation of the Georgian population of Saingilo and would help create the type of environment in which cultural-economic prosperity realistically would be possible.[73]

Noting that Soviet power had brought improvements to the entire Soviet Union, he raised the issue of Saingilo, where, he argued, Ingilois experienced myriad economic and cultural shortcomings thanks to Azerbaijani officials.

Later petitions written by Georgian-Ingilois and Lezgins display some continuities with these earlier efforts, while also reflecting shifts in tone and argumentation. Available documents show that, from the Thaw onward, complainants more regularly emphasized the legal baseline of their claims to equality and used a direct, confident, and authoritative tone. Some of the phrases and words that appear across many of these letters and petitions include "illegal," "right," "law," references to violations of specific decrees and constitutional articles, examples of anti-Soviet and anti-Leninist nationality politics, defenses of the legality of writing petitions, and complaints about behaviors akin to the cult of personality criticized at the Twentieth Party Congress in 1956. Some Lezgin petitioners, for example, denounced the condemned Bagirov for his role in suppressing their national cultural development.

In one petition sent to the Soviet Minister of Culture in 1962, signatories from the Muslim Georgian-Ingiloi village Aliabad cited the 1961 decree while complaining about local officials who still refused to reopen Georgian schools:

> The current head of the [regional executive committee], Madiashov, in every way hinders the development of Georgian schools in our region. Despite the fact that there is a decree of the Central Committee of the Azerbaijan Communist Party from May 19,1961 about the restoration of Georgian schools in the villages where Georgian-Ingilo live, the regional leadership does not comply with this ruling. To this day, there is agitation against the admission of Georgian Muslim Ingilois to Georgian schools.[74]

In another long collective complaint from 1962, petitioners wrote, "We . . . call for the establishment of Leninist norms in both schools and in many other issues. Our demand is fully legal and one cannot consider it a dishonor or call it demagoguery."[75] Another individual petitioner from Aliabad requested help from Azerbaijan's new first secretary Vali Yusuf oglu Akhundov (Vəli Yusif oğlu Axundov) for the Ingiloi population, informing Akhundov that if he sent a commission and it found inconsistencies between his claims and the facts, then the petitioner was prepared to answer the commission with all of the applicable legal articles.[76]

Not only did Georgian-Ingiloi and Lezgin writers employ a legal language and invoke specific decrees, they occasionally denounced local officials by name, and never defined their subject position or marshaled their biographies to explain why they were compelling petitioners.[77] In a nineteen-page Rik'in Gaf letter, the authors cited multiple legal provisions, including an article from Azerbaijan's constitution that ensured national minorities in the republic "the right to free development and the use of their native language in their cultural and government activities."[78] In further contrast with Gamkharashvili and his contemporaries, there was a distinct lack of fawning supplicant language in these documents; rather, they addressed Khrushchev, Mzhvanadze, and Akhundov not as modern-day "benevolent tsars," but as "comrades" who were duty bound to protect the laws of the land. They were firm, but generally not aggressive.[79] One writer, for example, thanked Akhundov for his kind intervention with the 1962 decree, before launching into an explanation of why it was still insufficient.[80]

Definitions and uses of the concept of legal consciousness have been varied. Some have defined it narrowly as something that characterizes people in the legal profession who engage with legal theories and jurisprudence.[81] Others have invoked it to explain how law builds its own hegemony—that is, why people acquiesce to laws without overt violence forcing their compliance.[82] Still others focus on the courts, judicial processes, and other legal institutions to describe the belief that a judicial system will defend citizen rights and assist when violations of the law and its protective powers occur. How did Soviet citizens relate to the law in their actions and words? How did they understand and articulate their rights and entitlements? Soviet legal institutions had a limited scope; as William Pomeranz has pointed out, there were myriad sources of law, some of which were never published and thus knowable to the general public, and decrees both outnumbered laws and played a more significant role in governance. Rule of law was also weak in the sense that neither the head of the party nor the party itself necessarily recognized "absolute legal restraints" on them or their authority.[83] Yet this did not necessarily impede the development of legal consciousness among Soviet citizens. Not unlike courtroom lawyers, these Georgian-Ingilois and Lezgins used legal arguments (i.e., arguments based on constitutional articles, decrees, and precedent) to make their case and try to produce new norms and configurations. In so doing, they challenged the practices of local officials whom they understood to be in violation of Soviet law and ideology. They had expectations that the legal and political systems would guarantee meaningful and stable national rights. Quite clearly, they also believed that legal complaints could be challenged through the political hierarchy rather than through the courts.

Campaigns and the Thaw

Why did Georgian-Ingiloi and Lezgin grassroots movements emerge at nearly the same time and with such similar characteristics? Georgian-Ingiloi activism can be explained in part as a reaction to the rise of Azeri national consciousness and local events such as school closures after Stalin's death in the 1950s, but this does not explain why broad-based activism was possible. Further, that explanation does not take into account Lezgin petitioners. When I spoke with former members of Rik'in Gaf, they recalled that it formed at the same time the republican leadership was attempting to nationalize the republic (some cited in particular the 1956 Azerbaijani language constitutional amendment), but they did not have local flashpoints like school closures to rally around since Lezgin schools had been closed since the late 1930s. Cross-pollination between the movements is also an unsatisfactory explanation. Lezgins and Georgian-Ingilois who I spoke with, including many active petitioners, knew little if anything about one another's situation until I brought it up.[84]

The transformative influence of World War II cannot be overlooked. The war inculcated a sense of pride in the Soviet Union as well as a growing rights consciousness for both elites and everyday people.[85] According to Elena Zubkova, Soviet social psychology evolved during the war. While expectations of political liberalization were dashed afterward and political consciousness may not have changed right away, she argues that the population emerged from this experience less fearful than it once had been.[86] Many of the Georgian-Ingiloi and Lezgin activists were reared in this period. It was also the environment into which post-Stalin reforms were introduced, creating space for the bold to test the limits of the state's forbearance. In this way, they were not so different from those Azeris who were also experimenting with the boundaries of acceptable national behavior at this time.

Respondents often referenced Khrushchev when talking about why they or their neighbors decided to complain about proscribed national rights in their communities. Overall, the oral history interviews conveyed a generally negative impression of Khrushchev, with most people recalling crippling food shortages during his tenure. When I asked one respondent in Qusar whether Khrushchev had helped to build communism, he replied, "He became obsessed with that corn and at the end of the day everyone was hungry. You can't imagine the fight that would develop here over one sack of flour! They would give four families one bag of flour. I remember well that hard period."[87] An interviewee from Lerik similarly responded to a question about Khrushchev:

He messed up. In the Khrushchev period, the Soviet people starved . . . when I think of those years, I wonder how did we endure it? You've never seen such hunger. We never experienced such hunger, well, during the war, but in wartime . . . in war, everything is done for the war. And then when the war was over, then we said that we were advancing and developing, we talked like this. And then, all of a sudden, hunger! You understand? And we all suffered: not only Talyshes, not only Azerbaijanis, we all suffered.[88]

At the same time, however, many others—particularly those who participated in grassroots actions—acknowledged that Khrushchev's denunciation of Stalin and the regime's worst excesses fostered more open and direct engagement with the state. In this vein, one former Rik'in Gaf participant spoke to the strategic approach of group organizers:

When I joined the circle our goal was to establish lost rights, Lezgin language, culture, literature, and so on. But, well, when I joined I was very
young, you understand? And Rizvanov, the others, they were older, they
had finished the party school . . . We didn't discuss Khrushchev or ideological things, but they knew that the time was softer. After Stalin it was
good. At the time of Stalin nothing would have been possible.[89]

A former leader of Rik'in Gaf confirmed this impression:

In the Khrushchev period there was a little leverage, leverage that brought
some release. If it had been the Stalin period they would have put us all
in jail in one day! And in the Khrushchev period they didn't bother us as
much, it was a bit more free . . . democracy developed a little bit . . .
well, a type of democracy, which we used.[90]

A Muslim Georgian-speaker in Zaqatala similarly explained the rise of activism among Georgian-Ingilois in this period:

Then people could talk about their problems. There was a system like
this: If people from my village wanted to express their opinion, they
would write a letter to Baku. Then if there was no answer or reaction
they would address Moscow. If the letter would get to Moscow a special commission would be formed and would contact [them] via tele-
phone or some other way. They were interested in our problems.[91]

These sentiments are strikingly similar to the recollection of a Chechen speaking about unauthorized Chechen migration from Kazakhstan to Chechnya in
1956: "You have to grant it to Khrushchev, he didn't follow the old Russian policy of force, there was a real move at that time to get rid of the memory of
Stalin, and we exploited that."[92]

This is not to say there were no repercussions for national agitation—the
contours of the Thaw were ambiguous. When asked whether it was dangerous to agitate as they did in these post-reform decades, many former participants at first reflexively said no before describing the fears and problems they
experienced in the past or explaining this answer. Some of them initially responded in the negative because they did not consider post-Stalinist forms of
repression dangerous in comparison with Stalinist norms. Others defended
their answers by explaining how years of fear had conditioned their behavior.
One 80-year-old man, for example, told me that he had learned not to talk over
the years because talking could lead to arrest. According to him, everyone who
lived then knew what had happened but no one wanted to say anything. That
is, people were not lying if they told me they did not know something, they

were just keeping it to themselves. Others initially denied the risks involved in post-Stalinist agitation because they consider post-Soviet life to be more uncertain. Now that Baku is no longer afraid of Moscow, according to them, they have no protection from repression or help ameliorating inequalities. Indeed, for some people, memories of the Soviet past seem less threatening in the context of the post-Soviet present, where people's livelihoods, personal property, and personal safety, as well as their families, remain vulnerable. Indeed, threats and "consequences" often are extended to family members as a way of getting people to "cooperate." As one man stated, "Well, what can I say? What can I say today? Well, I can tell you, I can't say anything because they can fire me from my work or my son from where he works. This is something that happens regularly here."[93]

Despite these social factors, archives and oral histories are littered with evidence of low-level repression and arrests during and after the Thaw. Sometimes people openly referenced their fears. In one anonymous letter sent from a Georgian-Ingiloi community, the petitioner asked, "Why do they close our schools and if someone dares to protect the native language or native school he suffers persecution and all sorts of coercion?"[94] Other letter writers explained that they felt intimidated because people had been detained while trying to enroll students in Georgian schools in the Zaqatala region.[95] Because Moscow often forwarded these letters to republic officials with instructions to investigate and correct the situation, refusing to put one's name on a letter protected you if you were scared of Moscow, but also at home if those letters ended up in local hands. This fear frequently plays out in records related to investigations. In the summer of 1959, for example, the Central Statistical Administration oversaw a review of census procedures in Georgian-Ingiloi areas of Azerbaijan after receiving complaints from Georgian-Ingilois in Georgia, including Gamkharashvili, as well as others in Aliabad and elsewhere. The petitioners alleged that Georgian-Ingilois had incorrectly been categorized as Azerbaijani in the census. For example, a Georgian-Ingiloi man from Aliabad who helped conduct the census in Mosul informed the Administration that on the second day of census collection, the chairman of the Zaqatala Executive Committee and the secretary of the Aliabad Party Committee reprimanded the census workers, informing them that the inhabitants of Mosul were not Georgian-Ingilois but Azerbaijanis. They subsequently were instructed to scrap the census forms that had already been completed and fill out new ones so every resident of the village would be classified as Azerbaijani.[96]

The Administration in Moscow responded by ordering its Azerbaijani counterpart to follow up on these complaints and report back. The investigatory brigade was composed of workers from the Azerbaijan Central Statistical

Administration and local representatives—that is officials from the regions in question. They checked approximately six hundred homes in villages where "Georgians should have lived" and, as is common in these state reports, not a single person disagreed with how they had been characterized—including people who had been listed as Georgian. This latter finding should not have been surprising as Christian Georgian-Ingilois were usually categorized as Georgian in Soviet censuses and passports. The question should have been whether residents of Muslim Georgian-Ingiloi villages were categorized as such or whether they were all labeled Azerbaijani as these were the communities at the center of battles over Georgian-Ingilois' national orientation.

They further found no evidence that Mosul census workers had been unduly influenced by local authorities. Having been informed of these findings, the original complainants protested that people had been afraid to speak truthfully to the brigade because it was made up of local officials who intimidated them, but the Administration's response was that this could not have been the case. As evidence for this position, they pointed out that one of the census workers who had accused local authorities of improperly influencing the census in Mosul did not repeat these claims when confronted in person by the investigators.[97] This conclusion, however, was drawn despite this same census worker informing the Central Statistical Administration in Moscow that he told the investigators nothing happened because he was afraid of reprisals.[98] The Moscow-based officials, unable to convince these complainants that the census did not need to be retaken, turned to Mzhvanadze for advice, but it is not known how he responded.

A similar situation unfolded in 1988 when a group of Lezgins from Piral village in Qusar petitioned Moscow for the creation of an autonomous Lezgin republic in the RSFSR that would include northern Azerbaijani regions like Quba and Shaki. In making their argument, they detailed violations of their national rights in Azerbaijan, but also explained that they wanted to join Russia because the quality of life was better there than in Azerbaijan. The Azerbaijani officials who Moscow asked to investigate this manner downplayed these grievances in their report back to Moscow, explaining that some of the people who signed the letter told them they did not know what they were endorsing. Nonetheless, the Azerbaijani officials vaguely promised to attend to some of the social issues that generated the complaint.[99]

It is the case that some people did not know what they were signing or felt pressured to do so by their friends or family members—in one interview a Georgian-Ingiloi woman told me she sometimes signed letters she didn't read because she was bored or felt social pressure when she was traveling by bus to Tbilisi with other Georgian-Ingilois studying there—but it is also possible that these Piral villagers lied to the inspectors out of fear. I heard stories like this in interviews, where people explained that they had signed complaint letters and then tried to get out of trouble by claiming someone else had signed their name or they did not know what they were signing when confronted by local officials.

There are other concrete examples of repression in Lezgin areas. In interviews, several people declined to discuss Rik'in Gaf because they still considered the topic dangerous. One individual close to Rizvanov would not speak about the movement but did say that Rizvanov isolated himself from relatives and friends to protect them.[100] Another individual, who characterized the Khrushchev period as being softer, later explained how his association with Rik'in Gaf had derailed his career in Azerbaijan. That disclosure prompted a more serious reflection. He added, "There was, eh, repression did happen in 1962 . . . we wrote several letters to Moscow with requests for help, help in terms of supporting Lezgin culture, development of the national culture and literature of Lezgins. But several people didn't like this, you understand. Therefore, there were some difficult years then. I . . . I myself lived through a lot then."[101]

In these accounts of repression, people tend to blame local officials and place Moscow politicians in the role of arbitrators and guarantors of stability. Archival sources provide multiple examples, including telegrams in which Rik'in Gaf members asked Moscow to intervene and protect them from local officials who were pressuring or threatening them.[102] According to oral history sources, several group members left Azerbaijan out of fear or because they experienced some form of repression there, mostly ending up in Dagestan.[103] Rizvanov also addresses the question of repression in his written account of Rik'in Gaf:

> There were opponents to this process [of Lezgin national rights expansion] . . . All the participants were taken under control, their biographies were studied, quiet surveillance was established. Partly they . . . tried to find in [participants'] creative works, in their actions, in their conversations elements contradicting Soviet morality. They thus infringed on their rights as citizens . . . After interviews with workers from the KGB, many talented poets stopped their participation in "K'vat'al" meetings and several were completely scared off . . . [104]

Yet it was not just local officials in the Azerbaijan SSR who drew these sorts of complaints. In a letter sent in the mid-1970s, a Lezgin musician from Dagestan reported to Moscow that Lezgins needed their own autonomous *oblast'* in the RSFSR *or* in Azerbaijan because Avars and Dargins were repressing Lezgins in Dagestan to assert their own dominance in the republic. According to this petitioner, Lezgin cultural figures—including Rik'in Gaf members Bairam Salimov and Rizvanov—had recently been criticized at a Dagestan party plenum and the KGB had expelled some Lezgin students from Dagestan State University. He explained that he was writing his letter anonymously because otherwise it would be hard to live in Makhachkala, and also took care to write in a non-identifying style of penmanship.[105]

Blaming local authorities is a common trope in Soviet letter writing.[106] Petitioners of all kinds long recognized that pitting officials against one another and exploiting divisions among the powerful were effective strategies. In Lezgin and Georgian-Ingiloi rights campaigns this approach appears to have worked sometimes, as there are concrete examples of Moscow-based officials intervening on the petitioners' side and especially around the time that Khrushchev fell out with the Azerbaijani leadership in the late 1950s. At a time when harsh repression was a recent memory, and the potential for violence still felt very real, attacking specific officials who represented the government rather than directly criticizing the government or its policies could also be an effective means of shielding oneself from more severe consequences.[107]

How did the Thaw alter national relations in the republic? Even though they experienced low-level repression in Azerbaijan, minority interviewees explicitly cite it to explain why they felt empowered to do things they might not have done earlier. They were not the only national actors emboldened by the shifting political and social landscape, however. At least some of these nontitular rights advocates took action in response to Azerbaijan SSR officials taking advantage of somewhat relaxed central controls in the 1950s to implement nation-building measures aimed at promoting the role and status of the Azerbaijani language in the lives of all Soviet Azerbaijan residents. Both minorities and republic officials could do this work because the opening of Soviet society after Stalin's death had real meaning in everyday lives.

This chapter tells many stories. Nationality practices often looked different in different parts of the Soviet Union, and, sometimes, even within republics, but the core values and features of nationality policies that were developed at the start of the Soviet era—namely the discourse of equality, the organizational principle of ethnoterritorialism, and the development of select national languages, cadres, and cultures—remained central features of the Soviet system and markers of national status long after terms like *korenizatsiia* fell out of common use. This also meant that they were the battleground over which many national disputes continued to be fought. The limited space available for subrepublic minority cultural expression and development contracted in Azerbaijan as party and state officials worked to increase Azeri linguistic and cultural hege-mony in the republic. In this way, Georgian-Ingiloi and Lezgin rights activists were responding to titular nationalism, just as some of the people supporting Azerbaijani nation-building were reacting against Russian hegemony and mi-nority nationalism. While Georgian-Ingiloi and Lezgin movements made little headway immediately after Stalin's death, they gained some traction as Mos-cow and Baku's interests diverged at the close of the 1950s.

The chapter offers a deeper glimpse into the history of two nontitular mi-nority communities that through grassroots mobilization achieved re-newed—if still limited—access to national cultural support in the 1960s. In so doing, they relied less explicitly than earlier activists on the clout of sympa-thetic elites in a neighboring kin republic to give meaning to their ascribed rights. Charkviani's intervention on Gamkharashvili's behalf resulted in an inter-republic agreement and temporary reversals of national practices in Georgian-Ingiloi communities, but the Azerbaijani Communist Party issued decrees in 1961, 1962, and 1966 in direct response to activism among Georgian-Ingilois and Lezgins. Even though local officials still often undermined these decrees in practice, these nontitular minority actors found some success in their rights negotiations with the state and established a new status quo that stayed in place, at least on paper, until the late 1980s, when the shifting politi-cal landscape renewed debates about the meaning of Leninist nationality ideas in daily life and political practice.

Yet these examples also show that kin republics still mattered. Georgian-Ingilois and Lezgins drew inspiration from the example of their co-ethnics, took advantage of cultural, educational, and political opportunities in neigh-boring kin republics, and learned that their trajectories remained linked to those bonds. These connections ultimately helped them gain access to national cultural resources in Azerbaijan that remained out of reach for most other non-titular populations there, including Talyshes and Kurds, whose co-ethnics abroad were also suppressed—and thus not an example to draw inspiration from—and who Soviet authorities had marked as potentially disloyal.

There are few traces of Georgian-Ingilois and Lezgins in Azerbaijani ar-chives after the 1930s, but other nontitular minorities including Talyshes, Tats, Tsakhurs, and Kurds are almost entirely absent. Azerbaijani archives have their own specificities, but they also reflect some broader institutional and ide-ological influences in state record-keeping. Among the files that are available, there are only fragmentary records related to nontitular populations after the 1930s because most of these communities lacked the native-language schools, ensembles, and newspapers that tended to generated bureaucratic documenta-tion. There are additional obstacles in those cases where nontitular minorities were deemed assimilated because state and popular use of their preassimilation ethnonyms often precipitously declined afterward. In the Azerbaijan state archive, there are also chronological constraints. Available records for many of the ministries that coordinated national cultural institutions (schools, theaters, ensembles, printing presses, etc.) extend only to the mid-1960s, making it difficult to follow stories after that point. Party archive collections are richer for these later decades, but researchers studying politically sensitive topics like this one have had difficulty accessing this archive in Baku.

In this politicized context, the Georgian-Ingiloi and Lezgin examples highlight why co-ethnic connections make it easier to tell some stories over others. When silences or access issues arise in the archives of one former Soviet republic, obscuring minority voices and histories there, archives in neighboring republics sometimes help fill those gaps. The record is often still constrained to flashpoints like the rights contests described in this chapter, but populations with neighboring kin republics can be visible and findable in a way that other minorities are not. The relative success of nontitular activists with kin republic connections also increases the likelihood that there will be relevant paper trails in state and party archives. In Azerbaijan, complaints, letters, and petitions from this era were generally preserved alongside the party decrees that ordered officials to renew national cultural resources in those communities. Multiple factors, meanwhile, worked against nontitular minorities who agitated for, but did not achieve, renewed rights recognition at that time.

The Kurds are a good example here. With their history of suspect foreign ties, deportations, and assimilation, Kurds faced an uphill battle for national recognition and rights in Azerbaijan. In April 1959, Soviet ethnographer and Kurdish specialist Tat'iana Fedorovna Aristova sent a scathing letter to Sergei Tolstov, then director of the Institute of Ethnography at the Academy of Sciences in Moscow, documenting problems she observed in Kurdish areas of the republic. She was incensed to find Kurdish villages with people ill from living in "damp, cold, completely dark dugouts" or "cave-like" conditions and students staying home from school because they didn't understand Azerbaijani and lacked access to Kurdish schools. Comparing Kurds in Azerbaijan to those in Armenia, she explained that Kurdish villages in Armenia were relatively well-maintained and many Kurds there had access to a small network of Kurdish-language schools. She also described an expanding national cultural scene for Kurds in Armenia but a stagnant situation in Azerbaijan. The Kurdish-language newspaper *Ria Taza* reopened in Armenia in 1955, presses there were once again producing Kurdish-language texts, and, by the early 1960s, Kurdish radio broadcasts originating in Armenia extended as far away as Turkey, Iran, and Iraq. In Azerbaijan, meanwhile, the Kurdish newspaper, *Sovetskii Kurdis-*

tan, was only printed in Azerbaijani. Aristova implored Tolstov to help her ameliorate these "abnormalities." Tolstov, in turn, drafted a message to Secretary Mukhitdinov, explaining that he was forwarding Aristova's letter about nationality politics in the South Caucasus, but a penciled notation at the top of this letter indicates that his note was never sent.[108]

Aristova constructs a comparison between Azerbaijan and Armenia that might make one think that minorities were uniquely disadvantaged in Azerbaijan. In terms of national identification and resources, Kurds were comparatively worse off in Azerbaijan, where Kurdish national cultural development had long been hampered by an insistence in some governing circles in Baku that most people categorized as Kurds in Azerbaijan either did not know the Kurdish language or were actually Azerbaijanis. This was a dominant line of contention in publications about Kurds in the 1920s and early 1930s, as well as in party and state meetings about Kurdish matters.[109] During debates about developing the Kurdish Latin script in 1931, for example, when the question arose about where to base a committee for Kurdish alphabet reform, representatives from both Georgia and Armenia banded together to reject the suggestion of Baku, criticizing it for a variety of sins, including undercounting the Kurdish population, refusing to send Kurds from Azerbaijan to learn the new alphabet, and mistakenly claiming that few Kurds in Azerbaijan knew Kurdish. Azerbaijani representatives, meanwhile, argued that Armenia was a poor choice because Armenians and Kurds had a recent history of interethnic fighting and Armenians had tried to Armenianize Kurds living there. Others defended Armenia on the basis that, like Georgia, it had nonetheless supported more Kurdish development work than Azerbaijan. Representatives from Georgia, meanwhile, suggested that Tiflis was the ideal center for this work because Tiflis had more of a presence in Kurdish areas than Baku and lacked the baggage of Musavat and Dashnak discriminatory treatment of Kurds (essentially amounting to a critique of the way that Kurds were handled in the independent states of Azerbaijan and Armenia that existed between the Russian Revolution and Sovietization in the early 1920s).[110]

Indeed, despite Aristova's overwhelming frustration with Azerbaijan, problems existed in Armenia as well. The Kurdish population in Armenia included both Sunni Muslims and Yezidis. As in Azerbaijan, from the very start of the Soviet project there were voices within Armenian society who favored Kurdish and Yezidi assimilation. These pressures intensified in the final years of the Soviet Union and early post-Soviet period. As the Nagorno-Karabakh conflict escalated, Muslim Kurds were pushed out of the republic and more effort was put into reshaping Yezidis as a people separate from Kurds or at least as fundamentally different from Muslim Kurds, leading some Yezidis to complain that they experienced discrimination when embracing a broader Kurdish identification.[111] To be sure, each Soviet republic had its own particularities that intersected with broader patterns of majority-minority relations in the Soviet Union.

Yet, as it had for Georgian-Ingilois and Lezgins, the opening after Stalin's death renewed Kurdish rights agitation in the USSR. An observable increase in autonomist sentiment among both deported Kurds in Central Asia and those remaining in the South Caucasus surfaced in the 1950s, intensifying over the next couple of decades. Many of the Kurds who had been expelled to Kazakhstan and Kyrgyzstan were frustrated with discrimination they experienced there. They wanted to return to the South Caucasus, register as Kurds in their Soviet passports, and, ideally, create a Kurdish republic in Azerbaijan. A series of decrees from the presidium of the Supreme Soviet of the USSR in 1956, 1957, 1968, and 1974 lifted restrictions on Kurdish special settlements in Central Asia and created a path for their return to the South Caucasus. By 1979, the Soviet census recognized 115,000 Kurds in the Soviet Union. Of this number, the majority resided in the Caucasus (6,000 in Azerbaijan, more than 50,000 in Armenia, and 25,000 in Georgia), but nearly 30,000 remained in Central Asia (17,700 in Kazakhstan and around 10,000 in Kyrgyzstan).[112]

Kurdish activists failed to achieve autonomy in Soviet Azerbaijan and fell short of the national cultural support (schools, newspapers, radio transmissions, etc.) they sought there, highlighting what variables helped some minorities achieve measured success while others continued to struggle for basic cultural investment and recognition. Their story reminds us that there is still much we have yet to learn and that archives often obscure more than they reveal, but their rights negotiations nonetheless reinforce what the Georgian-Ingiloi and Lezgin examples tell us about the promise of citizenship and the rise of nontitular organizing and rights demands from the mid-1950s onward.

Many scholars have challenged glorifications of the Thaw and representations of Khrushchev as a halcyon figure in the Soviet storm. Polly Jones, for instance, has questioned depictions of the era as a "turning point" marking a definitive decline in Stalinist practices. She recast the word "Thaw" to capture the fragility of the period, "the potential for reversal (or 'freeze'), which each tentative step forward carried."[113] This chapter embraces this conceptualization, while also emphasizing the ways that Soviet citizens located changing possibilities for social mobilization and rights negotiation in the transition from Stalinism. Respondents often criticized Khrushchev except when explaining why they challenged local rights norms, crediting him for fostering an environment that they felt comfortable stepping out into. As one Rik'in Gaf member recalled, he was terrified in the 1940s when someone asked him to help write a complaint letter about "Lezgi pulu," but recognized that something had intangibly shifted when he started agitating for Lezgin rights in the late 1950s. There is no doubt that the Soviet Union—like other countries—failed to realize full and equal rights for its citizens, whether Georgian-Ingilois, Lezgins, Kurds, Talyshes, Azeris, or people from other national communities. Nonetheless, the existence of Leninist nationalities politics and constitutionally guaranteed national rights for Soviet citizens both inspired belief in those rights and offered people the possibility of contesting practices that proscribed them.

Conclusion

In spring 2011, the First World Forum on Intercultural Dialogue took place in Baku, Azerbaijan. In front of the gathered international assembly, Azerbaijani President İlham Aliyev lauded Azerbaijan as a model of tolerance and assured the audience that "everyone lives like one family in Azerbaijan. No national or religious confrontations or misunderstandings have existed here."[1] There is a domestic audience for this discourse, but the conference also contributed to an ongoing effort by the government to increase its global prestige and economic ties while simultaneously detracting from international criticism of human rights violations, political repression, and corruption. In the words of the president's office, Azerbaijan seeks to be recognized "in the world as the center of multiculturalism" and they have bolstered this image through a strategic public relations campaign that includes concerts, conferences, sponsored trips, and publications.[2]

One can easily find examples that contradict Aliyev's absolutist claim of eternal national and religious harmony in Azerbaijan. In the late 1980s and early 1990s, for instance, several minority communities there harbored autonomy or separatist movements—Armenian nationalists fought to separate Nagorno-Karabakh from Azerbaijan; the Sadval movement spread among Lezgins in Dagestan and Azerbaijan seeking to territorially unify their community; Kurds renewed their calls for autonomy; and Talyshes in the south experimented with a short-lived Talysh-Mughan Autonomous Republic in the summer of 1993. Ongoing violence in and around Nagorno-Karabakh is perhaps the most obvious example, but the official interpretation of this discord portrays it as something of an aberration and constructs the people of Azerbaijan as victims who played no role in generating Armenian grievances or nationalism. In other words, the Azerbaijani government argues that the conflict is the product solely of Armenian intolerance (to be sure, the Armenian government has cultivated a similar refusal to engage in self-reflection). In this interpretive framework, the Azerbaijani government rejects the notion that what has happened in Nagorno-Karabakh damages its reputation as a global center of multiculturalism and instead upholds it as an example of why Azerbaijan is a model of tolerance par excellence, claiming it has respected Armenians and Armenian cultural artifacts despite Armenians violating Azerbaijanis and their historical objects.[3] Indeed, if Soviet diversity and ethnic harmony were discursively juxtaposed to Jim Crow racism and violence in the United States in order to promote the Soviet model abroad, the Azerbaijani government has contrasted its rhetoric of tolerance with Armenian nationalism, terrorism, and destruction to advance the Azerbaijani model of multiculturalism on the world stage.

The Nagorno-Karabakh conflict erupted in the late 1980s amidst renewed demands for the Nagorno-Karabakh Autonomous Oblast' to be transferred to Armenia. Large-scale population displacement and incidents of mass violence marked the final years of Soviet rule in the Armenian and Azerbaijani SSRs before transitioning after Soviet collapse into open military conflict that lasted from 1992 to 1994 and caused further mass dislocations and deaths. A negotiated ceasefire in 1994 initiated a new stage of this war, which is far from settled, with Armenian forces still occupying all or part of seven Azerbaijani regions (Jabrayıl, Zangilan, Qubadlı, Lachın, Kalbajar, Aghdam, and Füzuli) surrounding the breakaway Nagorno-Karabakh Republic. Armenia also politically, militarily, and financially supports the self-proclaimed republic and its Armenian inhabitants. To date, tens of thousands of people have died as a result of this conflict and more than one million Azeris, Armenians, Kurds, and others have been forcibly displaced from their homes, essentially eradicating the Azeri population, Nagorno-Karabakh, and surrounding areas under Armenian occupation, as well as the Armenian population in Azerbaijan (excluding areas of Azerbaijan currently under Armenian occupation).[4]

The ongoing violence and displacement associated with Armenian-Azerbaijani conflict have aggravated long-standing national insecurities in Azerbaijan and raised the domestic stakes of disputing Aliyev's claim that "everyone lives like one family" there. Many minorities in Azerbaijan favor a minority identification (Talysh, Lezgin, etc.) over an Azerbaijani one because they think "Azerbaijani" describes the Azeri people, language, and culture rather than a broader civic community of people living in the country. This preference often provokes resentment and suspicion, however, especially among those who interpret it as a worrisome sign of minority disloyalty to the Azerbaijani nation. The minority question is so sensitive in Azerbaijan that people who study the history of national relations there or question the treatment of minorities are frequently accused of treasonous thoughts and behaviors, such as harboring pro-Armenian sympathies.[5] When told I was studying Soviet nationality policies in nontitular communities, for example, Yaqub Mikayıl oğlu Mahmudov, the director of the Institute of History at the Academy of Sciences in Baku and a long-time member of Azerbaijan's legislative branch—the Milli Majlis (Milli Məclis)—angrily shouted that I was a spy who had come to Azerbaijan to commit treason and sow separatism.

Subtler examples also paint a more complicated picture of lived minority experience in Azerbaijan. When Aliyev was standing in front of the 2011 international audience, I was working in various minority communities researching the practices and politics of managing nontitular minorities in the Soviet Union, as well as the consequences of these efforts. As part of my daily routine and while conducting interviews, I often witnessed or was told about microaggressions, overt acts of violence, structural inequalities, and the effects of slow violence—violence that has been defined as relatively invisible in that it "is neither spectacular nor instantaneous, but rather incremental and accretive"—among Lezgins, Georgian-Ingilois, Avars, Laks, Tsakhurs, Talyshes, and other nontitular peoples in Azerbaijan.[6]

These dynamics can generate frustration, embarrassment, resentment, and anger, affecting the way in which people who experience them relate to minority identifications, to the communities around them, and to the state. Popular jokes about Georgian-Ingilois being poor and Talyshes being slow or unintelligent stigmatize those identifications, while informal restrictions on minority-language business signs and unspoken rules mandating Azerbaijani language use in public performances marginalize minority cultures in those communities. Targeted political repression has also had a pedagogical effect in minority areas where the state has undercut independent organizing and cultural movements. Rules restricting the names that people can give their children, fears of arrest and intimidation, battles over toponyms and local heritage sites, surveillance culture in villages, and arrests of prominent minority cultural figures have created incentives for assimilation by encouraging people to give up their alternative ways of understanding themselves and fit in lest they be accused of nefarious thoughts or actions.[7]

Restrictions on minority cultural expression and identifications have thus had the unintended effect of alienating some people from the "Azerbaijani national idea," succinctly defined by Azerbaijani scholar Tair Faradov as the notion that "Representatives of all nations and *narodnosti*, Azerbaijanis [*azerbaidzhantsy*], Russians, Tatars, Ukrainians, Avars, Lezgins, Tsakhurs, Jews, Talyshes, Tats, Ingilois, members of different ethnic groups, see themselves as part of a unified civil and ethnocultural community—the Azerbaijani people [*azerbaidzhanskii narod*]."[8] Faradov describes an idealized notion of civic belonging, yet his double use of *azerbaidzhantsy* to indicate both a civic Azerbaijani nation and the Turkic Azeri people neatly captures a problem that many minorities have with this Azerbaijani identification. This national idea, a product of the Soviet-era project to turn "Turks," "Tatars," and "Muslims" into Azerbaijanis rooted in the history of Azerbaijan's ancient states (Albania, Media Atropatene, etc.) and indigenous peoples, tells minorities that identifying themselves as Azerbaijanis connects them to a civic identification while disregarding the ways in which it is defined in practice by the Turkic Azeri nation and culture.

This is not to imply that all minorities in Azerbaijan reject the Azerbaijani identification. Far from it. There are different ways of imagining the Azerbaijani nation, plus some people recognize themselves as both a nontitular minority and Azerbaijani, two identifications that do not necessarily rule out the other. As Frederick Cooper and Rogers Brubaker argue, "The formal institutionalization and codification of ethnic and national categories implies nothing about the *depth*, *resonance*, or *power* of such categories in the lived experience of the persons so categorized."[9] Because national and ethnic categories obscure human agency and tend to homogenize "ethnic experiences," they reveal little about the fluidity of identification and individual self-understanding in the communities that they are describing.

Oral history interviews can bring necessary nuance to these discussions of national orientations and self-understandings. Indeed, many people from minority communities explained to me that Azerbaijani was a natural identification for them but also expressed a variety of understandings about what it meant. For example, an Ingiloi scholar who supports the idea that Georgian-Ingilois are ethnographically closer to Azeris than Georgians, reasons that people from small ethnic groups in Azerbaijan consider themselves to be Azerbaijani because their own populations do not constitute nations (*natsiia*): "Since the Ingiloi are not a nation [*natsiia*] and not even a *narod* but an ethnographic group, we consider that Ingilois participated in the process of forming the Azerbaijani nation [*natsiia*]. Therefore, I think that I am an Azerbaijani whose roots are Ingiloi. That's what I say. But there are also Azerbaijanis . . . the majority of Azerbaijanis, that is, are Turkic-speaking, but I am not a Turkic-speaking Azerbaijani, I am an Azerbaijani with Ingiloi ancestry."[10]

Others seemed to identify with Azerbaijani-ness but emphasized that this is true only when it is defined in a civic or territorial manner rather than in an ethnic or national one. This was the case with a Talysh woman who tried to explain the Azerbaijani nationality listed in her Soviet passport:

> I am Talysh, I was born here, and my mother is Talysh. She spoke with us then in Talysh and even now speaks in the Talysh language. But I studied in an Azerbaijani school, that is, we had to know Azerbaijani. But this was not the Azerbaijani language, this was the Turk language. Azerbaijani Turk. That is, as far as I understand it, there is no Azerbaijani nationality [*natsional'nost'*], this is my personal opinion. Here [in Azerbaijan] there are nations [*natsiia*]—there are Turks, there are Talyshes, like us, there are Ingilois, Lezgins, Udins . . . these are the nations [*natsiia*].

She further explained that Talyshes are indigenous to Azerbaijan so they would never deny being Azerbaijani. For this reason, and because she had no problems with her "Turk" neighbors, she did not question her Azerbaijani categorization in the Soviet period. Yet, she clarified, "If they had written Turk, if they had registered me as a Turchanka, or some Talysh man as Turok, that would not have been good."[11] Another Talysh man reasoned, "If a Talysh person says that they are Azerbaijani this means that Azerbaijan is his or her motherland . . . Talyshes never called *them* Azerbaijanis, for Talyshes they were always Turks. It's the same today."[12]

Still others, however, explained why they could not connect with the Azerbaijani identification. They argued that the concept of Azerbaijani was ethnically defined and thus not representative of the broader community of people living in Azerbaijan. Many of these individuals were classified as Azerbaijani in Soviet censuses and passports, but clarified that they never considered themselves to be Azerbaijani as they equated it with being a Tatar, Turk, or Muslim.[13] When asked whether or not he considered himself to be Azerbaijani, a Lezgin man responded that he was a citizen of the Azerbaijan SSR and post-Soviet Azerbaijan, but he was not Azerbaijani. He explained that Lezgins could not be Azerbaijanis because Azerbaijanis had Turkish origins.[14] This was a particularly common response among Christian Georgian-Ingilois. These respondents were adamant that they were citizens of Azerbaijan, but they also equated the Azerbaijani nationality in Soviet passports with "Tatars."[15] Speaking about the Soviet period, a Talysh man similarly explained:

> We are all Azerbaijanis [*azerbaidzhantsy*]. An Azerbaijani should be identified with the place, but the state took this over for the nation. And

when they said Azerbaijani, they thought Turk, that everyone was Turk. This is not true. Azerbaijan is not made up only of Turks.

In other words, many interviewees indicated that, at least from their perspective, Soviet and post-Soviet Azerbaijan have lacked a robust territorial or civic identification unmoored from the Azeri nation, culture, and language. They may be from Azerbaijan, but many hesitate to say that they are Azerbaijanis (and certainly do not want to be conflated with those they call Turks, or Tatars).

There are concerns that identifying oneself as Azerbaijani implies a denial of self or an acceptance of Turkicness, but there is also a related discomfort about the dominant role that Azeris have played in this multiethnic country. As a commentator argued in a 2009 online discussion about banned Lezgin-language signs in Qusar, a majority Lezgin town in northern Azerbaijan, "In the end, we declare everywhere that we are all brothers in Azerbaijan and Azerbaijan is our common home, but then we get such a strange analogy: your younger brother comes to you and says, 'Brother, you have a television in your room and I want one in my room,' and you tell him, 'You know, brother, this is our shared home so watch television in my room and watch the channels that I watch.'"[16] In drawing this analogy, the commentator brings to mind the nested nationalism concept highlighted in the title of this book. Non-Russians living in the former Soviet Union sometimes evaluate their Soviet experiences through a postcolonial framework of analysis, considering their nations and national cultures to have been "damaged by the colonial experience" dominated by their Russian "big brothers."[17] Yet, experiences ranged widely in the Soviet Union between titular majorities and nontitular minorities in the republics and even within and between different minority communities. For some nontitular minorities in Azerbaijan, the "big brothers" that they most resented or distrusted were representatives of Soviet Azerbaijan rather than of Moscow. Further, the nationalist behaviors of those titular majorities often intersected with nationalisms that emerged among nontitular minorities and vice versa.

The online commentator also touched on an important dynamic that undergirds the discourse of tolerance in Azerbaijan: embedded within that rhetoric is the belief among many Azeris that, as the titular nation, they are first among all others in Azerbaijan, they are the truest embodiment of Azerbaijan's historical heritage, and tolerance is a gift that they have bestowed upon the other peoples of Azerbaijan. Social philosopher Ilham Abbasov argues that the contemporary discourse of tolerance is the embodiment of Soviet ideas about titular nations and the "Soviet people." He writes, "The state, following Soviet tradition, is thought of as belonging to one dominant ('titular') group—ethnic Azerbaijanis (or Azerbaijani Turks) . . . those who are not eth-nic Azerbaijani have a right to citizenship primarily by virtue of the tolerance of the dominant group. For their part, they are obliged to demonstrate their gratitude and loyalty to [ethnic Azerbaijanis]." This dynamic undercuts legal guarantees of equality among all peoples in contemporary Azerbaijan just as violations of Leninist nationality practices contradicted the constitutional amendments, decrees, and discourses of egalitarianism that characterized the Soviet period.[18]

That national imbalances and misunderstandings exist in Azerbaijan is un-surprising. What state is devoid of inequalities? Yet a popular refusal to ac-knowledge assimilatory and discriminatory practices in Azerbaijan has had many unintended effects, including masking the ways in which past experi-ences and practices continue to shape its present. Soviet nationality policies have frequently been invoked to explain the dissolution of the Soviet Union and the attendant emergence of ethnically framed violence in the Caucasus and else-where, but most of these studies connect the early decades of these policies to Soviet collapse fifty to sixty years later. The resulting chronological gap has gen-erated ahistorical analyses of minority organizing across the USSR and post-Soviet space. Unaware of the historical grievances, experiences, and expectations that motivated minority activists in, for example, Sadval and the Talysh-Mughan Autonomous Republic, scholars and commentators have portrayed Lezgin and Talysh efforts to achieve autonomy as spontaneous products of a weakened So-viet center in the late 1980s and early 1990s rather than as movements connected to longer historical timelines and complaints rooted in specific experiences of inequality.[19] In contrast, this book has shown that, while *korenizatsiia* practices were suspended in most nontitular communities in the late 1930s, nationality policies, relations, and experiences continued to evolve in subsequent decades. This sometimes led to a revival of minority national-cultural support. Further, communities did not simply cease to exist or fall out of historical time when they were declared assimilated or lost access to national cultural resources. The history of these minority communities after the 1930s—the majority of the So-viet period—matters and must also be taken into account.

What are some of the ways in which a more developed picture of Soviet history can help explain post-Soviet national relations? One way would be to explore and acknowledge the ongoing relevance of Soviet ethnogenesis theo-ries, national experiences, rights debates, expectations of titular hegemony rooted in claims to territorial legitimacy, and autonomy movements. In the late Soviet and early post-Soviet periods, the evolving political environment triggered public conversations about these topics in the USSR. After Mikhail Sergeevich Gorbachev was appointed General Secretary of the CPSU in

March 1985, he ushered in the twin policies of *perestroika* (restructuring) and *glasnost'* (openness or transparency) that are popularly credited with reshaping Soviet political, economic, and social norms. These policies were inspired by Gorbachev's sense that changes needed to occur, but also by signal events that disrupted the equilibrium, inspiring his evolution from early tentative reform measures to more ambitious efforts. Most notable, perhaps, is the April 1986 nuclear disaster at the Chernobyl power plant, which played a significant role in eroding state control over political organizing and information, pushing the Communist Party toward more open communication and critical public discussions more than a year before *glasnost'* formally embraced these practices.[20] Gorbachev also confronted ethnically motivated protests in Soviet republics that year. In April, fights in Yakutsk between Sakha students and Russians provoked days of demonstrations after locals perceived a pro-Russian bias in the initial police response. Later that year, when Gorbachev replaced the ethnically Kazakh first secretary of Kazakhstan, Dinmukhamed Kunaev, with an outsider Russian, protests broke out there as well, escalating to violence, and leaving nearly a hundred people dead.[21]

By the close of 1987, Armenian organizing around the question of Nagorno-Karabakh had started to approach a mass scale, raising tensions in Azerbaijan, but also in Armenia. That November, the first train arrived in Baku carrying Azeris fleeing interethnic violence in Armenia. A few months later, in February 1988, Armenian deputies in the Nagorno-Karabakh regional soviet formally requested unification with Armenia while hundreds of thousands of Armenians rallied under this call in Yerevan. Within days, anti-Armenian pogroms—sparked by the stories of Azeris who had been forced out of Armenia and anger over the resolution in Nagorno-Karabakh—broke out in the Azerbaijani city Sumqayıt, leaving 26 Armenians and 6 Azerbaijanis dead (according to official reports) and driving nearly the entire Armenian population of 14,000 people out of the city. Incidents of mass violence and forced displacements immediately escalated in both Armenia and Azerbaijan. By the end of the Soviet Union, almost all Armenians in Azerbaijan (excluding those in the Karabakh region) and Azeris in Armenia—hundreds of thousands of people—had been expelled from their home republic,[22] drastically altering the demographic composition of these two SSRs.

Self-determination was on the agenda not only in the South Caucasus, but elsewhere in the region as well, including in Warsaw Pact countries where there was growing civil unrest (a non-Communist government had already come to power in Poland); in the Baltics, where the Supreme Soviets had made declarations of national sovereignty; and in other Soviet republics that harbored national movements advancing similar conversations. That month, the CPSU Central Committee plenum adopted a report by Gorbachev titled "On the National Politics of the Party in Modern Conditions," wherein he acknowledged past distortions of Soviet nationality politics, including national deportations, and urged the party to reaffirm the Leninist principle of national self-determination in an attempt, no doubt, to reclaim control over a rapidly deteriorating political situation. To his mind, the solution was a greater devolution of decision-making power to the republics to preserve their national identities, enjoy sovereignty, and manage their economies within the bounds of a "voluntary union of republics." In short, he did not propose concrete measures to radically change the power structure of the Soviet Union to meet the demands of people agitating for national independence. At the same time, however, he suggested new autonomous national regions should be created in areas where minorities lived compactly, opening the party up to the possibility of renegotiating republic boundaries.[23] This expanded an earlier statement Gorbachev made in a November 1988 Supreme Soviet meeting, where he reaffirmed the ongoing relevance of nationalities and national identifications in the Soviet Union and committed the party to strengthening the federal structure of the state in order to develop nations and national cultures. In his words, it would be a mistake if nations, which were the "wealth not the weakness" of the Soviet Union were to disappear.

The proposal to expand national autonomies touched on an issue that was clearly on the minds of many Soviet citizens. For years now, people had written letters to Moscow proposing new administrative-territorial delineations and autonomies—Nogais wanted a Nogai republic, *oblast'*, or *okrug*; Ossetians demanded the unification of South and North Ossetia; Abkhazians asked Russia to incorporate the Abkhaz ASSR into Russia; Uyghurs proposed a new Uyghur ASSR in Kazakhstan; Germans hoped to renew their autonomy in the Volga region; Ingushes dreamed of self-rule; Bashkirs marked out a new national okrug in Chelyabinsk; Kumyks wanted to carve out a piece of Dagestan for a Kumyk ASSR; Kurds from across the Soviet Union agitated in favor of a Kurdish autonomous region in Azerbaijan; and, of course, Armenians demanded the transfer of Nagorno-Karabakh to Armenia. After the party plenum in September 1989, a draft CPSU platform reproducing Gorbachev's speech was distributed via newspapers and party meetings to encourage public discussion and debate. In Azerbaijan, the epicenter of the growing Karabakh conflict, people who attended these workplace meetings sent mountains of letters to Moscow.

Though many of their communications were fairly formulaic, indicating centrally coordinated responses, it is nonetheless clear that Gorbachev's endorsement of new autonomies provoked a sense of panic in Azerbaijan given

the precarious situation with Nagorno-Karabakh. People were also clearly outraged that Gorbachev had failed to recognize Azeri victimhood at the hands
of Armenians, and at his suggestion that Kurds might deserve autonomy for
the persecution they had faced (particularly since this autonomy would likely
come at the expense of Azerbaijan). Why, they asked, did he not validate Azeri suffering? Tensions that had been building up between Baku and Moscow
since the outbreak of Karabakh-related violence reached a breaking point in
January 1990. Ethnonationalists, many affiliated with the Popular Front political movement, which by this point posed a serious challenge to the authority of the Azerbaijan Communist Party, incited people to attack Armenians in
Baku, leading to a spree of anti-Armenian violence between January 13–15 that
left at least a hundred, perhaps more, Armenians dead and forced authorities
to evacuate thousands of other Armenians still in Baku. This interethnic violence gave way to rallies, including one that saw a gallows erected in front of
the Central Committee building in Baku. Finally, during the night of January 19–20, 1990, Ministry of Interior troops and tanks, which had silently
stood by during days of anti-Armenian violence, were sent out into the streets
of Azerbaijan's main city, resulting in the death of more than 130 Azerbaijanis
and injuries to hundreds of others.

Thomas de Waal concludes that at this point, "Moscow essentially lost Azerbaijan."[24] Hundreds of thousands of people turned out for the funerals of
these victims of state violence. The Communist Party soon after replaced the
first secretary of Azerbaijan with Ayaz Mütallibov (Ayaz Niyazi oğlu Mütəllibov),
but Laurence Broers argues that the party only "clung to power" in Azerbaijan by embracing some of the Popular Front's nationalist agenda, including
the demand to reassert dominance over Nagorno-Karabakh.[25] Mütallibov
was later elected Azerbaijan's first president in September 1991, one month
before Azerbaijan's Supreme Council declared Azerbaijan's independence
and three months before the Soviet Union dissolved. He was later deposed
(after first briefly resigning) by the Popular Front in May 1992 following devas-
tating defeats on the Karabakh front, including an Armenian massacre of several hundred Azerbaijani civilians near Khojalı (Xocalı) in late February and,
in May, the loss of Shusha, militarily strategic high ground and the last Azeri-
occupied town in Nagorno-Karabakh.[26]

The violence that people in Azerbaijan experienced in these final years of the
Soviet Union only exacerbated long-standing national grievances in the republic,
including some concerning the status of the Azerbaijani language and ethnogenesis narratives that continued to downplay Azeris' Turkic heritage. Newspaper editorials in the late 1980s decried the low prestige of the Azerbaijani language
in Azerbaijan, calling for greater adherence to constitutional provisions defining

Azerbaijani as the official language of the republic. Aliagha Mammadli argues that "these discussions eventually coalesced into a powerful movement" centered around language politics, which were a "key point of ethnic mobilization." Critical discussions about the Azerbaijani national identity also developed in the final years of Soviet rule, sometimes challenging the narratives that had previously been developed according to Communist Party preferences. In 1983, for example, the Azerbaijani Academy of Sciences hosted a workshop examining Azerbaijani ethnogenesis that led to an open discussion about a widespread theory—rarely openly articulated at the time—that Azerbaijan was ethnically Turkic.[27] The stakes of these discussions were heightened during the 1992–1993 presidency of Abülfaz Elchibey (Əbülfəz Elçibəy), an Arab philologist and historian who specialized in the history of the Middle East and had studied under Ziya Bünyadov. Elchibey was also a dissident, who spent two years in a Soviet prison in the mid-1970s as a "nationalist anti-Soviet propagandist." He was caught up for leading a secret university group that discussed various transgressive and sensitive topics, including breaking Azerbaijan free from Soviet rule and the national independence movement in Iranian Azerbaijan.[28] Elchibey played a central role in building the national movement in Soviet Azerbaijan, and at the close of the end of the 1980s emerged as a leader of the Popular Front. During his presidency, Elchibey embraced a pan-Turkic orientation for Azerbaijanis, reinforcing the sense among many minorities that the Azerbaijani identification connoted Turkicness rather than territorial belonging.[29]

New publications that were produced by, and offered a voice to, members of minority communities also confronted decades of muted scholarly engagement and raised pressing questions about community identifications and histories in these transitional years. In Azerbaijan, where ethnogenesis has played a significant role in legitimating Azeri titularity and in coopting the counterclaims of various minorities, "who are we" questions and historical revisionism flourished in minority journalism and historical publications in the late 1980s and early 1990s. Many of these articles and books contradicted the official line that minorities had ancient links to the Azeri nation or should identify with the Azerbaijani nationality as a multiethnic civic identifier.[30]

In the early 1990s, for example, Zabit Rizvanov, one of the founders of Rik'in Gaf, produced a samizdat publication that detailed his grievances against Baku, including his frustration with Azeri ethnogenesis narratives and toponymic claims that supplanted Lezgin indigeneity by asserting (or, in his words, fabricating) ancient Azeri roots in northern Azerbaijan.[31] When Sadval and Lezgin National Soviet leaders petitioned the Supreme Soviet of the Russian Federation in 1992, asking for help unifying the divided Lezgin nation, they similarly asserted that Lezgins embodied the ancient heritage of

FIGURE 17.   The front cover of the third issue of *Moambe* newspaper in 1990. Author photo.

northern Azerbaijan and endorsed Rizvanov's legacy and ideas, advising the Russian Supreme Soviet that he was one of the Lezgin nation's foremost ethnographic and historical specialists.[32]

Similar conversations dominated the pages of *Moambe*, a Georgian-language newspaper published in 1990 by the Mose Janashvili Society, which was established by Georgian-Ingilois interested in improving relations with Azeris (amid concerns that the nationalist Popular Front movement might redirect its anti-Armenian anger to other Christians in Azerbaijan) and building a stronger Georgian-Ingiloi community. Born in the mid-nineteenth century, Janashvili was an ethnographer and historian from Qakh, who supported Christian missionary work among Georgian-Ingilois and distinguished himself in Tiflis (now Tbilisi) as an educator and prolific author of Georgian historical publications. In naming their organization after Janashvili, society members definitively showed where they stood in debates about whether Georgian-Ingilois are ethnographically and historically closer to Azeris than Georgians.[33]

If the editors of *Moambe* had a clear vision of their Georgian past and identification, the content of the newspaper itself reveals that these issues were still unsettled within the broader Georgian-Ingiloi community. Soviet nationality categories made it difficult for people to situate themselves in the in-between spaces; in the eyes of the state, you were either Georgian or Azerbaijani, but you were not both. If you considered yourself to be Ingiloi, meanwhile, there was no way to represent yourself as such in state records, including in the internal Soviet passports that recorded the official nationality of each Soviet citizen. The Georgian-Ingiloi "community" also lacked much of the coherence that Georgians and others ascribed to it. Georgian-Ingiloi national activists came from both Christian and Muslim communities, embraced unity in their advocacy, and subordinated religious differences to national variables, but there were also very real divisions and pressures to pick a side.

There were also many people who did not identify themselves and their lives by nationality and instead gravitated toward alternative or complementary ways of ordering themselves and their communities, whether by religion, status, region, or some other classification. In fact, when asked whether nationality was important in the Soviet period, many of the people I spoke with reflexively answered "no," referencing discourses of Soviet nationhood and friendship rather than conversations about national disagreements and contestations. They frequently invoked World War II to explain this reasoning. As one Talysh woman argued, "If there had not been friendship, if every people [*narod*], every nation [*natsiia*] thought only about themselves, then there would never have been such a great victory . . . probably you understand what kind of an army the Germans had! Hitler conquered all of Europe and then the Soviet Union conquered him."[34] Still others would point to the example of intermarriage, arguing that neighbors were neighbors regardless of their language or categorization. Stories about mixed marriages, however, made clear that religious and national identifications were often layered onto one another. As one man clarified, "In the Soviet Union, all people, all nationalities were very close to one another. You understand? They communicated with one another, they created families together. So many of our people married Russians, Georgians, Ukrainians, Belarusians. But! But it was the women who were from the other nationality. Not one of our Talysh women married into another nation [*natsiia*]. Pay attention to that. Religion is another matter."[35] Other respondents pointed to Soviet mobility to illustrate that nationality held meaning in political rather than personal terms. As a Lezgin man explained, "Nationality—this was a government matter but I'm speaking about the people [*narod*] . . . in the Soviet Union with regards to the ordinary people, everything was the same for everyone. I, for example, traveled to Moscow without a passport. Without a passport! And no one asked me where I was from, why I had gone there. That is, no one bothered you. For the simple people it wasn't important, but when you dealt with political or official affairs then it became important."[36]

As Tara Zahra has shown, however, indifference to nationalism itself can be both a central category of analysis and a factor of historical change.[37] The nationalized actors or ethnopolitical entrepreneurs, as Brubaker likes to call them, who are highlighted in this book—Ibragimov, Mustafayev Gamkharashvili, Rizvanov, Charkviani, and others—had an interest in nationalizing those around them in order to form cohesive groups and demands. When the broader population did not respond in predictable ways to their campaigning, they sometimes employed other means to shape community self-understanding. Indeed, difference and belonging were often complementary. Soviet citizens for the most part got along with their neighbors, fought alongside one another in wars, and carried the same Soviet passport, but that passport also assigned them to a nationality category that carried instrumental significance while sometimes contradicting the way in which they felt about themselves.

Although I have chosen to use the term Georgian-Ingiloi in this book in an attempt to recognize the different ways that people identified themselves to me—as Georgian, Ingiloi (Ingilo), and Georgian-Ingiloi (Georgian-Ingilo)—the existence of multiple names for this population is telling. Some Christians reject the Ingiloi label because they do not want to be associated with what it means: that at some point their ancestors had given up the Christian faith, becoming Muslims or "Tatars" before reclaiming Christianity and a Georgian identity. There is a definite stigma associated with this history of conversion in the Christian community.[38] A retired teacher from one of Qakh's Georgian schools explained to me that many Christians living there deny being Ingiloi and refer to themselves only as Georgian because accepting an Ingiloi public identity or being affiliated too closely with Muslim Georgian-Ingiloi villages exposes them to assimilationist politics and the Azerbaijani argument that Ingilois are not Georgians. She also pointed out, however, that many of these same people would identify themselves to one another as Ingiloi or would have no problem "being Ingiloi" in Georgia. Although some Georgians in Georgia look down on Georgian-Ingilois from Azerbaijan, again, mostly because of this history of Muslim conversion, Georgian-Ingilois could also benefit from the accommodations that Georgian nationalists created to cultivate connections between Georgia and Georgian-Ingilois. This includes exemptions from qualifying exams that made it easier for Georgian-Ingilois to enroll in Georgian institutes and universities.[39]

Georgian-Ingilois occasionally mentioned discriminatory comments directed toward them in Georgia, but Georgian-Ingilois from Muslim villages also complained to me about Christian Georgian-Ingilois looking down on them because they "failed" to reconvert to Christianity.[40] Indeed, some Christians I interviewed in Qakh confirmed this uneven relationship and a general reluctance to categorize Muslims as Georgian. One man explained that he did not get involved in Georgian-Ingiloi advocacy in the Soviet period because the authorities did not hassle the Christian communities as much and he felt as though Muslim Georgian-Ingilois were not really Georgian. He elaborated, "How could I consider them Georgian if they had mosques?" To him, they were simply Ingiloi (and that was not necessarily a good thing to be).[41] Another man with a similar viewpoint reported that Georgian-Ingilois in Aliabad were "Muslims who two or three centuries ago used to be Georgian."[42] Yet another person from Qoraghan, a village in Qakh with both Muslim Ingilois and Christian Georgians—and from which most of the Christians nervously migrated to Georgia in 1930—explained to me that he had relatives who "first were Georgians, were Christians, but then became Muslims and Azerbaijanis."[43]

This confusion about who is Georgian, who is Ingiloi, and whether or not there is a coherent Georgian-Ingiloi identity or community was also on display in *Moambe*. In an early issue, one of the editors wrote,

> Among our numerous problems, the most noteworthy is the issue of relations among Georgian villages in Saingilo. In fact, our future depends on solving it. There are literally no relations that serve the mutual interests of Georgian villagers in Saingilo. On the contrary, we have a lot of demands against one another. This is strategically used by the government to make hostile relations even worse . . . [and] relations between Qakh and Zaqatala-Balakan [where there were Muslim Georgian-Ingiloi villages] are even worse.

Letters written by people from various villages in all three regions—Zaqatala, Balakan, and Qakh—about Georgian-Ingiloi relations reinforced the issues raised in this editorial. For example, a teacher from Kötüklü (a Qakh region "Georgian" Christian village) argued the following:

Regarding relations between Qakh and Zaqatala-Balakan inhabitants, I don't consider them normal. In my opinion this is our fault [Qakh region]. There are occasions when acts of humiliation and insults come from us [as opposed to from Azerbaijanis]. These acts shouldn't take place, and we should befriend them. The more we help them and support them, the friendlier they will be.

A teacher from Aliabad (a Zaqatala "Ingiloi" Muslim village) also weighed in on the Muslim/Christian dichotomy:

Some Georgians from Qakh don't know anything about the problems in Aliabad and sometimes make the situation worse (by calling us Tatars).[44] These people should understand that if they don't want to help us then they should at least stop hindering us.[45]

Decades of divisive policies and practices, including differentiated treatment by state officials, have deepened differences that were long in play—and often exploited—among Georgian-Ingilois.

In addition to internal disagreements about the boundaries of the Georgian-Ingiloi community, there are also ongoing disputes about Georgian-Ingilois' "place" in their home regions. These debates are often mired in ethnogenesis theories that originated in the midcentury decades of the Soviet period. A church on the outskirts of Qakh provides one such example. According to

FIGURE 18. A view of Kurmukhi Church of Saint George. Author photo.

Georgian-Ingilois, Kurmukhi Church of Saint George is a prominent symbol of their local heritage and indigeneity, a place where Georgian-Ingilois— Muslim and Christian alike—mark Saint George's Day (Giorgoba) twice a year (Saint George is one of Georgia's patron saints and Giorgoba is a public holiday there). According to the Azerbaijani government and many others in the region, however, the church site is most notable not for its Georgian Orthodox heritage but for its association with ancient Albania, which helps position Azeris as mutual inheritors—with Ingilois, Udis, Tsakhurs, and others—of its legacy. At the site itself, an Azerbaijan Ministry of Culture and Tourism sign emphasizes these links to Albania while excluding any mention of Georgian-Ingilois' connection to the nineteenth-century Kurmukhi church that stands there next to the ruins of an ancient Albanian temple.

In recent years, there has been a broad state-led effort to claim and advertise Giorgoba to the people of Azerbaijan but also to a foreign, English-speaking audience as a quintessential symbol of Azerbaijani multiculturalism and tolerance, as a time when Muslims and Christians (Georgian-Ingilois, Tsakhurs, Azeris, and others) peacefully gather with family, friends, and neighbors. In this new discourse, the holiday is usually billed under an alternate name, Kürmükoba (holiday of Kürmük), rather than Giorgoba (or, at least, never as simply Giorgoba), downplaying its connection to St. George's Day and the Georgian Orthodox faith. These narrators also frequently argue that the true origins of this holiday lie in a pre-Christian Pagan ritual that Georgians coopted and turned into a Christian holiday. Following this logic, Georgians are the guests here as they have a later historical claim to Kürmükoba than others who can trace their origins to Caucasian Albania, such as Tsakhurs, Azeris, and Ingilois— who, it must be remembered, according to Azerbaijani ethnogenesis theories are not Georgian.[46] This helps make it a shared holiday for all the people of Qakh, rather than a Georgian holiday that others participate in. These ideas are transmitted in English-language articles for an international audience, but also promoted and taken up on the local level. For example, Ahmad Shahidov, who recently ran to represent Qakh in the Milli Majlis and positions himself as a human rights defender, highlighted the multicultural significance of the holiday during his campaign, arguing that it "symbolizes [the] unity of Georgians and Azerbaijanis" and is a "holiday of both Azerbaijanis and Georgians."[47] When talking about Kürmükoba, an Azeri from Qakh similarly explained that, "the best part is we live together in peace because our ancestors were the same people."[48]

For some Georgian-Ingilois, the growing assertion that this is a site of interethnic worship and Albanian heritage has been unnerving, not necessarily because they reject in principle the presence of non-Ingiloi Muslims at the church or don't get along with their Azeri neighbors but because they feel that their holiday and heritage site are being coopted, which changes the culture of their own religious celebration. They also complain about their connection to the church being downplayed, describing this dynamic not as an example of tolerance but of something that imposes an unwanted identification on them. Transforming Kurmukhi Church and St. George's Day into evidence of shared Albanian heritage inscribes Georgian-Ingilois as Azerbaijani, denying the self-understanding of many Georgian-Ingilois who consider themselves ethnic Georgians who live in Azerbaijan. The number of non-Georgian-Ingilois visiting the site has steadily grown as its image has been transformed in recent years. As one Georgian from Qakh explained to me, some Georgians also now worry that they will soon be unable to worship there because the government will use the excuse of the site's Albanian heritage to close the church's doors and fully claim it as their own.[49]

The Talysh example offers another productive opportunity to explore how the past is intertwined with contemporary national relations. A standard narrative surrounding the Talysh-Mughan Autonomous Republic that lasted from June–August, 1993 is that it amounted to little more than a power grab by Colonel Alakram Hümmatov (Gummatzoda), garnered little public support, and had "minimal" Talysh character. Although very little has been written about the republic, this Baku-sourced description has coalesced across numerous sources with few details provided about the republic itself.[50] The story that some participants tell is more complicated. According to them, Heydar Aliyev (Heydər Əlirza oğlu Əliyev)—among other things the former head of the Committee for State Security (KGB) in Soviet Azerbaijan, long-time first secretary of the Azerbaijan Communist Party and member of the CPSU Politburo—manipulated the situation to seize power in the summer of 1993. This came amid more Azerbaijani losses in Nagorno-Karabakh and an insurrectionist showdown between Elchibey and Colonel Surat Hüseynov (Surət Davud oğlu Hüseynov), who had gained prominence while leading Azerbaijani militias against the Armenians. In fact, Aliyev managed to force through a popular vote of no confidence for Elichbey that August. Seeking a victory that could help him cement his rise to power, Aliyev looked south rather than west to Nagorno-Karabakh, whipped up demonstrations in Lankaran, and brought down the inchoate Talysh-Mughan republic.[51] He was elected president of Azerbaijan soon after and remained in that position for the next decade, only stepping down shortly before his death in December 2003. His son, İlham, has been president ever since.

The claim that the republic had no Talysh character is meant to discredit it, but also minimizes the history of Talysh organizing leading up to its establishment and during its brief existence. Talyshes had poorer access to national rights in the Soviet period than some other minorities in Azerbaijan and do not have the same strong collective memory of national organizing in the midcentury period, but members of the community started to agitate more aggressively for Talysh cultural and national recognition in the 1970s. It took until 1989 for them to regain census recognition, but before that some Talyshes managed to form a number of folkloric groups that achieved fame in Soviet cultural circles.

Nineteen eighty-nine also brought significant cultural development, including the establishment of a Talysh Cultural Center and the creation of a community-produced half-typed, half-handwritten Talysh-language publication titled Tolyshi Sado. Articles and letters printed in this newspaper show that Talyshes were now publicly tackling many of the same issues raised in Lezgin, Georgian-Ingiloi, and other national publications in the late 1980s. One letter originating from Shaghlaser village attacked the notion that Talyshes had merged with Azerbaijanis: "Leninist politics provided unique rights for the development of all peoples of the USSR. The Azerbaijani and Talysh languages are oriented toward completely different families and are absolutely different. 'Talyshes merged with Azerbaijanis?' . . . If this is not national assimilation then what is it?" (*Им ды зу ассимиласија кардэ ни бэс чиче?*).[52] Some ethnographers, politicians, and others had lauded Talysh assimilation as a sign of Soviet ethnohistorical advancement, but, assimilation was not always welcome, and particularly not in those communities that were said to be experiencing it. There, assimilation could represent experiences of inequality and discrimination rather than positive Soviet achievement.

In another article, titled "Who Are the Talysh?" the author wrote, "Our history has been hidden for already half a century. Now is *glasnost'*. No one will tell us our history except us. If we don't take this on now then our children will not know our history! And those who do not know their history are called mankurts. History is our memory. If we do not know our history then we are mankurts." This was a reference to Chinghiz Aitmatov's novel *The Day Lasts More Than a Hundred Years*, which was published in 1980 in *Novy Mir*. The legend of the mankurt, as Aitmatov related it, described how slaves were created from prisoners whose memories were stolen from them through a grueling, often deadly process in which raw camel hides were wrapped then dried on their shaven heads in the hot sun. According to historian Michael Rouland, Aitmatov's mankurt symbolized the destructive force of the Soviet era and was "a violent reminder that Central Asians should struggle to hold onto their cultural past, traditions, and languages."[53] As this Talysh writer shows, however, the warning of the mankurt traveled well beyond Central Asia in the Soviet

Union. Detailing his version of Talysh ethnogenesis, he rewrote the history of various historical figures and states that Azerbaijani ethnogenesis scholars had linked to the Azeri people. Soviet Azerbaijani historians like Ziya Bünyadov, for example, had singled out Babek, who lived in what is now Iranian Azerbaijan in the ninth century, as an example of Azeris' heroic history of struggling for national liberation. In this article, however, this Talysh writer described both Babek and the ancient Media-Atropatene state as essential components of the Talysh past rather than of Azeri history.[54] Yet another article in that same issue explored ancient Talysh history and challenged Azeri ethnogenesis theories through an analysis of local toponyms.[55]

Hümmatov, who had been a leading figure in the Popular Front and at one point served as deputy defense minister, controlled the military unit stationed in Lankaran and, with its support, established the republic in June 1993. Some space had been carved out in preceding years for Talysh cultural and political organizing, with the first Talysh political organizing emerging in the late 1980s, helping to build a new self-awareness and political movement among Talyshes. In fact, when helping draft the program for the Azerbaijan Popular Front, Hümmatov and the poet Ali Nasir, who jointly headed its Lankaran branch, made sure the program included a demand for Talysh autonomy.[56] The program, it should be noted, also supported minority cultural rights, although stated in such a way to demonstrate the largesse of "Azerbaijanis," who were deemed the primary nationality and thus able to gift this to others. Although Elchibey pursued an overall Turkifying agenda, he also issued a decree on the protection of the rights of national minorities in Azerbaijan, which enabled the creation of the Talysh Cultural Center and the official registration of a Talysh political party.

The national character of the Talysh-Mughan Autonomous Republic developed over the course of the summer and attracted the participation of some of Azerbaijan's most prominent Talysh intellectuals and cultural figures, whom all had their own ideas about what this opportunity might offer the Talysh nation. Among these participants were Hilal Mammadov, a mathematician at the Academy of Sciences and head of the Azerbaijan National Equality Party (renamed from Talysh People's Party to gain official registration), and Novruzali Mammadov, a linguist at the Academy of Sciences and head of the Talysh Cultural Center.[57] Novruzali Mammadov was well regarded for his cultural work and studies of the Talysh language, and participated in conversations and debates in the Talysh region during the summer of 1993, including some about whether autonomy was the right path forward for Talyshes.[58]

Once Hümmatov took control in Lankaran, the leadership of the Azerbaijan National Equality Party relocated from Baku to Lankaran to support him.

Hilal Mammadov was a political force in the republic, helping to shape its character and communicate its message to the local population via newspaper articles and television reports. Fakhraddin Aboszoda, who later edited *Tolyshi Sado* (1993–1995), became chairman of the republic's *majlis* (parliament) after first helping to create it. Aboszoda joined the Talysh movement after the creation of the republic, but assumed a central role in its leadership after Hümmatov asked him to write its constitution. The *majlis* was formed on the basis of local councils of people's deputies leftover from the Soviet period and first convened in August 1993. Several hundred representatives from all districts in the area participated in the *majlis*, including deputies from areas populated mostly by Azeris. Its first orders of business were to transfer military power to the civilian authorities, officially declare the creation of an autonomous Talysh-Mughan republic that would remain a constituent part of Azerbaijan, elect Hümmatov president, and appoint Aboszoda head of the *majlis*.

Although the republic has since been disparaged as an artificial project that garnered little to no local support, by the time Hümmatov took control in June, several thousand Talyshes were already participating in Talysh political and cultural movements that then pledged support to Hümmatov. Talyshes had gotten a slower start to national organizing than some other national minorities in Azerbaijan due to obstacles they faced in the Soviet period, including their official assimilation, near complete lack of national cultural infrastructure after the 1930s, and collective fear of potential consequences for Talysh organizing, but by this point a stronger self-understanding had started to coalesce. Republic leaders over the course of the summer traveled around the region, campaigning in the villages, explaining what autonomy would mean in people's lives. According to some of those who undertook this organizing work, people they encountered sometimes had a weak Talysh national consciousness, but they generally didn't challenge the premise of the republic; they mainly wanted to be reassured that the republic would not make their lives more difficult during an already precarious time of political transition and war by causing breakdowns in supply lines for necessities like gasoline. Thus, hundreds of people actively participated in the parliament, and thousands more engaged with it through formal and informal discussions and debates.[59]

The republic's leadership scattered when Baku reasserted control over Lankaran at the end of August in 1993. Repression was swift. A Milli Majlis decree immediately condemned the republic's supporters as separatists, nationalists, and terrorists who betrayed Azerbaijan's statehood and territorial integrity. It singled out Hümmatov but also Hilal Mammadov as the "initiator" of the "so-called" republic, and explicitly linked it to Armenian territorial gains against Azerbaijani forces around Karabakh, portraying its creation as a treasonous, pro-Armenian act.[60] More than thirty republic participants were subsequently arrested and convicted under various articles in the Azerbaijani Criminal Code. Some of these prisoners died in custody. Hümmatov initially fled to the mountains, was captured, charged with treason and various other crimes, escaped, was recaptured, and, ultimately, sentenced to death in 1995. While in custody, the United Nations classified him as a political prisoner and at one point his sentence was eventually commuted to life in prison. In 2004, Hümmatov was pardoned and gained asylum in the Netherlands. Three years later, he won a case against Azerbaijan at the European Court of Human Rights, which ordered Azerbaijan to pay him restitution.[61]

Many other participants, including Hilal Mammadov, fled to Russia after the republic was defeated in 1993 and stayed there for more than a decade, returning to Azerbaijan only when they saw an opportunity to do so in 2005. This spirit of reconciliation did not last long, however, as the government soon renewed repression of independent cultural organizing in the Talysh community. Multiple Talysh newspapers had sprung up in Talysh communities in both Azerbaijan and Russia since the late 1980s, but in 2007, not long after *Tolyshi Sado* published articles about Talysh connections to Nizami Ganjavi and Babek—historical figures brought to the forefront of the Azeri national canon in the Soviet period—its editor, Novruzali Mammadov, was arrested and charged with treason and collaboration with Iranian intelligence services. In 2008, he was sentenced to ten years in prison. He died the following year in detention. Repression also extended to his family and, by 2011, both of his sons were dead.[62] His wife, Maryam, eventually achieved asylum in the Netherlands, and in 2019 the European Court of Human Rights found that Azerbaijan had violated Novruzali Mammadov's rights, including the right to protection from inhumane and degrading treatment, the right to medical care, the right to an investigation into allegations of mistreatment, the right to proper recording of detention, the right to an effective investigation into his death, and entitlement to trial within a reasonable time or to release pending trial.[63]

Three years after Novruzali Mammadov died, Hilal Mammadov was arrested. Although initially held on manufactured accusations of heroin possession, he was soon charged with almost identical crimes to Novruzali: treason (for conspiring with Iranian intelligence services) and inciting ethnic hatred.[64] This type of arrest is common in contemporary Azerbaijan, where trumped up charges ranging from drug possession to hooliganism are regularly used to detain people targeted for political reasons. Hilal Mammadov, who led the Committee for the Defense of Novruzali Mammadov, had since revived and taken over as editor of *Tolyshi Sado*. Although there still is no clear sense of why

Hilal Mammadov was arrested in 2012, there has been speculation that he was arrested in response to the popularity of a meykhana video he posted online, "Ty kto takoi? Davai, do svidaniia!" Filmed at a Talysh wedding in the Astara region of Azerbaijan, the video featured the Talysh, Azerbaijani, and Russian languages and gained extreme popularity in the former Soviet Union, particularly as a phrase of political protest, propelling Talysh culture into the mainstream and overwhelming the Azerbaijani government's expensive investment in hosting Eurovision that year.[65]

The Azerbaijani government accused him of spreading misinformation about Azerbaijan in discussions with foreigners about Talysh issues, raised the issue of his participation in the Talysh-Mughan Autonomous Republic, and insinuated that Mammadov was friendly with Armenians when he was in Russia. The latter accusation, which equated minority organizing with treason and implied that national minority activists in Azerbaijan are somehow motivated by loyalty to Armenia, sparked outrage among Hilal Mammadov supporters, who argued that the allegation was deeply offensive and disrespected the memory of Talyshes who died fighting for Azerbaijan in Karabakh. The accusation was, in effect, a denial of space for Talysh cultural activists in the Azerbaijani nation. In 2013, Hilal Mammadov was found guilty and sentenced to five years imprisonment, but in 2016 he was released early via presidential pardon. One month before his release, the European Court of Human Rights found that Azerbaijan had violated his right to humane treatment, his right to an investigation, and his right to an individual petition.[66] Although minority repression garners comparatively little attention in Azerbaijan, where paranoia about minority separatism and distrust of minority activism remain strong even among the political opposition, the Azerbaijan Institute of Peace and Democracy awarded Mammadov the Isakhan Ashurov Prize in recognition of his human rights work while he was on trial.[67]

In February 2019, Fakhraddin Aboszoda became the third editor of *Tolyshi Sado*—and final leader of the Talysh Mughan Autonomous Republic—to be arrested in Azerbaijan. Since the end of the republic, Aboszoda has edited multiple Talysh newspapers—including *Tolyshi Sado*, *Tolysh*, and *Shavnysht*—and published a series of Talysh-Russian and Talysh-English dictionaries, the first completed since Novruzali Mammadov's Talysh-Russian-Azerbaijani dictionary in 2006. Leading up to his arrest, Aboszoda had been a longtime resident of Russian. He first fled Azerbaijan in 1995 fearing that arrest was imminent for his participation in the republic. Like others, he returned in 2005, but left again in 2007 after Novruzali Mammadov's arrest signaled renewed repression of Talysh activists.

Perhaps in recognition of the fact that he harbored no hope of returning to Azerbaijan, after several years in Moscow, Aboszoda started to debate whether separatism could be the solution to Talysh problems in Azerbaijan. In one of his more provocative actions from Baku's perspective, he attended a conference in Yerevan, where he criticized Azerbaijan's treatment of Talyshes. In 2018, Azerbaijan formally petitioned the Russian government to arrest and deport Aboszoda to Azerbaijan on the grounds that he had threatened Azerbaijan's territorial integrity and incited ethnic hostility. Russian authorities detained Aboszoda in September 2018 and deported him to Azerbaijan in February 2019 despite a pending application for asylum. Aboszoda was arrested immediately upon arrival in Baku and nearly a year later, in February 2020, sentenced to 16 years in prison after being found guilty of public appeals against the state, inciting ethnic hatred, and treason.

Azerbaijan is clearly still contending with the republic's legacy today, as well as with older patterns, relations, and frustrations. Since the 1920s, centralizers in Baku have successfully impeded minority—namely, Talysh, Kurdish, and Lezgin—autonomies in Azerbaijan as well as Georgian attempts to annex Zaqatala, Balakan, and Qakh. Yet the ongoing disjuncture between promises of national equality for nontitular minorities and a differentiated lived experience have also motivated cultural and political actors intent on realizing actual equality for Azerbaijan's varied minority populations. Pitched battles over ethnogenesis testify to the embeddedness and ongoing relevance of Soviet models of titularity, with Azeris and other titular nations in the former Soviet Union still using ethnogenesis to legitimate their claims to dominance.

Perhaps the most striking pattern that has emerged from the Soviet period and transition to independence, however, is the tendency to conflate minority expression and demands for actualized equal rights with separatism. Madeleine Reeves, writing about the Ferghana Valley, analyzes a similarly instrumental and interventionist discourse of *konfliktogennost'* which "incites practices of anticipation; it invites intervention before conflict appears." She links this language to the underlying rationale of Soviet-era ethnoterritorialism, which sought to ensure that state and ethnic boundaries coincided. The inability to realize this ideal meant that "mismatches (*nesovpadeniia*) between ethnic and territorial boundaries" led to some areas known for their minority populations, density, and ethnic heterogeneity being identified as fundamentally unstable, prone to conflict, and in need of preemptive intervention.[68] In Azerbaijan, extreme sensitivity, even paranoia, surrounding minority organizing has guided assumptions about imminent separatism and incited "preventive" practices, mostly disciplining ones that punish participants or, at a minimum, seek to silence their complaints. This reaction belies Azeris' own anxiety about their place in Azerbaijan as well as a general ignorance of—or refusal to acknowledge—the grievances that have generated minority dissatisfaction. In the online chat room discussion about restrictions on Lezgin language signs in Qusar, for example, one of the participants wrote,

> Yeah, today they want the status of a regional language and tomorrow they will want autonomy as well . . . From the north, Avars and Lezgins, from the south Talyshes and it's still unknown how Karabakh will end and everything . . . Goodbye Azerbaijan . . .
>
> Such questions should be radically suppressed. All of us live in Azerbaijan and the state language is Azerbaijani . . . Minorities can converse in their language as much as they want to but nothing else . . . [69]

This quick link of cultural rights to autonomy (and then to separatism) reflects the sense among many people in Azerbaijan—government officials included—that minorities and minority identifications pose an existential threat to Azerbaijan and to the viability of the Azerbaijani nation. Limits on minority expression and organizing, pressure to acclimate to the Azerbaijani identification, and demonstrative repression of cultural activists affect minorities as well, coding minority identifications as nonviable, empty, and potentially dangerous. Among Talyshes, for example, if the case of Zulfugar Ahmedzade sparked a fear that silenced some, what has happened to Talysh cultural leaders and national activists more recently has been similarly disciplining.

The Soviet Union fostered many expectations, including some that contradicted one another. Practices that established and sustained titular hegemony (and defined the titular nationality as an ethnic belonging defined by a titular national culture and language rather than as a civic belonging) clashed with discourses about Soviet unity and national minority equality. While many minorities experienced a downturn in national cultural resources and recognition at the end of the 1930s, people in those communities continued to find inspiration in the promise of national equality, the example of co-ethnics and other nationalities around them, and the remnants of national minority *korenizatsiia*, which still inspired demands that the discourses of equality start to actually mean something in the Soviet system.

Some rights were regained, but others remained out of reach. Among those who continued to see themselves as Talysh, Lezgin, Avar, Kurdish, or something other than simply Azerbaijani, frustration with enduring national inequalities sometimes found expression in autonomy or separatist movements, the former sanctioned by precedence in the Soviet Union and the latter always an off-limits concept. And these ideas, in turn, fed Azeri insecurities. It is not that tensions or problems do not and have not existed, but that for a long time there has not been public space for productive expression of these ideas and critical discussion of what they mean. The persistence of different ways of imagining what it means to be Azerbaijani ultimately means that while it is a natural way of ordering oneself for many people in Azerbaijan, some minorities continue to reject this identification while still others find a way to acclimate and fit into it without achieving a substantive sense of belonging.

NOTES

Introduction

1. Archive of Political Documents of the Administrative Department of the President of the Republic of Azerbaijan [*Azərbaycan Respublikası Prezidentinin İşlər İdarəsinin Siyasi Sənədlər Arxivi*], 1.48.405.90 (hereafter ARPİİSSA). There is no uniform agreement about the definition and usage of the terms Ingiloi and Georgian in this community (and in the region in general). I use "Georgian-Ingiloi" in order to be inclusive of the different ways in which people from these communities in the Qakh, Balakan, and Zaqatala regions of Azerbaijan have identified themselves to me and categorized themselves in archived complaint letters—as Ingiloi, Ingiloi, Georgian, and Georgian-Ingiloi. Indeed, it is not unusual for state authorities or people from these communities to switch among these ethnonyms in the same document or conversation.

2. S. I. Bruk and V. S. Apenchenko, eds., *Atlas narodov mira* (Nauka: Moscow, 1964), preface.

3. RGASPI 558.1.4490.9, cited in Terry Martin, *The Affirmative Action Empire: Nations and Nationalism in the Soviet Union, 1923–1939* (Ithaca, NY: Cornell University Press, 2001), 5.

4. Martin, *The Affirmative Action Empire*, 15.

5. Francine Hirsch, *Empire of Nations: Ethnographic Knowledge and the Making of the Soviet Union* (Ithaca, NY: Cornell University Press, 2005), 14.

6. Some scholars have argued that Soviet Central Asia more closely resembled other modern states than colonial empires (see, for example, Adeeb Khalid, "Backwardness and the Quest for Civilization: Early Soviet Central Asia in Comparative Perspective," *Slavic Review* 65, no. 2 [2006]: 232), but others have adopted a more ambivalent view, finding, as Adrienne Edgar does, that the Soviet Union "was neither an empire nor a unitary state but had features of both." Edgar, "Bolshevism, Patriarchy, and the Nation: The Soviet 'Emancipation' of Muslim Women in Pan-Islamic Perspective," *Slavic Review* 65, no. 2 (2006): 272. Botakoz Kassymbekova questions the dominant role that Central Asia has played in debates about Soviet colonialism, but similarly pushes for a more flexible and less binary understanding of Soviet rule, one that treats modern state building and colonialism as complex and interrelated "repertoires of power." Kassymbekova, *Despite Cultures: Early Soviet Rule in Tajikistan* (Pittsburgh: University of Pittsburgh Press, 2016), 15–16. Looking more broadly at the Soviet Union, Valerie Kivelson and Ron Suny make the case for the USSR as a nationalizing empire. Kivelson and Suny, *Russia's Empires* (New York: Oxford University Press, 2017).

7. Moritz Florin, "Beyond Colonialism? Agency, Power, and the Making of Soviet Central Asia," *Kritika: Explorations in Russian and Eurasian History* 18, no.4 (Fall 2017): 828.

8. Maria Todorova, "Balkanism and Postcolonialism, or On the Beauty of the Airplane View," in *Marx's Shadow: Knowledge, Power, and Intellectuals in Eastern Europe and Russia*, ed. Costica Bradatan and Serguei Alex. Oushakine (New York: Lexington Books, 2010), 181, cited in Oushakine "Political Estrangements"; and Serguei Alex. Oushakine, "Political Estrangements: Claiming a Space Between Stalin and Hitler," in *Rites of Place: Public Commemoration in Russia and Eastern Europe*, ed. Julie Buckler and Emily D. Johnson (Evanston, IL: Northwestern University Press), 287.

9. Irada Ismail kyzy Kasumova, "Kul'turnoe stroitel'stvo v Azerbaidzhane v 20-30-e gody/na primere natsional'nykh men'shinstv i malochislennykh narodov," Kandidat istoricheskikh nauk diss., Bakinskii gosudarstvennyi universitet im. M. E. Rasulzade, 1996, 9.

10. The concept of "leapfrogging" is borrowed from Frederick Cooper, who criticizes a similar tendency in colonial and postcolonial histories. Cooper, *Colonialism in Question: Theory, Knowledge, History* (Berkeley: University of California Press, 2005), 17. Crafting arguments about the trajectory of nationality policies from 1917 to 1991 is difficult based on the current historiography, which remains overly dependent on histories of the 1920s and 1930s. Jeremy Smith, for instance, has posited that there was no coherent nationality policy in the Soviet Union after the 1920s and that the "final acts in Soviet nationality policies" occurred in the early 1930s. In making this sweeping argument, however, he maintains an overwhelming focus on the first two decades of Soviet history, more clearly illustrating the chronological failures of the field than the absence of a nationality policy engagement over the long term. Smith, "Was There a Soviet Nationality Policy?" *Europe-Asia Studies* 71, no. 6 (2019): 972–993.

11. For early examples of this genre, see Ronald Grigor Suny, *The Revenge of the Past: Nationalism, Revolution, and the Collapse of the Soviet Union* (Stanford, CA: Stanford University Press, 1993); and Yuri Slezkine, "The USSR as a Communal Apartment, or How a Socialist State Promoted Ethnic Particularism," *Slavic Review* 53, no. 2 (Summer 1994).

12. For examples of this literature, Robert Conquest, *The Last Empire* (London: Ampersand Books, 1962); Robert Conquest, *Stalin: Breaker of Nations* (New York: Penguin Books, 1992); Walter Kolarz, *The Peoples of the Soviet Far East* (New York: Praeger, 1954); Walter Kolarz, *Russia and her Colonies* (New York: Praeger, 1952); and Richard Pipes, *The Formation of the Soviet Union: Communism and Nationalism, 1917–1923* (Cambridge, MA: Harvard University Press, 1954). There was also variance in these earlier years, however. In Alexander Park's 1957 study of Turkestan, he established a middle ground between two diametrically opposed interpretive frameworks: a pre–World War II tendency to acknowledge Soviet success in building equality and progress and an ascendant postwar narrative that emphasized the artificial and divisive characteristics of these nationality politics. Park concluded that a mix of theoretical and practical shortcomings inadvertently cultivated colonial divisions and inequalities between Moscow and the "national" periphery, but also argued that the Bolsheviks were often sincere in their efforts to achieve national equality. Alexander G. Park, *Bolshevism in Turkestan: 1917–1927* (New York: Columbia University Press, 1957). For more background on Cold War–era historiography and its ideological underpinnings,

see David Engerman, *Know Your Enemy: The Rise and Fall of America's Soviet Experts* (New York: Oxford University Press, 2009).

13. See, for example, Kate Brown, *A Biography of No Place: From Ethnic Borderland to Soviet Heartland* (Cambridge, MA: Harvard University Press, 2004); Bruce Grant, *In the Soviet House of Culture: A Century of Perestroikas* (Princeton, NJ: Princeton University Press, 1995); and Alaina Lemon, *Between Two Fires: Gypsy Performance and Romani Memory from Pushkin to Postsocialism* (Durham, NC: Duke University Press, 2000).

14. The dynamic that plays out across internal Soviet republic borders is similar to what Rogers Brubaker finds with homeland nationalisms and ethnonational kin abroad. Brubaker, *Nationalism Reframed: Nationhood and the National Question in the New Europe* (Cambridge: Cambridge University Press, 1996).

15. Rogers Brubaker, *Ethnicity Without Groups* (Cambridge, MA: Harvard University Press, 2004), 8.

16. Ann Laura Stoler, "Colonial Archives and the Arts of Governance: On the Content in the Form," in *Archives, Documentation, and Institutions of Social Memory*, ed. Francis X. Blouin Jr. and William G. Rosenberg (Ann Arbor: University of Michigan Press, 2006), 271.

17. Kirsten Weld, *Paper Cadavers: The Archives of Dictatorship in Guatemala* (Durham, NC: Duke University Press, 2014).

18. Antonio Gramsci, *Selections from the Prison Notebooks*, ed. Quintin Hoare and Geoffrey Nowell Smith (London, 1971), 54–55, cited in Gyanendra Pandey, *Routine Violence: Nations, Fragments, Histories* (Stanford, CA: Stanford University Press, 2006), quote on 60.

19. Michel-Rolph Trouillot, *Silencing the Past: Power and the Production of History* (Boston: Beacon, 1995); Ann Laura Stoler, *Along the Archival Grain: Epistemic Anxieties and Colonial Common Sense* (Princeton, NJ: Princeton University Press, 2010).

20. Irina Sherbakova, "The Gulag in Memory," in *Memory and Totalitarianism*, ed. Luisa Passerini (New Brunswick, NJ: Transaction, 2009), 103.

21. Daria Khubova, Andrei Ivankiev, and Tonia Sharova, "After Glasnost: Oral History in the Soviet Union," in *Memory and Totalitarianism*, ed. Luisa Passerini (New Brunswick, NJ: Transaction, 2009), 96.

22. Khubova, Ivankiev, and Sharova, "After Glasnost," 89.

23. In his anthropography of violence, E. Valentine Daniel discusses the "drone of silence" in interviews with people who experienced torture. He describes it as "a silence that does not settle for the anthropologist whether it is a silence of not-being-able-to-speak or of an ought-not-to-speak." Daniel, *Charred Lullabies: Chapters in an Anthropology of Violence* (Princeton, NJ: Princeton University Press, 1996), 150. Urvashi Butalia, meanwhile, writes about the "other side of silence" in her study of the violence, particularly against women, that occurred during the Partition of India. She calls attention to the nuances, half-said things, ambiguous phrasings, and hidden histories that are masked by oral and textual silences. Butalia also pushes researchers to take responsibility for what it means for informants to break their silence in an interview, and to recognize those times when silences are more important—and less invasive—than speech. Butalia, *The Other Side of Silence: Voices from the Partition of India* (Durham, NC: Duke University Press, 2000).

24. Alessandro Portelli differentiates between remembering and memory. Remembering calls to mind an active and ongoing process, whereas memory implies that

something is stabilized and known. Portelli, "Response to Commentaries," *Oral History Review* 32, no. 1 (Winter–Spring 2005): 30. Luisa Passerini, meanwhile, valuably draws our attention to the interplay between remembering and forgetting: "silences, oblivions, and memories are aspects of the same process, and the art of memory cannot but be also an art of forgetting, through the mediation of silence and the alteration of silence and sound." Passerini, "Memories between Silence and Oblivion," in *Memory, History, Nation: Contested Pasts*, ed. Katharine Hodgkin and Susannah Radstone (New Brunswick, NJ: Transaction, 2006), 250. Their observations underscore the point that Anika Walke has made about the collaborative work of interviews and their afterlives: "Recalling the past is an activity, it is work: memory work. Memory work also involves listening to those who remember and talk about their lives, about violence and its effects on their lives and relationships, and then arranging these recollections." Walke, *Pioneers and Partisans: An Oral History of Nazi Genocide in Belorussia* (Oxford: Oxford University Press, 2015), 25.

25. This is similar to a point that Irada Ismail kyzy Kasumova makes in her dissertation. She argues that the 1936–1937 repression of scholars who studied national minorities in Azerbaijan suppressed further work in that sphere. She cites the arrest of historian A. Bukshpan, who published a study of the Kurds in the early 1930s, as one example (Kasumova, "Kul'turnoe stroitel'stvo," 7). Other nontitular minority cultural leaders were also targeted at this time.

26. The leader of the Talysh-Mughan Autonomous Republic, Alakram Hümmatov (Hümmətov), was sentenced to death. This sentence was later commuted to a life sentence before he was stripped of his citizenship and exiled to the Netherlands in 2004. Other key participants who remained in Azerbaijan or the broader region have faced ongoing repression.

27. Interview, March 2011. K'vat'al can roughly be translated as circle, meeting, or association. Zabit Rizvanov, *Kniga pravdy: sbornik statei, 1980–90 gg.* (Qusar: Samizdat, n.d.), 115.

28. In some cases, people in minority zones reported that local police or government officials questioned them simply because they invited a foreigner (me) into their home.

29. Interview, April 2011.

30. Interview, November 2010.

31. Nergis Canefe, "Communal Memory and Turkish Cypriot National History: Missing Links," in *Balkan Identities: Nation and Memory*, ed. Maria Todorova (New York: New York University Press, 2004), 79.

32. RFE/RL, "Azerbaijan a Model of Tolerance—Aliyev," *Eurasianet*, April 7, 2011, https://eurasianet.org/azerbaijan-a-model-of-tolerance-aliyev.

33. Rogers Brubaker et al., *Nationalist Politics and Everyday Ethnicity in a Transylvanian Town* (Princeton, NJ: Princeton University Press, 2006), 207–208.

34. See, for example, Jennifer Solveig Wistrand, "Becoming Azerbaijani: Uncertainty, Belonging, and Getting by in a Post-Soviet Society," PhD diss., Washington University, 2011.

35. Marianne Kamp, for example, cites Trevor Lummis's argument that "the individual oral history accounts from the memories of those who actually lived that experience are very different from 'popular' presentations" and contrasts this interpretation with that of the "popular memory school," which Lummis summarizes as be-

lieving that "memory cannot simply be a memory of life as it was ... anyone's memory must be selectively distorted by the class power behind the projection of these images." See, Kamp, *The New Woman in Uzbekistan: Islam, Modernity, and Unveiling under Communism* (Seattle: University of Washington Press, 2006), 15; and Trevor Lummis, *Listening to History: The Authenticity of Oral Evidence* (Totowa, NJ: Barnes & Noble, 1988), 123, 126. Elsewhere, Kamp draws attention to the way in which politics intrude on personal remembrances, but describes a trajectory in which the collapse of the Soviet Union allows for both spontaneous individual release from ideological narratives and the emergence of an interviewee's agency rather than turning an equally critical eye to external influences that filled the vacuum left by the Soviet system. Marianne Kamp, "Three Lives of Saodat: Communist, Uzbek, Survivor," *Oral History Review* 28, no. 2 (Summer–Autumn 2001): 21–58.

36. Alessandro Portelli, "What Makes Oral History Different," in *The Oral History Reader*, ed. Robert Perks and Alistair Thomson (Abingdon, UK: Routledge, 1998), 68.

37. Liisa Malkki, *Purity and Exile: Violence, Memory, and National Cosmology among Hutu Refugees in Tanzania* (Chicago: University of Chicago Press, 1995), 104.

1. Making Minorities and National Hierarchies

1. The spelling of Ayyub as Əjjub reflects the Latin alphabet from the time that Zulfugar Ahmedzade wrote these telegrams and letters. According to the Latin alphabet used now in Azerbaijan, Əjjub is more often written as Əyyub, hence my use of Ayyub here.

2. Deputy head of Azerbaijan SSR Supreme Court S. Imanov, spravka no. 7-0/826, November 1956, private document collection.

3. Tsentral'nyi gosudarstvennyi arkhiv Oktiabr'skoi revoliutsii i sotsialisticheskogo stroitel'stva, arkhivnaia spravka, Baku, October 12, 1989, private document collection.

4. M. Iu. Gasan-Dzhalalova, Azerneshr arkhivnaia spravka, Baku, August 30, 1989, private document collection.

5. Deputy head of Azerbaijan SSR Supreme Court S. Imanov, spravka no. 7-0/826, November 1956, private document collection.

6. For some examples of these elite negotiations in other Soviet national communities, see Adrienne Edgar, *Tribal Nation: The Making of Soviet Turkmenistan* (Princeton, NJ: Princeton University Press, 2004); Adeeb Khalid, *Making Uzbekistan: Nation, Empire, and Revolution in the Early USSR* (Ithaca, NY: Cornell University Press, 2015); and Brigid O'Keeffe, *New Soviet Gypsies: Nationality, Performance, and Selfhood in the Early Soviet Union* (Toronto: University of Toronto Press, 2013).

7. For an example of this tendency see Audrey L. Altstadt, *The Politics of Culture in Soviet Azerbaijan, 1920–1940* (London: Routledge, 2016).

8. Khalid, *Making Uzbekistan*, 267.

9. The TSFSR, comprised of the Armenian, Azerbaijani, and Georgian republics, existed from 1922 to 1936. Based in Tbilisi, it oversaw military decisions, foreign affairs, infrastructure, economic and fiscal matters, interrepublic disputes, public health, communications, transportation, and cultural development. The TSFSR functioned as an added layer of bureaucracy between the republics and Moscow and had the power to

overrule republic decisions, although republics also gained the right of appeal. The battle over its establishment climaxed in the Georgian Affair, a clash between Stalin and Ordzhonikidze, who both favored centralization, and the Georgian Communist Party (especially Polikarp "Budu" Mdivani), who opposed the Federation. The conflict also reflected a broader power struggle between Lenin and Stalin. For more on the Georgian Affair, see Moshe Lewin, *Lenin's Last Struggle*, trans. A. M. Sheridan Smith (Ann Arbor: University of Michigan Press, 2005); and Jeremy Smith, *The Bolsheviks and the National Question*, Studies in Russia and East Europe (New York: St. Martin's Press, 1999).

10. For more on Azerbaijani identity and nation-building in Azerbaijan prior to Sovietization, see Altstadt, *Politics of Culture*, chap. 1; Leah Feldman, *On the Threshold of Eurasia: Revolutionary Poetics in the Caucasus* (Ithaca, NY: Cornell University Press, 2018); James H. Meyer, *Turks Across Empires: Marketing Muslim Identity in the Russian-Ottoman Borderlands, 1856–1914* (Oxford: Oxford University Press, 2014); and Kelsey Rice, "Forging the Progressive Path: Literary Assemblies and Enlightenment Societies in Azerbaijan, 1850–1928," PhD diss., University of Pennsylvania, 2018.

11. Today, the term is often used in Russian everyday speech as an ethnic slur to refer to someone who is not of Russian origin (usually someone from Central Asia or the Caucasus).

12. Janet Klein, "Making Minorities in the Eurasian Borderlands: A Comparative Perspective from the Russian and Ottoman Empires," in *Empire and Belonging in the Eurasian Borderlands*, ed. Krista A. Goff and Lewis H. Siegelbaum (Ithaca, NY: Cornell University Press, 2019), 17–18.

13. See, for example, Francine Hirsch, *Empire of Nations*, 9; Terry Martin, *Affirmative Action Empire*, chap. 10; and Nicholas Timasheff, *The Great Retreat: The Growth and Decline of Communism in Russia* (New York: E.P. Dutton and Company, 1946).

14. ARDA 57.1.151.11. Azeris are generally referred to as "Tiurk" in state documents in the 1920s and early 1930s. "Azerbaijani" gained traction in official and popular use in the latter half of the 1930s. I follow the same practice here to stay true to the language used in primary sources but also to highlight how official ethnonyms changed over time.

15. M. G. Veliev (Bakharly), *Azerbaidzhan (Fiziko-geograficheskii, etnograficheskii i ekonomicheskii ocherk)* (Baku: Izd-vo Sov. Nar. Khoz., 1921), 50, cited in A. Bukshpan, *Azerbaidzhanskie kurdy: Lachin, Kel'badzhary, Nakhkrai: Zametki* (Baku: Azerbaidzhanskii gos. nauchno-issledovat. institut. Otdelenie Vostoka, 1932), 75–76.

16. See the Archive of the Ministry of Internal Affairs of Georgia II (sakartvelos šinagan sakmeta saministros arqivi, or sšssa [II]), 13.3.103.10-17. For more on discourses of backwardness tied to women, see Northrop, *Veiled Empire: Gender and Power in Stalinist Central Asia* (Ithaca, NY: Cornell University Press, 2004).

17. ARDA 57.1.538.57.

18. Mountain Jews, or Juhuro as they self-identify, consider themselves to be descendants of the ten lost tribes and date their origin in Dagestan and northern Azerbaijan to the First Temple period. Many linguists and historians have estimated, however, that Mountain Jews migrated to this area in the fifth century. Mikhail A. Chlenov, "Rasselenie evreiskikh etnicheskikh grupp na Kavkaze," in *Materialy mezhdunarodnogo nauchnogo simpoziuma "Gorskie evrei Kavkaza," 24–26 aprelia 2001 g. Baku-Kuba-Krasnaia Sloboda* (Baku: Elm, 2002), 25–26.

19. sšssa (II), 13.3.103.18-19.

20. Aleksei Lund, "At the Center of the Periphery: Oil, Land, and Power in Baku, 1905–1917," PhD diss., Stanford University, 2013, 142–143; Ronald Suny, *The Baku Commune 1917–1918: Class and Nationality in the Russian Revolution* (Princeton, NJ: Princeton University Press, 1972), chap. 1.

21. sšssa (II) 13.3.103.10.

22. Hüseynov was chairman of the Presidium of the Central Committee, not first secretary.

23. A celebration of Baku's pluralist past contrasts with the nativist interpretation of Baku's modern history. For more on the history of Azerbaijan's multicultural capital city, see Bruce Grant, "'Cosmopolitan Baku,'" *Ethnos: Journal of Anthropology* 75, no. 2 (June 2010): 123–147.

24. The specifics of how this played out for the titular nationality are beyond the scope of this book. See Altstadt, *Politics of Culture*, for details about the ways in which the implementation of Tiurk korenizatsiia was hampered in Azerbaijan.

25. ARDA 57.1.153.11, 11ob. See also Kasumova, "Kul'turnoe stroitel'stvo."

26. ARDA 57.1.864.125.

27. Thus far, of course, the Transcaucasian Federation had mainly been a source of conflict. Its establishment had generated the Georgian Affair the previous year and, at this Congress, Stalin and Ordzhonikidze battled once more with Georgian "deviationists" (principally Philip Makharadze and Mdivani) over the federation and, ultimately, political centralization. Russian State Archive of Socio-Political History (Rossiiskii gosudarstvennyi arkhiv sotsial'no-politicheskoi istorii), or RGASPI, 64.1.215.108. Stalin and Ordzhonikidze envisioned a type of institutional organization that would unify what had been three independent states, neutralize economic devastation in the region, create a network of self-help that would localize costs for rebuilding after lengthy conflicts, and allow disputes to be resolved in the Caucasus rather than Moscow. Despite Georgian opposition to this plan, others supported this effort, including the Central Committee of the Azerbaijan Communist Party, which feared Bolshevik rule might otherwise collapse. See, Brinegar, "Baku at All Costs: The Politics of Oil in the New Soviet State," PhD diss., University of Wisconsin–Madison, 2014, 61–65; Etienne Forestier-Peyrat, "Soviet Federalism at Work: Lessons from the History of the Transcaucasian Federation, 1922–1936," *Jahrbücher für Geschichte Osteuropas* 65, no. 4 (2017): 529–559.

28. For example, ARDA 57.1.538.51. In documents from this period, the settlement is generally referred to as Jewish Slobodka (Evreiskaia slobodka) or simply slobodka. It is known as Qırmızı Qasaba (Qəsəbə) in Azerbaijani, but I use the Russian name (Krasnaia Sloboda) as it is more commonly used in English-language sources.

29. ARDA 379.9.17.1-2. Miudzhi Gavtaran is also referred to as Medzhi-Kaftaran in some documents.

30. ARDA 379.9.16.30.

31. ARDA 379.9.16.10.

32. ARDA 57.1.39-45.

33. Bukshpan, *Azerbaidzhanskie kurdy*, 50–53. Harun Yilmaz indicates that two factions—one that favored autonomy and a "pro-Turkic or centralist" group that wanted to create an "ordinary" Kurdistan *uezd* with no special status—hashed out Kurdistan's status at a meeting of the presidium of the Central Executive Committee

in late 1922, but discussions about Kurdistan's composition extended into the summer of 1923 and included multiple proposals. Yilmaz, "The Rise of Red Kurdistan," *Iranian Studies* 47, no. 5 (2014): 803.

34. It took more than a year to resolve Karabakh's borders and legal status after the initial declaration of its creation in July 1923. The Autonomous Oblast' of Nagorno-Karabakh was renamed the Nagorno-Karabakh Autonomous Oblast' in 1937. For more on the creation of Karabakh Armenian autonomy in Azerbaijan, see Arsène Saparov, *From Conflict to Autonomy in the Caucasus: The Soviet Union and the Making of Abkhazia, South Ossetia, and Nagorno Karabakh* (Abingdon, Oxon: Routledge, 2015).

35. ARDA 57.1.864.110. See also "Obrazovan Kurdistanskii okrug," *Zaria Vostoka*, June 2, 1930, and ARDA 379.1.3247.1.

36. Bugai and Mamaev, *Kurdy SSSR*, 96.

37. Arsène Saparov, "Between the Russian Empire and the USSR: The independence of Transcaucasia as a socio-political transformation," in *Routledge Handbook of the Caucasus*, ed. Galina M. Yemelianova and Laurence Broers, 133 (Abingdon, Oxon: Routledge, 2020).

38. For more on this case, see Timothy Blauvelt, "The 'Mingrelian Question': Institutional Resources and the Limits of Soviet Nationality Policy," *Europe-Asia Studies* 66, no. 6 (May 2014): 993–1013.

39. Michael Reynolds, *Shattering Empires: The Clash and Collapse of the Ottoman and Russian Empires 1908–1918* (Cambridge: Cambridge University Press, 2011), 46.

40. See, for example, the report written by Russian army captain P. I. Aver'yanov from 1900, recently republished as *Kurdy v voinakh Rossii s Persiei i Turtsiei v techenie XIX stoletiia* (Tiflis: Tipografiia Shtaba Kavkazskago voennago okruga, 1900; reprint, Moscow: Ripol Klassik, 2013).

41. See, for example, Jo Laycock, "Developing a Soviet Armenian Nation: Refugees and Resettlement in the Early Soviet South Caucasus," in *Empire and Belonging in the Eurasian Borderlands*, ed. Krista A. Goff and Lewis H. Siegelbaum (Ithaca, NY: Cornell University Press, 2019); and Jeremy Johnson, "Speaking Soviet with an Armenian Accent: Literacy, Language Ideology, and Belonging in Early Soviet Armenia," in *Empire and Belonging in the Eurasian Borderlands*.

42. See Uğur Ümit Üngör, *The Making of Modern Turkey: Nation and State in Eastern Anatolia, 1913–1950* (Oxford: Oxford University Press, 2011), esp. chap. 3; and Zharmukhamed Zardykhan, "Ottoman Kurds of the First World War Era: Reflections in Russian Sources," *Middle Eastern Studies* 42, no. 1 (January 2006): 67.

43. Martin van Bruinessen, *Agha, Shaikh and State: The Social and Political Structures of Kurdistan* (London: Zed Books, 1992), 280.

44. sšssa (II) 13.9.153.

45. ARDA 411s.20.13.10.

46. Sabina Rafik kyzy Gadzhieva, "Razvitie shkoly natsional'nykh men'shinstv i malochislennykh narodov Azerbaidzhana: 1920–1940 gody," Kandidat pedagogicheskikh nauk diss., Azerbaidzhanskii gosudarstvennyi pedagogicheskii universitet, 2005, 44.

47. Gadzhieva, "Razvitie shkoly," 86.

48. Gadzhieva, "Razvitie shkoly," 87.

49. Gadzhieva, "Razvitie shkoly," 81.

50. ARDA 379.7.16.7, 9.

51. Gadzhieva, "Razvitie shkoly," 84–86.

52. Sheila Fitzpatrick, "Cultural Revolution in Russia 1928–32," *Journal of Contemporary History* 9, no. 1 (January 1974): 33–52.

53. Martin, *Affirmative Action Empire*, 7.

54. RGASPI 64.1.215.108-111.

55. Slezkine, "Communal Apartment," 438–439.

56. Martin, *Affirmative Action Empire*, 154–155, 178; Altstadt, *Politics of Culture*, 52.

57. Khalid, *Making Uzbekistan*, 20.

58. Khalid, *Making Uzbekistan*, 363. The disciplining of titular nations and elites looked different in different republics. In Turkmenistan, for example, the purge of titular communists and elites hit a little later than in Uzbekistan. Adrienne Lynn Edgar, *Tribal Nation*, 124–128.

59. Khalid, *Making Uzbekistan*, 280–281.

60. Brigid O'Keeffe's study of Roma national policies, meanwhile, reminds us of the diversity of nontitular minority experiences and chronologies. As early as 1928, the NKVD liquidated the Gypsy Union, declaring it a "lifeless organization." O'Keeffe, *New Soviet Gypsies*, 59–60.

61. ARDA 57.1.538.72.

62. ARDA 57.1.571.22.

63. ARDA 57.11.7.30-31, 57.1.571.21-22, and 57.1.864.9-11.

64. ARDA 57.1.864.112-113.

65. ARDA 57.11.7.49.

66. ARDA 57.1.560.25.

67. ARDA 57.1.560.13-26.

68. State Archive of the Russian Federation (Gosudarstvennyi arkhiv Rossiiskoi Federatsii, or GARF) 9478.1.469.6561-6565. Bruce Grant conducted a fascinating case study of a Shaki rebellion in, "An Average Azeri Village (1930): Remembering Rebellion in the Caucasus Mountains," *Slavic Review* 63, no. 4 (Winter 2004): 705–731.

69. sšssa (II) 13.9.195.47.

70. sšssa (II) 13.9.195.47. In 1931, the national breakdown in Azerbaijan was reported as the following: 1,648,788 (62.1 percent) Tiurks out of a total population of 2,653,758 people in Azerbaijan. The rest of the population was categorized as: Armenian (323,494, or 12.2 percent), Russian (273,859, or 10.3 percent), Talysh (88,636, or 3.3 percent), Kurdish (46,444, or 1.8 percent), Lezgins (42,726, or 1.6 percent), Tat (34,641, or 1.3 percent), Jewish (22,026, or 0.8 percent), and Georgian (10,830, or 0.4 percent). The remaining 162,314 people (6.1 percent) were Avars, Tsakhurs, Germans, Mountain Jews, Tatars, Greeks, Persians, Udins, Assyrians, and others.

71. sšssa (II) 13.9.195.61.

72. sšssa (II) 13.9.195.49-50.

73. Suny, *Modern Georgian Nation*, 254.

74. sšssa (II) 13.9.195.121; Suny, *Modern Georgian Nation*, 253.

75. sšssa (II) 13.9.195.122.

76. ARDA 57.1.873.6-9.

77. Regions in Nagorno-Karabakh and Nakhchıvan were excluded from this count.

78. Although called "Annenfal'" in this document (the city had previously been named Annenfeld by the German colony there), the settlement by now was known as

Annino. In 1938, it was renamed Shamkhor, in reference to a historical name (Shamkir) for this settlement area. It is now Shamkir. Central Archive of the Contemporary History of Georgia (sakartvelos uaxlesi istoriis centraluri arqivi), or suica, 607.1.33 36.74.

79. Talysh was taught in the Lankaran region until sixth grade, and in other regions until fourth grade. Gadzhieva, "Razvitie shkoly," 109–110.

80. Gadzhieva, "Razvitie shkoly," 110.

81. ARDA 57.11.32.17, ARDA 57.11.32.26.

82. Interview conducted in the Lankaran region, 2008. ARDA 57.11.32.40, 47.

83. ARDA 57.1.864.11, ARDA 57.11.7.24 / 24a; sšssa (II) 13.9.195.56.

84. Gadzhieva, "Razvitie shkoly," 96–115.

85. Gadzhieva, "Razvitie shkoly," 124.

86. Central State Archive of the Republic of Dagestan (Tsentral'nyi gosudarstvennyi arkhiv Respubliki Dagestan), or TsGA RD, 645p.2.18.22.

87. TsGA RD, 37r.22.38.17-25.

88. ARDA 57.1.864.111-112.

89. For example, ARDA 57.1.395.2ob.

90. In the document, Lezgins and Mountain Jews are combined. ARDA 57.1.864.110.

91. ARDA 57.1.864.112.

92. ARDA 57.11.7.21.

93. ARDA 379.1.6907.10.

94. ARDA 379.1.6907.1-12.

95. Martin, *Affirmative Action Empire*, 439.

96. GARF R3316.29.575.17-18.

97. ARDA 894.2.39.24-25 and 894.7.18-39.

98. GARF R3316.29.576.1-3.

99. Hirsch, *Empire of Nations*, 274.

100. Hirsch, *Empire of Nations*, 287–291.

101. Pavel Polian, *Against Their Will: The History and Geography of Forced Migrations in the USSR*, trans. Anna Yastrzhembska (Budapest: Central European University Press, 2003), 102.

102. GARF 9479.1.55.24-28, cited in Bugai and Mamaev, *Kurdy SSSR*, 158.

103. Svetlana Alieva, ed., *Tak eto bylo: Natsional'nye repressii v SSSR, 1919–1952 gody*, t. 1 (Moscow: Insan, 1993), 104.

104. RGASPI 17.162.17.134 reprinted in Bugai and Mamaev, *Kurdy SSSR*, 118.

105. The idea was first proposed in 1926. ARDA 379.28.243.1, 1ob.

106. Relevant interviews were conducted by the author between 2011 and 2016.

107. sšssa (II) 13.9.195.58.

108. ARDA 57.1.864.9.

109. For example, ARDA 411.20.61.

110. On the uprisings, see GARF 9478.1.469.6566-6569.

111. sšssa (II) 13.9.195.58.

112. sšssa (II) 13.9.195.61.

113. Oral history interviews with Talyshes whose relatives were deported. Interviews conducted by the author between 2011 and 2016.

114. ARDA 57.11.32.35-38ob.

115. ARDA 379.1.6907.9-12.

116. ARDA 379.1.6907.1-2.

117. ARDA 379.1.7047.1.

118. ARDA Shaki Filial (ARDASF) 216.1.217.61.

119. For example, ARDA 57.11.332.

120. RGANI 89.62.7.1; RGANI 89.62.4.1; Martin, *Affirmative Action Empire*, 411–412.

121. In Azerbaijan, the Sovnarkom and Central Committee of the Communist Party adopted the decree on March 23, 1938. ARDA 411.35.39.146-147.

122. Martin, *Affirmative Action Empire*, chap. 10.

123. Peter Blitstein, "Nation-Building or Russification? Obligatory Russian Instruction in the Soviet Non-Russian School, 1938–1953," in *A State of Nations*, ed. Ronald Grigor Suny and Terry Dean Martin (New York: Oxford University Press, 2001), 255–258.

124. ARDA 57.1.1292.106, 206.

125. For example, ARDA 57.1.1292.130.

126. ARDA 57.1.1292.85-86; ARDA 57.1.1292.204.

127. ARDA 57.1.1292.94.

128. ARDA 57.1.1292.165-167.

129. ARDA 57.1.1292.167.

130. ARDA 57.1.1292.96.

131. ARDA 57.1.1292.94-99.

132. ARDA SF 197.1.84.3-22.

133. ARDA 57.11.32.20.

134. ARDA 57.1.1292.171-172.

135. ARPİİSSA 1.74.103.218.

136. El'dar Ismailov, *Istoriia "bol'shogo terrora" v Azerbaidzhane* (Moscow: ROSSPEN, 2015), 156.

137. GARF 3316.27.766 (1934), 125–126, quoted in Martin, *Affirmative Action Empire*, 408.

138. Hirsch, *Empire of Nations*, 290.

139. Baberowski, *Der Feind ist überall:Stalinismus im Kaukasus* (Munich: Deutsche Verlags-Anstalt, 2003), 814–815; Altstadt, *Politics of Culture*, 188; and Ismailov, *Istoriia 'bol'shogo terrora' v Azerbaidzhane*, 5.

140. Altstadt, *Politics of Culture*, xiii, 200.

141. Isabelle Ruth Kaplan, "The Art of Nation-Building: National Culture and Soviet Politics in Stalin-Era Azerbaijan and Other Minority Republics," PhD diss., Georgetown University, 2017, 164 and 177; Baberowski, *Der Feind ist überall*, 814–829.

142. Zulfugar Ahmedzade letters from private collection.

2. Territory, War, and Nation-Building in the South Caucasus

1. Ablet Kamalov provides a succinct overview of different historiographical, oral history, and memoir interpretations of Soviet involvement in the Ili Rebellion and ETR (1944–1949), as well as its effect on Uyghur nation-building. Kamalov, "Uyghur Memoir Literature in Central Asia on Eastern Turkestan Republic (1944–49)," in James A.

Millward, Shinmen Yasushi, and Jun Sugawara, eds., *Studies on Xinjiang Historical Sources in 17–20th Centuries* (Tokyo: Toyo Bunko, 2010), 257–278.

2. Nikki Keddie, *Modern Iran: Roots and Results of Revolution* (New Haven, CT: Yale University Press, 2006), 105. See also Nikolay A. Kozhanov, "The Pretexts and Reasons for the Allied Invasion of Iran in 1941," *Iranian Studies* 45, no. 4 (2012): 479–497; and Richard A. Stewart, *Sunrise at Abadan: The British and Soviet Invasion of Iran, 1941* (New York: Praeger, 1988). Reza Shah's pro-German orientation unnerved the Soviet leadership, which had viewed Iranian state documents indicating that Iran planned to seize territory in the Soviet south if Hitler's invasion of the USSR succeeded. Dzhamil' Gasanly, *SSSR-Iran: Azerbaidzhanskii krizis i nachalo kholodnoi voiny, 1941–1946 gg.* (Moscow: Geroi Otechestva, 2006), 15–16. For a detailed examination of Soviet involvement in Iran during the war, see Gasanly, *SSSR-Iran*; and Fernande Beatrice Scheid, "Stalin, Bagirov and Soviet Policies in Iran, 1939–1946," PhD diss., Yale University, 2000, 72–75.

3. *Sto sorok besed s Molotovym: Iz dnevnika Feliksa Chueva* (Moscow: Terra, 1991), 14. This story is widely cited, including in Fernande Scheid Raine, "Stalin and the Creation of the Azerbaijani Democratic Party in Iran, 1945," *Cold War History* 2, no. 1 (October 2001): 1.

4. ARPIISSA 1.89.90.4. The political composition of Iran has changed since the Soviet occupation of northern Iran. Tehran divided Iranian Azerbaijan into West Azerbaijan and East Azerbaijan not long after World War II. The province of Ardabil was later carved out of East Azerbaijan, and the province of Golestan was split from Mazandaran. Khorasan, meanwhile, has since been dvided into three separate provinces—North Khorasan, Razavi Khorasan, and South Khorasan.

5. Joanne Laycock, "The Repatriation of Armenians to Soviet Armenia, 1945–1949," in *Warlands: Population Resettlement and State Reconstruction in the Soviet-East European Borderlands, 1945–50*, ed. Peter Gatrell and Nick Baron (New York: Palgrave Macmillan, 2009), 143; Gasanly, *SSSR-Turtsiia: ot neitraliteta k kholodnoi voine (1939–1953)* (Moscow: Tsentr Propagandy, 2008), 278–279.

6. Archive of Foreign Policy of the Russian Federation [*Arkhiv vneshnei politiki Rossiiskoi Federatsii*], or AVPRF 6.8.35.552.20-21.

7. Stalin absorbed pressure, including a UN Security Council resolution, when he kept his troops in Iran after the March 2, 1946 withdrawal deadline. The United States and Britain withdrew their troops on time, but continued to interfere in Iranian affairs. That summer, for example, Britain supported a tribal rebellion in southern Iran in part to put anti-Soviet pressure on Tehran. Irina Morozova, "Contemporary Azerbaijani Historiography on the Problem of 'Southern Azerbaijan' after World War II," *Iran and the Caucasus* 9, no. 1 (2005): 117–118. This behavior was reminiscent of the 1920s, when Britain delayed troop withdrawal after World War I and supported an autonomy movement in the oil-producing region of Khuzistan. Keddie, *Modern Iran*, 84–85. The United States, meanwhile, established a lasting presence in Iran while helping to faciliate Lend-Lease aid to the Soviet Union. For more on the U.S. story, see Louise Fawcett, *Iran and the Cold War: The Azerbaijan Crisis of 1946* (Cambridge: Cambridge University Press, 1992), chap. 5.

8. Hasanli argues that this standoff over Soviet troop withdrawal—known as the Iranian Crisis of 1946—damaged relations with Turkey, marked Stalin's first defeat in his new war with the West, and constituted the start of the Cold War. Gasanly, *SSSR-*

Iran. Geoffrey Roberts disagrees with this assessment, finding that Stalin invested comparatively little in wartime efforts to pull Greece, Turkey, and Iran into his orbit and was more willing to sacrifice the southern periphery than his sphere of influence in Eastern Europe. Geoffrey Roberts, "Moscow's Cold War on the Periphery: Soviet Policy in Greece, Iran, and Turkey, 1943–8," *Journal of Contemporary History* 46, no. 1 (January 2011): 58–81.

9. V. A. Barmin, *Sin'tszian v sovetsko-kitaiskikh otnosheniiakh 1941–1949 gg.* (Barnaul: Izdatel'stvo BGPU, 1999), cited in David Wolff, "Stalin's Postwar Border-Making Tactics: East and West," *Cahiers du Monde russe* 52, no. 2–3 (April–September 2011): 284–285. For more on the ETR and the history of grievances there, see James Millward, *Eurasian Crossroads: A History of Xinjiang* (New York: Columbia University Press, 2007), 229. See also memorandums documenting Soviet negotiations with Zhou Enlai and Mao Zedong in 1949 in the Wilson Center's "China and the Soviet Union in Xinjiang, 1934–1949," digital primary source collection.

10. Raine, "Stalin and the Creation of the Azerbaijan Democratic Party," 31; and Natalia I. Yegorova, "The 'Iran Crisis' of 1945–1946: A View from the Russian Archives," Cold War International History Project Working Paper Series No. 15 (Washington, DC: Woodrow Wilson International Center for Scholars, May 1996), 19–20. Irina Morozova is more cautious than Raine and Yegorova, concluding that, despite Stalin's concerns about foreign interest in Baku's oil "reserves, 'the Soviet quest for oil did have certain political, geopolitical, and diplomatic motives, and it is difficult to come to the final conclusion what was predominant and what was secondary in the Stalin's desire to obtain an oil concession in the Northern Iran'" (*sic*). Morozova, "Contemporary Azerbaijani Historiography," 93, 111.

11. Ronald Grigor Suny, *Looking toward Ararat: Armenia in Modern History* (Bloomington: Indiana University Press, 1993), chap. 10.

12. More specifically, in his 1913 treatise *Marxism and the National Question*, Stalin writes that "*a common territory* is one of the characteristic features of a nation," but only when coupled with a common economic life facilitated by shared political borders. Thus territorial continuity became a hallmark of how Soviet nations were defined, most notably through the establishment of ethnoterritorial units (such as the Azerbaijan SSR) that made up the organizational infrastructure of the USSR. J. V. Stalin, "Marxism and the National Question," *Works* (Moscow: Foreign Languages Publishing House, 1954), 304–307. This meant that until Stalin's foreign interventions endorsed national extraterritoriality, it was politically risky to conceive of the Azerbaijani, Georgian, or Armenian nations as extending beyond the borders of their respective republics. At the same time, however, the Soviet leadership had long propagandized among co-ethnics who lived across Soviet-international borders.

13. Martin, *Affirmative Action Empire*, 26–27, 328.

14. Raine, for instance, writes that "As of 1945, Stalin's activities in Iran had no more than a six-year history." Raine, "Stalin and the Creation of the Azerbaijan Democratic Party," 1. For an example of a more extended timeline of engagement, see Etienne Peyrat, "Fighting Locusts Together: Pest Control and the Birth of Soviet Development Aid, 1920–1939," *Global Environment* 7 (2014): 536–571.

15. The Soviet occupation of Iran covered most of the northern and eastern parts of Iranian Azerbaijan, but only extended as far south as Oshnavieh and Miandoab (on the northern side of Iran's Kurdish territories). There there were territories in the

Kurdish lands between the Soviet and British occupying forces, with areas in British or Soviet spheres of influence but outside direct military control. David McDowall, *A Modern History of the Kurds* (London: Tauris, 2000), 231.

16. ARPİİSSA 1.89.1.21.

17. Inviting them to Baku was a strategic move, particularly with Kurdish tribal chiefs who had already initiated conversations with Britain about negotiated protectorate status. On their return to Iran, some of the Kurdish emissaries, including Qazi Muhammad, future leader of the Kurdish Republic of Mahabad, tried to settle intertribal disputes and raise the question of Kurdish self-determination but struggled to build on the Baku summit. The fickle Soviet leadership for many years subordinated Kurdish interests to other priorities. See McDowall, *Modern History of the Kurds*, 236–239; and Scheid, "Stalin, Bagirov and Soviet Policies," 183–185.

18. ARPİİSSA 1.89.1.15, 31. Bagirov frequently reported directly to Stalin, but also to collective groups of Party leaders, generally Stalin, Molotov, Beria, and Malenkov.

19. For details about local grievances, see Ervand Abrahamian, "Communism and Communalism in Iran: The Tudah and the Firqah-i Dimukrat," *International Journal of Middle East Studies* 1, no. 4 (October 1970): 296; Touraj Atabaki, *Azerbaijan: Ethnicity and the Struggle for Power in Iran* (New York: Tauris, 2000), 59; and Afshin Matin-Asgari, "The Impact of Imperial Russia and the Soviet Union on Qajar and Pahlavi Iran: Notes Toward a Revisionist Historiography," in *Iranian-Russian Encounters: Empires and Revolutions Since 1800*, ed. Stephanie Cronin (Abingdon, Oxon: Routledge, 2013), 11–46.

20. Central Archive of the Ministry of Defense of the Russian Federation (Tsentral'nyi arkhiv Ministerstva oborony Rossiiskoi Federatsii), or TsAMO RF, 400.9450.4.127-127ob.

21. TsAMO RF 400.9450.4.76 and 126; ARPİİSSA 1.89.1.24.

22. For examples of how these techniques were developed in previous decades, see Michael David-Fox, *Showcasing the Great Experiment: Cultural Diplomacy and Western Visitors to the Soviet Union, 1921–1941* (New York: Oxford University Press, 2012). See also James Pickett, "Soviet Civilization through a Persian Lens: Iranian Intellectuals, Cultural Diplomacy and Socialist Modernity 1941–1955," *Iranian Studies* 48, no. 5 (September 2015): 805–826.

23. See, for example, sšssa (II) 14.16.201.8, 14.19.209.45, and 14.16.201.5. For more on the history of Georgian engagement with the Fereydan Georgian population, see Claire Kaiser, "Lived Nationality: Policy and Practice in Soviet Georgia, 1945–1978," PhD diss., University of Pennsylvania, 2015, chap. 5. Georgians often claim that Fereydan Georgians are from eastern Georgia and converted to Islam after Shah Abbas forcibly relocated them to Iran. The preservation of their "Georgian-ness" despite three centuries of "exile" forms the basis of a sentimental narrative in which they are lauded as heroes of an enduring Georgian nation (see, for example, sšssa [II] 14.38.329.6). Babak Rezvani disputes this narrative, arguing that hundreds of thousands of Georgians moved to Iran in the Safavid, Afsharid, and Qajar eras. More specifically, he asserts that Fereydan Georgians originate from elite families in Georgia that converted to Shi'i Islam before migrating to Iran. See Rezvani, "Iranian Georgians: Prerequisites for Research," *Iran and the Caucasus* 13, no. 1 (2009): 197–203; and "The Islamization and Ethnogenesis of the Fereydani Georgians," *Nationalities Papers* 36, no. 4 (September 2008): 593–623.

24. ARPİİSSA 1.89.104.93-103, cited in Scheid, "Creation of the Azerbaijan Democratic Party," 254.

25. ARPİİSSA 1.89.104.1-3.

26. ARPİİSSA 1.89.90.4-5. The plan in several provinces was to appeal to economic complaints while organizing separatist movements, but in Gorgan province, they also aimed to address national issues by calling essentially for the *korenizatsiia* of the educational and state apparatus to accommodate the local Turkmen population. ARPİİSSA 1.89.90.12.

27. Bagirov, former Commissar for Azerbaijani Internal Affairs Mir Teymur Yakubov, Commissar of Azerbaijan State Security Stepan Emel'ianov, and the Commander of the Baku Military District Ivan Maslennikov oversaw this Tabriz troika from Baku.

28. ARPİİSSA 1.89.90.19.

29. ARPİİSSA 1.89.90.19; and Abrahamian, "Communism and Communalism in Iran," 306. For background on Pishevari's relationship with Tudeh, see M. Reza Ghods, "The Iranian Communist Movement under Reza Shah," *Middle Eastern Studies* 26, no. 4 (October 1990): 506–513.

30. ARPİİSSA 1.89.90.40.

31. Different stories are told about this meeting. According to William Eagleton, who wrote a history of the Kurdish Republic of Mahabad based largely on the remembrances of participants, the Soviet side informed Qazi Muhammad "that the time had come" to meet again in Baku. Eagleton, *The Kurdish Republic of 1946* (London: Oxford University Press, 1963), 43. In a report Bagirov sent to Stalin at the time, however, Bagirov claimed that the Kurds "urged us to receive their delegation" after the creation of the ADP and Azerbaijan separatist movement inspired them to create a Kurdish democratic party and separatist movement (ARPİİSSA 1.89.90.39).

32. ARPİİSSA 1.89.90.39.

33. The complete KDPI program is available in Eagleton. Eagleton, *Kurdish Republic*, 57. For discussions around the formation of the ADP program, see ARPİİSSA 1.89.90.

34. For example, Swietochowski in 1995 noted that Pishevari was vague in his memoir about the ADP's origins, but assumes Pishevari "suddenly" established it upon his own initiative with Red Army troops in the background. Swietochowski's interpretation of what happened between the Kurds and Bagirov is also missing important insights that later emerged from the Baku archives. Tadeusz Swietochowski, *Russia and Azerbaijan: A Borderland in Transition* (New York: Columbia University Press, 1995), 141–148. Scheid/Raine and Hasanli's access to key archival documents have changed our understanding of the Soviet Union's role in northern Iranian autonomy movements among Kurds and Azeris.

35. ARPİİSSA 1.89.90.294.

36. Massoud Barzani, *Mustafa Barzani and the Kurdish Liberation Movement (1931–1961)* (New York: Palgrave Macmillan, 2003), 244, 100–101. Eagleton documents claims that Barzani was a British agent (*The Kurdish Republic*, 45–46).

37. ARPİİSSA 1.89.90.294. Hasanli argues that Bagirov also supported Kurdish autonomy to block Soviet Armenian political elites, including Foreign Affairs Commissar of Armenia Saak Karapetyan, from using the Kurdish example to foster Armenian autonomy in Iran. Gasanly, *SSSR-Iran*, 226–229.

38. For more on division among Kurds, see Farideh Koohi-Kamali, *The Political Development of the Kurds in Iran: Pastoral Nationalism* (New York: Palgrave Macmillan, 2003).

39. Shortly after Qavam's army took control of Iranian Azerbaijan, 760 people were executed by court martial. Within a matter of days, perhaps as many as 3,000 had been killed while thousands more were imprisoned or exiled to southern Iran. Gasanly, *SSSR-Iran*, 453.

40. Bagirov quickly and confidentially ordered Ibragimov, Emel'ianov, A. Rusov, and Atakishiyev to make arrangements for the Iranian emigrant population, including Azeris and Kurds receiving military training in Soviet Azerbaijan. ARDA 411.25.588.58-59.

41. ARDA 411.25.588. See also Morozova, "Contemporary Azerbaijani Historiography," 119.

42. Swietochowski, *Russia and Azerbaijan*, 163–165. Hamid Molla-Zadeh claims that Pishevari entered his partnership with the Soviet leadership knowing that he might be betrayed. See Hamīd Mollā-Zādeh, *Rāzhā-ye sar-be-mohr: Nāgoftehā-ye 'vaqāy'e Āzarbāiǰān* (Tabriz: 1976, 1998), 20, cited in Morozova, "Contemporary Azerbaijani Historiography," 112.

43. *Mir Cəfər Bağırovun məhkəməsi: arxiv materialları* (Baku: Yazıçı, 1993), 98, cited in Swietochowski, *Russia and Azerbaijan*, 164. Atabaki also reports that "well-informed sources . . . maintain that Pishevari was murdered by agents of Stalin and Bagirov in the hospital where he was taken after the car accident." Atabaki, *Azerbaijan*, 119. Scheid, meanwhile, interviewed Aga Farughian about his experiences with the Soviet intervention. He claimed that Pishevari's death was a true accident that occurred while he was traveling to dissolve partisan units. Scheid, "Stalin, Bagirov, and Soviet Policies," 352.

44. Koohi-Kamali, *Political Development*, 121.

45. There is some disagreement over the dates. In an archived report (number 519k) from Soviet Minister of Internal Affairs S. Kruglov to Stalin dated February 10, 1949, Kruglov dates their entry into the Soviet Union as May 17–18, 1947. GARF 9401.2.234.180-182, reprinted in N. F. Bugai and M. I. Mamaev, *Kurdy SSSR*, 245. Barzani's son, Massoud, meanwhile, reports that they entered the Soviet Union in mid-June. Barzani, *Mustafa Barzani*, 125–134.

46. The text of his speech is in Barzani, *Mustafa Barzani*, 251–261.

47. Barzani, *Mustafa Barzani*, 137–139. Based on his conversations with his father, Massoud Barzani characterizes Bagirov as "racist and arrogant" in his treatment of Kurds.

48. GARF 9401.2.234.180-182, reprinted in Bugai and Mamaev, *Kurdy SSSR*, 246.

49. Bugai and Mamaev, *Kurdy SSSR*, 246

50. The Norashen region was renamed Il'ichevsk in 1964 and Sharur in 1991. GARF 9401.2.234.180-182, reprinted in Bugai and Mamaev, *Kurdy SSSR*, 246.

51. Yevgeny Primakov, *Russia and the Arabs: Behind the Scenes in the Middle East from the Cold War to the Present*, trans. Paul Gould (New York: Basic Books, 2009), 326.

52. There is some disagreement over the number of people repatriated to Iraq. These figures are from a report on their repatriation written by the head of the Union of the Red Cross and Red Crescent Societies delegation that accompanied the repatriated Kurds

to Iraq. It is unclear whether only 456 men returned to Iraq because the rest decided to stay in the Soviet Union or if some died in the interim. GARF 9501.5.610.1-13, reprinted in Bugai and Mamaev, *Kurdy SSSR*, 305–318. Massoud Barzani, meanwhile, reports that 784 people were on the boat. Barzani, *Mustafa Barzani*, 185.

53. Morozova, "Contemporary Azerbaijani Historiography," 107.

54. Interview conducted in Astara region, March 2011.

55. ARDA 411.25.539 and 411.25.488.

56. For an example with Armenia, see National Archive of Armenia (Hayastani Azgayin Arkhiv), or HAA, 326.1.100A.10, available in Arman Kirakosyan, ed., *Armeniia i sovetsko-turetskie otnosheniia v diplomaticheskikh dokumentakh 1945–1946 gg.* (Yerevan: Tigran Mets, 2010), 61.

57. Kirakosyan, *Armeniia i sovetsko-turetskie otnosheniia*, 75–76.

58. sšssa (II) 14.19.209.49-57.

59. Arsène Saparov, "Re-negotiating the Boundaries of the Permissible: The National(ist) Revival in Soviet Armenia and Moscow's Response," *Europe-Asia Studies* 70, no. 6 (2018): 868.

60. Gasanly, *SSSR-Turtsiia*, 314–316; Kaiser, "Lived Nationality," 75–84; Kirakosyan, *Armeniia i sovetsko-turetskie otnosheniia*, 32.

61. Kaiser, "Lived Nationality," 75–84.

62. Kirakosyan, *Armeniia i sovetsko-turetskie otnosheniia*, 76.

63. A Georgian Society for Cultural Relations with Foreign Countries (GOKS) was created in 1946 to advance Georgian interests in Iran, but declining Soviet influence in Iran frustrated plans to support and repatriate Fereydan Georgians. sšssa (II) 14.45.388.10. Georgian national leaders repeatedly revisited the issue and around one hundred Fereydan Georgians repatriated in the early 1970s. sšssa (II) 14.45.388.6. As Kaiser has shown, however, repatriation did not go as planned. Centuries of separation had sown myriad differences between Soviet and Iranian Georgians, including religious ones that proved hard to overcome. Of the twenty-three families that repatriated to the Georgian SSR in the 1970s, nine had asked to return home by the close of the decade. As of 2013, only two of these families remained in Georgia. Kaiser, "Lived Nationality," 289–290.

64. The figure of 96,000 Armenian repatriates is based on a resettlement agency survey from 1949 (RGAE 5675.1.413.40). Different sources use different numbers. Joanne Laycock proposes that around 110,000 Armenians were repatriated, but Maike Lehmann uses a figure of 89,637 diaspora Armenians repatriated post-1946. She qualifies this statistic by noting that tens of thousands of diaspora Armenians also moved to Soviet Armenia in the interwar period. Laycock, "The Repatriation of Armenians to Soviet Armenia, 1945–1949," in *Warlands: Population Resettlement and State Reconstruction in the Soviet-East European Borderlands, 1945–1950*, ed. Peter Gatrell and Nick Baron (New York: Palgrave Macmillan, 2009), 156; and Lehmann, "A Different Kind of Brothers: Exclusion and Partial Integration after Repatriation to a Soviet 'Homeland,'" *Ab Imperio* 3 (2012): 179, 182. In a more recent article, Saparov cites a KGB report from 1966 that documents around 82,000 Armenian repatriates between 1946 and 1948. Saparov, "Re-negotiating the Boundaries," 868.

65. National Archives of Armenia Division of Socio-Political Documentation (Hayastani Azgayin Arkhiv Hasarakakan Qaghaqakan Pastatghteri Bazhin), or HAAHQPB, 1.27.47.137-138.

66. See, for example, ARDA 411.9.442.88-88ob and ARDA 411.9.12.20-21.

67. See *Ocherki obshchei etnografii: Aziatskaia chast' SSSR*, ed. S. P. Tolstov, M. G. Levin, and N. N. Cheboksarov (Moscow: Izdatel'stvo Akademii nauk SSSR, 1960), 75–76; and J. Stalin, *Speeches Delivered at Meetings of Voters of the Stalin Electoral District, Moscow* (Moscow: Foreign Languages Publishing House, 1950), 31.

68. For example, the Main Resettlement Administration planned to move 78,584 households in 1949 (RGAE 5675.1.456.84), 147,897 in 1950, 94,833 in 1951, and 89,173 in 1952 (RGAE 5675.1.388.7).

69. We do have the proposal that Bagirov and Arutiunov sent to Stalin shortly before Stalin decreed the resettlement on December 23, 1947, as chairman of the Council of Ministers. HAAHQPB, 1.27.47.137-138. On plans to relocate Azeri national-cultural infrastructure from Armenia to Azerbaijan, see ARDA 411.28.681.113-115.

70. For example, ARDA 417.36.407.159.

71. See, for example, ARDA 411.26.34.65; HAA 113.49.499; and RGAE 5675.1.466.20.

72. ARDA 411.9.734.232; HAA 113.49.449.73; ARDA 417.36.407.150-151.

73. See ARDA 411.26s.296.62. For comparison with a simultaneous resettlement happening in Ukraine, see RGAE 5675.1.515.13.

74. RGAE 5675.1.678.59 and ARDA 411sp.26s.330.4.

75. Maike Lehmann, "A Different Kind of Brothers: Exclusion and Partial Integration after Repatriation to a Soviet 'Homeland,'" *Ab Imperio* 3 (2012); Jo Laycock, "Belongings: People and Possessions in the Armenian Repatriations, 1945–1949," *Kritika* 18, no. 3 (Summer 2017).

76. HAAHQPB 1.28.94.6-8.

77. HAAHQPB 1.27.47.76-77.

78. Vastly different figures have been used for the number of repatriates deported during Operation Volna. Maike Lehmann has cited estimates of 40,000 deported repatriates. If true, this would mean that nearly half of repatriates were expelled from Soviet Armenia. Jo Laycock, meanwhile, references a much lower figure, writing that "repatriates were among the 12,000 Armenians targeted" in Operation Volna deportations. See Maike Lehmann, *Eine sowjetische Nation. Nationale Sozialismusinterpretationen in Armenien seit 1945* (Frankfurt am Main: Campus, 2012), 110–111; and Laycock, "Belongings," 512.

79. ARPiiSSA 1.169.249 (part 1), 8–12, cited in Gasanly, *SSSR-Turtsiia*, 449.

80. The North Ossetian ASSR, Stavropol Krai, Georgian SSR, and Dagestan ASSR all gained land after Balkars, Chechens, and Ingushes were deported, the Kabardino-Balkar ASSR was converted into the Kabardian ASSR, and the Chechen-Ingush ASSR was dissolved. ARDA 411.25.335.5-10.

81. Kandid Charkviani, *Gantsdili da naazrevi: 1906–1994* (Tbilisi: Merani, 2004), 500–503. Selection translated for the author from Georgian to Russian by Timothy Blauvelt.

82. M. G. Seidov, *Obshchestvenno-politicheskaia obstanovka v Azerbaidzhane v 1940-e–nachale 1950-kh godov*, book manuscript, 27, cited in Gasanly, *SSSR-Turtsiia*, 458.

83. For more on Beria's patronage network, see Timothy Blauvelt, "March of the Chekists: Beria's Secret Police Patronage Network and Soviet Crypto-politics," *Communist and Post-Communist Studies* 44, no. 1 (March 2011): 71–88; and Oleg Khlevniuk, "Kremlin-Tbilisi: Purges, Control and Georgian Nationalism in the First

Half of the 1950s," in *Georgia after Stalin: Nationalism and Soviet Power*, ed. Timothy K. Blauvelt and Jeremy Smith (New York: Routledge, 2016), 13–31. Stalin likely appointed Charkviani as first secretary because he was not in Beria's network, but Charkviani nonetheless developed a patron-client relationship with Beria while maintaining his own network and power base in the republic. Ronald Grigor Suny, *The Making of the Modern Georgian Nation* (Bloomington: Indiana University Press, 1994), 277–278, 288.

84. Timothy Blauvelt, "Abkhazia: Patronage and Power in the Stalin Era," *Nationalities Papers* 35, no. 2 (2007): 213–219.

85. Mgeladze continued Beria's policy of promoting a Georgian national identification and culture in Abkhazia, but Blauvelt argues that Mgeladze was "Stalin's man" and was appointed in part to disrupt Beria's power monopoly in the republic. Blauvelt, "Abkhazia," 220. Beria still maintained a strong hold in the republic, however. Genuflections to Beria in party reports are one sign of his continuing influence. sšssa (II) 14.20.255.7.

86. sšssa (II) 14.21.298.67. See also sšssa (II) 14.20.255.1-9, 14.21.298.1-86, and 14.26.380.13-50.

87. sšssa (II) 14.20.255.5.

88. Blauvelt, "Abkhazia," 221.

89. This "Turk" ethnonym is complicated. Various terms—Tatar, Turk, Tiurk, Meskhetian Turk, Muslim Georgian, and Azerbaijani—are used at different times in Russian imperial and Soviet documents to describe the Muslim population in the Akhaltsikhe, Aspindza, Akhalkalaki, and Bogdanov districts of Georgia. The majority of "Turk" deportees were Turkish-speaking Sunni Muslims who called themselves Ahıska or Meskhetians, but they were rarely categorized as such in state documents. For example, in the 1926 census Meskhetians were classified as Turks, then as Azerbaijanis in 1939. When they were deported they were once again "Turks," but those who moved to Azerbaijan from Central Asia in 1957 became Azerbaijani once again (ARPİİSSA 1.45.84). For more on this community, their experience of displacement, and their ethnonym, see Irina Levin, "Caught in a Bad Romance: Displaced People and the Georgian State," *Citizenship Studies* 22, no. 1 (2018): 19–36; and Hulya Dogan, "Conceptions of Homeland and Identity among Meskhetian Turk Refugees in the U.S. and Turkey," PhD diss., Texas A&M University, 2016.

90. *"Ikh nado deportirovat'"*: *dokumenty, fakty, kommentarii* (Moscow: Druzhba narodov, 1992), 155.

91. Reported numbers of deportees vary across sources but reliably increase over time, indicating that more people were deported after the initial operations. For example, in late November 1944, Beria reported to Stalin, Molotov, and Malenkov that 91,095 Turks, Khemshins, and Kurds had been deported. The next month, the head of the NKVD's Department of Special Settlements, V. V. Chernyshova, informed Beria that 92,307 people from Georgia had been resettled in Uzbekistan, Kazakhstan, and Kyrgyzstan. A few years later, in January 1949, Soviet Minister of Internal Affairs Kruglov and Prosecutor General Grigorii Nikolaevich Safonov referenced a figure of 94,955 deportees in a draft report to Beria. *"Ikh nado deportirovat'*," 155–169. Over the next three years, an additional 894 "Turks," Khemshins, and Kurds and 690 "Vlasovtsy" accused of collaborating with the Germans followed the initial deportees into exile.

92. An official report on the deportation referenced just over 450 deaths during this earlier deportation. GARF 9479.1.184.229, reprinted in Bugai and Mamaev, *Kurdy*

SSSR, 202. Deportees also perished as a result of special settlement conditions. In January 1949, head of the MVD's Department of Special Settlements Colonel V. Shiian reported that, as of October 1948, 44,887 deportees from Crimea had died; 16,594 Kalmyks; 146,892 Chechens, Ingushes, Karachays, and Balkars; 45,275 Germans; and 14,432 Kurds, Turks, and Khemshins from Georgia (approximately 15 percent of the total population of deported Kurds, Turks, and Khemshins). GARF 9479.1.436.14, reprinted in Bugai and Mamaev, *Kurdy SSSR*, 233.

93. Numbers, again, vary across time and sources. In 1949, the Georgian Minister of State Security Nikolai Maksimovich Rukhadze and A. Valis from the Soviet MGB informed Deputy Minister of State Security of the USSR Nikolai Nikolaevich Selivanovskii that they had expelled 36,705 people from Georgia in the Volna operation, including 2,548 Turks, 31,386 Greeks, and 2,771 Dashnaks (sšssa [II] 14.27.252.75-76). In April 1953, Major General V. Kakuchaia from the Georgian MVD reported that 43,344 people were deported from Georgia over the course of 1949–1950. Archive of the Ministry of Internal Affairs of Georgia (sakartvelos šinagan sakmeta saministros arqivi), or sšssa (I) 13.27.1-3, cited in Claire P. Kaiser, "'What Are They Doing? After All, We're Not Germans': Expulsion, Belonging, and Postwar Experience in the Caucasus," in *Empire and Belonging in the Eurasian Borderlands*, ed. Krista A. Goff and Lewis H. Siegelbaum (Ithaca, NY: Cornell University Press, 2019). As with the Iranian label in the Soviet Union, "Turk" in Soviet documents can indicate more than ethnicity or nationality. Sometimes it is used more broadly to refer to a person's citizenship or language affiliation. Some Laz with a history of Turkish citizenship, for example, were linked to this deportation. On Laz deportations, see Mathijs Pelkmans, *Defending the Border: Identity, Religion, and Modernity in the Republic of Georgia* (Ithaca, NY: Cornell University Press, 2006), 34–35.

94. According to an MVD report dated June 20, 1949, the 2,096,102 deportees included 1,098,490 Germans; 372,257 Chechens and Ingushes; 192,953 Crimean Tatars, Bulgarians, Greeks, and Armenians from Crimea; 94,799 "kulaks, nationalists, bandits, and members of their families evicted [*vyselennye*] from Lithuania, Latvia, and Estonia"; 81,575 Khemshins, Kurds, and Turks (deported from Georgia in 1944); 77,663 Kalmyks; 58,854 Karachays; 57,246 Greeks, Turks, Dashnaks evicted from Georgia, Armenia, Azerbaijan, and the Black Sea coast; 34,763 "kulaks, participants in profascist organizations, associates [*posobniki*] of Germans and members of their families" evicted from Moldova; and 32,522 Balkars. The 466,729 special settlers in the report, meanwhile, included people targeted for affiliation with Germany, OUN, and poor work behavior or antisocial activities. GARF 9401.2.235.356-362, reprinted in Bugai and Mamaev, *Kurdy SSSR*, 248–250.

95. Kaiser, "Lived Nationality," 134.

96. sšssa (II) 14.31.248.1.

97. sšssa (II) 14.18.266.3-8.

98. sšssa (II) 14.18.266.20. Chechens, Ingushes, and Balkars were deported to Central Asia and stripped of their autonomous republics earlier that year. Chechens and Ingushes were accused of collaborating with German occupiers against the Red Army, being saboteurs and spies, and raiding and robbing neighboring farms rather than productively participating in kolkhozes (ARDA 411.25.335.5). Balkars were accused of collaborating with the Germans against the Red Army and Soviet power (ARDA 411.25.335.9).

99. sšssa (II) 14.18.266.3-8.

100. sšssa (II) 14.27.252.

101. Kaiser, "Lived Nationality," 109–112.

102. Kaiser, "What Are They Doing?," 86–90.

103. Although Kurds were also swept into the deportations, they only accounted for 3 percent of the regional population in that year's census. Bugai and Mamaev, *Kurdy SSSR*, 160.

104. Representatives of the Mountainous Republic argued at the 1919 Paris Peace Conference that 90 percent of the population in the Zaqatala okrug were Dagestanis who desired this unification. They claimed that Armenians and Georgians comprised the remaining ten percent of the local population. M. M. Vachagaev, *Soiuz gortsev Severnogo Kavkaza i Gorskaia respublika: Istoriia nesostoiavshegosia gosudarstva, 1917–1920* (Moscow: Tsentrpoligraf, 2018).

105. GARF R9559.4.11293.

106. Central Historical Archive of Georgia (*sakartvelos centraluri saistoriis arqivi*, or *scsa*) 1833.1.903.

107. RGASPI 64.1.61.7.

108. In 1901, for instance, P. P. Nadezhdin emphasized Zaqatala's Kakhetian past and classified "Georgian-Engilo" in the Karvetlian group alongside Imeretians, Tushins, Adjarans, Khevsurs, and others. Nadezhdin, *Kavkazskii krai: Priroda i liudi* (Tula: Tipografiia Vladimira Nikolaievicha Sokolova, 1901), 167, 382. The next year, Karl von Hahn (Gan), a Tbilisi-based German ethnographer, explained that "engiloi"—Muslim and Christian alike—maintained a Georgian cultural orientation despite being enumerated separately from Georgians in the 1897 census, which documented 8,727 "engliois" and 3,709 "Georgians." *Sbornik materialov dlia opisaniia městnostei i plemen Kavkaza* 31 (Tiflis: Izdanie Upravleniia Kavkazskago uchebnago okruga, 1902), 57–61.

109. A. I. Von-Plotto, "Priroda i liudi Zakatal'skogo okruga," *Sbornik svedenii o kavkazskikh gortsakh* 4 (Tiflis, 1870).

110. Republic of Azerbaijan State Historical Archive (Azərbaycan Respublikası Dövlət Tarix Arxivi), or ARDTA, 571.1.1 and 571.1.3.

111. Liaister and Chursin, *Geografiia Kavkaza*, 282. This book was co-written. I suspect that Chursin wrote the ethnographic descriptions. The "convert" reference ties into speculation about the origin of the "Ingilo" term. According to many people with whom I spoke in Qakh and Zaqatala, the word "Ingilo" refers to *yeni* and *yol*, which mean "new path" in Azerbaijani, and refers to their forced conversion to Islam by Shah Abbas. In a report written by Georgian-Ingiloi activist Georgii Gamkharashvili about his community, he explained it differently, attributing the label to Georgian-Ingiloi reconversion to Christianity under Russian rule in the nineteenth century. Gamkharashvili claimed that the word came from the "Tiurko-Tatar" word *engi*, which meant "again" (*snogo*) in Russian, "that is, 'again' returned to the Orthodox church." sšssa [II] 14.18.180. 37. N. Ia. Marr also categorized the Ingilo as part of the eastern branch of the Kartvelian group in his report on the tribal structure of the Caucasus population in 1920. Marr, *Plemennoi sostav naseleniia Kavkaza: Trudy Komissii po izucheniiu plemennogo sostava naseleniia Rossii (Rabochii konspekt)* (Petrograd: Rossiiskaia gosudarstvennaia akademicheskaia tipografiia, 1920), 43.

112. ARDA 57.1.297.125ob.

113. For the case of Turkey, see Soner Çağaptay, "Reconfiguring the Turkish Nation in the 1930s," *Nationalism and Ethnic Politics* 8, no. 2 (2002): 76.

114. Interviews, fall 2010 and spring 2011.

115. ARDA 379.1.7047 and ARDA SF 216.1.27.61.

116. ARDA 57.11.650.26.

117. He writes Khoshtari, but is likely referring to Semyon Khoshtaria, a deputy in the Soviet of Nationalities at this time.

118. sšssa (II) 14.18.180.30-31.

119. For example, sšssa (II) 14.20.271.2 and 14.24.296.1.

120. sšssa (II) 14.18.180.34-41 (Gamkharashvili), 14.18.180.46-73 (Dzhanashvili), and 14.18.180.74-94 (Dzhanashvili).

121. sšssa (II) 14.18.161.1-19.

122. sšssa (II) 14.18.180.125.

123. sšssa (II) 14.18.180.22-27.

124. sšssa (II) 14.18.180.5-7.

125. Charkviani, *Gantsdili da naazrevi*, 500–503.

126. sšssa (II) 14.18.180.5-13.

127. sšssa (II) 14.18.180.3.

128. sšssa (II) 14.18.180.17.

129. sšssa (II) 14.18.180.4. Georgian-speakers in Azerbaijan and Georgians in Georgia often refer to Azeri and other Muslims in Azerbaijan as "Tatars," regardless of ethnic differentiation. When used in this way, it can carry a pejorative connotation.

130. sšssa (II) 14.18.180.110.

131. sšssa (II) 14.18.161.160-165.

132. ARDA 411.25.521.156.

133. ARPİİSSA 1.226.54.27-37, cited in Gasanly, *SSSR-Turtsiia*, 461–464.

134. ARDA 411.8.284.320-338.

135. Charkviani indicates that this was in 1947, but it more likely occurred in 1944, when he met Bagirov in the region. Charkviani, *Ganstdili da naazrevi*, 500–503; sšssa (II) 14.18.180.3-10.

Interlude

1. Jan Plamper, *The Stalin Cult: A Study in the Alchemy of Power* (New Haven, CT: Yale University Press, 2012), 221.

2. Irina Ghughunishvili, interview with Lamara Akhvlediani, July 13, 2013, https://thestalinproject.org.

3. Ghughunishvili, interview.

4. Oleg Khlevniuk, *Stalin: New Biography of a Dictator* (New Haven, CT: Yale University Press, 2015), 319.

5. Sheila Fitzpatrick, *On Stalin's Team: The Years of Living Dangerously in Soviet Politics* (Princeton, NJ: Princeton University Press, 2015), 223. When Akhvlediani entered the Hall of Columns to view Stalin's body, she crossed paths with Kaganovich, Molotov, and Beria as they exited the building. She recalls, "What surprised me is that I saw a smile on Beria's face and it remained a sort of unpleasant memory for me" (Ghughunishvili, interview).

6. Yoram Gorlizki and Oleg Khlevniuk, *Cold Peace: Stalin and the Soviet Ruling Circle, 1945–1953* (New York: Oxford University Press, 2005).

7. Fitzpatrick, *On Stalin's Team*, 224.

8. *Memoirs of Nikita Khrushchev*, vol. 2, *Reformer (1945–1964)*, ed. Sergei Khrushchev, trans. George Shriver and Stephen Shenfield (University Park, PA: Pennsylvania State University Press, 2006), 183.

9. Amy Knight, *Beria: Stalin's First Lieutenant* (Princeton, NJ: Princeton University Press, 1993), 194.

10. Jeff Hardy, *The Gulag After Stalin: Redefining Punishment in Khrushchev's Soviet Union, 1953–1964* (Ithaca, NY: Cornell University Press, 2016), 23–26.

11. Elena Zubkova, "Vlast' i razvitie etnokonfliktnoi situatsii v SSSR, 1953–1982 gody," *Otechestvennaia istoriia* 4 (2004): 4.

12. Timothy Blauvelt discusses Beria's patronage networks in Georgia in "March of the Chekists: Beria's Secret Police Patronage Network and Soviet Crypto-Politics," *Communist and Post-Communist Studies* 44 (2001): 73–88; and "Abkhazia," 203–232. Charles H. Fairbanks analyzed late Stalinist Georgian cadre changes in Fairbanks, "Clientelism and Higher Politics in Georgia, 1949–1953," in *Transcaucasia: Nationalism and Social Change*, ed. Ronald Grigor Suny (Ann Arbor: University of Michigan Press, 1983), 339–368.

13. Knight, *Beria*, 187–191; Zubkova, "Vlast' i razvitie," 4.

14. Fitzpatrick, *On Stalin's Team*, 230–233.

15. Beria ultimately was blamed when Walter Ulbricht, first secretary of the Socialist Unity Party of Germany, resisted his recommendation to compromise with the workers, resulting in the Berlin Uprising of 1953. Amy Knight argues that if the Moscow leadership had stood united behind Beria, they might have been able to force Ulbricht's hand and avoid both the uprising and the subsequent violent intervention. Knight, *Beria*, 191–193. See also Fitzpatrick, *On Stalin's Team*, 231–233.

16. Knight, *Beria*, 176–225.

17. Amir Weiner, "The Empires Pay a Visit: Gulag Returnees, East European Rebellions, and Soviet Frontier Politics," in *The Thaw: Soviet Society and Culture during the 1950s and 1960s*, ed. Denis Kozlov and Eleonory Gilburd (Toronto: University of Toronto Press, 2013), 308–361.

18. TsGA RD 1.2.1894.141-142 and 1.2.1686.131-132.

19. RGASPI 82.2.148.30-33.

20. RGASPI 82.2.148.34-38.

21. RGASPI 82.2.148.186-191.

22. Timothy Blauvelt, "Language Education and Ethnic Resentment in Soviet Abkhazia, 1939–1953," *Ab Imperio* 1 (2020): 216.

23. Nikita Khrushchev, "Speech to 20th Congress of the CPSU," February 24–25, 1956, https://www.marxists.org/archive/khrushchev/1956/02/24.htm.

24. Levan Avalishvili, "The March 1956 Events in Georgia: Based on Oral History Interviews and Archival Documents," in *Georgia After Stalin: Nationalism and Soviet Power*, ed. Timothy K. Blauvelt and Jeremy Smith (London: Routledge, 2016), 37.

25. Giorgi Kldiashvili, "Nationalism After the March 1956 Events and the Origins of the National-Independence Movement in Georgia," in *Georgia After Stalin: Nationalism and Soviet Power*, ed. Timothy K. Blauvelt and Jeremy Smith (London: Routledge, 2016), 77–91.

26. RGANI 5.31.25.

27. The second trial, held concurrently with the Twentieth Party Congress in February 1956, was of Boris Rodos, one of the NKVD's most well-known interrogators during the terror. He was executed that April. Samuel Arthur Casper, "The Bolshevik Afterlife: Posthumous Rehabilitation in the Post-Stalin Soviet Union, 1953-1970," PhD diss., University of Pennsylvania, 2018, 206.

28. GARF R-7523.89a.8444.128.

29. GARF R-7523.89a.8444.24.

30. GARF R-7523.89a.8444.14-15.

31. Casper, "The Bolshevik Afterlife," 246–247.

32. GARF R-7523.89a.8444.135.

33. GARF R-7523.89a.8444.59.

34. Baberowski, *Der Feind ist überall*, 791–794.

35. In *Le goût de l'archive*, for example, Arlette Farge discusses how police statements are articulated between "a power that obliges, a desire to convince, and a practice of words," as well as a legal procedure that structures these forces. Farge, *Le goût de l'archive* (Paris: Seuil, 1997), 39. See also, Peter Holquist, "'Information is the Alpha and Omega of Our Work': Bolshevik Surveillance in Its Pan-European Context," *The Journal of Modern History* 69, no. 3 (September 1997): 415–450; and Tracy McDonald, *Face to the Village: The Riazan Countryside Under Soviet Rule, 1921–1930* (Toronto: University of Toronto Press, 2011), 24–26.

36. ARDA 411sg.26s.338.136-141.

3. Defining the Azerbaijan Soviet Socialist Republic

1. Both Ibragimov's personal file and the official decree on his departure in Azerbaijan indicate that he chose to give up his governmental duties in order to focus on his cultural work (ARDA 2941.9.76.18 and 340.4.261.33-35). Similarly, available paperwork archived at RGANI notes that Ibragimov's retirement from the Supreme Soviet was associated with health problems and a desire to return to his literary career (RGANI 5.31.101.3).

2. A. A. Fursenko, ed., *Prezidium TsK KPSS 1954–1964: Chernovye protokol'nye zapisi zasedanii. Stenogrammy. Postanovleniia*, vol. 1 (Moscow: ROSSPEN, 2004), 365.

3. See Fursenko, 356–387; and ARPİİSSA 1.46.87.67-68.

4. See, for example, *Bakinskii rabochii*, July 11, 1959.

5. *Bakinskii rabochii*, December 11, 1959. Ibragimov ultimately maintained a public profile as a celebrated writer, deputy in convocations of the Supreme Soviet of the USSR and first secretary of the Azerbaijan Writers' Union. Mustafayev, meanwhile, turned to an academic career at the Academy of Sciences in Baku.

6. Hirsch, *Empire of Nations*, 14.

7. The deputy chairman of Latvia's Council of Ministers, Eduards Berklāvs, was criticized in Moscow at the same time as Mustafayev and publicly dismissed from his post just days after Mustafayev's fate was announced in the newspapers of Azerbaijan. As this case shows, disputes between different factions of the party sometimes played out in these conflicts. Michael Loader, "A Stalinist Purge in the Khrushchev Era? The Latvian Communist Party Purge, 1959–1963," *The Slavonic and East European Review* 96, no. 2 (April 2018): 244–282.

8. Bilinsky, "The Soviet Education Laws," 138–157.

9. Jeremy Smith, "Leadership and Nationalism in the Soviet Republics, 1951–1959," in *Khrushchev in the Kremlin: Policy and Government in the Soviet Union, 1953–1964*, ed. Melanie Ilic and Jeremy Smith (New York: Routledge, 2011), 85.

10. Smith, "Leadership and Nationalism," 79.

11. For example, Ismailov, *Ocherki po istorii*, 358.

12. Dzhamil' Gasanly, *Khrushchevskaia "ottepel'" i natsional'nyi vopros v Azerbaidzhane (1954–1959)* (Moscow: Flinta, 2009), 616. He is referring here to the 1956 constitutional amendment, which made Azerbaijani the official language of the Azerbaijan SSR. It is discussed in more detail later in the chapter.

13. Marlene Laruelle, "The Concept of Ethnogenesis in Central Asia: Political Context and Institutional Mediators (1940–1950)," *Kritika: Explorations in Russian and Eurasian History* 9, no. 1 (Winter 2008): 181. Ethnogenesis also helped foster primordialized national identities in the Soviet Union. For more on this aspect of ethnogenesis and the consequences of creating fixed nationalities in the Soviet Union, see Ronald Grigor Suny, "Constructing Primordialism: Old Histories for New Nations," *Journal of Modern History* 73, no. 4 (December 2001): 862–896.

14. A discrete Azerbaijani (*Azərbaycanlı*) national identity had started to form in the late nineteenth century among Azerbaijani elites, but it did not make significant gains in the official or popular sphere until the 1920s/1930s when the Soviet state embraced this term of identification. Feldman, *On the Threshold of Eurasia*, 10–11.

15. Concern about Soviet Turkic ties to Turkey in part motivated the decision to switch Turkic scripts from the Latin alphabet to Cyrillic in 1939, only a few years after Arabic alphabets used by Soviet Turkic peoples were scrapped in favor of Latin.

16. Liaister and Chursin, *Geografiia Kavkaza*, 329.

17. Harun Yilmaz argues that the Soviet leadership fostered the Soviet Azerbaijani nationality to separate Azeris from Turkish and Iranian links as tensions rose with those countries. Yilmaz, "The Soviet Union and the Construction of Azerbaijani National Identity in the 1930s," *Iranian Studies: Journal of the International Society of Iranian Studies* 46, no. 5 (2013): 1–23.

18. Victor A. Shnirelman, *The Value of the Past: Myths, Identity and Politics in Transcaucasia* (Osaka, Japan: National Museum of Ethnology, 2001), 104.

19. Shnirelman, *The Value of the Past*, 105.

20. Shnirelman, *The Value of the Past*, 106–109. This theme continues in successive history books, including Dzh. B. Guliev, ed., *Istoriia Azerbaidzhana* (Baku: Elm, 1979).

21. Adil' Iusif ogly Nadzhafov, *Formirovanie i razvitie azerbaidzhanskoi sotsialisticheskoi natsii* (Baku: Izd. Akademii nauk Azerbaidzhanskoi SSR, 1955), 27–28. Similar ideas were disseminated to students in history textbooks. A history of Azerbaijan for seventh and eighth graders written in 1964, for example, traced Russian involvement with Azerbaijan back to the tenth century (before the arrival of the Turkic Seljuk tribes). In this textbook, Russian engagement generally received a positive spin, while the negative and disruptive elements of Turkic and Persian interactions with Azerbaijan and its people were emphasized. A. N. Guliev and E. I. Mamedov, *Istoriia Azerbaidzhana dlia 7–8 klassov* (Baku: Azeruchpedgiz, 1964).

22. *Istoriia Azerbaidzhana* (Baku: Izd. Akademii nauk Azerbaidzhanskoi SSR, 1958) was the first of a multivolume history of Azerbaijan from ancient times to the present.

23. On Armenian and Azerbaijani competition over Caucasian Albanian heritage, see Nora Dudwick, "The Case of the Caucasian Albanians: Ethnohistory and Ethnic Politics," *Cahiers du Monde russe et soviétique* 31, no. 2–3 (April–September 1990): 377–384.

24. Shnirelman, *The Value of the Past*, 109–111. Language had been an essential part of defining nationhood in the Soviet Union. As Stalin wrote in "Marxism and the National Question," a nation without a common language was not a nation. See https://www.marxists.org/reference/archive/stalin/works/1913/03a.htm#s1.

25. Shnirelman, *The Value of the Past*, 112; Altstadt, *Azerbaijani Turks*, 173.

26. Aliaga Mammadli, "Peculiarities of the Formation of Azerbaijanis' Ethnic Identity in the Soviet Era," in *"Azerbaijani" and Beyond: Perspectives on the Construction of National Identity*, ed. Aliaga Mammadli, Adeline Braux, and Ceyhun Mahmudlu (Berlin: Verlag Dr. Köster, 2017), 63.

27. Mammadli, 181; and Aliagha Mammadli, "Soviet-Era Anthropology by Azerbaijani Scholars," in *Exploring the Edge of Empire: Soviet Era Anthropology in the Caucasus and Central Asia*, ed. Florian Mühlfried and Sergey Sokolovskiy, Halle Studies in the Anthropology of Eurasia, vol. 25 (Berlin: LitVerlag, 2011), 179.

28. ARPİİSSA 1.44.67.62-66.

29. Shnirelman, *The Value of the Past*, 105; Ismailov, *Vlast' i Narod*, 281.

30. sšssa (II) 14.18.180.167, 178.

31. Barbara L. Voss, *The Archaeology of Ethnogenesis: Race and Sexuality in Colonial San Francisco* (Gainesville: University Press of Florida, 2015), 37.

32. Laruelle, "Concept of Ethnogenesis," 184.

33. ARPİİSSA 1.48.405.36.

34. Archive of the Russian Academy of Sciences (Arkhiv Rossiiskoi akademii nauk), or ARAN, 142.10.346.46-48; ARPİİSSA 1.48.405.31-39.

35. ARPİİSSA 1.48.405.38.

36. Suha Bölükbaşı, "Nation-Building in Azerbaijan: The Soviet Legacy and the Impact of the Karabakh Conflict," in *Identity Politics in Central Asia and the Muslim World*, ed. Willem van Schendel and Erik J. Zürcher (London: Tauris, 2001), 46.

37. Although Bünyadov was a prominent Azerbaijani historian, he has been accused of plagiarism and historical misrepresentation. See, for example, Thomas de Waal, *Black Garden: Armenia and Azerbaijan Through Peace and War* (New York: New York University Press, 2003), 165–166.

38. For a detailed study of this violence, see Leslie Sargent, "The 'Armeno-Tatar War' in the South Caucasus, 1905–1906: Multiple Causes, Interpreted Meanings," *Ab Imperio* 4 (2010): 143–169.

39. Saparov, *From Conflict to Autonomy*, 93.

40. Baberowski, *Der Feind ist überall*, 245–246.

41. Saparov, "Between the Russian Empire and the USSR," 129.

42. Georgi M. Derluguian, *Bourdieu's Secret Admirer in the Caucasus: A World-System Biography* (Chicago and London: The University of Chicago Press, 2005), 186.

43. RGANI 5.59.3.108-118.

44. Suny, *Looking Toward Ararat*, 195.

45. The question of Nagorno-Karabakh's placement in Azerbaijan was revisited once again, of course, during *glasnost'*. This time it resulted in a formal request by Armenian deputies in the NKAO soviet to join Armenia in February 1988. The popu-

lar response to this request provoked interethnic violence and mass expulsions of Azeris from Armenia and Armenians from Azerbaijan over the course of the next couple of years. This escalation of violence in the waning years of the Soviet Union led to the Nagorno-Karabakh war, which has since entered a "frozen" stage of conflict in which Armenia helps sustain—militarily, economically, and politically—a Nagorno-Karabakh separatist state inside Azerbaijan and occupies several Azerbaijani regions surrounding the Karabakh region.

46. Rashid Khalidi, *Palestinian Identity: The Construction of Modern National Consciousness* (New York: Columbia University Press, 2010), 15.

47. Amir Weiner, *Making Sense of War: The Second World War and the Fate of the Bolshevik Revolution* (Princeton, NJ: Princeton University Press, 2001).

48. Dzhamil' Gasanly, *Khrushchevskaia "ottepel'" i natsional'nyi vopros v Azerbaidzhane (1954–1959)* (Moscow: Flinta, 2009), 11.

49. David Nissman, "The Origin and Development of the Literature of 'Longing' in Azerbaijan," *Journal of Turkish Studies* 8 (1984): 200.

50. Shnirelman, *The Value of the Past*, 108.

51. ARDA 411.26s.357.68-76.

52. Nissman, "Origin and Development," 201. For other pan-Azerbaijani publications produced in the late 1940s and early 1950s, see Swietochowski, *Russia and Azerbaijan*, 166–167.

53. The one-third estimate is from Altstadt, *Politics of Culture*, 209.

54. Ismailov, *Ocherki po istorii*, 346–347.

55. ARPIISSA 1.43.91.135.

56. ARPIISSA 1.43.91.151-152.

57. ARPIISSA 1.43.91.153-156.

58. ARPIISSA 1.43.91.144 and 146.

59. ARPIISSA 1.43.91.138.

60. ARPIISSA 1.43.91.135.

61. ARDA 2941.7.951.253.

62. *Constitution of the Georgian Soviet Socialist Republic of February 13, 1937 as Amended through July 24, 1947* (New York: American Russian Institute, April 1950), 23; *Constitution of the Armenian Soviet Socialist Republic of March 23, 1937 as Amended through July 11, 1947* (New York: American Russian Institute, April 1950), 17.

63. ARPIISSA 1.43.87.116.

64. It was printed in the August 24, 1956, edition of *Bakinskii rabochii* (ARDA 2941.7.951.252).

65. Mirza Ibragimov, "Third Session of the Supreme Council of the Azerbaijan SSR: Speech of Deputy Mirza Ibragimov," *Bakinskii rabochii*, August 29, 1956.

66. RGANI 5.30.60.16-20. Titled "Azerbaidzhanskii iazyk v gosudarstvennykh uchrezhdeniiakh," the article appeared in *Kommunist* on October 28, 1956.

67. "Azerbaidzhanskii iazyk."

68. ARDA 2941.7.976.142-143.

69. ARPIISSA 1.43.107.258-259.

70. ARPIISSA 1.43.107.253.

71. RGANI 5.31.60.10-11.

72. Hasanli, *Khrushchev's Thaw*, chap. 4.

73. ARPİİSSA 1.45.101.7; ARDA 3034.1.185.82-83.

74. Aidyn Balaev, *Etnoiazykovye protsessy v Azerbaidzhane v XIX–XX vv.* (Baku: Nurlar, 2005), 124.

75. Jeremy Smith goes into great detail about this law and discussions surrounding it in his article "The Battle for Language: Opposition to Khrushchev's Education Reform in the Soviet Republics, 1958–59," *Slavic Review* 76, no. 4 (Winter 2017): 983–1002.

76. During closed-door discussions over Mustafayev's departure in the summer of 1959, Azerbaijan Communist Party secretaries argued that they thought they did nothing wrong because they followed the precedent set by Latvia earlier in the year (ARPİİSSA 1.46.87). See also ARDA 57.14.99.238 for local discussions and measures related to this issue.

77. RGANI 5.31.60.13, cited in Hasanli, *Khrushchev's Thaw*, 111–112.

78. Republic of Azerbaijan State Literature and Art Archive, or ARDAIA, 340.1.606.1-8, cited in Hasanli, *Khrushchev's Thaw*, 317–318.

79. ARDA 2941.7.951.253.

80. Hasanli, *Khrushchev's Thaw*, 91.

81. Interview in St. Petersburg, Russia, May 2003.

82. In 1959, the Soviet Azerbaijan census reported that Georgians comprised 0.3 percent of the population of Azerbaijan. This figure underrepresented the number of people who identified as Georgian or Ingiloi in the republic, however, since Muslim Ingilois were registered as Azerbaijani rather than as Georgian. Interviews in Ingiloi communities show that many Ingiloi consider themselves to be a part of the Georgian nation and would have categorized themselves as Georgian or Ingiloi in Soviet censuses had it been allowed.

83. ARPİİSSA 1.46.110.324-325.

84. ARPİİSSA 1.43.107.258.

85. Hirsch, *Empire of Nations*, 14.

86. Dominque Arel, "Demography and Politics in the First Post-Soviet Censuses: Mistrusted State, Contested Identities," *Population* 57, no. 6 (November–December 2002): 801–827.

87. *Vsesoiuznaia perepis' naseleniia 1939 goda*, 71.

88. G. M. Maksimova, ed., *Vsesoiuznaia perepis' naseleniia 1970 goda: sbornik statei* (Moscow: Statistika, 1976), 203.

89. Maksimova, *Vsesoiuznaia perepis'*, 140.

90. The Russian population in Azerbaijan declined from 528,318 in 1939 to 475,255 in 1979.

91. Ismailov, *Ocherki po istorii*, 355–356. Hasanli (*Khrushchev's Thaw*, 174) repeats this interpretation, but the effect of these demographic changes, including increased rural to urban migration, likely would have become significant factors only after the constitutional amendment and complementary policies were put into motion in the mid-1950s.

92. Süha Bölükbaşı, *Azerbaijan: A Political History* (London: Tauris, 2011), 51.

93. See, for example, Brown, *Biography*; and Sarah Cameron, *The Hungry Steppe: Famine, Violence, and the Making of Soviet Kazakhstan* (Ithaca, NY: Cornell University Press, 2018).

94. The phrase "technologies of population policies" comes from Uğur Ümit Üngör's study of the ethnic homogenization of East Anatolia between 1913 and 1950.

Üngör, *The Making of Modern Turkey: Nation and State in Eastern Anatolia, 1913–1950* (Oxford: Oxford University Press, 2011), vii. Census trends look different elsewhere. In a number of Central Asian republics, such as Kazakhstan and Kyrgyzstan, the titular nation as a percentage of republic population declined in the 1939 and 1959 censuses in part due to the mass resettlement of Russians and deportees in these republics.

95. The Azerbaijani government has claimed that as many as 150,000 Azeris were moved to Azerbaijan from Armenia at this time, but 45,000 is a reliable estimate based on available documentation. The original decree called for the resettlement of 100,000 Azeris, but archival records show that resettlement officials consistently mismanaged the migration and that both potential Azeri migrants and some officials became resistant to resettlement over time. In 1954, the Azerbaijan Resettlement Administration reported that they resettled 11,914 households (52,956 people) to the Kura-Araks zone of Azerbaijan between 1948 and 1953, including 9,875 households (83 percent) from Armenia and 2,039 from mountainous and foothill regions of Azerbaijan (17 percent). RGAE 5675.1.772.66.

96. See, for example, Bəxtiyar Nəcəfov, *Deportasiya* (Baku: Çaşıoğlu, 2006); Atakhan Pashayev, "Deportatsiia (1948–1953 gody)," *Azerbaidzhan* (June and July 1997), issue numbers 132, 134, 139, 143, 144, 145; Əsad Qurbanlı, *Azərbaycan Türklərinin Ermənistandan Deportasiyası, 1947-1953-cü illər* (Baku: Monoqrafiya, 2004); and Karim Shukurov, "Great Tragedy: Deportation of Azerbaijanis from Armenia," *Visions of Azerbaijan* (November–December 2010), 61.

97. Krista Goff, "Postwar rebuilding and national migration in the Soviet Union: A case of Azeri resettlement, 1948–1953," *Slavic Review*, forthcoming 2021.

98. Between 1948 and 1950, 451 *families* (2,116 people) reportedly returned to Armenia (RGAE 5675.1.466.29). An additional 2,000 families moved back to Armenia between 1950 and 1956 (ARDA 417.36.407.150-151), but census figures indicate many more eventually returned.

99. GARF 9479.1.55.24-28, reprinted in Bugai and Mamaev, *Kurdy SSSR*, 158.

100. For 1931, see sšssa (II) 13.9.195.47. The 1937 census figures are available in "Iz arkhivov Goskomstata SSSR: Itogi Vsesoiuznoi perepisi naseleniia 1937 g.," *Vestnik statistiki* 7 (1990): 77. The 1939 census statistics are included in *Vsesoiuznaia perepis' naseleniia 1939 goda: Osnovnye itogi* (Moscow: Nauka, 1992), while comprehensive figures from 1959 are in ARDA 2511.15.202.313.

101. Daniel Müller, "The Kurds of Soviet Azerbaijan, 1920–91," *Central Asian Survey* 19, no. 1 (2000): 62–65.

102. RGANI 100.5.738.27.

103. N. F. Bugai and A. M. Gonov, *Kavkaz: narody v eshelonakh (20-60-e gody)* (Moscow: Insan, 1998), 105; oral history interviews conducted in 2011 and 2016.

104. *Vsesoiuznaia perepis' naseleniia 1939 goda*, 71; Irina Mukhina, *The Germans of the Soviet Union* (Abingdon, Oxon: Routledge, 2007), 46. Most Germans in the South Caucasus descended from migrants who moved from German territories between the early nineteenth and early twentieth centuries. The earliest settlements, such as Helenendorf (which was renamed Khanlar in the late 1930s and then Göygöl in 2008), were founded after the Treaty of Gulistan when the Russian Tsars sought to populate and remake their new Caucasian territories. Religious sectarians also played a role in colonizing the Caucasus, often after having arrived there as exiles. Nicholas Breyfogle

explores this history in his book, *Heretics and Colonizers: Forging Russia's Empire in the South Caucasus* (Ithaca, NY: Cornell University Press, 2005).

105. This amount was miniscule in comparison with the numbers of people deported from Georgia (36,705 people) and Armenia (12,000) during Operation Volna. The figures for Operation Volna deportations from Azerbaijan are from GARF R-9479.1.476.22, 29, 36, 38, cited in Kaiser, "'What Are They Doing?'" See also Pavel Polian, *Ne po svoei vole . . . Istoriia i geografiia prinuditel'nykh migratsii v SSSR* (Moscow: OGI-Memorial, 2001), 141.

106. As discussed earlier, "Turks" deported from Georgia were mostly Meskhetian Turks. ARPİİSSA 1.45.84.16.

107. RGAE 1562.336.1565.226.

108. Document from Central Statistical Administration to Talysh man in Lankaran explaining that the Talysh category would not be added to the 1979 census for this reason (private archive).

109. S. I. Bruk and V. I. Kozlov, "Etnograficheskaia nauka i perepis' naseleniia 1970 goda," *Sovetskaia etnografiia* 6 (1967): 8.

110. By "fill in the other lines," he meant that he would be asked to provide information for the rest of the census form (oral history interview conducted in March 2010).

111. Interviews conducted between June 2007 and July 2013.

112. Interviews conducted between November 2010 and July 2013, as well as archived complaint letters in the Azerbaijan and Georgian Communist Party Archives. Ingiloi would have been a difficult category of registration because scientists in Moscow and Georgia classified Ingilois as an ethnographic group of the Georgian nation rather than as an independent nationality, but Muslim Georgian-Ingilois who preferred to be identified as Georgian were often denied the right to register as such and instead were categorized as Azerbaijani.

113. *Vsesoiuznaia perepis' naseleniia 1939 goda*, 71; *Tsentral'noe statisticheskoe upravelnie SSSR* (1963), 134–135. In the 1970 census, the number of Lezgins was greater in comparison with the 1959 census (from 98,211 to 137,250), but the percentage of Lezgins relative to the population of Azerbaijan remained the same—2.7 percent. *Tsentral'noe statisticheskoe upravelnie SSSR* (1973), 263. This is lower than 1939, when Lezgins comprised 3.5 percent of the population. *Vsesoiuznaia perepis' naseleniia 1939 goda*, 71. By 1970, the titular nationality accounted for nearly 75 percent of Soviet Azerbaijan's population and had more than doubled in comparison with 1939.

114. Interview, July 2007.

115. Interview, March 2011.

116. ARPİİSSA 1.56.38.372.

117. See, for example, Ismailov, *Ocherki po istorii*, 355.

118. ARDA 411.35.22.231; Ismailov, *Vlast' i narod*, 281.

119. ARDA 57.11.326.2.

120. See, for example, ARDA 2941.7.990.49-56, cited in Hasanli, *Khrushchev's Thaw*, 133; and ARPİİSSA 1.45.2.272-275, cited in Hasanli, *Khrushchev's Thaw*, 309.

121. RGANI 5.30.141.91.

122. RGANI 5.30.141.91-93.

123. Iosif Shikin reported this anecdote during a meeting of the presidium of the Central Committee about Mustafayev's dismissal. Mustafayev confirmed its accuracy at the time. Fursenko, *Prezidium TsK KPSS*, 365.

124. ARPİİSSA 1.46.16.128, cited in Hasanli, *Khrushchev's Thaw*, 131.

125. Hasanli, *Khrushchev's Thaw*, 113.

126. Fitzpatrick, *On Stalin's Team*, 230–231.

127. Weiner, "The Empires Pay a Visit," 331–333.

128. ARPİİSSA 1.46.87.30.

129. ARPİİSSA 1.46.87.50-52, 67–68.

130. ARPİİSSA 1.46.87.50-52.

131. Interview, June 2008. Adrienne Edgar has written about the choices that children in mixed marriages had to make in the Soviet Union to "reconcile their multiple identities with the Soviet requirement that each citizen possess a single 'official' nationality" and the pain that this could cause when they felt a disconnect between how the state viewed them and the way they saw themselves. Adrienne Edgar, "Children of Mixed Marriage in Soviet Central Asia: Dilemmas of Identity and Belonging," in *Ideologies of Race: Imperial Russia and the Soviet Union in Global Context*, ed. David Rainbow (Montreal: McGill-Queen's University Press, 2019), 209–210.

132. Interview, March 2011.

133. Les W. Field, "Mapping Erasure: The Power of Nominative Cartography in the Past and Present of the Muwekma Ohlones of the San Francisco Bay Area," in *Recognition, Sovereignty Struggles, and Indigenous Rights in the United States*, ed. Amy E. Den Ouden and Jean M. O'Brien (Chapel Hill: University of North Carolina Press, 2013), 288.

134. Interview, March 2011.

135. Interview, July 2008.

136. Interview, July 2008.

137. Elena Zubkova, *Russia After the War: Hopes, Illusions, and Disappointments, 1945–1957* (Armonk, NY: Sharpe, 1998), 5.

138. Brubaker, *Nationalist Politics*, 39.

4. The Vanishing Minority

1. A. A. Isupov, Central Statistical Administration letter number 32-02-1/i-3-1, January 17, 1979, private archive; A. A. Isupov, Central Statistical Administration letter number 32-01-9/kl-16-1, March 27, 1979, private archive.

2. Isupov, letter number 32-02-1/I-3-1, January 17, 1979, private archive.

3. State officials viewed those characterized as part of a diaspora or foreign nationality (Poles, Greeks, Koreans, Germans, Iranians, Japanese, etc.) as suspicious outsiders, concerned that their loyalty lay more with their co-ethnics abroad than at home with the Soviet Union. Oirots from the Russian Altai region are another interesting example from the 1959 census. The Oirot category was included in the 1939 census and, like the Talysh nationality, was removed for the first time in 1959. The difference between the two examples is that the Oirot category was removed because Oirots were rebranded (rather than assimilated into another group). In 1948, the word "Oirot" was deemed counterrevolutionary following charges that local nationalists were pro-Japanese. The name of the Oirot Autonomous Oblast' was thus changed in 1948 to the Gorno-Altai Autonomous Oblast'. This lexical adjustment is elucidated in documents generated by the Institute of Ethnography, where the Altai category of 1959 is listed as replacing the Oirot category of 1939. ARAN 142.1.980.39. There was no similar renaming of the Talysh category that year.

4. Kasumova, "Kul'turnoe stroitel'stvo," 7–8.

5. Genko's official cause of death was extreme exhaustion and heart disease. He was rehabilitated thirteen years later and his grammar text of the Abkhaz language was published shortly thereafter. N. G. Volkova and G. A. Sergeeva, "Anatolii Nestorovich Genko: Tragic Pages from the History of Caucasus Studies," *Anthropology and Archeology of Eurasia* 42, no. 2 (Fall 2003): 47.

6. N. G. Volkova, ed., *Stranitsy otechestvennogo kavkazovedeniia* (Moscow: Nauka, 1992), 32.

7. Hirsch, *Empire of Nations*, 320.

8. ARAN 142.1.1050.67.

9. ARAN 142.1.1050.57.

10. Nicholas Dirks, "Forward," in Bernard Cohn, *Colonialism and Its Forms of Knowledge: The British in India* (Princeton, NJ: Princeton University Press, 1996), ix, cited in Hirsch, *Empire of Nations*, 146.

11. Nicholas Dirks, *Castes of Mind: Colonialism and the Making of Modern India* (Princeton, NJ: Princeton University Press, 2001).

12. Hirsch, *Empire of Nations*, 13. The point Hirsch makes here overlaps with a broader debate about whether the Soviet Union was a modern colonial empire that pursued what Partha Chatterjee calls the "colonial rule of difference" or more akin to what Adeeb Khalid has termed modern mobilizational states that "tended to homogenize populations in order to attain universal goals." See Chatterjee, *The Nation and Its Fragments: Colonial and Postcolonial Histories*, 19. For more on these conversations, see Khalid, "Backwardness and the Quest for Civilization," 233, 236; Northrop, *Veiled Empire*, 19–24; and Yuri Slezkine, "Imperialism as the Highest Stage of Socialism," *Russian Review* 59, no. 2 (April 2000): 227–234.

13. ARAN 142.10.119.9.

14. These ideas harken to Marx and Engels' discussion about peoples with and without history (*geschichtslosen Völker*), and specifically the belief that the assimilation of so-called nonhistoric peoples would benefit social progress because they were counterrevolutionary at their very core. V. I. Lenin, "The Socialist Revolution and the Right of Nations to Self-Determination," in *Collected Works*, vol. 22, ed. George Hanna, trans. Yuri Sdobnikov (Moscow: Progress Publishers, 1974), 147.

15. ARAN 142.10.21.13-16. For more on the example of the Far North, see Yuri Slezkine, *Arctic Mirrors: Russia and the Small Peoples of the North* (Ithaca, NY: Cornell University Press, 1996).

16. ARAN 142.1.324.48. The decade began with a two-year (1950–1952) investigation of Dagestani national consolidation, followed by numerous other studies. The initial proposal was for a five-year research program that would culminate in 1955 with the publication of a book about the consolidation of Dagestani *narodnosti*.

17. Volkova, *Stranitsy*, 32–33.

18. A. D. Danialov, "Speech by Comrade A. D. Danialov, Dagestan Autonomous Republic," *Pravda*, February 21, 1956, 7–8, reprinted in *Current Digest of the Russian Press* 10, no. 8 (April 18, 1956): 27–29.

19. Ikhilov worked in the Institute of History, Language, and Literature in the Dagestani branch of the Academy of Sciences. M. M. Ikhilov, "K voprosu o natsional'noi konsolidatsii narodov Dagestana," *Sovetskaia etnografiia* 6 (1965): 101.

20. Ikhilov, "K voprosu."

21. Lavrov is referencing Shaki, a town in Azerbaijan known at this time as Nukha. Although Nukha was in the Azerbaijan SSR, Soviet political borders crossed historical economic, social, political, and demographic zones. Nukha had long been part of a broader region comprising parts of Georgia, northern Azerbaijan, and southern Dagestan. The well-traveled path between Nukha and Khnov, for instance, had once been an important trade route through the Caucasus Mountains from Tbilisi to the Caspian coastal settlement of Derbent.

22. L. I. Lavrov, *Etnografiia Kavkaza: (Po polevym materialam 1924–1978 gg.)* (Leningrad: Nauka, 1982), 140–141.

23. M. M. Ikhilov, *Narodnosti lezginskoi gruppy: Etnograficheskoe issledovanie proshlogo i nastoiashchego lezgin, tabasarantsev, rutulov, tsakhurov, agulov* (Moscow: Avtoreferat, 1968), 42–43.

24. V. I. Kozlov, "K voprosu ob izuchenii etnicheskikh protsessov u narodov SSSR (opyt issledovaniia na primere mordvy)," *Sovetskaia etnografiia* 4 (1961): 59. Kozlov, based at the Academy of Sciences in Moscow, published extensively on nationality theory and ethno-demographic processes.

25. Kozlov, "K voprosu ob izuchenii etnicheskikh protsessov," 60.

26. "Materialy XXII s"ezda KPSS," 405. The program's original draft used the more aggressive language of *sliianie*. The switch to *sblizhenie* in the final version perhaps reflects the leadership's awareness that this was a sensitive agenda item. Alexander Titov, "The 1961 Party Programme and the Fate of Khrushchev's Reforms," in *Soviet State and Society Under Nikita Khrushchev*, ed. Melanie Ilic and Jeremy Smith (Abingdon, Oxon: Routledge, 2009), 15.

27. It was renamed the Patrice Lumumba People's Friendship University after the Congolese independence leader's execution in 1961.

28. Odd Arne Westad, *The Global Cold War: Third World Interventions and the Making of Our Times* (Cambridge: Cambridge University Press, 2007), 68. There were similar efforts in the United States during the Cold War, leading to the creation of the area studies discipline in American academia. See Christopher Simpson, ed., *Universities and Empire: Money and Politics in the Social Sciences during the Cold War* (New York: New Press, 1998); and Engerman, *Know Your Enemy*.

29. Titov, "The 1961 Party Programme," 8.

30. For example, V. P. Murat, "Novyi etap v osvoboditel'noi bor'be negrov SShA," *Sovetskaia etnografiia* 2 (1962): 51–59.

31. G. A. Agranat, "Polozhenie korennogo naseleniia Krainego Severa Ameriki," *Sovetskaia etnografiia* 4 (1961): 100–113. See also I. A. Zolotarevskaiia, "Nekotorye materialy ob assimiliatsii indeitsev Oklakhomy," *Kratkie soobshcheniia Instituta etnografii im. N. N. Miklukho-Maklaia AN SSSR* 33 (Moscow: Izdatel'stvo Akademii nauk SSSR, 1960), 84–89; and B. G. Gafurov, "Stroitel'stvo kommunizma i natsional'nyi vopros," *Voprosy stroitel'stva kommunizma v SSSR: Materialy nauchnoi sessii otdelenii obshchestvennykh nauk Akademii nauk SSSR* (Moscow: Izdatel'stvo Akademii nauk SSSR, 1959), 88–104.

32. These distinctions were also articulated in Institute of Ethnography discussions about ethnographic museums. Capitalist countries used these museums to display cultural remnants of the past, it was argued, but Soviet ethnographic museums advertised the progressive traditions of Soviet peoples. ARAN 142.10.307.1.

33. RGAE 1562.327.1002.38.

34. Potekhin was a prominent scholar who worked on processes of ethnic consolidation and national studies, largely in the African context. From the late 1940s through the 1950s, he was deputy director of the Institute of Ethnography. Starting in 1959, he headed the newly established Institute of African Studies and Association for Friendship with the Peoples of Africa. Terent'eva specialized in the Baltic regions of the USSR and ethnic processes there. At one point she also served as deputy director of the Institute of Ethnography.

35. ARAN 142.1.980.91.

36. ARAN 142.1.980.74.

37. RGAE 1562.327.1002.38-43.

38. For example, ARAN 142.1.980.62, RGAE 1562.327.1002.42, and RGAE 1562.36.15.12.

39. For example, ARAN 142.10.346.40, 5.

40. ARDA 2511.8.27, 2511.8.29, 2511.8.30.

41. ARDA 2511.8.27.2787.

42. ARDA 2511.15.202.167.

43. For examples of traveler accounts published around this time, see Baron von Haxthausen, *Transcaucasia: Sketches of the Nations and Races Between the Black Sea and the Caspian*, trans. J. E. Taylor (London: Chapman and Hall, 1854); Alexandre Dumas, *Adventures in Caucasia* (Philadelphia: Chilton Books, 1962); Gustav Radde, *Reisen an der Persisch-Russischen Grenze. Talysch und seine Bewohner* (Leipzig: Brockhaus, 1886); and Gustav Radde, *Talysch, das Nordwestende des Alburs und sein Tiefland* (Petermanns: Mittheilungen, 1885).

44. Based in Tbilisi (then Tiflis), the *Caucasus Calendar* was published annually from 1845 to 1916. This particular analysis of Talyshes aligned with the work of L. P. Zagurskii, the long-time head of the Caucasus Division of the Geographical Society. Zagurskii, *Etnologicheskaia klassifikatsiia kavkazskikh narodov: (Izvlecheno iz rukopisnago truda L. P. Zagurskago): Prilozhenie k Kavkazskomu kalendariu na 1888 g.* (Tiflis, 1887), 2.

45. Nadezhdin, *Kavkazskii krai*, 154. Another example is the 1888 study by Evgenii Gustavovich Veidenbaum, who held various positions in the imperial government in the Caucasus and participated in the Caucasus Division of the Geographic Society. While he questions whether another Iranian-speaking people, Tats, were defined by lifestyle or social condition rather than shared ethnicity, he confidently positions the Talysh as a separate ethnicity. E. Veidenbaum, *Putevoditel' po Kavkazu: Po porucheniiu gen.-ad"iutanta kn. Dondukova-Korsakova, Glavnonachal'stvuiushchego grazhd. chast'iu na Kavkaze, sostavil E. Veidenbaum* (Tiflis: tip. Kantsel[iarii] Glavnonachal'stvuiushchego grazhd. chast'iu na Kavkaze, 1888), 75–76.

46. Florian Mühlfried, "Caucasus Paradigms Revisited," *Routledge Handbook of the Caucasus*, 22.

47. See chapter 3 of Sara Brinegar's dissertation for more information about the Gilan Soviet Republic. She argues that it was an "unintended consequence of the Bolshevik drive to possess Azerbaijan's oil." Brinegar, "Baku at All Costs," 122.

48. The Sovietization of Azerbaijan is a complicated story outside the scope of this study. For more detailed examinations of this period, see Jamil Hasanli, *The Sovietization of Azerbaijan: The South Caucasus in the Triangle of Russia, Turkey, and Iran, 1920–1922* (Salt Lake City: University of Utah Press, 2018); Reynolds, *Shattering Empires*; Suny, *The Baku Commune*.

49. N. Ia. Marr, *Plemennoi sostav naseleniia Kavkaza*, 25.

50. N. Ia. Marr, *Talyshi* (Petrograd: Rossiiskaia gosudarstvennaia akademicheskaia tipografiia, 1922), 1.

51. Marr, *Talyshi*, 2, 22. While Azerbaijanis were generally referred to as "Tiurks" in Russian, authors sometimes also called them "Turks" or used both terms in the same publication.

52. Liaister and Chursin, *Geografiia Kavkaza*, 315. This book was cowritten, but I believe that Chursin wrote the ethnographic descriptions based on his academic specialization and other publications.

53. G. F. Chursin, *Talyshi* (Tiflis: Izvestiia Kavkazskogo istoriko-arkheologicheskogo instituta, 1926), 15–16.

54. Figures in the table from Nadezhdin, *Kavkazskii krai*, 244–245; Chursin, *Talyshi*, 16–17; Marr, *Talyshi*, 2.

55. Chursin, *Talyshi*, 16–17.

56. ARDA 57.1.1222 and ARDA 57.11.7.30-31.

57. B. V. Miller, *Predvaritel'nyi otchet o poezdke v Talysh letom 1925 g. (Doklad, chitannyi na zasedanii Istoriko-Etnograficheskoi Sektsii Obshchestva 14-go sentiabria 1925 goda)* (Baku: Izdanie Ob-va Issledovaniia i Izucheniia Azerbaidzhana, 1926), 5.

58. sšssa [II]) 13.9.195.58.

59. B. V. Miller, *Talyshskii iazyk* (Moscow: Izdatel'stvo Akademii nauk SSSR, 1953), 9. The 1931 census included 87,991 Talyshes and a document from 1934 registers 93,009 Talysh in the Azerbaijan SSR. suica 607.1.2404.104 and 106.

60. Miller, *Talyshskii iazyk*, 11.

61. In 1962, Aleksandra Grigor'evna Trofimova published the first post-census ethnographic description of the Talysh population in *Narody Kavkaza (Peoples of the Caucasus)*. Although not entirely representative of the script that developed in subsequent publications, she accepted Talysh assimilation and emphasized their close ties to Azerbaijanis. A. G. Trofimova, "Talyshi," in *Narody Kavkaza*, ed. B. A. Gardanov et al. (Moscow: Izdatel'stvo Akademii nauk SSSR, 1962), 187–194.

62. Isaev, born in North Ossetia, was a well-known scholar of languages in the Iranian language family, including Ossetian, and published frequently on ethnolinguistics and Esperanto. M. I. Isaev, *Sto tridtsat' ravnopravnykh: O iazykakh narodov SSSR* (Moscow: Nauka, 1970), 61.

63. ARAN 142.10.386.19.

64. ARAN 142.10.386.20.

65. ARAN 142.10.386.21.

66. ARAN 142.10.346.27 and 30.

67. ARAN 142.10.346.40.

68. ARAN 142.10.346.41.

69. ARAN 142.10.346.42.

70. ARAN 142.10.346.46-47.

71. ARAN 142.10.346.40.

72. Sergei Alymov, "The Concept of the 'Survival' and Soviet Social Science in the 1950s and 1960s," *Forum for Anthropology and Culture* 9 (2013): 165–166.

73. The term *otstalye* (backward) is applied to Tiurks in the 1920s by some critics of the slow progress of *korenizatsiia* in Azerbaijan, but that descriptor fades away in the 1930s as it became less expedient to describe titular nations as backward survivals. By

the 1950s, the Azerbaijanis had evolved from a backward people to a modern socialist nation. ssssa (II) 14.4.131.

74. Julie Fairbanks, "Narratives of Progress: Soviet Ethnographic Discourse and the Study of the Caucasus," workshop paper, University of Michigan, Eurasia Collective Workshop, 2013.

75. ARAN 142.10.432.69-70; ARAN 142.19.346.11.

76. ARAN 142.10.346.

77. A. A. Izmailova, "O narodnoi odezhde naseleniia iugo-vostochnykh raionov Azerbaidzhana," *Izvestiia Akademii nauk Azerbaidzhanskoi SSR* 4 (1964): 93.

78. Bruno Latour, *We Have Never Been Modern*, trans. Catherine Porter (Cambridge, MA: Harvard University Press, 1991), 10. Cited in Jean M. O'Brien, *Firsting and Lasting: Writing Indians Out of Existence in New England* (Minneapolis: University of Minnesota Press, 2010), 4.

79. O'Brien, *Firsting and Lasting*, xv.

80. O'Brien, *Firsting and Lasting*, xxii.

81. Interview, May 2010.

82. ARAN 142.1.1050.67-68.

83. ARAN 142.10.346.35-36. Vinnikov, born and raised in Kazakhstan, joined the Institute of Ethnography at the Academy of Sciences in 1946.

84. ARAN 142.10.346.40-41. A similar debate about assimilation in Azerbaijan erupted a decade earlier during a December 1953 meeting about G. A. Guliev's defense of his dissertation, "Socialist Culture and Lifestyle [*byt*] of Collective Farmworkers [*krest'ianstvo*] of Azerbaijan (Based on Materials of the Quba Region)." There, ethnographer Pavel Ivanovich Kushner criticized Guliev's dissertation, arguing that Lezgins and Tats also lived in the Quba region and that, although they used the Azerbaijani language alongside their native languages, they were still separate *narodnosti*. According to Kushner, it was incorrect for Guliev to overlook the culture and lifestyle of the Tats and Lezgins and act as though only Azerbaijanis lived in the Quba region. Kushner suggested that Guliev's dissertation would be more properly titled "Socialist Culture and Lifestyle of Collective Farmworkers-Azerbaijanis of the Quba Region." Guliev saw no problem with his homogeneous portrayal of Quba, however, responding that Lezgins and Tats had merged with Azerbaijanis and all shared a similar lifestyle and culture. ARAN 142.1.520.32-43.

85. Bruk and Kozlov, "Etnograficheskaia nauka," 8.

86. Bruk and Kozlov, "Etnograficheskaia nauka," 8.

87. ARAN 142.10.346.30.

88. Nauchno-redaktsionnoi kartosostavitel'skoi chast'iu GUGK i Institutom etnografii im. N. N. Miklukho-Maklaia AN SSSR pod obshchim rukovodstvom S. I. Bruka (spetsial'nuiu nagruzku karty sostavili S. I. Bruk, Ia. R. Vinnikov, V. I. Kozlov, V. V. Andrianov), ed., E. A. Shishkin, *Glavnoe upravlenie geologii i okhrany nedr SSSR* (Moscow, 1962), retrieved from Harvard Map Collection, Pusey Library.

89. S. I. Bruk, V. I. Kozlov, and M. G. Levin, "O predmete i zadachakh etnogeografii," *Sovetskaia etnografiia* 1 (1963): 11–25.

90. *Atlas narodov mira* (Moscow: Glavnoe upravlenie geodezii i kartografii Gosudarstvennogo geologicheskogo komiteta SSSR: Institut etnografii im. N. N. Miklukho-Maklaia Akademii nauk SSSR, 1964), 18–19.

91. A. M. Prokhorov, ed., *Bol'shaia sovetskaia entsiklopediia (v 20-ti t.)*, vol. 24, no. 2 (Moscow: Sovetskaia entsiklopediia, 1977), inset between 32–33.

92. *Atlas SSSR* (Moscow: Glavnoe upravlenie geodezii i kartografii pri Sovete ministrov SSSR, 1983).

93. Iu. S. Gambarov, V. Ia. Zheleznov, M. M. Kovalevskii, S. A. Muromtsev, K. A. Timiriazev, *Entsiklopedicheskii slovar' Russkogo bibliograficheskogo instituta Granat*, vol. 41, no. 6 (Moscow: Russkii bibliograficheskii institut Granat, 1926), 746.

94. K. E. Voroshilov et al., *Bol'shaia sovetskaia entsiklopediia*, vol. 53 (Moscow: OGIZ RSFSR, 1946), 514–515.

95. B. A. Vvedenskii, *Bol'shaia sovetskaia entsiklopediia*, vol. 41 (Moscow: Bol'shaia sovetskaia entsiklopediia, 1956), 562.

96. A. M. Prokhorov, *Bol'shaia sovetskaia entsiklopediia*, vol. 25 (Moscow: Sovetskaia entsiklopediia, 1976), 237.

97. Interview with Pireiko, 2010.

98. Liia Aleksandrovna Pireiko, *Talyshsko-russkii slovar'* (Izd-vo "Russkii iazyk," 1976).

99. Alexander Formozov, "Azerbaidzhanskij 'Dikii Zapad' v seredine 1980-kh: vzgliad moskovskogo etnosotsiologa: Viktor Karlov v besede s Aleksandrom Formozovym," *Laboratorium: Zhurnal sotsial'nykh issledovanii* 1 (2010): 230.

100. ARPiISSA 1.46.87; Fursenko, *Prezidium TsK KPSS*, 357–387.

101. Pelkmans, *Defending the Border*, 27–37.

102. Oral history interviews with people whose family members were relocated and deported in the 1930s, 2010–2011.

103. The villages were in the Bandasar sel'sovet (Unuz, Tangov, Armudy, Siyov, Dilmadi, Bandasar, Novushtarud, Tatarmaglya, Vanabidzhar, Chaiagzy, Isabidzhar, Geimatullamagla, Godon, Piyakenarud, and Zanguliash).

104. ARDA 411.26s.330.1.

105. Interview, July 2008.

106. Interview, April 2010.

107. Interviews, March 2011.

108. Interview, July 2008.

109. Adzhiev, "Skazhi svoe imia, talysh," 11–15.

110. Interviews, 2010 and 2011.

111. "Population by Ethnic Groups," http://www.stat.gov.az/source/demoqraphy/ap/indexen.php.

112. James Minahan, *The Former Soviet Union's Diverse Peoples: A Reference Sourcebook* (Santa Barbara, CA: ABC-CLIO, 2004), 303. By 2004, when Minahan's book was published, the 1999 census had recorded 77,000 Talysh in Azerbaijan. Qəmərşah Cavadov presents an alternative approach to Minahan's attempt to explain how an assimilated people still existed. In his detailed ethnographic study of Talyshes, Cavadov offers an analysis of Talysh modern demographic history. When it comes to the 1959, 1970, and 1979 censuses, however, he simply notes, but does not try to explain, their absence. Qəmərşah Cavadov, *Talışlar (tarixi-etnoqrafik tədqiqat)* (Baku: Elm, 2004), 109–112.

113. Suny, *Revenge of the Past*, 3.

114. Michael Taussig, *Defacement: Public Secrecy and the Labor of the Negative* (Stanford, CA: Stanford University Press, 1999), 7.

115. Taussig, *Defacement*, 6 (italics in the original).

116. See also Daphne Berdahl's work for an exploration of how secrets in East German border areas were sustained by the interplay of their public nature and the power of the regime. Berdahl, *Where the World Ended: Re-Unification and Identity in the German Borderland* (Berkeley, CA: University of California Press, 1999), chap. 2.

117. Adzhiev, "Skazhi svoe imia, talysh"; "Talysh, charuzh i drugie," *Vokrug sveta* 11 (1991): 38–43.

5. Minority Activism and Citizenship After Stalin

1. ARPİİSSA, 1.48.405.90.

2. Crimean Tatar activists succeeded in meeting with Presidium member and first deputy chairman of the Council of Ministers of the Soviet Union Anastas Mikoyan in the late 1950s and other high-ranking officials such as KGB head Yuri Andropov in the 1960s, but were unable to secure the right of return at that time. State Archive of the Russian Federation, or GARF, r-5446.58.92.889. See also Greta Uehling, "Squatting, Self-Immolation, and the Repatriation of Crimean Tatars," *Nationalities Papers* 28, no. 2 (2000): 317–341.

3. See, for example, Vladimir A. Kozlov, *Mass Uprisings in the USSR: Protest and Rebellion in the Post-Stalin Years* (London: Sharpe, 2002); Pohl, "'It Cannot Be that Our Graves Will Be Here': The Survival of Chechen and Ingush Deportees in Kazakhstan, 1944–1957," *Journal of Genocide Research* 4, no. 3 (September 2002): 401–430; Alan Fisher, *The Crimean Tatars* (Stanford, CA: Hoover Institution, 1978); Edward A. Allworth, *The Tatars of Crimea: Return to the Homeland* (Durham, NC: Duke University Press, 1998); Brian G. Williams, *The Crimean Tatars: The Diaspora Experience and the Forging of a Nation* (Leiden: Brill, 2001); and Greta Lynn Uehling, *Beyond Memory: The Crimean Tatars' Deportation and Return* (New York: Palgrave Macmillan, 2004).

4. William Clark and Ablet Kamalov, "Uighur Migration Across Central Asian Frontiers," *Central Asian Survey* 23, no. 2 (June 2004): 167–182.

5. Archive of the President of the Republic of Kazakhstan (Qazaqstan Respublikasy Prezidentīnīng Arxivī), or QRPA, 708.30.1527.1-5, 15.

6. For the imperial period, see, for example, Jane Burbank, "An Imperial Rights Regime: Law and Citizenship in the Russian Empire," *Kritika: Explorations in Russian and Eurasian History* 7, no. 3 (Summer 2006): 397–431; and Burbank, *Russian Peasants Go to Court: Legal Culture in the Countryside, 1905–1917* (Bloomington: Indiana University Press, 2004). For the earlier period, see Valerie Kivelson, "Muscovite 'Citizenship': Rights without Freedom," *Journal of Modern History* 74 (September 2002): 465–489; and Nancy Kollmann, *By Honor Bound: State and Society in Early Modern Russia* (Ithaca, NY: Cornell University Press, 1999).

7. Golfo Alexopoulos, for instance, uses T. H. Marshall's study of England to define citizenship as the marriage of civil, political, and social protections. Marshall, *Class, Citizenship, and Social Development* (New York: Doubleday, 1964), 71–72. Alexopoulos juxtaposes Soviet citizenship with this triad and finds that only social citizenship (or "the right to a modicum of economic welfare and security") was meaningful in the USSR since economic rights were "reasonably protected." Alexopoulos, "Soviet Citizenship, More or Less: Rights, Emotions, and States of Civic Belonging," *Kritika: Explorations in Russian and Eurasian History* 7, no. 3 (Summer 2006): 495. Alexopoulos

also notes that the failure to achieve social and legal equality is a marker not only of the Soviet system but of modernity in general. Alexopoulos, "Soviet Citizenship," 487. Christine Varga-Harris also uses Marshall to define citizenship. Varga-Harris, "Forging Citizenship on the Home Front: Reviving the Socialist Contract and Constructing Soviet Identity during the Thaw," in *The Dilemmas of De-Stalinization: Negotiating Cultural and Social Change in the Khrushchev Era*, ed. Polly Jones (Abingdon, Oxon: Routledge, 2006), 101–116.

8. In keeping with the temporal focus on the late 1920s and 1930s, Soviet-era petitions are frequently used to document resistance among the peasantry. See, for example, Chris J. Chulos, "Peasants' Attempts to Reopen their Church, 1929–1936," *Russian History/Histoire Russe* 24, nos. 1–2 (Spring-Summer 1997): 203–213; Lynne Viola, *Peasant Rebels Under Stalin: Collectivization and the Culture of Peasant Resistance* (New York: Oxford University Press, 1996); and Sheila Fitzpatrick, *Stalin's Peasants: Resistance and Survival in the Russian Village After Collectivization* (New York: Oxford University Press, 1994).

9. See, for example, Hasanli, *Khrushchev's Thaw*, 130.

10. Hasanli, *Khrushchev's Thaw*, 372–373.

11. This resonates with Vladimir Kozlov's argument that moments of disorder in the post-Stalin years often reflected popular investment in the regime rather than conscious political dissent or disillusionment. Kozlov, *Mass Uprisings*. Kevin O'Brien's notion of "rightful resistance," based on his work on China, is useful for thinking about the Soviet case. According to O'Brien, rightful resistance "entails the innovative use of laws, policies, and other officially promoted values to defy 'disloyal' political and economic elites; it is a kind of partially sanctioned resistance that uses influential advocates and recognized principles to apply pressure on those in power who have failed to live up to some professed ideal or who have not implemented some beneficial measure." O'Brien, "Rightful Resistance," *World Politics* 49, no. 1 (1996): 33.

12. Alexei Yurchak, *Everything Was Forever, Until It Was No More: The Last Soviet Generation* (Princeton, NJ: Princeton University Press, 2005), 8.

13. Social theorist Margaret Somers's approach to defining citizenship is more helpful in judging the Soviet context than studies that use Marshall or other universalized measures. In her work, Somers acknowledges the localized and uneven nature of rights regimes everywhere, and proposes that we explore citizenship formation through the "relational settings of contested but patterned relations among people and institutions . . . to see that citizenship identities and practices developed in analytic autonomy from the bundle of attributes associated a priori with the categories of feudalism and capitalism." Somers, "Rights, Relationality, and Membership: Rethinking the Making and Meaning of Citizenship," in *Public Rights, Public Rules: Constituting Citizens in the World Polity and National Policy*, ed. Connie L. McNeely (New York: Garland, 1998), 161. Somers further defines citizenship as "the right to have rights," with the access to enjoy political and social membership serving as baseline parameters. Somers, *Genealogies of Citizenship: Markets, Statelessness, and the Right to Have Rights* (Cambridge: Cambridge University Press, 2008), 5. James Holston also offers a productive critique of the universalizing uses of Marshall's theories in his study of citizenship and modernity in Brazil. Although he sees Marshall as helpful for showing how we might "expand the analysis of citizenship beyond political institutionalization," like Somers, Holston emphasizes that the "spread, timing, and substance of

citizenship vary substantially with historical and national context." Holston, *Insurgent Citizenship: Disjunctions of Democracy and Modernity in Brazil* (Princeton, NJ: Princeton University Press, 2008), 317.

14. GARF R3316.29.576.1-3, and oral history interview, March 2011.

15. See, for example, sšssa (II) 14.18.180.94, 14.18.161.1-19, and 14.24.296.1.

16. sšssa (II) 14.18.180.5-7.

17. ARPİİSSA 1.53.36.123 and ARPİİSSA 1.46.110.324-325.

18. ARPİİSSA 1.48.405.89-93, 1.48.405.100-103, 1.48.405.117, 1.48.405.119, 1.48.405.123-126, 1.48.405.141-144, 1.48.405.145, 1.48.405.146-151.

19. ARPİİSSA 1.48.405.72.

20. ARPİİSSA 1.48.405.89-90.

21. Interview, December 2010.

22. Interview, December 2010.

23. Interviews, 2007–2011.

24. Anna Whittington, "Forging Soviet Citizens: Ideology, Identity, and Stability in the Soviet Union, 1930–1991," PhD diss., University of Michigan, 2018, 227–238.

25. Interview, July 2008.

26. Interviews, 2008–2011.

27. ARPİİSSA 1.48.405.40-42. Hasanli focuses on these sources in his version of events, using them to discredit demands for Georgian language instruction and assert that Georgian-Ingilois demanded access to Azerbaijani-language schools. To bolster this interpretation, he leaves out contradictory state sources that validate Georgian-Ingiloi complaints about assimilatory pressures and local dissatisfaction about school closures. Hasanli, *Khrushchev's Thaw*, 373.

28. ARPİİSSA 1.48.405.138.

29. ARPİİSSA 1.48.405.4.

30. ARPİİSSA 1.46.110.318-319. The name of Qakh-gürcü village was changed to Qakhingiloy. Replacing the word Georgian (*gürcü*) with Ingiloi reflects an effort to distance this community from connections to Georgia and Georgians.

31. ARPİİSSA 1.45.405.13-14.

32. ARPİİSSA 1.48.405.27. The draft document is undated, but references in the letter indicate that it is from 1961.

33. ARDA 411.8.536.58.

34. ARDA 411.8.536.60-61.

35. ARPİİSSA 1.48.405.58-59.

36. ARPİİSSA 1.48.405.6-8.

37. ARPİİSSA 1.48.405.129 and ARPİİSSA 1.48.405.123-128.

38. Interview, November 2010.

39. ARPİİSSA 1.53.36.123-134.

40. ARPİİSSA 1.53.36.126.

41. ARPİİSSA 1.48.405.8. No date is given on the document, but the content suggests it was written in 1962.

42. Interviews, October 2010 to March 2011.

43. Interview, December 2010.

44. Examples drawn from oral histories, as well as from Nino Aivazishvili-Gehne, "The Power of the Shrine and Creative Performances in Ingiloi Sacred Ritu-

als," in *Sacred Places, Emerging Spaces: Religious Pluralism in the Post-Soviet Caucasus*, ed. Tsypylma Darieva, Florian Mühlfried, and Kevin Tuite (New York: Berghahn Books, 2018), 127.

45. Khrushchev called for a return to socialist legality in his Secret Speech. It was a euphemism for due process, stronger legal institutions, and better adherence to laws and legal norms.

46. Interview, December 2010.

47. Rik'in Gaf is also often referred to in shorthand as K'vat'al (circle, society). It first met on October 18, 1959, and functioned until 1988. Rizvanov, *Kniga pravdy*, 115.

48. Rizvanov, *Kniga pravdy*, 115–116.

49. Interview, May 2011.

50. ARPİİSSA 1.56.38.357-360. The Lezgin decree was adopted on August 25, 1962.

51. ARDA 57.13.141.2-3.

52. ARDA 57.13.141.4-5.

53. Republic of Azerbaijan State Literature and Art Archive (Azərbaycan Respublikası Dövlət Ədəbiyyat və İncəsənət Arxivi, or ARDAİA), 340.1.990.39-40.

54. ARDAİA 340.1.1141.7.

55. ARDAİA 340.1.1141.1-7.

56. ARPİİSSA 1.56.38.348.

57. RGANI 100.5.433.9-10.

58. RGANI 100.5.433.1-5.

59. RGANI 100.5.432.11.

60. RGANI 100.5.432.43-44.

61. RGANI 100.5.432.2-6.

62. Interview, 2011.

63. Interview, July 2013.

64. For example, Emily Pyle shows that peasants seeking state assistance during World War I sometimes invoked legal rights but also appealed to informal rules or moral principles. Pyle, "Peasant Strategies for Obtaining State Aid: A Study of Petitions During World War I," *Russian History/Histoire Russe* 24, nos. 1–2 (Spring/Summer 1997): 60.

65. Golfo Alexopoulos, "The Ritual Lament: A Narrative of Appeal in the 1920s and 1930s," *Russian History/Histoire Russe* 24, no. 1–2 (Spring/Summer 1997): 119.

66. Fitzpatrick, "Supplicants," 91. Fitzpatrick also identifies a contrasting citizen type who invokes a language of rights, criticizes policies, officials, or miscarriages of justice, and claims to act in the public interest (or conceals private motives for writing).

67. sšssa (II) 14.18.161.12.

68. sšssa (II) 14.18.161.19 and 14.20.271.5.

69. sšssa (II) 14.20.271.13.

70. sšssa (II) 14.18.180.30.

71. sšssa (II) 14.20.271.2.

72. sšssa (II) 14.18.180.31.

73. sšssa (II) 14.18.180.75.

74. ARPİİSSA 1.48.405.79-80.

75. ARPİİSSA 1.48.405.100.

76. ARPİİSSA 1.48.405.144.

77. In her study of housing petitions in Khrushchev-era St. Petersburg, Varga-Harris similarly argues that a new mode of negotiation developed during the Thaw. She finds, however, that complainants in her study often blurred the lines between supplicant and citizen "types" by invoking rights while seeking justice. The autobiographical forms of the "supplicant type" also remained prominent in the letters with which she worked. Varga-Harris, "Forging Citizenship," 111.

78. ARPİİSSA 1.56.38.373.

79. ARPİİSSA 1.56.38.344.

80. ARPİİSSA 1.56.38.333.

81. Richard Wortman, *The Development of a Russian Legal Consciousness* (Chicago: University of Chicago Press, 1976).

82. Patricia Ewick and Susan S. Silbey, *The Common Place of Law: Stories from Everyday Life* (Chicago: University of Chicago Press, 1998).

83. William Pomeranz, *Law and the Russian State: Russia's Legal Evolution from Peter the Great to Vladimir Putin* (London: Bloomsbury Academic, 2019), 93, 101.

84. Interviews, 2010–2013.

85. Benjamin Nathans argues that the growth in postwar Soviet rights consciousness was part of a broader global phenomenon. Nathans, "Soviet Rights-Talk in the Post-Stalin Era," in *Human Rights in the Twentieth Century*, ed. Stefan-Ludwig Hoffmann (New York: Cambridge University Press, 2011), 166–190.

86. Elena Zubkova, *Russia After the War: Hopes, Illusions and Disappointments, 1945–1957* (Armonk, NY: Sharpe, 1998).

87. Interview, May 2011.

88. Interview, March 2011.

89. Interview, May 2011.

90. Interview, April 2011.

91. Interview, December 2010.

92. Pohl, "It Cannot Be that Our Graves Will Be Here," 424.

93. Interviews conducted in 2008, 2010, and 2011 in Azerbaijan.

94. ARPİİSSA 1.48.405.90.

95. ARPİİSSA 1.48.405.141-144, 119.

96. The Administration alludes to an earlier complaint not available in the archival file, but the following record details what happened: sšssa (II) 14.34.242g.10.

97. sšssa (II) 14.34.242g.2.

98. sšssa (II) 14.34.242g.10.

99. RGANI 100.5.433.11-13.

100. Interview, March 2011.

101. Interview, May 2011.

102. ARPİİSSA 1.56.38.364-366.

103. Interview, May 2011.

104. Rizvanov, *Kniga pravdy*, 116. Specific examples of repression directed toward Lezgi Niamet and Bagishev were echoed in multiple oral history interviews, but Rizvanov gives the most complete account.

105. RGANI 100.6.382.9.

106. Varga-Harris also found this reliance on Moscow in her study of housing petitions in the Khrushchev period. Varga-Harris, "Forging Citizenship," 109. Daniel Peris linked this pattern to a historical belief in the benevolence of authority figures,

but found in his case that senior officials and central ministries often just forwarded complaints back to the local level instead of dealing with them directly. Daniel Peris, "'God Is Now on Our Side': The Religious Revival on Unoccupied Soviet Territory during World War II," *Kritika: Explorations in Russian and Eurasian History* 1, no. 1 (Winter 2000): 110.

107. See Daphne Berdahl, *Where the World Ended: Re-Unification and Identity in the German Borderland* (Berkeley, CA: University of California Press, 1999), 54.

108. ARAN 142.1.1038.30-32.

109. For example, in 1925 Chursin reported after an expedition to the Kurdistan *uezd* for the Transcaucasian Scientific Association that more than 80 percent of the 44,000 people living in the Kurdistan *uezd* were Kurdish. Half of them reportedly only knew the Kurmanji dialect of Kurdish, while the other half had lost their "native language" and only spoke the Azerbaijani dialect of the Tiurk language. A few years later, after the *uezd* had already been eliminated, Bukshpan argued the opposite, that Kurds comprised a minority in major areas of the former uezd and only negligible amounts spoke Kurdish as a primary language. See G.F. Chursin, "Azerbaidzhanskie Kurdy," *Izvestia Kavkazskogo istoriko-arkheologicheskogo instituta*, vol. 3 (Tiflis, 1925), 2; A. Bukshpan, *Azerbaidzhanskie kurdy: Lachin, Kel'badzhary, Nakhkrai: Zametki* (Baku: Azerbaidzhanskii gos. nauchno-issledovat. institut. Otdelenie Vostoka, 1932), 59–66.

110. sšssa (II) 13.9.153.

111. Khanna Omarkhali, "The Kurds in the former Soviet States from the Historical and Cultural Perspectives," *The Copernicus Journal of Political Studies* 2, no. 4 (2013): 137–139.

112. RGANI 100.5.738.33.

113. Polly Jones, "Introduction: The Dilemmas of de-Stalinization," in Jones, ed., *The Dilemmas of De-Stalinization: Negotiating Cultural and Social Change in the Khrushchev Era* (Abingdon, Oxon: Routledge, 2006), 14. Stephen Bittner employs a similar approach to Khrushchev's Thaw in *The Many Lives of Khrushchev's Thaw: Experience and Memory in Moscow's Arbat* (Ithaca, NY: Cornell University Press, 2008).

Conclusion

1. RFE/RL, "Azerbaijan a Model of Tolerance—Aliyev," *Eurasianet*, April 7, 2011, https://eurasianet.org/azerbaijan-a-model-of-tolerance-aliyev.

2. Azerbaijan Presidential Library, "Azerbaijani Multiculturalism: General Information," http://multiculturalism.preslib.az/en_a1.html, accessed March 3, 2020. This message has found some foreign cheerleaders who have written superficial promotional articles positioning Azerbaijan as "an oasis of tolerance" surrounded by "less tolerant neighbors." Most of these publications, however, are linked to government-sponsored trips or events. See, David Wolpe, "Azerbaijan Is an Oasis of Tolerance in the Middle East," *Time*, November 5, 2015, http://time.com/4099548/azerbaijan-is-an-oasis-of-tolerance-in-the-middle-east/; Adelle Nazarian, "Azerbaijan: A Nation that Bears the Torch, and Burden, of Bringing Religious Freedom to Its Less Tolerant Neighbours in the Region," May 13, 2019, https://observatoryihr.org/priority_posts/azerbaijan-a-nation-that-bears-the-torch-and-burden-of-bringing-religious-freedom-to-its-less-tolerant-neighbours-in-the-region/.

3. For an example of this discourse, see Azerbaijan State News Agency, "Azerbaijani model of multiculturalism and tolerance as tool to prevent conflicts highlighted at landmark conference in Geneva," http://multiculturalism.preslib.az/en_events-BUbhjzSyRX.html. The reality, of course, is much more complicated. Azerbaijani ethnogenesis theories have long been used to discursively erase Armenian heritage in Azerbaijan by recasting churches and other historical monuments as part of the legacy of Caucasian Albania and portraying Armenians as recent migrants to the Caucasus, just as Armenians have used ethnogenesis to undercut Azeri historical roots in the region. Similarly, both sides have accused the other of destroying artwork, cemeteries, religious structures and other historical objects. For more on these ethnogenesis battles, see Dudwick, "The case of the Caucasian Albanians"; V. A. Shnirel'man, *Voiny pamiati: mify, identichnost' i politika v Zakavkaz'e* (Moscow: Akademkniga, 2003), esp. chap. 13.

4. There is substantial variance in reported numbers of refugees and internally displaced persons, but Azerbaijan absorbed the majority of these persons due to Azeris and smaller numbers of Kurds being forced out of both Armenia and areas of Azerbaijan under Armenian occupation. Though this impasse between Armenia and Azerbaijan has popularly been termed a frozen conflict, Laurence Broers has rejected this label, describing instead a dynamic situation prone to violence rather than stasis and complacency. He characterizes Nagorno-Karabakh as part of an enduring rivalry between Azerbaijan and Armenia that encompasses broad interstate dynamics extending beyond territorial issues. Laurence Broers, *Armenia and Azerbaijan: Anatomy of a Rivalry* (Edinburgh: Edinburgh University Press, 2019), 10–12.

5. As Jennifer Wistrand has pointed out, an "inflexible script" of Azerbaijani citizenship has developed in Azerbaijan around issues of loyalty and national identification. Fidelity to the idea that Karabakh will once again be part of Azerbaijan is a central part of this narrative, as well as a willingness to accept that "Armenia is responsible for *all* of Azerbaijan's . . . present-day problems." Jennifer Solveig Wistrand, "Becoming Azerbaijani: Uncertainty, Belonging, and Getting by in a Post-Soviet Society," PhD diss., Washington University, 2011, 93–94, 390. This has become a test of loyalty to the state and reinforces a sense of emotional stability and security at a time of Armenian occupation.

6. Rob Nixon, *Slow Violence and the Environmentalism of the Poor* (Cambridge, MA: Harvard University Press, 2011), 2.

7. In Muslim Georgian-Ingiloi villages, many people complained in oral history interviews about not being able to give their children "Georgian" names. They stated that there were lists of "Muslim" names they have to adhere to or they risk not being able to register their children with the state, something that is necessary in order to enroll children in school, acquire state documents, etc. Others have reported that they feel pressure to retain a Muslim identity in these communities.

8. There is some frustration with the English term "Azeri" in Azerbaijan. Some people who reject the use of this term favor an Azerbaijani Turk identification, but others prefer to be known simply as "Azerbaijani," referring to the fact that this is the term used in the constitution, in the Azerbaijani language, and other mediums.

9. Frederick Cooper and Rogers Brubaker, "Identity," in *Colonialism in Question: Theory, Knowledge, History*, ed. Frederick Cooper (Berkeley: University of California Press, 2005), 82.

10. Interview, December 2010.

11. Interview, July 2008.

12. Interview, May 2010.

13. Interviews conducted between 2007 and 2016.

14. Interview, February 2011.

15. Interviews conducted between 2010 and 2012.

16. "Vyveski na lezginskom iazyke v Gusare pod zapretom?" December 16, 2009, https://www.disput.az/topic/163552-вывески-на-лезгинском-языке-в-гусаре-под-запретом/page/2/.

17. This view has been taken up by some scholars outside Azerbaijan as well. See, for example, Altstadt, *The Politics of Culture*; and Shouleh Vatanabadi, "Past, Present, Future, and Postcolonial Discourse in Modern Azerbaijani Literature," *World Literature Today* 70, no. 3 (Summer 1996): 493.

18. Ilham Abbasov, "From 'Friendship of Peoples' to a Discourse of 'Tolerance': Constructing Ethnic Boundaries in Post-Soviet Azerbaijan," in *Caucasus Conflict Culture: Anthropological Perspectives on Times of Crisis*, ed. Stéphane Voell and Ketevan Khutsishvili (Marburg: Curupira, 2013), 150.

19. See, for example, Frederick Coene, *The Caucasus—An Introduction* (London: Routledge, 2009); and Svante Cornell, *Azerbaijan Since Independence* (Armonk, NY: Sharpe, 2011).

20. Serhii Plokhy, *Chernobyl: The History of a Nuclear Catastrophe* (New York: Basic Books, 2018), chap. 15.

21. Smith, *Red Nations*, 259–260.

22. This is a simplified chronology of events driving the escalation of the Nagorno-Karabakh conflict. For a more detailed overview, see de Waal, *Black Garden*.

23. *Materialy Plenuma Tsentral'nogo Komiteta KPSS, 19–20 sentiabria 1989 g.* (Moscow: Politizdat, 1989).

24. de Waal, *Black Garden*, 94. For detailed accountings of this period, see de Waal, *Black Garden*, chap. 6, and Broers, *Armenia and Azerbaijan*, chap. 1.

25. Broers, *Armenia and Azerbaijan*, 36.

26. To now, Khojaly has been the worst atrocity of the Nagorno-Karabakh War. Considered in Azerbaijan to have been a genocide, the Azerbaijani government has spent millions of dollars at home and abroad memorializing it as such and characterizing Armenians as *génocidaires* to offset their global reputation as victims of genocide due to the Armenian Genocide of 1915. See, for example, an English-language article by the Ministry of Defense of the Republic of Azerbaijan titled "The Khojaly genocide," https://mod.gov.az/en/khodjali-genocide-411/. Less attention is paid to a retributive massacre Azerbaijani soldiers executed that April of around fifty Armenian civilians in Maragha. See, Broers, *Armenia and Azerbaijan,* 37.

27. Mammadli, "Soviet-era Anthropology," 179, 189.

28. Gasanly, *Khrushchevskaia "ottepel'" i natsional'nyi vopros*, 632–634.

29. "Otkrytoe pis'mo Prezidentu Azerbaidzhanskogo gosudarstva gospodinu Abul'fazu El'chibeiu," *Lezginskii vestnik* 9, no. 5 (1992): 2.

30. Tair Faradov, "Etnokul'turnaia identichnost' i nekotorye aspekty psikhologii mezhnatsional'nogo obshcheniia v Azerbaidzhane," in *Aktual'nye problemy sovremennykh etnosotsiologicheskikh issledovanii v Azerbaidzhane (sbornik statei)*, ed. A. Mamedli (Baku: Elm, 2007), 54. *Narod* can be translated as people or nation.

31. Zabit Rizvanov, *Kniga pravdy*.

32. Letter from G. Abduragimov, N. Ramazanov, and M. Melik Mammadov to I. Khasbulatov, April 20, 1992, GARF 10026.4.707.19-20.

33. *Moambe*, July 1990, 1. Shirinbay Aliyev explores the Ingilo-as-Azerbaijani ethnogenesis theory criticized by Mose Janashvili Society members. Şirinbəy Hacıəli Əliyev, *Şimal-Qərbi Azərbaycan: İngiloylar* (Bakı: Təhsil, 2007).

34. Interview, June 2008.

35. Interview, July 2008.

36. Interview, April 2011.

37. Tara Zahra, *Kidnapped Souls: National Indifference and the Battle for Children in the Bohemian Lands, 1900–1948* (Ithaca, NY: Cornell University Press, 2008).

38. Nino Aivazishvili-Gehne also noted this in her fieldwork among Ingilois in Azerbaijan. See, Aivazishvili-Gehne, "Ingiloy-Ingiloi: The Ethnicity and Identity of a Minority in Azerbaijan," in *Caucasus Conflict Culture: Anthropological Perspectives on Times of Crisis*, ed. Stéphane Voell and Ketevan Khutsishvili (Marburg: Curupira, 2013), 275.

39. Interview, December 2010.

40. Interviews, November and December 2010.

41. Interview, October 2010.

42. Interview, November 2010.

43. Interview, October 2010. These migrants left Azerbaijan apparently out of fear that past events from the Tsarist era and period of the Azerbaijan Democratic Republic would repeat themselves, but this was also a moment of great unrest and rebellion due to collectivization efforts in the area. See ARDA 379.3.2649.4.

44. In this context, the ethnonym "Tatar" can be used in a pejorative manner.

45. *Moambe*, July 1990, 12.

46. Martha Lawry, "Kurmukoba: Mingling Faiths in Qakh," *Visions of Azerbaijan* (Winter 2018), http://www.visions.az/en/news/1013/9995267/. This online magazine targets an international audience. It is edited by Tale Heydarov, the son of Kamaladdin Heydarov, Azerbaijan's Minister of Emergency Situations. See also the accompanying video "Mingling Faiths: Kurmukoba/Giorgoba in Qakh," https://www.youtube.com/watch?v=_Ipzd6ZpdPA.

47. See, for example, a video and article he has posted on his professional website: http://shahidov.com/en/?p=10055.

48. Interview, May 2020.

49. Interview, May 2020.

50. See, for example, Svante Cornell, *Azerbaijan Since Independence* (Armonk, NY: Sharpe, 2011), 84.

51. Conversations with various participants of the government of the Talysh-Mughan Autonomous Republic.

52. "Бэ Ын Соэлон Чэвоб Ни," *Толыши Садо* 1 (1989): 1.

53. Michael Rouland, "mankurt," http://www.pitt.edu/~filmst/events/Turk menFilmSeries/mankurt.htm.

54. "Толошон Кин?" *Толыши Садо* 1 (1989): 2. The connection to Babek has become a particularly strong one in post-Soviet Talysh historical thought. A Talysh newspaper published in Moscow, *Talyshskii vestnik*, even started to run a Babek

"quote" in its header—"One day in freedom is better than forty years in slavery." *Taly-shskii Vestnik* 9 (September–October 2002).

55. "Толошон Топонимон Барәдә Кали Fеjдон," *Толыши садо* 1 (1989): 3.

56. Shnirelman, "Value of the Past," 90.

57. The National (or People's) Equality Party was registered in 1993, but it was the successor party of the Talysh National Revival Party, which was created in 1989 and renamed the Talysh People's Party in 1991.

58. Interviews with Talysh-Mughan Autonomous Republic participants and Mammadov's widow, Maryam Mammadova, in Azerbaijan, Russia, and the Netherlands, 2008–2019.

59. This narrative is reconstructed from interviews with many people who participated in and observed the republic in 1993.

60. Milli Majlis, "Azərbaycan Respublikasının Lənkəran, Astara, Masallı, Lerik, Yardımlı, Cəlilabad və Biləsuvar rayonlarında yaranmış vəziyyət haqqında Azərbaycan Respublikası Milli Məclisinin Qərarı," August 17, 1993, http://www.meclis.gov.az/?/az/topcontent/50.

61. *Hummatov v. Azerbaijan*, 9852/03 and 13413/04, Council of Europe: European Court of Human Rights, November 29, 2007.

62. According to Mar'yam Mammadova, both sons died prematurely as a result of repression and violence they experienced after their father's arrest. Interviews with Mammadova from 2014 to 2019; and Mar'yam Mammadova, *Tragediia Odnoi Sem'i* (Moscow: 2013).

63. European Court of Human Rights, "Case of *Mammadov and Others v. Azerbaijan*," February 21, 2019, http://hudoc.echr.coe.int/eng?i=001-189960.

64. Political arrests in Azerbaijan are often predicated on bogus charges such as drug possession, tax-related offenses, and hooliganism.

65. ToloshiSado, "Ty kto takoi, davai do svidaniia!" January 25, 2012, https://www.youtube.com/watch?v=UFUtDdgEYwk.

66. The Commissioner for Human Rights for the Council of Europe also intervened on Hilal Mammadov's side, alleging that he was being punished for exposing human rights violations in Azerbaijan. Commissioner for Human Rights, "Third Party Intervention by the Council of Europe Commissioner for Human Rights Under Article 36, Paragraph 3, of the European Convention on Human Rights, Application No. 81553/12, *Hilal Mammadov v. Azerbaijan*" (Strasbourg, February 19, 2015), https://rm.coe.int/third-party-intervention-by-the-council-of-europe-commissioner-for-hum/16806daae3.

67. Approximately one year after conferring this award on Hilal Mammadov, Leyla Yunus, the head of the institute, was arrested along with her husband, Arif, on charges of fraud and tax evasion. Leyla, a trained historian and well-known human rights campaigner in Azerbaijan had been an active member of Azerbaijani civil society since the late 1980s. Her husband, also a historian, worked with her at the institute, both promoting conflict resolution between Armenians and Azerbaijanis. Both were also accused of spying for Armenia. They were found guilty of the financial charges and sentenced to 8.5 and 7 years in custody, respectively, but were released after more than a year in prison amid significant international uproar over their detention and deteriorating health in custody. They now live in the Netherlands.

68. Madeleine Reeves, *Border Work: Spatial Lives of the State in Rural Central Asia* (Ithaca, NY: Cornell University Press, 2014), 89–91.

69. "Vyveski na lezginskom iazyke v Gusare pod zapretom?" December 16, 2009, https://www.disput.az/topic/163552-вывески-на-лезгинском-языке-в-гусаре-под -запретом/page/2/.

Bibliography

Archives
Armenia

HAA   National Archive of Armenia (Hayastani Azgayin Arkhiv)
HAAHQPB   National Archive of Armenia Division of Socio-Political Documenta-
           tion (Hayastani Azgayin Arkhiv Hasarakakan Qaghaqakan Pastat-
           ghteri Bazhin)

Azerbaijan

ARDA   Republic of Azerbaijan State Archive (Azərbaycan Respublikası
           Dövlət Arxivi)
ARDAİA   Republic of Azerbaijan State Literature and Art Archive (Azərbaycan
           Respublikası Dövlət Ədəbiyyat və İncəsənət Arxivi)
ARDA SF   Shaki Filial of the Republic of Azerbaijan State Archive (Azərbaycan
           Respublikası Dövlət Arxivinin Şəki filialı)
ARDKFSA   Republic of Azerbaijan State Archive of Film and Photo Documents
           (Azərbaycan Respublikasının Dövlət Kino-Foto Sənədləri Arxivi)
ARDTA   Republic of Azerbaijan State Historical Archive (Azərbaycan
           Respublikası Dövlət Tarix Arxivi)
ARPİİSSA   Archive of Political Documents of the Administrative Department of
           the President of the Republic of Azerbaijan (Azərbaycan Respublikası
           Prezidentinin İşlər İdarəsinin Siyasi Sənədlər Arxivi)

Georgia

sšssa (I) Archive of the Ministry of Internal Affairs of Georgia I (sakartvelos
           šinagan sakmeta saministros arqivi I)
sšssa (II) Archive of the Ministry of Internal Affairs of Georgia II (sakartvelos
           šinagan sakmeta saministros arqivi II)
scsa   Central Historical Archive of Georgia (sakartvelos centraluri saistoriis
           arqivi)
suica   Central Archive of the Contemporary History of Georgia (sakart-
           velos uaxlesi istoriis centraluri arqivi)

Kazakhstan

QRPA   Archive of the President of the Republic of Kazakhstan (Qazaqstan
              Respublikasy Prezidentīnīñg Arxivī)

Russia

Makhachkala, Dagestan

TsGA RD   Central State Archive of the Republic of Dagestan (Tsentral'nyi
              gosudarstvennyi arkhiv Respubliki Dagestan)

Moscow

ARAN   Archive of the Russian Academy of Sciences (Arkhiv Rossiiskoi
              akademii nauk)
GARF   State Archive of the Russian Federation (Gosudarstvennyi arkhiv
              Rossiiskoi Federatsii)
RGAE   Russian State Archive of the Economy (Rossiiskii gosudarstvennyi
              arkhiv ekonomiki)
RGANI   Russian State Archive of Contemporary History (Rossiiskii gosudarst-
              vennyi arkhiv noveishei istorii)
RGASPI   Russian State Archive of Socio-Political History (Rossiiskii gosudarst-
              vennyi arkhiv sotsial'no-politicheskoi istorii)

Documents and Photos Cited from Private Archives/Collections

A. A. Isupov, Central Statistical Administration letter number 32-02-1/i-3-1, Janu-
    ary 17, 1979.
A. A. Isupov, Central Statistical Administration letter number 32-01-9/kl-16-1,
    March 27, 1979.
Zulfugar Ahmedzade letters and photos from private collection.
Ethnographic photos from the archive of Atiga Izmailova.
Images from the Photolibrary of Kurdistan.
Soviet Information Bureau Photograph Collection, Fung Library, Harvard University.

Select Published Primary Sources

Journals and Newspapers

Bakinskii rabochii
Lezginskii vestnik
Moambe
Pravda
Shavnysht

Talyshskii vestnik
Tolishi sado
Tolysh
Zaria Vostoka

Articles and Books

Adzhiev, Murad. "Skazhi Svoe Imia, Talysh." *Vokrug sveta* 7 (1989): 11–15.

——. "Talysh, Charuzh i Drugie." *Vokrug sveta* 11 (1991): 38–43.

Agranat, G. A. "Polozhenie korennogo naseleniia Krainego Severa Ameriki." *Sovetskaia etnografiia* 4 (1961): 100–113.

Alieva, Svetlana, ed. *Tak eto bylo: Natsional'nye repressii v SSSR, 1919–1952 gody*. Tom 1. Moscow: Insan, 1993.

Aver'yanov, P. I. *Kurdy v voinakh Rossii s Persiei i Turtsiei v techenie XIX stoletiia*. Tiflis: Tipografiia Shtaba Kavkazskago voennago okruga, 1900. Reprint, Moscow: Ripol Klassik, 2013.

Bugai, N. F., ed. *Iosif, Stalin - Lavrentiiu Berii: "Ikh nado deportirovat'": Dokumenty, fakty, kommentarii*. Moscow: Druzhba narodov, 1992.

Bruk, S. I., and V. S. Apenchenko, eds. *Atlas narodov mira*. Moscow: Nauka, 1964.

Bruk, S. I., and V. I. Kozlov. "Etnograficheskaia nauka i perepis' naseleniia 1970 goda." *Sovetskaia etnografiia* 6 (1967): 3–20.

Bruk, S. I., V. I. Kozlov, and M. G. Levin. "O predmete i zadachakh etnogeografii." *Sovetskaia etnografiia* 1 (1963): 11–25.

Bugai, N. F., and M. I. Mamaev. *Kurdy SSSR—Rossii: trassa dlinoiu v 100 let . . . : dokumental'naia istoriia*. Tula: Akvarius, 2014.

Bukshpan, A. *Azerbaidzhanskie kurdy: Lachin, Kel'badzhary, Nakhkrai: Zametki*. Baku: Azerbaidzhanskii gos. nauchno-issledovat. institut. Otdelenie Vostoka, 1932.

Charkviani, Kandid. *Gantsdili da naazrevi: 1906–1994*. Tbilisi: Merani, 2004.

Chuev, Feliks. *Sto sorok besed s Molotovym: Iz dnevnika F. Chueva*. Moscow: Terra, 1991.

Chursin. G.F. "Azerbaidzhanskie Kurdy." *Izvestia Kavkazskogo istoriko-arkheologicheskogo instituta* 3. Tiflis, 1925.

Chursin, G. F. *Talyshi. Izvestiia Kavkazskogo istoriko-arkheologicheskogo instituta* 4. Tiflis, 1926.

Commissioner for Human Rights. "Third Party Intervention by the Council of Europe Commissioner for Human Rights Under Article 36, Paragraph 3, of the European Convention on Human Rights, Application No. 81553/12. *Hilal Mammadov v. Azerbaijan*." Strasbourg, February 19, 2015. https://rm.coe.int /third-party-intervention-by-the-council-of-europe-commissioner-for-hum /16806daae3.

"Constitution of the Armenian Soviet Socialist Republic of March 23, 1937 as Amended Through July 11, 1947." New York: American Russian Institute, 1950.

"Constitution of the Azerbaijan Soviet Socialist Republic of March 14, 1937 as Amended Through July 29, 1947." New York: American Russian Institute, 1950.

"Constitution of the Georgian Soviet Socialist Republic of February 13, 1937 as Amended Through July 24, 1947." New York: American Russian Institute, 1950.

Danialov, A. D. "Speech by Comrade A. D. Danialov, Dagestan Autonomous Republic." *Pravda*, February 21, 1956, 7–8. Reprinted in *Current Digest of the Russian Press* 10, no. 8 (1956): 27–29.

Dumas, Alexandre. *Adventures in Caucasia.* Philadelphia: Chilton, 1962.

European Court of Human Rights. "Case of *Mammadov and Others v. Azerbaijan.*" February 21, 2019. http://hudoc.echr.coe.int/eng?i=001-189960.

——. *Hummatov v. Azerbaijan.* 9852/03 and 13413/04. November 29, 2007.

Formozov, Alexander. "Azerbaidzhanskij 'Dikii Zapad' v seredine 1980-kh: vzgliad moskovskogo etnosotsiologa: Viktor Karlov v besede s Aleksandrom Formozovym." *Laboratorium: Zhurnal sotsial'nykh issledovanii* 1 (2010).

Fursenko, A. A., ed. *Prezidium TsK KPSS 1954–1964: Chernovye protokol'nye zapisi zasedanii. Stenogrammy. Postanovleniia.* Vol. 1. Moscow: ROSSPEN, 2004.

Gafurov, B. G. "Stroitel'stvo kommunizma i natsional'nyi vopros." *Voprosy stroitel'stva kommunizma v SSSR: Materialy nauchnoi sessii otdelenii obshchestvennykh nauk Akademii nauk SSSR*, 88–104. Moscow: Izdatel'stvo Akademii nauk SSSR, 1959.

Gambarov, Iu. S., V. Ia. Zheleznov, M. M. Kovalevskii, S. A. Muromtsev, K. A. Timiriazev. *Entsiklopedicheskii slovar' Russkogo bibliograficheskogo instituta Granat.* Vol. 41. No. 6. Moscow: Russkii bibliograficheskii institut Granat, 1926.

Ghughunishvili, Irina. Interview with Lamara Akhvlediani, July 13, 2013. https://thestalinproject.org.

Guliev, A. N., and E. I. Mamedov. *Istoriia Azerbaidzhana dlia 7–8 klassov.* Baku: Azeruchpedgiz, 1964.

Guliev, Dzh. B., ed. *Istoriia Azerbaidzhana.* Baku: Elm, 1979.

Ikhilov, M. M. "K voprosu o natsional'noi konsolidatsii narodov Dagestana." *Sovetskaia etnografiia* 6 (1965): 92–101.

——. *Narodnosti lezginskoi gruppy: etnograficheskoe issledovanie proshlogo i nastoiashchego lezgin, tabasarantsev, rutulov, tsakhurov, agulov.* Moscow: Avtoreferat, 1968.

Isaev, M. I. *Sto tridtsat' ravnopravnykh: O iazykakh narodov SSSR.* Moscow: Nauka, 1970.

Istoriia Azerbaidzhanskoi SSR: Uchebnik dlia 8 i 9 klassov. Baku: AzFAN, 1939.

Istoriia Azerbaidzhana (kratkiiocherk). Baku: AzFAN, 1941.

Istoriia Azerbaidzhana. Baku: Izd. Akademii nauk Azerbaidzhanskoi SSR, 1958.

Izmailova, A. A. "O narodnoi odezhde naseleniia iugo-vostochnykh raionov Azerbaidzhana." *Izvestiia Akademii nauk Azerbaidzhanskoi SSR* 4 (1964): 93–100.

"Iz arkhivov Goskomstata SSSR: Itogi Vsesoiuznoi perepisi naseleniia 1937 g." *Vestnik statistiki* 7 (1990).

Kirakosyan, Arman, ed. *Armeniia i sovetsko-turetskie otnosheniia v diplomaticheskikh dokumentakh 1945–1946 gg.* Yerevan: Tigran Mets, 2010.

Khrushchev, Nikita. "Speech to 20th Congress of the CPSU." February 24–25, 1956. https://www.marxists.org/archive/khrushchev/1956/02/24.htm.

Kozlov, V. I. "K voprosu ob izuchenii etnicheskikh protsessov u narodov SSSR (opyt issledovaniia na primere mordvy)." *Sovetskaia etnografiia* 4 (1961): 58–73.

Lavrov, L. I. *Etnografiia Kavkaza: (Po polevym materialam 1924–1978 gg.).* Leningrad: Nauka, 1982.

Lawry, Martha. "Kurmukoba: Mingling Faiths in Qakh." *Visions of Azerbaijan* (Winter 2018). http://www.visions.az/en/news/1013/9995267/.

Lenin, V. I. "The Socialist Revolution and the Right of Nations to Self-Determination." In *Collected Works*. Vol. 2. Edited by George Hanna and translated by Yuri Sdobnikov, 143–156. Moscow: Progress Publishers, 1974.

Liaister, A. F., and G. F. Chursin. *Geografiia Kavkaza: priroda i naselenie.* Tiflis: Izdanie Zakavk. kommunist. universitet. imeni 26-ti, 1924.

Maksimova, G. M. ed. *Vsesoiuznaia perepis' naseleniia 1970 goda: sbornik statei.* Moscow: Statistika, 1976.

Mamedov, Novruzali. *Talyshsko-russko-azerbaidzhanskii slovar'.* Baku: Nurlan, 2006.

Mammadova, Mar'yam. *Tragediia odnoi sem'i.* Moscow: 2013.

Marr, N. Ia. *Plemennoi sostav naseleniia Kavkaza: Trudy Komissii po izucheniiu plemen-nogo sostava naseleniia Rossii (Rabochii konspekt).* Petrograd: Rossiiskaia gosudarstvennaia akademicheskaia tipografiia, 1920.

——. *Talyshi.* Petrograd: Rossiiskaia gosudarstvennaia akademicheskaia tipografiia, 1922.

Materialy Plenuma Tsentral'nogo Komiteta KPSS, 19–20 sentiabria 1989 g. Moscow: Politizdat, 1989.

Memoirs of Nikita Khrushchev. Vol. 2. *Reformer (1945–1964).* Edited by Sergei Khrushchev and translated by George Shriver and Stephen Shenfield. University Park, PA: Pennsylvania State University Press, 2006.

Mgeladze, Akaki. *Stalin, kakim ia ego znal: stranitsy nedavnego proshlogo.* Tbilisi, 2001.

Miller, B. V. *Predvaritel'nyi otchet o poezdke v Talysh letom 1925 g. (Doklad, chitannyi na zasedanii Istoriko-Etnograficheskoi Sektsii Obshchestva 14-go sentiabria 1925 goda).* Baku: Izdanie Ob-va Issledovaniia i Izucheniia Azerbaidzhana, 1926.

——. *Talyshskii iazyk.* Moscow: Izdatel'stvo Akademii nauk SSSR, 1953.

Milli Majlis. "Azərbaycan Respublikasının Lənkəran, Astara, Masallı, Lerik, Yardımlı, Cəlilabad və Biləsuvar rayonlarında yaranmış vəziyyət haqqında Azərbaycan Respublikası Milli Məclisinin Qərarı." August 17, 1993. http://www.meclis.gov.az/?/az/topcontent/50.

Murat, V. P. "Novyi etap v osvoboditel'noi bor'be negrov SShA." *Sovetskaia etnografiia* 2 (1962): 51–59.

Nadezhdin, P. P. *Kavkazskii krai: Priroda i liudi.* Tula: Tipografiia Vladimira Nikolaievicha Sokolova, 1901.

Nadzhafov, Adil'. *Formirovanie i razvitie azerbaidzhanskoi sotsialisticheskoi natsii.* Baku: Izd. Akademii nauk Azerbaidzhanskoi SSR, 1955.

Pireiko, Liia Aleksandrovna. Izd-vo "Russkii iazyk," *Talyshko-russkii slovar',* 1976.

Prokhorov, A.M., ed. *Bol'shaia sovetskaia entsiklopediia.* Vol. 25. Moscow: Sovetskaia entsiklopediia, 1976.

Radde, Gustav. *Reisen an der persisch-russischen Grenze. Talysch und seine Bewohner.* Leipzig: Brockhaus, 1886.

Radde, Gustav. *Talysch, das Nordwestende des Alburs und sein Tiefland.* Petermanns: Mittheilungen, 1885.

Rizvanov, Zabit. *Kniga pravdy: sbornik statei, 1980–90 gg.* Qusar: samizdat, n.d.

Sbornik materialov dlia opisaniia mestnostei i plemen Kavkaza. Tiflis: Izdanie Upravleniia Kavkazskago uchebnago okruga, 1902.

Speeches Delivered at Meetings of Voters of the Stalin Electoral District, Moscow. Moscow: Foreign Languages Publishing House, 1950.

Stalin, J. V. *Works.* Moscow: Foreign Languages Publishing House, 1954.

State Statistical Committee of the Republic of Azerbaijan. "Population by Ethnic Groups." https://www.stat.gov.az/source/demoqraphy/ap/?lang=en.

ToloshiSado. "Ty kto takoi, davai do svidaniia!" January 25, 2012. https://www.youtube.com/watch?v=UFUtDdgEYwk.

Tolstov, S. P., M. G. Levin, and N. N. Cheboksarov, eds. *Ocherki obshchei etnografii: Aziatskaia chast' SSSR.* Moscow: Izdatel'stvo Akademii nauk SSSR, 1960.

Trofimova, A. G. "Talyshi." In *Narody Kavkaza,* edited by B. A. Gardanov, A. N. Guliev, S. T. Eremyan, L. I. Lavrov, G. A. Nersesov, G. C. Chitaia, 187–194. Moscow: Izdatel'stvo Akademii nauk SSSR, 1962.

Tsentral'noe statisticheskoe upravlenie SSSR. *Itogi Vsesoiuznoi perepisi naseleniia 1959 goda: Azerbaidzhanskaia SSR.* Moscow: Gosstatizdat, 1963.

——. *Itogi Vsesoiuznoi perepisi naseleniia 1970 goda.* Vol 4. Moscow: Statistika, 1973.

Veidenbaum, E. *Putevoditel' po Kavkazu: Po porucheniiu gen.-ad"iutanta kn. Dondukova-Korsakova, Glavnonachal'stvuiushchego grazhd. chast'iu na Kavkaze, sostavil E. Veidenbaum.* Tiflis: tip. Kantsel[iarii] Glavnonachal'stvuiushchego grazhd. chast'iu na Kavkaze, 1888.

Veliev (Bakharly), M. G. *Azerbaidzhan (Fiziko-geograficheskii, etnograficheskii i ekonomicheskii ocherk).* Baku: Izd-vo Sov. Nar. Khoz., 1921.

von Haxthausen, Baron. *Transcaucasia: Sketches of the Nations and Races between the Black Sea and the Caspian.* Translated by J. E. Taylor. London: Chapman and Hall, 1854.

Von-Plotto, A. I. "Priroda i liudi Zakatal'skogo okruga." *Sbornik svedenii o kavka-zskikh gortsakh.* Vol. 4. Tiflis, 1870.

Voroshilov, K. E., A. Ia. Vyshinskii, S. I. Vavilov, A. Lozovskii, P. I. Lebedev-Polianskii, F. N. Petrov, F. A. Rotshtein, O. Iu. Shmidt, eds. *Bol'shaia sovetskaia entsiklopediia.* Vol. 53. Moscow: OGIZ RSFSR, 1946.

Vsesoiuznaia perepis' naseleniia 1939 goda: Osnovnye itogi. Moscow: Nauka, 1992.

Vvedenskii, B. A., ed. *Bol'shaia sovetskaia entsiklopediia.* Vol. 41. Moscow: Bol'shaia sovetskaia entsiklopediia, 1956.

Zagurskii, L. P. *Etnologicheskaia klassifikatsiia kavkazskikh narodov: (Izvlecheno iz rukopisnago truda L. P. Zagurskago): Prilozhenie k Kavkazskomu kalendariu na 1888 g.* Tiflis, 1887.

Zolotarevskaiia, I. A. "Nekotorye materialy ob assimiliatsii indeitsev Oklakhomy." *Kratkie soobshcheniia Instituta etnografii im. N. N. Miklukho-Maklaia AN SSSR.* Vol. 33. Moscow: Izdatel'stvo Akademii nauk SSSR, 1960.

Maps

Atlas narodov mira. Moscow: Glavnoe upravlenie geodezii i kartografii Gosudarstven-nogo geologicheskogo komiteta SSSR: Institut etnografii im. N. N. Miklukho-Maklaia Akademii nauk SSSR, 1964.

Atlas SSSR. Moscow: Glavnoe upravlenie geodezii i kartografii pri Sovete ministrov SSSR, 1983.

Nauchno-redaktsionnoi kartosostavitel'skoi chast'iu GUGK i Institutom etnografii im. N. N. Miklukho-Maklaia AN SSSR pod obshchim rukovodstvom S. I. Bruka (spetsial'nuiu nagruzku karty sostavili S. I. Bruk, Ia. R. Vinnikov, V. I. Kozlov, V. V. Andrianov). *Glavnoe upravlenie geologii i okhrany nedr SSSR*. Edited by E. A. Shishkin. Moscow, 1962. Retrieved from Harvard Map Collection, Pusey Library.

Prokhorov, A. M., ed. *Bol'shaia sovetskaia entsiklopediia (v 20-ti t.)*. Vol. 24. No. 2. Moscow: Sovetskaia entsiklopediia, 1977.

Secondary Sources

Abbasov, Ilham. "From 'Friendship of Peoples' to a Discourse of 'Tolerance': Constructing Ethnic Boundaries in Post-Soviet Azerbaijan." In *Caucasus Conflict Culture: Anthropological Perspectives on Times of Crisis*, edited by Stéphane Voell and Ketevan Khutsishvili. Marburg: Curupira, 2013.

Abrahamian, Ervand. "Communism and Communalism in Iran: The Tudah and the Firqah-i Dimukrat." *International Journal of Middle East Studies* 1, no. 4 (October 1970): 291–316.

Aivazishvili-Gehne, Nino. "Ingiloy-Ingilo: The Ethnicity and Identity of a Minority in Azerbaijan." In *Caucasus Conflict Culture: Anthropological Perspectives on Times of Crisis*, edited by Stéphane Voell and Ketevan Khutsishvili. Marburg: Curupira, 2013.

——. "The Power of the Shrine and Creative Performances in Ingiloi Sacred Rituals." In *Sacred Places, Emerging Spaces: Religious Pluralism in the Post-Soviet Caucasus*, edited by Tsypylma Darieva, Florian Mühlfried, and Kevin Tuite. New York: Berghahn Books, 2018.

Alexopoulos, Golfo. "The Ritual Lament: A Narrative of Appeal in the 1920s and 1930s." *Russian History/Histoire Russe* 24, no. 1–2 (Spring–Summer 1997): 117–129.

——. "Soviet Citizenship, More or Less: Rights, Emotions, and States of Civic Belonging." *Kritika: Explorations in Russian and Eurasian History* 7, no. 3 (Summer 2006): 487–528.

Alymov, Sergei. "The Concept of the 'Survival' and Soviet Social Science in the 1950s and 1960s." *Forum for Anthropology and Culture* 9 (2013): 157–183.

Allworth, Edward A. *The Tatars of Crimea: Return to the Homeland*. Durham, NC: Duke University Press, 1998.

Altstadt, Audrey L. *The Azerbaijani Turks: Power and Identity Under Russian Rule*. Stanford: Hoover Institution Press, 1992.

——. *The Politics of Culture in Soviet Azerbaijan, 1920–1940*. London: Routledge, 2016.

Arel, Dominque. "Demography and Politics in the First Post-Soviet Censuses: Mistrusted State, Contested Identities." *Population* 57, no. 6 (November–December 2002): 801–827.

Atabaki, Touraj. *Azerbaijan: Ethnicity and the Struggle for Power in Iran*. New York: Tauris, 2000.

Avalishvili, Levan. "The March 1956 Events in Georgia: Based on Oral History Interviews and Archival Documents." In *Georgia After Stalin: Nationalism and*

Soviet Power, edited by Timothy K. Blauvelt and Jeremy Smith, 32–52. London: Routledge, 2016.

Baberowski, Jörg. *Der Feind ist überall: Stalinismus im Kaukasus*. Munich: Deutsche Verlags-Anstalt, 2003.

Balaev, Aidyn. *Etnoiazykovye protsessy v Azerbaidzhane v XIX–XX vv.* Baku: Nurlar, 2005.

Barmin, V. A. *Sin'tszian v sovetsko-kitaiskikh otnosheniiakh (1941–1949)*. Barnaul: Izdatel'stvo BGPU, 1999.

Barzani, Massoud. *Mustafa Barzani and the Kurdish Liberation Movement (1931–1961)*. New York: Palgrave Macmillan, 2003.

Berdahl, Daphne. *Where the World Ended: Re-Unification and Identity in the German Borderland*. Berkeley, CA: University of California Press, 1999.

Bilinsky, Yaroslav. "The Soviet Education Laws of 1958–9 and Soviet Nationality Policy." *Soviet Studies* 14, no. 2 (October 1962): 138–157.

Bittner, Stephen. *The Many Lives of Khrushchev's Thaw: Experience and Memory in Moscow's Arbat*. Ithaca, NY: Cornell University Press, 2008.

Blauvelt, Timothy. "Abkhazia: Patronage and Power in the Stalin Era." *Nationalities Papers* 35, no. 2 (May 2007): 203–232.

——. "Language Education and Ethnic Resentment in Soviet Abkhazia, 1939–1953." *Ab Imperio* 1 (2020): 197–219.

——. "March of the Chekists: Beria's Secret Police Patronage Network and Soviet Crypto-Politics." *Communist and Post-Communist Studies* 44 (March 2001): 73–88.

——. "The 'Mingrelian Question': Institutional Resources and the Limits of Soviet Nationality Policy." *Europe-Asia Studies* 66, no. 6 (May 2014): 993–1013.

Blitstein, Peter. "Nation-Building or Russification? Obligatory Russian Instruction in the Soviet Non-Russian School, 1938–1953." In *A State of Nations: Empire and Nation-Making in the Age of Lenin and Stalin*, edited by Ronald Grigor Suny and Terry Dean Martin. New York: Oxford University Press, 2001.

——. "Researching Nationality Policy in the Archives." *Cahiers du Monde russe* 40, no. 1–2 (January–June 1999).

Blium, Alen, and Martina Mespule. *Biurokraticheskaia anarkhiia: Statistika i vlast' pri Staline*. Translated by V. M. Volodina. Moscow: ROSSPEN, 2006.

Bölükbaşı, Süha. "Nation-Building in Azerbaijan: The Soviet Legacy and the Impact of the Karabakh Conflict." In *Identity Politics in Central Asia and the Muslim World*, edited by Willem van Schendel and Erik J. Zürcher, 35–64. London: Tauris, 2001.

——. *Azerbaijan: A Political History*. London: Tauris, 2011.

Breyfogle, Nicholas. *Heretics and Colonizers: Forging Russia's Empire in the South Caucasus*. Ithaca, NY: Cornell University Press, 2005.

Brinegar, Sara. "Baku at All Costs: The Politics of Oil in the New Soviet State." PhD diss., University of Wisconsin–Madison, 2014.

Broers, Laurence. *Armenia and Azerbaijan: Anatomy of a Rivalry*. Edinburgh: Edinburgh University Press, 2019.

Brown, Kate. *A Biography of No Place: From Ethnic Borderland to Soviet Heartland*. Cambridge, MA: Harvard University Press, 2004.

Brubaker, Rogers. *Ethnicity Without Groups*. Cambridge, MA: Harvard University Press, 2004.

——. *Nationalism Reframed: Nationhood and the National Question in the New Europe*. Cambridge: Cambridge University Press, 1996.

Brubaker, Rogers, et al. *Nationalist Politics and Everyday Ethnicity in a Transylvanian Town*. Princeton, NJ: Princeton University Press, 2006.

Bugai, N. F., and A. M. Gonov. *Kavkaz: narody v eshelonakh (20-60-e gody)*. Moscow: Insan, 1998.

Burbank, Jane. "An Imperial Rights Regime: Law and Citizenship in the Russian Empire." *Kritika: Explorations in Russian and Eurasian History* 7, no. 3 (Summer 2006): 397–431.

——. *Russian Peasants Go to Court: Legal Culture in the Countryside, 1905–1917*. Bloomington: Indiana University Press, 2004.

Butalia, Urvashi. *The Other Side of Silence: Voices from the Partition of India*. Durham, NC: Duke University Press, 2000.

Çağaptay, Soner. "Reconfiguring the Turkish Nation in the 1930s." *Nationalism and Ethnic Politics* 8, no. 2 (2002): 67–82.

Cameron, Sarah. *The Hungry Steppe: Famine, Violence, and the Making of Soviet Kazakhstan*. Ithaca, NY: Cornell University Press, 2018.

Canefe, Nergis. "Communal Memory and Turkish Cypriot National History: Missing Links." In *Balkan Identities: Nation and Memory*, edited by Maria Todorova. New York: New York University Press, 2004.

Casper, Samuel Arthur. "The Bolshevik Afterlife: Posthumous Rehabilitation in the Post-Stalin Soviet Union, 1953–1970." PhD diss., University of Pennsylvania, 2018.

Cavadov, Qəmərşah. *Talışlar (tarixi-etnoqrafik tədqiqat)*. Baku: Elm, 2004.

Chatterjee, Partha. *The Nation and Its Fragments: Colonial and Postcolonial Histories*. Princeton, NJ: Princeton University Press, 1993.

Chlenov, Mikhail A. "Rasselenie evreiskikh etnicheskikh grupp na Kavkaze." In *Materialy mezhdunarodnogo nauchnogo simpoziuma "Gorskie evrei Kavkaza," 24–26 aprelia 2001 g. Baku-Kuba-Krasnaia Sloboda*, 17–34. Baku: Elm, 2002.

Chulos, Chris J. "Peasants' Attempts to Reopen Their Church, 1929–1936." *Russian History/Histoire Russe* 24, no. 1–2 (Spring–Summer 1997): 203–213.

Clark, William, and Ablet Kamalov. "Uighur Migration Across Central Asian Frontiers." *Central Asian Survey* 23, no. 2 (June 2004): 167–182.

Coene, Frederick. *The Caucasus—An Introduction*. London: Routledge, 2009.

Conquest, Robert. *The Last Empire*. London: Ampersand Books, 1962.

——. *Stalin: Breaker of Nations*. New York: Penguin Books, 1992.

Cooper, Frederick. *Colonialism in Question: Theory, Knowledge, History*. Berkeley: University of California Press, 2005.

Cooper, Frederick, and Rogers Brubaker. "Identity." In *Colonialism in Question: Theory, Knowledge, History*, edited by Frederick Cooper. Berkeley: University of California Press, 2005.

Cornell, Svante. *Azerbaijan Since Independence*. Armonk, NY: Sharpe, 2011.

Daniel, E. Valentine. *Charred Lullabies: Chapters in an Anthropology of Violence*. Princeton, NJ: Princeton University Press, 1996.

David-Fox, Michael. *Showcasing the Great Experiment: Cultural Diplomacy and Western Visitors to the Soviet Union, 1921–1941*. New York: Oxford University Press, 2012.

Derlugian, Georgi M. *Bourdieu's Secret Admirer in the Caucasus: A World-System Biography*. Chicago: University of Chicago Press, 2005.

de Waal, Thomas. *Black Garden: Armenia and Azerbaijan Through Peace and War*. New York: New York University Press, 2003.

Dirks, Nicholas. *Castes of Mind: Colonialism and the Making of Modern India*. Princeton, NJ: Princeton University Press, 2001.

——. "Forward." In *Colonialism and Its Forms of Knowledge: The British in India*, edited by Bernard Cohn. Princeton, NJ: Princeton University Press, 1996.

Dogan, Hulya. "Conceptions of Homeland and Identity Among Meskhetian Turk Refugees in the U.S. and Turkey." PhD diss., Texas A&M University, 2016.

Dudwick, Nora. "The Case of the Caucasian Albanians: Ethnohistory and Ethnic Politics." *Cahiers du Monde russe et soviétique* 31, no. 2–3 (April–September 1990): 377–383.

Eagleton, William. *The Kurdish Republic of 1946*. London: Oxford University Press, 1963.

Edgar, Adrienne Lynn. "Bolshevism, Patriarchy, and the Nation: The Soviet 'Emancipation' of Muslim Women in Pan-Islamic Perspective." *Slavic Review* 65, no. 2 (2006): 252–272.

——. "Children of Mixed Marriages in Soviet Central Asia: Dilemmas of Identity and Belonging." In *Ideologies of Race: Imperial Russia and the Soviet Union in Global Context*, edited by David Rainbow. Montreal: McGill-Queen's University Press, 2019.

——. *Tribal Nation: The Making of Soviet Turkmenistan*. Princeton, NJ: Princeton University Press, 2004.

Engerman, David. *Know Your Enemy: The Rise and Fall of America's Soviet Experts*. New York: Oxford University Press, 2009.

Ewick, Patricia, and Susan S. Silbey. *The Common Place of Law: Stories from Everyday Life*. Chicago: University of Chicago Press, 1998.

Əliyev, Şirinbəy Hacıəli. *Şimal-Qərbi Azərbaycan: İngiloylar*. Bakı: Təhsil, 2007.

Fairbanks, Charles H. "Clientelism and Higher Politics in Georgia, 1949–1953." In *Transcaucasia: Nationalism and Social Change*, edited by Ronald Grigor Suny, 339–368. Ann Arbor: University of Michigan Press, 1983.

Fairbanks, Julie. "Narratives of Progress: Soviet Ethnographic Discourse and the Study of the Caucasus," Workshop paper, University of Michigan, Eurasia Collective Workshop, 2013.

Faradov, Tair. "Etnokul'turnaia identichnost' i nekotorye aspekty psikhologii mezhnatsional'nogo obshcheniia v Azerbaidzhane." In *Aktual'nye problemy sovremennykh etnosotsiologicheskikh issledovanii v Azerbaidzhane (sbornik statei)*, edited by A. Mamedli, 53–88. Baku: Elm, 2007.

Farge, Arlette. *Le goût de l'archive*. Paris: Seuil, 1997.

Fawcett, Louise. *Iran and the Cold War: The Azerbaijan Crisis of 1946*. Cambridge: Cambridge University Press, 1992.

Feldman, Leah. *On the Threshold of Eurasia: Revolutionary Poetics in the Caucasus*. Ithaca, NY: Cornell University Press, 2018.

Field, Les W. "Mapping Erasure: The Power of Nominative Cartography in the Past and Present of the Muwekma Ohlones of the San Francisco Bay Area." In *Recognition, Sovereignty Struggles, and Indigenous Rights in the United States*, edited by Amy E. Den Ouden and Jean M. O'Brien. Chapel Hill: University of North Carolina Press, 2013.

Fisher, Alan. *The Crimean Tatars*. Stanford, CA: Hoover Institution, 1978.

Fitzpatrick, Sheila. "Cultural Revolution in Russia 1928–32." *Journal of Contemporary History* 9, no. 1 (January 1974): 33–52.

——. *On Stalin's Team: The Years of Living Dangerously in Soviet Politics*. Princeton, NJ: Princeton University Press, 2015.

——. *Stalin's Peasants: Resistance and Survival in the Russian Village After Collectivization*. New York: Oxford University Press, 1994.

——. "Supplicants and Citizens: Public Letter-Writing in Soviet Russia in the 1930s." *Slavic Review* 55, no. 1 (Spring 1996): 78–105.

Florin, Moritz. "Beyond Colonialism? Agency, Power, and the Making of Soviet Central Asia." *Kritika: Explorations in Russian and Eurasian History* 18, no. 4 (Fall 2017): 827–838.

Forestier-Peyrat, Etienne. "Fighting Locusts Together: Pest Control and the Birth of Soviet Development Aid, 1920–1939." *Global Environment* 7, no. 2 (2014): 536–571.

——. "Soviet Federalism at Work: Lessons from the History of the Transcaucasian Federation, 1922–1936." *Jahrbücher für Geschichte Osteuropas* 65, no. 4 (2017): 529–559.

Gadzhieva, Sabina Rafik kyzy. "Razvitie shkoly natsional'nykh men'shinstv i malochislennykh narodov Azerbaidzhana: 1920–1940 gody." Kandidat pedagogicheskikh nauk diss., Azerbaidzhanskii gosudarstvennyi pedagogicheskii universitet, 2005.

Gasanly, Dzhamil'. *Khrushchevskaia "ottepel'" i natsional'nyi vopros v Azerbaidzhane (1954–1959)*. Moscow: Flinta, 2009.

——. *SSSR-Iran: Azerbaidzhanskii krizis i nachalo kholodnoi voiny, 1941–1946*. Moscow: Geroi Otechestva, 2006.

——. *SSSR-Turtsiia: ot neitraliteta k kholodnoi voine (1939–1953)*. Moscow: Tsentr Propagandy, 2008.

Ghods, M. Reza. "The Iranian Communist Movement Under Reza Shah." *Middle Eastern Studies* 26, no. 4 (October 1990): 506–513.

Goff, Krista. "Postwar rebuilding and national migration in the Soviet Union: A case of Azeri resettlement, 1948–1953." *Slavic Review*, forthcoming 2021.

Gorlizki, Yoram, and Oleg Khlevniuk. *Cold Peace: Stalin and the Soviet Ruling Circle, 1945–1953*. New York: Oxford University Press, 2005.

Gramsci, Antonio. *Selections from the Prison Notebooks*. Edited by Quintin Hoare and Geoffrey Nowell Smith. London, 1971.

Grant, Bruce. "An Average Azeri Village: Remembering Rebellion in the Caucasus Mountains." *Slavic Review* 63, no. 4 (Winter 2004): 705–731.

——. "'Cosmopolitan Baku.'" *Ethnos: Journal of Anthropology* 75, no. 2 (June 2010): 123–147.

——. *In the Soviet House of Culture: A Century of Perestroikas*. Princeton, NJ: Princeton University Press, 1995.

Hardy, Jeff. *The Gulag After Stalin: Redefining Punishment in Khrushchev's Soviet Union, 1953–1964*. Ithaca, NY: Cornell University Press, 2016.

Hasanli, Jamil. *Khrushchev's Thaw and National Identity in Soviet Azerbaijan, 1954–1959*. Lanham, MD: Lexington Books, 2015.

——. *The Sovietization of Azerbaijan: The South Caucasus in the Triangle of Russia, Turkey, and Iran, 1920–1922*. Salt Lake City: University of Utah, 2018.

Hirsch, Francine. *Empire of Nations: Ethnographic Knowledge and the Making of the Soviet Union*. Ithaca, NY: Cornell University Press, 2005.

Holquist, Peter. "'Information is the Alpha and Omega of Our Work': Bolshevik Surveillance in Its Pan-European Context." *The Journal of Modern History 69*, no. 3 (September 1997): 415–450.

Holston, James. *Insurgent Citizenship: Disjunctions of Democracy and Modernity in Brazil*. Princeton, NJ: Princeton University Press, 2008.

Ismailov, El'dar. *Istoriia "bol'shogo terrora" v Azerbaidzhane*. Moscow: ROSSPEN, 2015.

——. *Ocherki po istorii Azerbaidzhana*. Moscow: Flint, 2010.

——. *Vlast' i narod: poslevoennyi Stalinism v Azerbaidzhane: 1945–1953*. Baku: Adil'ogly, 2003.

Johnson, Jeremy. "Speaking Soviet with an Armenian Accent: Literacy, Language Ideology, and Belonging in Early Soviet Armenia." In *Empire and Belonging in the Eurasian Borderlands*, edited by Krista A. Goff and Lewis H. Siegelbaum, 129–143. Ithaca, NY: Cornell University Press, 2019.

Jones, Polly. "Introduction: The Dilemmas of De-Stalinization." In *The Dilemmas of De-Stalinization: Negotiating Cultural and Social Change in the Khrushchev Era*, edited by Polly Jones, 1–18. Abingdon, Oxon: Routledge, 2006.

Kaiser, Claire P. "Lived Nationality: Policy and Practice in Soviet Georgia, 1945–1978." PhD diss., University of Pennsylvania, 2015.

——. "'What Are They Doing? After All, We're Not Germans': Expulsion, Belonging, and Postwar Experience in the Caucasus." In *Empire and Belonging in the Eurasian Borderlands*, edited by Krista A. Goff and Lewis H. Siegelbaum, 80–94. Ithaca, NY: Cornell University Press, 2019.

Kamalov, Ablet. "Uyghur Memoir Literature in Central Asia on Eastern Turkestan Republic (1944–49)." In *Studies on Xinjiang Historical Sources in 17-20th Centuries*, edited by James A. Millward, Shinmen Yasushi, and Jun Sugawara, 257–278. Tokyo: Toyo Bunko, 2010.

Kamp, Marianne. *The New Woman in Uzbekistan: Islam, Modernity, and Unveiling Under Communism*. Seattle: University of Washington Press, 2006.

——. "Three Lives of Saodat: Communist, Uzbek, Survivor." *Oral History Review 28*, no. 2 (Summer–Autumn 2001): 21–58.

Kassymbekova, Botakoz. *Despite Cultures: Early Soviet Rule in Tajikistan*. Pittsburgh: University of Pittsburgh Press, 2016.

Kasumova, Irada Ismail kyzy. "Kul'turnoe stroitel'stvo v Azerbaidzhane v 20-30-e gody/na primere natsional'nykh men'shinstv i malochislennykh narodov/." Kandidat istoricheskikh nauk diss., Bakinskii gosudarstvennyi universitet im. M. E. Rasulzade, 1996.

Keddie, Nikki. *Modern Iran: Roots and Results of Revolution*. New Haven, CT: Yale University Press, 2006.

Khalid, Adeeb. "Backwardness and the Quest for Civilization: Early Soviet Central Asia in Comparative Perspective." *Slavic Review 65*, no. 2 (Summer 2006): 231–251.

——. *Making Uzbekistan: Nation, Empire, and Revolution in the Early USSR*. Ithaca, NY: Cornell University Press, 2015.

Khalidi, Rashid. *Palestinian Identity: The Construction of Modern National Consciousness*. New York: Columbia University Press, 2010.

Khlevniuk, Oleg. "Kremlin-Tbilisi: Purges, Control and Georgian Nationalism in the First Half of the 1950s." In *Georgia After Stalin: Nationalism and Soviet Power*, edited by Timothy K. Blauvelt and Jeremy Smith, 13–31. New York: Routledge, 2016.

——. *Stalin: New Biography of a Dictator*. New Haven, CT: Yale University Press, 2015.

Khubova, Daria, Andrei Ivankiev, and Tonia Sharova. "After Glasnost: Oral History in the Soviet Union." In *Memory and Totalitarianism,* edited by Luisa Passerini. New Brunswick, NJ: Transaction, 2009.

Kivelson, Valerie Ann. "Muscovite 'Citizenship': Rights without Freedom." *Journal of Modern History* 74, no. 3 (September 2002): 465–489.

Kivelson, Valerie Ann, and Ronald Grigor Suny. *Russia's Empires*. New York: Oxford University Press, 2017.

Kldiashvili, Giorgi. "Nationalism After the March 1956 Events and the Origins of the National-Independence Movement in Georgia." In *Georgia After Stalin: Nationalism and Soviet power*, edited by Timothy K. Blauvelt and Jeremy Smith, 77–91. London: Routledge, 2016.

Knight, Amy. *Beria: Stalin's First Lieutenant*. Princeton, NJ: Princeton University Press, 1993.

Kolarz, Walter. *Russia and her Colonies*. New York: Praeger, 1952.

Kollmann, Nancy. *By Honor Bound: State and Society in Early Modern Russia*. Ithaca, NY: Cornell University Press, 1999.

Koohi-Kamali, Farideh. *The Political Development of the Kurds in Iran: Pastoral Nationalism*. New York: Palgrave Macmillan, 2003.

Kozhanov, Nikolay A. "The Pretexts and Reasons for the Allied Invasion of Iran in 1941." *Iranian Studies* 45, no. 4 (2012): 479–497.

Kozlov, Denis, and Eleonory Gilburd. "The Thaw as Event in Russian History." In *The Thaw: Soviet Society and Culture during the 1950s and 1960s*, edited by Denis Kozlov and Eleonory Gilburd, 18–84. Toronto: University of Toronto Press, 2013.

Kozlov, Vladimir A. *Mass Uprisings in the USSR: Protest and Rebellion in the Post-Stalin Years*. London: Sharpe, 2002.

Laruelle, Marlene. "The Concept of Ethnogenesis in Central Asia: Political Context and Institutional Mediators (1940–1950)." *Kritika: Explorations in Russian and Eurasian History* 9, no. 1 (Winter 2008): 169–188.

Latour, Bruno. *We Have Never Been Modern*. Translated by Catherine Porter. Cambridge, MA: Harvard University Press, 1991.

Laycock, Joanne. "Belongings: People and Possessions in the Armenian Repatriations, 1945–1949." *Kritika* 18, no. 3 (Summer 2017): 511–537.

——. "Developing a Soviet Armenian Nation: Refugees and Resettlement in the Early Soviet South Caucasus." In *Empire and Belonging in the Eurasian Borderlands*, edited by Krista A. Goff and Lewis H. Siegelbaum, 97–111. Ithaca, NY: Cornell University Press, 2019.

——. "The Repatriation of Armenians to Soviet Armenia, 1945–1949." In *Warlands: Population Resettlement and State Reconstruction in the Soviet-East European Borderlands, 1945–50*, edited by Peter Gatrell and Nick Baron, 89–116. New York: Palgrave Macmillan, 2009.

Lehmann, Maike. "A Different Kind of Brothers: Exclusion and Partial Integration After Repatriation to a Soviet 'Homeland.'" *Ab Imperio* 3 (2012): 171–211.

——. *Eine sowjetische Nation. Nationale Sozialismusinterpretationen in Armenien seit 1945.* Frankfurt am Main: Campus, 2012.

Lemon, Alaina. *Between Two Fires: Gypsy Performance and Romani Memory from Pushkin to Postsocialism.* Durham, NC: Duke University Press, 2000.

Levin, Irina. "Caught in a Bad Romance: Displaced People and the Georgian State." *Citizenship Studies* 22, no. 1 (2018): 19–36.

Lewin, Moshe. *Lenin's Last Struggle.* Translated by A. M. Sheridan Smith. Ann Arbor: University of Michigan Press, 2005.

Loader, Michael. "A Stalinist Purge in the Khrushchev Era? The Latvian Communist Party Purge, 1959–1963." *The Slavonic and East European Review* 96, no. 2 (April 2018): 244–282.

Lummis, Trevor. *Listening to History: The Authenticity of Oral Evidence.* Totowa, NJ: Barnes & Noble, 1988.

Lund, Aleksei. "At the Center of the Periphery: Oil, Land, and Power in Baku, 1905–1917." PhD diss., Stanford University, 2013.

Malkki, Liisa. *Purity and Exile: Violence, Memory, and National Cosmology Among Hutu Refugees in Tanzania.* Chicago: University of Chicago Press, 1995.

Mammadli, Aliaga, ed. *Aktual'nye problemy sovremennykh etnosotsiologicheskikh issledovanii v Azerbaidzhane: sbornik statei.* Baku: Elm, 2007.

——. "Peculiarities of the Formation of Azerbaijanis' Ethnic Identity in the Soviet Era." In *"Azerbaijani" and Beyond: Perspectives on the Construction of National Identity,* edited by Aliaga Mammadli, Adeline Braux, and Ceyhun Mahmudlu, 65–90. Berlin: Verlag Dr. Köster, 2017.

Mammadli, Aliagha. "Soviet-Era Anthropology by Azerbaijani Scholars." In *Exploring the Edge of Empire: Soviet Era Anthropology in the Caucasus and Central Asia,* edited by Florian Mühlfried and Sergey Sokolovskiy. Halle Studies in the Anthropology of Eurasia, vol. 25. Berlin: LitVerlag, 2011.

Marshall, T. H. *Class, Citizenship, and Social Development.* New York: Doubleday, 1964.

Martin, Terry. *The Affirmative Action Empire: Nations and Nationalism in the Soviet Union, 1923–1939.* Ithaca, NY: Cornell University Press, 2001.

Matin-Asgari, Afshin. "The Impact of Imperial Russia and the Soviet Union on Qajar and Pahlavi Iran: Notes Toward a Revisionist Historiography." In *Iranian-Russian Encounters: Empires and Revolutions since 1800,* edited by Stephanie Cronin, 11–46. Abingdon, Oxon: Routledge, 2013.

McDonald, Tracy. *Face to the Village: The Riazan Countryside Under Soviet Rule, 1921–1930.* Toronto: University of Toronto Press, 2011.

McDowall, David. *A Modern History of the Kurds.* London: Tauris, 2000.

Millward, James. *Eurasian Crossroads: A History of Xinjiang.* New York: Columbia University Press, 2007.

Minahan, James. *The Former Soviet Union's Diverse Peoples: A Reference Sourcebook.* Santa Barbara, CA: ABC-CLIO, 2004.

Morozova, Irina. "Contemporary Azerbaijani Historiography on the Problem of 'Southern Azerbaijan' After World War II." *Iran and the Caucasus* 9, no. 1 (2005): 85–120.

Mühlfried, Florian. "Caucasus Paradigms Revisited." In *Routledge Handbook of the Caucasus,* edited by Galina M. Yemelianova and Laurence Broers, 19–31. Abingdon, Oxon: Routledge, 2020.

Mukhina, Irina. *The Germans of the Soviet Union.* Abingdon, Oxon: Routledge, 2007.

Müller, Daniel. "The Kurds of Soviet Azerbaijan, 1920–91." *Central Asian Survey* 19, no. 1 (2000): 41–77.

Nathans, Benjamin. "Soviet Rights-Talk in the Post-Stalin Era." In *Human Rights in the Twentieth Century*, edited by Stefan-Ludwig Hoffmann, 166–190. New York: Cambridge University Press, 2011.

Nəcəfov, Bəxtiyar. *Deportasiya.* Bakı: Çaşıoğlu, 2006.

Nissman, David. "The Origin and Development of the Literature of 'Longing' in Azerbaijan." *Journal of Turkish Studies* 8 (1984): 199–207.

Nixon, Rob. *Slow Violence and the Environmentalism of the Poor.* Cambridge, MA: Harvard University Press, 2011.

Northrop, Douglas. *Veiled Empire: Gender and Power in Stalinist Central Asia.* Ithaca, NY: Cornell University Press, 2004.

O'Brien, Jean M. *Firsting and Lasting: Writing Indians out of Existence in New England.* Minneapolis: University of Minnesota Press, 2010.

O'Brien, Kevin J. "Rightful Resistance." *World Politics* 49, no. 1 (1996): 31–55.

O'Keeffe, Brigid. *New Soviet Gypsies: Nationality, Performance, and Selfhood in the Early Soviet Union.* Toronto: University of Toronto Press, 2013.

Omarkhali, Khanna. "The Kurds in the former Soviet States from the Historical and Cultural Perspectives." *The Copernicus Journal of Political Studies* 2, no. 4 (2013): 128–142.

Oushakine, Serguei Alex. "Political Estrangements: Claiming a Space Between Stalin and Hitler." In *Rites of Place: Public Commemoration in Russia and Eastern Europe*, edited by Julie Buckler and Emily D. Johnson, 285–315. Evanston, IL: Northwestern University Press, 2013.

Pandey, Gyanendra. *Routine Violence: Nations, Fragments, Histories.* Stanford, CA: Stanford University Press, 2006.

Park, Alexander G. *Bolshevism in Turkestan: 1917–1927.* New York: Columbia University Press, 1957.

Pashayev, Atakhan. "Deportatsiia (1948–1953 gody)." *Azerbaidzhan* (June and July 1997), issue numbers 132, 134, 139, 143, 144, 145.

Passerini, Luisa. "Memories between silence and oblivion." In *Memory, History, Nation: Contested Pasts*, edited by Katharine Hodgkin and Susannah Radstone, 238–254. New Brunswick, NJ: Transaction, 2006.

Pelkmans, Mathijs. *Defending the Border: Identity, Religion, and Modernity in the Republic of Georgia.* Ithaca, NY: Cornell University Press, 2006.

Peris, Daniel. "'God Is Now on Our Side': The Religious Revival on Unoccupied Soviet Territory during World War II." *Kritika: Explorations in Russian and Eurasian History* 1, no. 1 (Winter 2000): 97–118.

Pickett, James. "Soviet Civilization through a Persian Lens: Iranian Intellectuals, Cultural Diplomacy and Socialist Modernity 1941–1955." *Iranian Studies* 48, no. 5 (September 2015): 805–826.

Pipes, Richard. *The Formation of the Soviet Union: Communism and Nationalism, 1917–1923.* Cambridge, MA: Harvard University Press, 1954.

Plamper, Jan. *The Stalin Cult: A Study in the Alchemy of Power.* New Haven, CT: Yale University Press, 2012.

Plokhy, Serhii. *Chernobyl: The History of a Nuclear Catastrophe*. New York: Basic Books, 2018.

Pohl, Michaela. "'It Cannot Be that Our Graves Will Be Here': The Survival of Chechen and Ingush Deportees in Kazakhstan, 1944–1957." *Journal of Genocide Research* 4, no. 3 (September 2002): 401–430.

Polian, Pavel. *Against Their Will: The History and Geography of Forced Migrations in the USSR*. Translated by Anna Yastrzhembska. Budapest: Central European University Press, 2003.

——. *Ne po svoei vole . . . Istoriia i geografiia prinuditel'nykh migratsii v SSSR*. Moscow: OGI-Memorial, 2001.

Pomeranz, William. *Law and the Russian State: Russia's Legal Evolution from Peter the Great to Vladimir Putin*. London: Bloomsbury Academic, 2019.

Portelli, Alessandro. "Response to Commentaries." *Oral History Review* 32, no. 1 (Winter–Spring 2005).

——. "What Makes Oral History Different." In *The Oral History Reader*, edited by Robert Perks and Alistair Thomson. Abingdon, Oxon: Routledge, 1998.

Primakov, Yevgeny. *Russia and the Arabs: Behind the Scenes in the Middle East from the Cold War to the Present*. Translated by Paul Gould. New York: Basic Books, 2009.

Pyle, Emily. "Peasant Strategies for Obtaining State Aid: A Study of Petitions during World War I." *Russian History/Histoire Russe* 24, no. 1–2 (Spring–Summer 1997): 41–64.

Qurbanlı, Əsəd Canəli oğlu. *Azərbaycan türklərinin Ermənistandan deportasiyası, 1947–1953-cü illər*. Bakı: Monoqrafiya, 2004.

Raine, Fernande Scheid. "Stalin and the Creation of the Azerbaijan Democratic Party in Iran, 1945." *Cold War History* 2, no. 1 (October 2001).

Reeves, Madeleine. *Border Work: Spatial Lives of the State in Rural Central Asia*. Ithaca, NY: Cornell University Press, 2014.

Reynolds, Michael. *Shattering Empires: The Clash and Collapse of the Ottoman and Russian Empires 1908–1918*. Cambridge: Cambridge University Press, 2011.

Rezvani, Babek. "Iranian Georgians: Prerequisites for Research." *Iran and the Caucasus* 13, no. 1 (2009): 197–203.

——. "The Islamization and Ethnogenesis of the Fereydani Georgians." *Nationalities Papers* 36, no. 4 (September 2008): 593–623.

Roberts, Geoffrey. "Moscow's Cold War on the Periphery: Soviet Policy in Greece, Iran, and Turkey, 1943–8." *Journal of Contemporary History* 46, no. 1 (January 2011): 58–81.

——. "Between the Russian Empire and the USSR: The Independence of Transcaucasia as a Socio-political Transformation." In *Routledge Handbook of the Caucasus*, edited by Galina M. Yemelianova and Laurence Broers, 121–135. Abingdon, Oxon: Routledge, 2020.

Saparov, Arsène. *From Conflict to Autonomy in the Caucasus: The Soviet Union and the Making of Abkhazia, South Ossetia, and Nagorno Karabakh*. Abingdon, Oxon: Routledge, 2015.

——. "Re-negotiating the Boundaries of the Permissible: The National(ist) Revival in Soviet Armenia and Moscow's Response." *Europe-Asia Studies* 70, no. 6 (2018).

Sargent, Leslie. "The 'Armeno-Tatar War' in the South Caucasus, 1905–1906: Multiple Causes, Interpreted Meanings." *Ab Imperio* 4 (2010): 143–169.

Scheid, Fernande Beatrice. "Stalin, Bagirov and Soviet Policies in Iran, 1939–1946." PhD diss., Yale University, 2000.

Sherbakova, Irina. "The Gulag in Memory." In *Memory and Totalitarianism*, edited by Luisa Passerini. New Brunswick, NJ: Transaction, 2009.

Shnirelman, Victor A. *The Value of the Past: Myths, Identity and Politics in Transcaucasia*. Osaka, Japan: National Museum of Ethnology, 2001.

Shnirel'man, V. A. *Voiny pamiati: mify, identichnost' i politika v Zakavkaz'e*. Moscow: Akademkniga, 2003.

Shukurov, Karim. "Great Tragedy: Deportation of Azerbaijanis from Armenia." *Visions of Azerbaijan* (November–December 2010).

Simpson, Christopher, ed. *Universities and Empire: Money and Politics in the Social Sciences during the Cold War*. New York: New Press, 1998.

Slezkine, Yuri. *Arctic Mirrors: Russia and the Small Peoples of the North*. Ithaca, NY: Cornell University Press, 1996.

——. "Imperialism as the Highest Stage of Socialism." *Russian Review* 59, no. 2 (April 2000): 227–234.

——. "The USSR as a Communal Apartment, or How a Socialist State Promoted Ethnic Particularism." *Slavic Review* 53, no. 2 (Summer 1994).

Smith, Jeremy. "The Battle for Language: Opposition to Khrushchev's Education Reform in the Soviet Republics, 1958–59." *Slavic Review* 76, no. 4 (Winter 2017): 983–1002.

——. *The Bolsheviks and the National Question*. New York: St. Martin's, 1999.

——. "Leadership and Nationalism in the Soviet Republics, 1951–1959." In *Khrushchev in the Kremlin: Policy and government in the Soviet Union, 1953–1964*, edited by Melanie Ilic and Jeremy Smith, 79–93. New York: Routledge, 2011.

——. *Red Nations: The Nationalities Experience in and after the USSR*. Cambridge: Cambridge University Press, 2013.

——. "Was There a Soviet Nationality Policy?" *Europe-Asia Studies* 71, no. 6 (2019): 972–993.

Somers, Margaret. *Genealogies of Citizenship: Markets, Statelessness, and the Right to Have Rights*. New York: Cambridge University Press, 2008.

——. "Rights, Relationality, and Membership: Rethinking the Making and Meaning of Citizenship." *Public Rights, Public Rules: Constituting Citizens in the World Polity and National Policy*, edited by Connie L. McNeely, 153–206. New York: Garland, 1998.

Stewart, Richard A. *Sunrise at Abadan: The British and Soviet Invasion of Iran, 1941*. New York: Praeger, 1988.

Stoler, Ann Laura. *Along the Archival Grain: Epistemic Anxieties and Colonial Common Sense*. Princeton, NJ: Princeton University Press, 2010.

Stoler, Ann Laura, and Frederick Cooper. "Between Metropole and Colony: Rethinking a Research Agenda." In *Tensions of Empire: Colonial Cultures in a Bourgeois World*, edited by Frederick Cooper and Ann Laura Stoler, 1–58. Berkeley: University of California Press, 1997.

Suny, Ronald Grigor. *The Baku Commune 1917–1918: Class and Nationality in the Russian Revolution*. Princeton: Princeton University Press, 1972.

——. "Constructing Primordialism: Old Histories for New Nations." *Journal of Modern History* 73, no. 4 (December 2001): 862–896.

——. *Looking toward Ararat: Armenia in Modern History*. Bloomington: Indiana University Press, 1993.

——. *The Making of the Modern Georgian Nation*. Bloomington: Indiana University Press, 1994.

——. *The Revenge of the Past: Nationalism, Revolution, and the Collapse of the Soviet Union*. Stanford, CA: Stanford University Press, 1993.

Swietochowski, Tadeusz. *Russia and Azerbaijan: A Borderland in Transition*. New York: Columbia University Press, 1995.

Taussig, Michael. *Defacement: Public Secrecy and the Labor of the Negative*. Stanford, CA: Stanford University Press, 1999.

Timasheff, Nicholas. *The Great Retreat: The Growth and Decline of Communism in Russia*. New York: E. P. Dutton and Company, 1946.

Tishkov, Valery. *Ethnicity, Nationalism, and Conflict in and After the Soviet Union: The Mind Aflame*. London: Sage, 1997.

Titov, Alexander. "The 1961 Party Programme and the Fate of Khrushchev's Reforms." In *Soviet State and Society Under Nikita Khrushchev*, edited by Melanie Ilic and Jeremy Smith, 8–25. Abingdon, Oxon: Routledge, 2009.

Todorova, Maria. "Balkanism and Postcolonialism, or On the Beauty of the Airplane View." In *Marx's Shadow: Knowledge, Power, and Intellectuals in Eastern Europe and Russia*, edited by Costica Bradatan and Serguei Alex. Oushakine, 175–196. New York: Lexington Books, 2010.

Trouillot, Michel-Rolph. *Silencing the Past: Power and the Production of History*. Boston: Beacon, 1995.

Uehling, Greta Lynn. *Beyond Memory: The Crimean Tatars' Deportation and Return*. New York: Palgrave Macmillan, 2004.

——. "Squatting, Self-Immolation, and the Repatriation of Crimean Tatars." *Nationalities Papers* 28, no. 2 (2000): 317–341.

Üngör, Uğur Ümit. *The Making of Modern Turkey: Nation and State in Eastern Anatolia, 1913–1950*. Oxford: Oxford University Press, 2011.

Vachagaev, Mairbek M. *Soiuz gortsev Severnogo Kavkaza i Gorskaia respublika: Istoriia nesostoiavshegosia gosudarstva, 1917–1920*. Moscow: Tsentrpoligraf, 2018.

van Bruinessen, Martin. *Agha, Shaikh and State: The Social and Political Structures of Kurdistan*. London: Zed Books, 1992.

Varga-Harris, Christine. "Forging Citizenship on the Home Front: Reviving the Socialist Contract and Constructing Soviet Identity during the Thaw." In *The Dilemmas of De-Stalinization: Negotiating Cultural and Social Change in the Khrushchev Era*, edited by Polly Jones, 101–116. Abingdon, Oxon: Routledge, 2006.

Vatanabadi, Shouleh. "Past, Present, Future, and Postcolonial Discourse in Modern Azerbaijani Literature." *World Literature Today* 70, no. 3 (Summer 1996): 493–497.

Vdovin, A. I. "Stalinskaia natsional'naia politika v 1930-e gody: istoricheskie sud'by natsional'nykh men'shinstv." *Golos kurda*, no. 6–7 (December 1991).

Viola, Lynne. *Peasant Rebels Under Stalin: Collectivization and the Culture of Peasant Resistance*. New York: Oxford University Press, 1996.

Volkova, N. G., ed. *Stranitsy otechestvennogo kavkazovedeniia*. Moscow: Nauka, 1992.

Volkova, N. G., and G. A. Sergeeva. "Anatolii Nestorovich Genko: Tragic Pages from the History of Caucasus Studies." *Anthropology and Archeology of Eurasia* 42, no. 2 (Fall 2003).

Voss, Barbara L. *The Archaeology of Ethnogenesis: Race and Sexuality in Colonial San Francisco*. Gainesville: University Press of Florida, 2015.

Walke, Anika. *Pioneers and Partisans: An Oral History of Nazi Genocide in Belorussia*. Oxford: Oxford University Press, 2015.

Weiner, Amir. "The Empires Pay a Visit: Gulag Returnees, East European Rebellions, and Soviet Frontier Politics." In *The Thaw: Soviet Society and Culture during the 1950s and 1960s*, edited by Denis Kozlov and Eleonory Gilburd, 308–361. Toronto: University of Toronto Press, 2013.

———. *Making Sense of War: The Second World War and the Fate of the Bolshevik Revolution*. Princeton, NJ: Princeton University Press, 2001.

Weld, Kirsten. *Paper Cadavers: The Archives of Dictatorship in Guatemala*. Durham, NC: Duke University Press, 2014.

Westad, Odd Arne. *The Global Cold War: Third World Interventions and the Making of Our Times*. Cambridge: Cambridge University Press, 2007.

Whittington, Anna. "Forging Soviet Citizens: Ideology, Identity, and Stability in the Soviet Union, 1930–1991." PhD diss., University of Michigan, 2018.

Williams, Brian G. *The Crimean Tatars: The Diaspora Experience and the Forging of a Nation*. Leiden: Brill, 2001.

Wistrand, Jennifer Solveig. "Becoming Azerbaijani: Uncertainty, Belonging, and Getting by in a Post-Soviet Society." PhD diss., Washington University, 2011.

Wolff, David. "Stalin's Postwar Border-Making Tactics: East and West." *Cahiers du Monde russe* 52, no. 2–3 (April–September 2011): 273–291.

Wortman, Richard. *The Development of a Russian Legal Consciousness*. Chicago: University of Chicago Press, 1976.

Yegorova, Natalia. "The 'Iran Crisis' of 1945–1945: A View from the Russian Archives." *Cold War International History Project*. Working Paper 15 (May 1996): 1–24.

Yilmaz, Harun. "The Rise of Red Kurdistan." *Iranian Studies* 47, no. 5 (2014): 799–822.

———. "The Soviet Union and the Construction of Azerbaijani National Identity in the 1930s." *Iranian Studies* 46, no. 4 (2013).

Yurchak, Alexei. *Everything Was Forever, Until It Was No More: The Last Soviet Generation*. Princeton, NJ: Princeton University Press, 2005.

Zahra, Tara. *Kidnapped Souls: National Indifference and the Battle for Children in the Bohemian Lands, 1900–1948*. Ithaca, NY: Cornell University Press, 2008.

Zardykhan, Zharmukhamed. "Ottoman Kurds of the First World War Era: Reflections in Russian Sources," *Middle Eastern Studies* 42, no. 1 (January 2006): 67–85.

Zubkova, Elena. *Russia After the War: Hopes, Illusions, and Disappointments, 1945–1957*. Armonk, NY: Sharpe, 1998.

———. "Vlast' i razvitie etnokonfliktnoi situatsii v SSSR, 1953–1982 gody." *Otechestvennaia istoriia* 4 (2004): 3–32.

ACKNOWLEDGMENTS

I have experienced an enormous amount of support, and accumulated many debts, over the course of researching and writing this book and, before that, the dissertation that inspired it. Fellowships from Brown University and the University of Michigan supported my dissertation research in Armenia, Azerbaijan, Georgia, and Russia, and offered me dedicated time to write. A FLAS in Modern Turkish and a Title VIII Eurasian Regional Language Fellowship administered by American Councils helped me advance my Azerbaijani language knowledge. This proved essential over many years of research in Azerbaijan. A Fulbright-Hays Doctoral Dissertation Research Abroad Fellowship supported ten of the months I spent there. At the end of my graduate student career, a Social Sciences Research Council Eurasia Program Dissertation Development Award and Doris G. Quinn Foundation Dissertation Completion Fellowship helped get me over the line to completion.

I owe a great debt to faculty members and graduate students at the University of Michigan for their encouragement and support in the early stages of this project. First and foremost, my dissertation committee—Douglas Northrop, Ronald Suny, Bruce Grant, Pamela Ballinger, and Müge Göçek—guided me through the completion of my doctoral program and suggested how I might successfully transition to this manuscript. My co-chairs Douglas Northrop and Ronald Suny deserve special recognition for their flawless supervision, unwavering support, and investment in my work, as does Bruce Grant for his incredible generosity as both an advisor and a colleague. I can't think of a better place than Michigan to start this project, and give thanks to professors, colleagues, and friends who provided a scholarly home and warm sense of community there, including Ian Campbell, Pedro Cantisano, Jesús de Felipe Redondo, Jeremy Johnson, Valerie Kivelson, Gerard Libaridian, Kathy Lin, Anna Whittington, and my soccer teammates.

The University of Miami has supported this project with research funds from the College of Arts and Sciences and the Provost's Office, but also by allowing me to accept residential fellowships off campus—a postdoctoral fellowship at Harvard's Davis Center for Russian and Eurasian Studies, a Title VIII Research Scholarship at the Woodrow Wilson Center's Kennan Institute, and a fellowship at the Library of Congress's John W. Kluge Center—that provided me access to research materials as well as valuable time to write this manuscript. I would like to thank William Pomeranz, Mattison Brady, John Haskell, Travis Hensley, Michael Stratmoen, and Stephanie Plant for their support during those fellowships, as well as Laziza Ibragimova, my research assistant at the Kennan Institute.

I also give thanks to the colleagues who helped me develop this project during those research leaves, including Faith Hillis, Erin Hutchinson, Elena Ion, Rachel Koroloff, Terry Martin, and Hugh Truslow at Harvard, and Alda Benjamen, Kate Brown, Michael David-Fox, Katrin Horn, Jeremy Johnson, Claire Kaiser, and Amarilis Lugo de Fabritz in Washington, D.C. I am particularly grateful for Sarah Cameron, who was a generous mentor throughout this period. At my academic home in Coral Gables, I am thankful for my exceptional departmental chair, Mary Lindemann, and others who supported me through the development of this book, including my colleagues in the Department of History, Karl Gunther, Aleksandra Perisic, Dominique Reill, and my students.

Many friends and colleagues offered critical feedback on this manuscript along the way. I workshopped versions of chapters 2, 3, and 4 at the Workshop on New Directions in the History of Central and Inner Asia at Harvard University, the Russian History Seminar of Washington, D.C., the Historians Seminar at Harvard's Davis Center, and the Nazarbayev University Arts and Sciences Workshop. I also shared related work at the Conflicting Narratives: History and Politics in the Caucasus Workshop at the University of Zurich and a Lithuanian Institute of History–sponsored workshop in Vilnius. I would like to recognize the participants of these workshops for their insightful comments and extend a special thanks to the organizers—Erin Hutchinson, Michael David-Fox, Terry Martin, Zbigniew Wojnowski, Jeronim Perović, and Darius Staliunas—for facilitating and inviting me to these collegial events. A version of chapter 5 also appeared as "'Why not love our language and our culture?' National rights and citizenship in Khrushchev's Soviet Union" in *Nationalities Papers* 43, no. 1 (2015).

I am fortunate as well that Tim Blauvelt, Julie Fairbanks, Aimee Genell, Isabelle Kaplan, Adeeb Khalid, Rachel Koroloff, Ceyhun Mahmudlu, and Kelly Shannon generously provided feedback on specific chapters, and that Sara Brinegar, Bruce Grant, Claire Kaiser, Lewis Siegelbaum, Ron Suny, and colleagues in Azerbaijan who prefer to remain anonymous here found the time to thoughtfully offer constructive criticism of the entire manuscript. Their feedback—as well as detailed and engaging reports from two anonymous readers—have helped make this a better book. It goes without saying that any remaining shortcomings are my responsibility.

Conducting research across this many years and places has required a collective effort. Dozens of archivists, librarians, and scholars, as well as more than 120 oral history interview participants in Armenia, Azerbaijan, Georgia, the Netherlands, and Russia (in both Moscow and Dagestan) made this project possible. With respect for the preferences of colleagues, friends, and collaborators in Azerbaijan, and a sad awareness of the precarity of personal safety there, I preserve their anonymity here, but want to acknowledge my wonderful colleagues in Azerbaijan, the archivists who helped me gain access to and navigate archives in Baku and elsewhere, many people who welcomed me into their homes and life stories, and my friends who kept me company and helped me learn more about the beautiful places where I lived and worked. I couldn't have researched or written this book without them. I would also like to offer a special thanks to Patimat Takhnaeva, who hosted me in Makhachkala; to Timothy Blauvelt and Jeremy Johnson, who seamlessly integrated me into Tbilisi's rich intellectual environment and, in the case of Jeremy, patiently answered questions about Georgian and Armenian transliteration over the years; to Levani Papashvili, Tatiana

Sossedskaya, and Liudmila Sharaya for research and copy editing assistance; to Donella Russell for good company in Moscow; and to Sara Brinegar, Michelle Brady, Reid Hamel, Melissa Lawrie, Aleksei Lund, Alison Mandaville, Marcy McCullaugh, Amy Petersen, and Kathy Taylor, for fostering a lively research community and providing good company in Azerbaijan over the years. Closer to home, Fernande Scheid Raine and Isabelle Kaplan graciously shared some archival documents with me, helping to ameliorate some archival obstacles I encountered in Azerbaijan and, in Fernande's case, allowing me to follow a story from Azerbaijan to the Archive of Foreign Policy of the Russian Federation (AVPRF) and Central Archive of the Ministry of Defense of the Russian Federation in Moscow (TsAMO RF).

It has been a pleasure working with Cornell University Press. I am fortunate that Roger Haydon took this project on, provided me with support and critical editorial suggestions along the way, and expertly saw this manuscript through review and production. I am grateful as well to Ellen Labbate for her assistance with this process, to Bill Nelson for making the maps used in this book, and to Eve McGlynn for map consultations. Kate Gibson was not only terrific at overseeing the copyediting for this project, but supportive through a challenging copyediting experience during which I first found myself stranded far from my academic home due to the Covid-19 pandemic and, unrelatedly, suddenly lost my father. I must also thank the ILL staff and Shatha Baydoun at the University of Miami Richter Library for providing excellent online support during this time.

My family has provided much needed encouragement over the course of this long project. Ali has been a steady source of support, welcome diversion, and love from the early days of this book's development through the end. My mother, Marianne Fattorini Goff, and father, Thomas Goff (February 28, 1942–April 10, 2020), opened their lively classrooms to me as a child. Watching them teach inspired me to become an educator. Their home libraries, travel stories, unending encouragement, and love of reading planted the seeds of this manuscript long before I realized what had happened. My siblings, Maria, Diana, and Tommy have similarly inspired me along the way and I hope they enjoy learning more about what has kept me so occupied. Without Mary Pugel Fattorini and John Fattorini, my maternal grandparents, who shared their Yugoslavian heritage with me, I might never have found myself drawn to the Communist world. I only wish that my grandmother, who passed away in my final weeks of graduate school and my father during the copy edits for this book, could see what came of all those trips that took me so far away from them. My father, the first and best historian I ever knew, couldn't wait to read this book and it is to him that I have dedicated it.

INDEX

Abkhazia and Abkhazians, 4, 83–84, 86, 99, 117, 153, 188, 222, 259n85

Aboszoda, Fakhraddin, 234, 236–37

Adjaran ASSR and Adjarans, 83, 85, 117, 152–53, 172

Ahmedzade, Zulfugar, 19–20, 41, 53, 54, 55–59, 145, 160, 175, 238

Aliabad
  Ingilois in, 88, 89, 188, 205, 228, 229
  language disputes in, 90, 91, 131, 185, 186, 187, 190, 191, 197, 201

Armenian SSR, 40, 48, 98
  claims to Azerbaijani territory, 29, 77, 81, 82, 93, 116–17, 157, 221
  claims to Turkish territory, 62, 75–76, 117
  deportations from, 47, 80, 135, 258n78, 260n94, 270n105
  See also Kura-Araks resettlement; Kurds; Nagorno-Karabakh Autonomous Oblast' (NKAO)

Armenians, 33, 40, 65, 66, 86, 117, 159, 197, 260n94
  in Azerbaijan, 10, 22, 23, 26, 27, 35, 40, 43–45, 51, 53, 122, 124, 127, 130–32, 155, 196, 215, 221, 223, 249n70
  and repatriation, 62, 75, 76–81, 257n64, 258n78
  See also Nagorno-Karabakh Autonomous Oblast' (NKAO)

Arutiunov, Grigor, 77, 78, 81, 82, 93, 98, 99, 117, 258n69

Assyrians, 33, 35, 40, 44, 45, 53, 66, 155, 249n70

Astara region, 19–20, 39, 40, 49, 74, 170, 172–75

Avars, 22, 41, 43, 45, 52–54, 86, 115, 148–49, 155, 207, 216, 238, 249n70

Azerbaijan, Republic of
  discourse of multiculturalism and tolerance, 15, 214–15, 216–20, 230, 235–38, 284n5

minority politics and research environment, 9–10, 13–14, 176, 215–16, 234, 236, 284n5, 287n67 (see also oral history methodology; national minority)
  See also Georgian-Ingilois; Lezgins; Nagorno-Karabakh Autonomous Oblast' (NKAO); Talyshes; Talysh-Mughan Autonomous Republic

Azerbaijan Democratic Party (ADP), 67–70, 255n34

Azerbaijan Democratic Republic (ADR), 86–87, 116, 157–58

Azerbaijan People's Government (APG), 62, 69–71, 74, 119

Azerbaijan SSR
  Central Executive Committee, 31, 39, 46, 48, 50, 117, 247n33
  Communist Party, 17, 24, 26, 27, 29, 31, 36, 54, 62, 64, 65, 68, 74, 92, 101–4, 106–7, 111, 115–16, 121–24, 128, 132, 140, 185, 189, 191, 194–96, 201, 209, 223, 247n27, 251n121, 268n76
  Council of Ministers, 92, 102, 106, 122, 125, 173, 185
  deportations from, 47–48, 80, 134–35
  forced resettlements in, 34, 48–49, 77–78, 134, 173–74
  Ministry of Enlightenment, 92, 122, 185, 191, 195
  People's Commissariat of Enlightenment, 20, 24, 28–29, 38–39, 40, 44, 52–53, 65, 68, 89, 90, 91
  question of Titular hegemony, 3, 5, 20, 23–24, 28, 35, 38–40, 41, 42, 44, 51, 52–55, 89–92, 114–18, 129–42, 145, 159–60, 161–64, 169–71, 175, 180–81, 188–89, 192, 196–98, 202, 222–24

Azerbaijan SSR (*continued*)
and Soviet pretensions to Iranian
territory, 62–72, 74–76, 81–82, 86, 93
Supreme Soviet, 65, 102, 106, 123–25, 128
See also Georgian-Ingilois; Kurds; Lezgins;
Kura-Araks resettlement; Nagorno-
Karabakh Autonomous Oblast'
(NKAO); national minority; Talyshes
Azeris (Tiurks/Türks), 24, 168–69, 197, 217,
222–23
in Armenia, 29, 77–78, 215, 221
ethnogenesis, 110–15, 117–18, 159,
161–63, 167, 176, 197, 224, 230, 232–33
naming of, 20–21, 46, 110, 217–19,
284n8
nation-building and national rights, 17,
21, 26–28, 32, 34, 35, 41, 56, 108–40,
168, 180–81, 219–20, 222–24 (*see also*
census; national minority)
repression of, 37, 47, 56, 78
See also Kura-Araks resettlement;
Nagorno-Karabakh Autonomous
Oblast' (NKAO)
Azeris in Iran (Iranian Azeris), 17, 48, 63–71,
74–76, 93, 111–12, 119–20

Bagirov, Mir Jafar
legacy, 27, 104, 108, 134
and nationality policies, 54, 77, 78, 91, 93,
108, 111, 121, 137–38, 184, 187, 201,
258n69
repression of, 17, 101–5
and Soviet intervention in Iran, 62, 64–75,
81, 82, 86, 254n18, 255n31, 255n34,
255n37, 256n40, 256n47
Bakradze, Valerian, 85, 86, 89, 99
Baku, 13, 26–28, 48, 124, 133, 157, 223,
247n23
Balakan region, 39, 50, 53, 81, 86–87, 89–93,
114, 117, 131, 157, 184, 186, 189–90,
192, 228–29, 237
Balkars, 82, 85, 146, 179, 258n80, 259n92,
260n94, 260n98
Barzani, Mustafa, 69, 71, 72–73, 74, 255n36,
256n45
Barzani, Sheikh Ahmed, 69, 71, 73, 74
Belarusian SSR/Belarusians, 61, 96, 97, 138
Beria, Lavrentiy
network, 28, 64, 97–99, 101–2, 104, 185,
258n83, 259n85
reforms, 95–97, 105, 106, 139, 263n15
role in nationality policies and deportations, 75–76, 82–86, 91–92, 184, 259n91

borderlands
anxieties about and forced migrations
from, 32–36, 47–49, 64, 66, 72, 78–80,
84–85, 111, 135–36, 157–58, 172–74,
181–82
See also deportations
Borshchev, Timofei Mikhailovich, 102–4
breakdown of USSR, 6, 11, 215, 220–24
Britain, 61, 62, 66, 69, 76, 252n7, 254n17
Bruk, Solomon Il'ich, 167–68, 169, 170
Bünyadov, Ziya, 113, 116, 117, 224, 233,
266n37

caucasian Albania, 112–13, 115–18, 189, 217,
230–31, 284n3
census
1921, 26–27, 160
1926, 46, 149, 259n89
1931, 135, 160, 275n59
1937, 46, 135
1939, 46, 55, 83, 86, 133, 134, 135, 136,
137, 145, 146, 152, 268n89
1959, 131, 133, 134, 135, 136, 137, 145,
155, 176
1970, 133, 167, 177, 198
1979, 177, 198, 212, 270n108
1989, 172, 174, 175–77, 232
design, 145–47, 152–55, 171, 271n3
debates about erasures in, 161–64,
166–69, 171–72, 205–6, 268n82
questions of national classification, 89,
110, 136, 259
recognition and erasure, 22, 23, 46, 55, 83,
89, 130, 134, 135–37, 144–47, 149,
153–54, 160–61, 166–68, 171, 174–75,
177–78, 198, 205–6, 218–19, 268n82,
277n112
role of, takers in assimilation, 136–37,
144, 154, 170–72, 176, 198, 205–6,
268n82, 270n110
titular bias in, 27, 55, 83, 89, 114, 130,
132–34, 135–37, 140–41, 152–54, 166–67,
171–72, 174–75, 205–6, 218–19, 268n82
Central Statistical Administration, 144,
152–53, 160, 167, 172, 205–6
Charkviani, Kandid, 114, 117, 184, 185, 199,
200, 209, 227, 258n83
Chechens, 82, 85, 98, 134, 146, 179, 204,
258n80, 259n92, 260n94, 260n98
Chursin, Grigorii Filippovich, 88, 110, 111,
157, 159, 160
citizenship, 8, 17, 182–84, 199–201, 212,
278n7, 279n13

collectivization, 39–40, 49, 95, 146
communism as stage of development, 2, 3, 4, 18, 46–47, 132, 145, 146, 149, 150
Communist Party of the Soviet Union, 94, 221, 223
    and nationality policies, 7, 20, 40, 107–8
Council of Ministers of the USSR, 72, 78, 85, 95, 122
    See also Azerbaijan SSR: Council of Ministers
Crimea, 7, 30–31, 179, 259n92, 260n94
Crimean Tatars, 7, 153, 179–80, 259n92, 260n94, 278n2

Dagestan, 77, 82, 86–88, 112, 157, 273n21
    kin relationship with minorities in Azerbaijan, 39, 43–44, 46, 52, 53, 87, 136, 157, 181, 195, 196, 198, 207
    as model of ethnohistorical progress, 148–50, 153, 272n16
    nationality politics, 13, 44, 98, 208–9, 214, 222, 258n80
Dargins, 43, 148, 149, 207
Dashnaks, 66, 80, 135, 211, 260n93, 260n94
deportation and return, 7, 22, 33, 47–49, 54–56, 63–64, 66, 73, 78, 80, 82, 84–86, 90, 95, 98, 111, 134–36, 143, 146, 173, 174, 179–80, 204, 210, 212, 222, 258n78, 258n80, 259n89, 259n91, 259n92, 260nn93–94, 260n98, 270n105
de-Stalinization, 18, 93, 94–105, 108–9, 180, 193
"diaspora" nationalities, 46–47, 50, 51, 55, 145, 271n3
discourse of "backwardness." *See* Kurds; Lezgins; Talyshes
double assimilation, 4, 107–8, 149, 150, 166
Dungans, 45–46, 180–81

East Germany, 96–97, 263n15, 278n116
East Turkestan Republic, 61, 180, 251n1
Emel'ianov, Stepan Fedorovich, 102, 173, 255n27, 256n40
empire
    colonialism/postcolonialism, 4–6, 108, 113–14, 123–24, 147, 219, 241n6
    Soviet condemnation of, 3, 109
Estonian SSR and Estonians, 47, 61, 96, 127, 139, 221, 260n94
ethnogenesis, 109–18, 128, 129, 159, 161–63, 167, 176, 197, 220, 223, 224, 229–30, 232–33, 237

ethnographers, 6, 87–88, 156, 157–61, 171, 210–11
    and censuses, 46, 89, 136, 144, 145–47, 152–55, 171, 172, 271n3
    theories of ethnohistorical progress/assimilation, 8, 46, 141, 145–51, 161–64, 166–67, 170, 232, 276n84
    See also ethnogenesis
ethnographic maps, 145, 155, 168–69
ethnoterritorialism, 3–4, 6, 110, 133, 142, 208, 222, 237, 253n12

Fereydan Georgians, 67, 76, 86, 254n23, 257n63

Gamkharashvili, Georgii, 89–90, 93, 114, 184–85, 193, 194, 199–201, 209, 227, 261n110
Georgian-Ingiloi and Georgians in Azerbaijan
    in ethnography and ethnogenesis, 87–88, 90, 114, 115, 117–18, 149, 187, 189, 217, 229–31, 261n107, 261n110
    kin relationship with Georgia, 22, 81–82, 86–87, 89–93, 117–18, 137, 181, 184–86, 188, 193–94, 197, 199–200, 209–10, 227–28, 230, 280n30
    naming and categorization, 87–89, 114, 137, 181, 182–83, 189–90, 198, 205–6, 217, 218, 225–31, 241n1, 249n70, 261n107, 261n110, 268n82, 270n112, 284n7
    national rights and lack thereof, 4, 14, 39, 44, 47, 49–50, 51, 86–92, 117–18, 122–24, 127, 129–32, 137, 139, 155, 184–92, 196–98, 201, 205–6, 209, 216, 284n7
    petitioning and activism, 1–3, 18, 89–91, 114, 137, 143, 181, 182–94, 196–206, 208–10, 212, 226, 280n27
Georgians, 110, 114, 156–57, 197
Georgian SSR, 2, 20, 28, 39, 99, 100–101, 110, 112, 125, 185–86, 245n9, 247n27
    and Fereydan Georgians in Iran, 67, 79, 193, 254n23, 257n63
    claims to Azerbaijani territory, 81–82, 86–88, 93, 117, 157, 184–85, 237
    claims to Turkish territory, 62, 75–76, 81, 82, 93
    Communist Party, 83–84, 90, 96, 98–100, 184–85, 246n9
    deportations from, 80, 84–86, 93, 134, 135–36, 258n80, 259n89, 259nn91–92, 260nn93–94, 270n105

Georgian SSR (*continued*)
  nationality policies in and assimilation,
    32, 34, 37, 40, 63–64, 82–86, 93, 99,
    116–17, 123, 129, 146, 152–53, 166–67,
    172, 211–12
Germans (in the Russian Empire and USSR),
    23, 35, 41, 43, 44, 45, 47, 51, 135, 146,
    155, 222, 249n70, 259n92, 260n94,
    269n104, 271n3
Germany, 61, 62, 64–67, 76, 252n2,
    260n98
Gilan, 62, 67, 68, 71, 157, 274n47
Glasnost', 175–78, 221, 225–26,
    232
Gorbachev, Mikhail Sergeevich,
    220–23
Great Terror, 6, 20, 21–22, 54–59, 83, 97,
    99–100, 102–4, 145–46, 175
Greeks, 23, 30, 35, 40, 43, 44, 45, 47, 80, 85,
    93, 111, 135, 249n70, 260nn93–94,
    271n3

Hümmatov (Gummatzoda / Gumbatov),
    Alakram, 231, 233–35, 244n26

Ibragimov, Mirza
  dismissal, 106–7, 264n1
  as head of Azerbaijan Supreme Soviet,
    17, 102, 108, 118, 121, 123, 125, 128,
    133, 138, 139, 227
  in Iran, 65, 67, 68, 119–20, 256n40
  involvement in Ingiloi matters, 91
Ingiloi. *See* Georgian-Ingiloi and Georgians
    in Azerbaijan
Ingushes, 40, 82, 85, 134, 179, 222, 258n80,
    259n92, 260n94, 260n98
Institute of Ethnography, 147–48, 152–53,
    161, 162, 167, 168, 172, 210–11, 271n3,
    273n32, 274n34
Iran, 2, 7, 17, 18, 21, 32–36, 47–49, 61–82,
    85–86, 93, 102, 111–12, 119–22, 135,
    156–58, 169, 170, 172–73, 181–82, 193,
    210, 224, 232, 235, 252n2, 252n4,
    252nn7–8, 253n15, 254n17, 254n23
See also Persian Empire
Iranian Azerbaijan, 62–71, 74–76, 81, 82, 86,
    93, 112–13, 119–21
Iranians, 66, 159
  repression in Soviet Union, 48, 63, 85,
    135, 146, 271n3
  in Soviet Azerbaijan, 23, 27, 48–49, 64,
    135, 249n70
Iraq, 35, 69–73, 210, 256n52

İtitala, 89, 90, 91, 131, 185, 189,
    191
Izmailova, Atiga, 161–65, 167–68

Japan, 61, 62, 271n3
Jews and Mountain Jews, 23, 24, 27, 30–31,
    35, 36, 38, 41, 43, 44, 155, 217, 246n18,
    249n70

Kalmyks, 179, 259n92, 260n94
Karachays, 179, 259n92, 260n94
Kazakhstan ASSR / SSR, 46, 47, 84, 135, 142,
    180–81, 204, 212, 221, 222, 259n91
Khanlar (Elendorf, Helenendorf, and
    Göygöl), 41, 78, 131, 269n104
Khemshins (Khemshils), 84, 85, 86, 93,
    259n91, 259n92, 260n94
Khorasan, 62, 66, 67, 252n4
Khrushchev, Nikita Sergeevich, 95, 97
  and building communism, 146, 150
  de-Stalinization and the Thaw, 17,
    99–105, 193–94, 198, 201, 203–8,
    212–13, 282n77
  and national relations, 1, 17, 106–7, 121,
    123, 127–28, 133, 138–39, 163, 174, 179,
    189
Korenizatsiia / indigenization. *See* Commu-
    nist Party of the Soviet Union:
    nationality policies
Kozlov, Viktor Ivanovich, 150, 167–68, 170,
    171
Kura-Araks resettlement, 77–78, 134, 173,
    258n69, 269n95, 269n98
Kurdish Republic of Mahabad, 62,
    69–71
Kurds, 34, 197, 211, 215, 284n4
  in Armenia, 34, 47–48, 135, 210–12
  in Azerbaijan, 22, 24, 35, 39, 40, 43, 45,
    47–48, 51, 53, 54, 55, 71–72, 74, 115,
    135, 155, 209–12, 222–23, 238, 249n70,
    283n109
  and Britain, 34–35, 69, 72
  and discourses of backwardness, 24, 34,
    40, 54
  and Iran, 17, 33, 35, 48, 62–72, 93, 181–82,
    210, 253n15, 254n17, 255n31, 266n31
  and Iraq, 35, 69–73, 210, 256n52
  language reform in Soviet Union, 34, 52,
    53, 54, 211
  repression in Soviet Union, 47–48, 49, 54,
    55, 63–64, 72–73, 84–86, 135, 145–46,
    212, 214, 244n25, 259n91, 259n92,
    260n94, 261n103

Soviet Kurdish autonomy, 31–32, 59, 73–74, 75, 135, 182, 212, 222–23, 237, 247n33, 283n109
and Turkey, 33–35, 48, 66, 70, 72, 84–85, 93, 181–82, 210
Kyrgyz ASSR/SSR, 45–46, 84, 108, 212, 259n91

Laks, 55, 81, 86, 148, 216
Lankaran region, 20, 32, 36, 39, 40, 42, 49, 157, 158, 160, 166, 169, 172, 173, 176, 231, 233–34
Latvian SSR and Latvians, 47, 61, 108, 127, 128, 139, 180, 260n94, 268n76
Laz, 83, 152, 260n93
Lenin, Vladimir Il'ich, 37, 147, 245n9, 272n14
Lerik, 42, 172, 173
Lezgins (Lezgians), 157
   and autonomy/unification, 13, 46, 59, 184, 196, 206, 207, 214, 220, 224–25, 237, 238
   in Azerbaijan, 22, 23, 27, 35, 38, 39, 40, 42–45, 49, 51–53, 81, 88, 92, 114, 130, 132, 136, 137, 155, 195, 196, 215, 218, 227, 249n70, 270n113, 276n84
   community fear, 12–14, 207–8
   and discourses of backwardness, 24, 40
   and Dagestan, 43, 46, 136, 148–50, 181, 195–96, 198, 207–8
   and discrimination, 12–13, 24, 38, 49, 115, 137–38, 141, 169, 184, 187, 196–97, 206–8, 216, 219
   and national activism in Azerbaijan, 46, 137, 143, 181, 184, 194–98, 200, 201–4, 206, 207–10, 212–13, 224–25
Lithuanian SSR and Lithuanians, 61, 96, 139–40, 221, 260n94

Malenkov, Georgii Maksimilianovich, 73, 95, 96, 97, 254n18, 259n91
Mammadov, Hilal, 14–15, 233–36
Mammadov, Novruzali, 12, 14–15, 233, 235, 236, 287n62
maps. *See* ethnographic maps
Mazandaran, 62, 66, 67, 156, 252n4
Meskhetian Turks
   deportation of, 7, 84, 85, 86, 93, 111, 136, 179, 259n89, 259n91, 259n92, 260n94
   naming of, as "Turks," 86, 136, 197, 259n89, 270n106
Mgeladze, Akaki, 83–84, 86, 98–99, 259n85
Miller, Boris Vsevolodovich, 157, 159, 160

Mingrelian Affair, 96, 98, 100, 185
Mingrelians, 83, 152, 166–67
Mirtskhulava, Aleksandr, 96, 98–99
Moambe newspaper, 225–26, 228
Moldovan SSR, 61, 97, 108, 260n94
Molotov, Viacheslav, 62, 73, 95, 97, 98, 254n18, 259n91
Mosul, 89, 91, 205–6
Mountain Jews, 24, 30, 38, 41, 43, 44, 55, 155, 246n18, 249n70
Mugals, 81, 88, 92, 114
Muhammad, Qazi, 68–72, 254n17, 255n31
Mustafayev, İmam Dashdamir oglu
   dismissal, 106–7, 128, 131, 132, 140, 172, 174, 189, 264n5, 268n76
   as first secretary, 17, 102, 108, 112, 118–21, 123, 125–27, 133–34, 138, 187
Mzhvanadze, Vasil Pavlovich, 99, 185, 201, 206

Nagorno-Karabakh Autonomous Oblast' (NKAO), 9–10, 29, 31–32, 40, 86, 105, 248n34
   attempts to adjoin it to Armenian SSR, 81–82, 93, 116–17, 157, 214, 221, 222
   autonomous oblast', 248n34
   related population displacement and conflict, 211, 215, 221, 223, 231, 234, 236, 238, 266n45, 284nn4–5, 285n26
Nakhchivan Autonomous Soviet Socialist Republic, 29, 31, 34, 39, 48, 73, 116
national question and policies
   Leninist nationality politics, 2–3, 6, 18, 22, 28, 47, 93, 124, 128, 181, 184, 194, 198, 200, 208, 220, 222, 242n10
   passport nationality, 22, 89, 110, 137–38, 140, 142, 145, 149, 171, 175, 188, 206, 212, 218, 226
   titularity/nontitularity, 1–10, 21–24, 28, 38, 44–45, 47, 51, 55, 63–64, 96, 107, 109–11, 113, 115, 118–19, 129–30, 133–34, 136, 140, 142–43, 145, 163–64, 166, 188, 217, 219, 238
   See also national minority
national minority (natsmen)
   and archives/research, 2, 6–8, 9–16, 182–83, 185–86, 204–7, 209–10
   definition, of, 3–4, 5–6, 21, 23–25, 46, 50–51, 55, 188
   and early national development, 22–23, 28–29, 35–36, 38–45, 49–52
   hierarchies of, 22, 23, 30, 43–45, 47, 49, 88–89, 181–82, 184, 212

national minority (*continued*)
  and minoritization, 14, 21–22, 47–49,
    50–55, 56, 59, 109, 216–17, 237–39
  minority assimilation and titular
    nation-building, 6, 8, 23, 29, 32, 46–47,
    54–55, 59, 64, 82–86, 109, 115–18,
    128–32, 134–43, 145–46, 150, 155,
    161–68, 170, 174–75, 177, 180, 182–83,
    208, 215–20
  See also Georgian-Ingilois; Kurds;
    Lezgins; Talyshes
nested nationalism, 4–6, 107–9, 113–15,
  128–29, 138–43, 180–81, 208, 209,
  216–17, 219–20, 237–39
  See also national minority; Russification/
    de-Russification
Nukha. *See* Shaki region (also Nukha)

Operation Volna, 80, 84, 85, 135, 258n78,
  260n93, 270n105
oral history methodology, 10–16
  and fear, 11–14, 192, 204–7, 216
Ordzhonikidze, Grigorii (Sergo), 29, 87,
  246n9, 247n27
Ossetians and South Ossetian, 83, 99, 117,
  153, 155, 197, 222

Pamiris, 152, 165–67, 172, 174
People's Commissariat of Internal Affairs, 47,
  48, 64, 66, 90, 104, 145, 259n91, 264n28
Persian Empire, 33, 48, 156, 265n21
petitioning, 182–83, 198–99
  See also Georgian-Ingilois; Lezgins;
    Talyshes
Pishevari, Ja'far, 68, 71, 75, 255n34, 256n43

Qakh region, 39, 40, 44, 49–50, 53, 81,
  86–93, 114, 117, 118, 131, 157, 184, 186,
  187, 189–91, 198, 228–31, 237
Quba region, 24, 30, 32, 38, 206, 276n84
Qusar region, 13, 46, 155, 157, 187, 194–97,
  206, 219

Ragimov, Sadıq Hajiyarali oglu, 17, 102,
  106–8, 122–23, 125
Reza Shah, 33, 61, 66, 71, 119, 252n2
Rik'in Gaf (Serdechnoe Slovo), 12–13, 194–96,
  201–4, 207–8, 212–13, 224, 281n47
Rizvanov, Zabit, 194, 195–96, 204, 207–8,
  224–25
Russian Empire, 62, 75, 86, 88, 182
  imperial legacy, 3, 33, 109, 123–24, 147,
    156, 162, 269n104

Russian Federation, 224–25, 235–38
Russian Soviet Federated Socialist Republic
  (RSFSR), 43, 61, 82, 103, 206, 222
Russians
  in Azerbaijan, 26–27, 36, 41, 124, 130, 133,
    136, 155, 157, 168–69, 217, 249n70,
    268n90
  as oppressor nation, 37, 96, 101, 104–5,
    113, 123–24, 138–40
Russification and de-Russification, 23, 51, 56,
  83, 96, 108, 139
  Russian hegemony, 4–5, 24, 36–37, 52,
    107–9, 112–13, 115, 119, 121–22,
    129–31, 138–39, 142–43, 148, 166, 180,
    181, 183, 188, 196, 209, 219, 221
  Russian language learning, 29, 35, 43, 44,
    45, 51–53, 83, 99, 109, 118, 122–24,
    127–31, 137, 149, 181, 196

Sadval, 13, 214, 220, 224
Serdechnoe Slovo. *See* Rik'in Gaf (Serdechnoe Slovo)
Shah Abbas, 67, 88, 254n23, 261n110
Shahsevans, 33, 48, 65, 66, 107, 152,
  153
Shaki region (also Nukha), 30, 32, 34, 39,
  149, 206, 273n21
socialism, as stage of development, 36–38,
  45–47, 50, 55, 56, 145–47, 150–51, 160,
  162–66
Soviet Socialist Republic of Gilan. *See* Gilan
Stalin, Joseph
  and internal national politics, 3, 28, 29,
    45–52, 54–57, 77–78, 81–85, 90–93, 180,
    184–85, 198–200, 245n9, 247n27,
    253n12, 259n91
  and patronage networks, 90–91, 99,
    258n83, 259n85 (*see also* Mingrelian
    Affair)
  transition from, 94–109, 119–21, 145–47,
    174, 180, 182, 187, 193, 202–4, 208,
    212–13
  See also World War II; deportations
Supreme Soviet of the USSR, 97, 123, 124,
  212, 222
  See also Azerbaijan SSR: Supreme Soviet

Tajiks and Tajikistan, 38, 108, 114–15, 152,
  166, 167, 172
Talyshes
  and assimilation, 18–19, 126, 141–42, 143,
    144–45, 149, 150, 152–55, 159–78, 180,
    209–10, 215–18

and autonomy, 36, 58–59, 182, 214–15, 220, 231–37, 238

censuses and erasure, 136, 141, 144–45, 152–54, 155, 159–61, 167–70, 176, 249n70, 277n112

community fear, 12, 175, 176–78, 234, 238

and discourses of backwardness, 24, 40, 44, 48, 54, 141, 162, 163–64, 166, 170, 177

ethnogenesis and ethnography, 115, 141, 144–45, 154–71, 218, 232–33, 275n61

forced resettlements, 48–49, 78, 135, 173–74

and Iran/Iranian borderlands, 33, 35–36, 48–49, 78, 135, 156–58, 169, 172–74, 181–82, 235

national rights and lack thereof, 4, 24, 35–45, 48–49, 51, 128, 132, 141–42, 144–45, 160, 198, 209, 213, 233 (*see also* Talyshes: assimilation)

petitioning and activism, 12, 175–76, 181–82

repression, 19–20, 47, 48–49, 57–59, 78, 170–71, 173–74, 175, 177–78, 235–37, 244n26 (*see also* Talyshes: assimilation)

Talysh-Mughan Autonomous Republic, 214, 220, 231–37

Tasmalı, 89, 131, 185, 187

Tats, 23, 24, 27, 38, 40, 45, 53, 55, 115, 149, 155, 159, 209, 217, 274n45, 276n84

Thaw, 186, 202–8

Tiurks. *See* Azeris

Tolstov, Sergei Pavlovich, 152, 166, 167, 210–11

Tolyshi Sado, 12, 15, 232, 234, 235, 236

Transcaucasian Socialist Federated Soviet Republic (TSFSR), 20, 29, 37, 40, 46, 135, 245n9, 247n27

Tsakhurs, 40, 41, 44, 47, 49–50, 51, 53, 54, 55, 81, 149, 209, 216, 217, 230, 249n70

Turkey, 2, 7, 66, 88, 116

in Azerbaijani ethnogenesis and national narratives, 111–13, 125

and Kurds, 33–35, 48, 66, 69–70, 71–73, 181–82, 210

Soviet pretensions to Turkish territory, 17, 61–64, 75–81, 82, 90, 93, 117

Soviet-Turkish borderlands, 66, 80–81, 84–85, 93, 111, 172, 181–82

relations with Soviet Union, 39, 48, 62–63, 75–81, 111, 120, 135, 157, 172, 252n8, 265n15

Turkmenistan SSR and Turkmen, 33, 103, 104, 108, 255n26

Turks, 7, 21, 33, 85, 135, 259n89, 260n93
See also Meskhetian Turks; Azeris

Udins, 44, 155, 249n70

Ukrainian SSR and Ukrainians, 37, 61, 96, 97, 127, 138, 139, 155

USSR

breakdown of, 6, 211–12, 220–23, 266n45

formation, 29–30, 86–87, 116, 157–58, 247n27

as model of socialist progress, 1–2, 34–35, 62–67, 69–70, 78–80, 113, 120, 150–51, 164–66, 180–81, 210
See also World War II

Uyghurs, 180–81, 222
See also East Turkestan Republic

Uzbekistan, 37–38, 72–73, 84, 108, 127, 136, 152, 259n91

Vinnikov, Iakov Romanovich, 167, 168, 170

Volga Tatars, 35, 43, 44, 45, 51

Voroshilov, Kliment Efremovich, 97, 123, 124, 139

World War II

Anglo-Soviet occupation of Iran in, 61–75

influence on postwar politics and society, 93, 119–21, 203, 226

Soviet pretensions to Turkish territory in, 62–64, 75–81
See also Armenians: repatriation; Azeris in Iran; deportation; Kurds

Xinjiang, 61, 63, 180

Yerevan, 47, 75, 77, 80, 117, 221, 237

Zangezur (Syunik), 29, 32, 116

Zaqatala region, 20, 29, 32, 38–39, 41, 50, 53, 81, 86–93, 114, 117, 131, 137, 184, 186, 187, 190–92, 197–98, 205, 228–29, 237, 261n107

Zayam, 89, 131, 185–87